The Research Foundations of Graduate Education

The Research Foundations of Graduate Education

Germany, Britain, France, United States, Japan

EDITED BY

Burton R. Clark

UNIVERSITY OF CALIFORNIA PRESS
Berkeley   Los Angeles   Oxford

University of California Press
Berkeley and Los Angeles, California

University of California Press
Oxford, England

Library of Congress Cataloging-in-Publication Data

The Research foundations of graduate education : Germany, Britain,
  France, United States, Japan / edited by Burton R. Clark.
    p. cm.
    Includes bibliographical references and index.
    ISBN 0-520-07997-3
    1. Research—Europe.   2. Research—United States.   3. Research—
Japan.   4. Education, Higher—Research.   5. Universities and
colleges—Research.   I. Clark, Burton R.
Q180.E9R47   1993
001.4'094—dc20   92-13407
                                                              CIP

Printed in the United States of America

1   2   3   4   5   6   7   8   9

The paper used in this publication meets the minimum requirements of American
National Standard for Information Sciences—Permanence of Paper for Printed Library
Materials, ANSI Z39.48-1984 ∞

CONTENTS

TABLES

vii

ACKNOWLEDGMENTS

This volume is based on a three-year study, undertaken between 1987 and 1990, which involved intensive analysis and cooperation on the part of scholars in five countries. Considerably open-ended at the outset, the study necessitated much collaborative effort to determine a common agenda. My colleagues had to engage in difficult fieldwork and to simultaneously adjust to emerging common frameworks appropriate for a cross-national statement. The completion of two long chapters on each country also subjected the involved scholars to considerable demand for revision of early drafts, which would turn disparate writings into a unified volume. Thus, as editor, I am deeply indebted to the colleagues named as authors of the individual chapters, and to their immediate collaborators and assistants, who did the research and then concentrated their extensive knowledge in the chapters that follow. International collaboration brings special problems not only of conceptualization but also of interpersonal relationships. Due to the ability and willingness of my colleagues, solutions to those problems for the most part were not hard to find.

On behalf of the entire research group, I wish to thank the Spencer Education Foundation for a generous research grant made in 1987, a grant that has supported all phases of the project, including the fieldwork in four countries outside of the United States. Under the leadership of the late Lawrence Cremin, Spencer has been in the forefront of research support in the field of education. The enthusiastic encouragement of Marion Faldet, Vice President of the Foundation, also materially assisted our efforts.

Patricia Smith, administrative assistant in the UCLA Comparative Higher Education Research Group, helped to organize two summer working-party conferences and to keep the preparation of this manuscript on course during revisions that stretched over eighteen months. Adele Clark ably provided the general editing that brought the clarity of clear English to the ambiguities inherent in language differences and the propensities of academics. Excellent copy editing that went beyond the call of duty was provided by Linda Benefield.

Burton R. Clark

Santa Monica, California
March, 1991

CONTRIBUTORS

Tony Becher is professor of education at the University of Sussex, England. A graduate in philosophy at the University of Cambridge, he served for some years on the editorial staff of Cambridge University Press while teaching at Cambridge. Later he was director of the Nuffield Higher Education Group, which studied innovations in undergraduate teaching. His principal publications include: "The Cultural View," in *Perspectives on Higher Education*, edited by Burton R. Clark, 1984; "The Disciplinary Shaping of the Profession," in *The Academic Profession*, edited by Burton R. Clark, 1987; (editor) *British Higher Education*, 1987; *Academic Tribes and Territories*, 1989; and (with Maurice Kogan) *Process and Structure in Higher Education*, 1991.

Burton R. Clark is Allan M. Cartter professor of higher education and sociology and chairman of the Comparative Higher Education Research Group, University of California, Los Angeles. He taught previously at Stanford and Harvard universities, the University of California, Berkeley, and Yale University in departments of sociology and schools of education; from 1974 to 1980 he was chairman of the Yale Higher Education Research Group. His publications include: *The Open Door College*, 1960; *The Distinctive College*, 1970; *Academic Power in Italy*, 1977; *The Higher Education System*, 1983; (editor) *Perspectives on Higher Education*, 1984; (editor) *The School and the University*, 1985; (editor) *The Academic Profession*, 1987; and *The Academic Life*, 1987.

Richard Edelstein is director of international affairs at the American Assembly of Collegiate Schools of Business (AACSB). He is also a Ph.D. candidate at the University of California, Berkeley, completing a dissertation tentatively entitled "French Business Education in the Post War Period: The Politics of Institutional Change." He was previously affiliated with the European Institute for Education and Social Policy in Paris, where he completed research for his dissertation, and with the Center for Studies in Higher Education at Berkeley, where he was a research associate. Prior to pursuing graduate study, he managed international projects for the Office of International Education and the Institute of International Studies on the Berkeley campus.

Claudius Gellert is research director at the European University Institute, Florence, Italy. He received an M.A. in sociology, philosophy, and psychology from Munich University and a Ph.D. in social and political sciences from Cambridge University. He has taught at Cambridge, Harvard, and Munich. His publications include: *Vergleich des Studiums an englischen und deutschen Universitäten*, 1988; *Alternatives to Universities in Higher Education*, Organisation for Economic Co-operation and Development, 1991; *Society, Politics and Universities in England and Germany*, 1991; and *Wettbewerb und Leistungsorientierung im amerikanischen Universitätssystem*, 1991.

Patricia J. Gumport is assistant professor of education and (by courtesy) sociology at Stanford University and deputy director of the Stanford Institute for Higher Education Research. After earning a doctorate from Stanford in 1987, she served for two years as a postdoctoral research scholar in the UCLA Comparative Higher Education Research Group. Her published and forthcoming articles and books include: "Feminist Scholarship as a Vocation," *Higher Education*, 1990; "The Research Imperative," in *Culture and Ideology in Higher Education*, edited by William G. Tierney, 1991; and *The Social Construction of Knowledge*, forthcoming.

Mary Henkel is lecturer in the Department of Government at Brunel University and member of the Centre for the Evaluation of Public Policy and Practice recently established there. She has undertaken research in the fields of research policy, higher education, and health and social welfare, seeking links between knowledge traditions, authority, and values, particularly as they emerge in evaluative policies and practice. Her publications include: (with Maurice Kogan) *Government and Research*, 1983; (with C. Boys, J. Brennan, J. Kirkland, M. Kogan, P. Youll) *Higher Education and the Preparation for Work*, 1988; *Government, Evaluation and Change*, 1991; and "The New Evaluative State" in *Public Administration*, Spring, 1991.

Tatsuo Kawashima is research associate (Joshu) in the Department of Education, Nagoya University, and also doctoral student in the Department of Education at the University of Chicago. His main interest lies in organizational analysis of Japanese schooling. His writings include: "Instructional and Sociological Approaches to 'Ability Grouping'," *Bulletin of the School of Education*, Nagoya University, 1986; and "Reconsideration of the Study of Schooling Effects: From the Input-Output Approach to the School Production Approach," *Bulletin of the School of Education*, Nagoya University, 1988.

Maurice Kogan is professor of government and social administration, and director of the Centre for the Evaluation of Public Policy and Practice at Brunel University, England. After graduating from Christ's College, Cambridge, he served for fifteen years in various posts in the Department of Education in the British government. While in his present post he has also served as Acting Vice-Chancellor at Brunel. His publications include: *The Politics of Education*, 1971; *Education Policy Making*, 1975; *Education Accountability*, 1988; and (with Tony Becher) *Process and Structure in Higher Education*, 1991.

Fumihiro Maruyama is associate professor of comparative education, Sugiyama Women's University, Nagoya, Japan. After completing his Ph.D. in comparative education at Michigan State University, he served on the research staff of the Research Institute for Higher Education, Hiroshima University. His current research focuses on the finance of higher education and the economic behavior of colleges and universities. His publications include: "The Process and Structure of Student Characteristics Formation in Japanese Higher Education," Ph.D. dissertation, 1983; and "Prospects and Problems in Japanese Higher Education," *Higher Education Expansion in Asia*, Research Institute for Higher Education, Hiroshima University, 1985.

Guy Neave is director of research at the International Association of Universities, Paris; joint editor with Ladislav Cerych of the *European Journal of Education*; and editor, *Higher Education Policy*, the quarterly journal of the International Association of Universities. He is a founder, with Ulrich Teichler and Frans van Vught, of the Consortium of Higher Education Researchers, a forum that brings together higher education researchers in Western and Eastern Europe. His publications include: *How They Fared*, 1975; *Patterns of Equality*, 1976; *The EEC and Education*, 1984; "France," in *The School and the University*, edited by Burton R. Clark, 1985; and (with van Vught) *Prometheus Bound*, 1990.

Morikazu Ushiogi is professor of sociology of education at Nagoya University, Japan. After graduating from the School of Education at Tokyo University, he served for several years as research associate there and at the National Institute for Educational Research. He has taught at Nagoya University since 1967 and served as dean of the School of Education from 1986 to 1988. His publications include: *Kindai Daigaku no Keisei to Henyou (The Emergence and Transformation of the Modern University)*, 1973; *Daigaku to Shakai (University and Society)*, 1982; *Kyouto Teikoku Daigaku no Chousen (The Challenge of the Kyoto Imperial University)*, 1984; *Doitu Daigaku heno Tabi (A History of the German University)*, 1986; and *Kyanpasu no Seitaisi (Ethnography of the Campus)*, 1986.

Introduction

Burton R. Clark

The coupling of research with teaching and learning is a basic feature of modern higher education. Since the fundamental reform of the German university in the early nineteenth century, about 180 years ago, academics in many countries have taken up research as a fundamental activity. Their intensified inquiry has caused disciplines and specialties to grow and multiply, thereby enlarging the cognitive territories and material claims of academic groups. Marrying science to higher education, academic research has brought prestige to universities and has enabled scholars to be something more than teachers and examiners. In various fields of study, professors assume they should produce knowledge and use the latest research results in their teaching. They should train students to conduct research, even directly involve them in research. Internationally, research is nearly everywhere at the center of the rewards of academic life and the status of academic enterprises. "Research university," a term now applied to the top one hundred American universities, is an appropriate label for the leading universities in most countries. It is arguably the case that the better the university, the more it engages in research; the higher the degree level within the university, the more it will have research foundations.

But just how sturdy are the research foundations in different national systems? There is ample reason to doubt the existence of a close research-teaching-study relationship throughout modern systems of higher education, even at the most advanced level known as graduate education in the United States. The transition from elite to mass higher education has greatly extended first-degree instruction that is often not closely linked with research. A large proportion of higher education is devoted to training for professions in which research is not a primary task. As research becomes more expensive, it is not distributed among all institutions in a national system. Research also develops outside universities in state-owned laboratories, business firms, and nonprofit research organizations. The marriage of science to higher education can turn into not only a partial separation within the academy but a sustained divorce. The unity option is not the only one.

The problem of the relationship between research organization and advanced education goes beyond the interests of the academy. Nations worry about their scientific capability and their capacity to recruit research talent and train new generations of researchers. As science and technology become more closely linked to economic health, military strength, and general national welfare, governments seek to extend and invigorate their research systems. They have greatly increased their research funding in and beyond the walls of the universities. Thus, at the beginning of the 1990s—and extending into the twenty-first century, we may safely predict—the comparative strength of national science and technology is and will be high on governmental agendas. Firmly anchored within this larger concern is the question of the capacity of universities to operate as centers of research, as places for research training, and as institutions where even students destined for nonacademic and nonresearch careers in professions, business, and government will learn about the nature of inquiry and have some sense of what research is all about.

Here is a topic worthy of sustained investigation involving cross-national analysis. This volume reports the results of a large study begun in 1987 and completed in 1990 to examine comparatively the historical development and current state of research organization and advanced education in the five leading countries of the Western world: the Federal Republic of Germany, Great Britain, France, the United States, and Japan. Ambitious in scope and considerably open-ended, the project was organized to include work done by experts in each country. Early discussion led to a decision to divide the study into two parts: a first-year probing of the general ("macro") structures found in each country for the support and implementation of research and advanced education (advanced education here meaning "graduate education" or "graduate school" in American terminology and its closest counterparts in the other countries), and a second-year analysis that would move inside the large national arrangements and examine faculty-student relationships within university departments. The latter "micro" investigation was intended to explore differences among disciplines and among institutions. It focused on the operating levels of national systems where patterns of behavior might be much more complicated, even radically different, than those portrayed or inferred in the broad strokes of national structures.

Five macro papers were first drafted at the end of the 1987–1988 academic year and were discussed at a working-party conference during the summer of 1988. These papers depended on analysis of national data, documents, and prior studies, supplemented by interviews with national officials and academic experts. Partial integration was attempted in the form of adjusted common categories, and the papers were left for further revision, especially in light of the second-year work. Agreement was reached on common plans for the following year: that three disciplines would be pursued in each country (physics to represent the sciences, economics for the social sciences, and history for the humanities); that an additional field ought to be pursued, time and resources permitting, where such a discipline loomed especially large in the national picture (hence engineering was added for Japan and the biological sciences for the United States); that the disciplines ought to be investigated in at least three varied institutional settings; and that this round of research ought to depend upon on-the-spot interviewing of faculty, graduate students, university administrators, and, if necessary, personnel in research institutes, such as the *Centre National de la Recherche Scientifique* (CNRS), an organization at the heart of the French research system.

The micro investigations, involving extensive fieldwork, were brought together in papers discussed at a second meeting during the summer of 1989. Further adjustments were made toward commonalities in perspective, coverage, and detail. Revisions of both sets of papers took place during 1989–1990, the third year of the study, toward the objective of having ten papers, two on each country, appear in an edited volume. This publication is the result.

As the organizer and coordinator of the project, I also initiated an additional volume that would build on the knowledge and experience gained in this study. The intent in the second book, tentatively entitled *Places of Inquiry: Graduate Education and Research in Modern Society*, is to clarify, through extended reanalysis of the project results and related literature, the conditions and trends that maintain the unity of research, teaching, and study along with the contrary forces that fragment this relation.

The following ten essays exhibit some common categories and comparative data. In varying fashion the papers attend to the historical development of higher education and science. For the contemporary period they explain the nature of the higher education system, the research system, and the funding system. In the micro accounts they describe the recruitment and selection of advanced university students, the nature of the main graduate degree programs, especially the doctorate, and the pathways by which students become involved in research. But the papers also vary greatly from one country to the next in analytical perspective and specific substantive focus. This variation was a deliberate choice, one dictated in part by the state of the art and the varied interests and analytical styles of colleagues available in different countries, and, most of all, by a determination to have the reports follow in a holistic fashion the special contours of tradition and structure each country offered. There was little prior research on which to build, especially of a cross-national nature. The talents of the assembled research group ranged across historical, sociological, anthropological, and policy perspectives. Critically, the histories of development dictated that the German analysis pursue a detailed explanation of the Humboldtian ideal, that the British analysis emphasize the driving force of governmental research policy and the recent move of the British government toward a *dirigiste* posture of control, that in France we understand above all else the powerful role played by a separate research establishment, that in the United States we fully grasp the dynamics of university development in a competitive decentralized system, which has led to great strength in Ph.D. production, and that in the Japanese case we come to see the interlocking set of conditions that has pushed engineering to the forefront but otherwise has weakened graduate work. To have forced the country reports into precisely parallel categories and sequences would have distorted the logics of the national arrangements, insisting, for example, that categories most appropriate for analysis of the American system must be used to explicate the quite different French schemes. Some price in common categories was deliberately paid to offer detailed accounts that might reveal the elaborate interplay of many nationally unique features among observable cross-national similarities.

We encountered difficulty in defining such apparently simple matters as parallel levels of advanced education and training. The American system offers a clear distinction between four-year undergraduate programs ending with a bachelor's degree and postbachelor programs leading to master's and doctoral degrees, which are formally organized in graduate schools. Oriented initially by the American definition, the project began as a study of the research foundations of "graduate education"—the title given finally to this volume. But parallels soon appeared in strange shapes. The British system is built on a three-year bachelor's program, one that is much more specialized than the American. In addition, "postgraduate" work is not formally organized in graduate schools and often does not involve "taught courses." The Japanese system possesses both a four-year undergraduate college and a graduate level organized in graduate schools, an imprint stemming in part from the post–World War II American Occupation, but it also has admissions practices, funding patterns, and degree requirements that make it qualitatively different, including a peculiar distancing of the doctorate from graduate work itself. Most important, universities in Germany, France, and elsewhere on the European continent have not had educational sequences that parallel the main breakpoints found in the American case. Students enter higher education to specialize in professional fields and academic disciplines. The historic first degree, awarded some five, six, or seven years later, is then more similar to the American master's than the U.S. bachelor's degree. Within the prolonged first-degree programs, several stages can sometimes be distinguished, but recent reforms, particularly in France, have only complicated matters. Terminological confusion abounds: the French use "college" to designate some secondary schools and "bacca-laureat" to refer to a secondary school degree. Thus, the papers that follow switch at times into a terminology of preadvanced and advanced education, or of introductory, intermediate, and advanced levels. A simple distinction between undergraduate and graduate cannot be upheld: "graduate" has different rough-and-ready counterparts in a good share of the national systems of higher education. But once the basic differences are grasped, they can be readily followed, as the authors of the papers go to some pains to explain.

The volume is organized by country. We begin in Part One with Germany, where the Humboldtian ideal of a close relationship between research, teaching, and study was established. We then take up the other two major European systems, the British and the French, where distinctively different national configurations of research organization and advanced education have developed. In modes of research support and means of advanced education, these three major systems could hardly be more different. We then turn to the imposing American case where another exceptional set of conditions has promoted an unique system now at the international forefront of academic research and research training. Here the dimensions of difference become even more extended. But whatever their differences, these four systems of higher education have been *the* international models of research and research training during the twentieth century; they have drawn scholars and students from elsewhere and their practices have been widely studied and freely imitated. The country analyses then conclude with Japan, a higher education system that has more recently come to the fore to join the select group. International cultural differences here are markedly prominent. It is enlightening for Americans and Europeans to grasp the inner workings of the Japanese university system and particularly to know how its most advanced level operates in relation to knowledge production and research training.

Brief comments by the editor introduce each of the five sets of chapters. For each country, the first chapter lays out the macro structures of research organization and advanced education, presents historical development, and points to basic contemporary strains and stresses. Here, the formal arrangement, even the "official" picture, receives much attention. The second chapter reports the findings of the micro study of disciplinary and institutional similarities and differences, breathing some of the everyday life of academic faculties, departments, chairs, and laboratories into the larger account. This approach reveals some informal arrangements that have emerged in the interactions of faculty and students. Professors often have considerable leeway to rearrange, or even circumvent, official systemwide rules and regulations. The assigned and accumulated powers of senior professors, their expertise, and their collegial ties can lead to extensive individual patronage and collective control at operating levels. Formal systemwide patterns may have broad unanticipated effects in actual practice.

The concluding chapter offers some integration of the country portraits by setting out common trends and problems revealed in the prior chapters or which lie just beneath the surface of descriptive knowledge. It then focuses on the distinctive capability of American graduate education in relation to research activities and presents an example of what the ideal type of research-centered graduate education looks like in a modern university setting near the end of the twentieth century. The final discussion highlights the importance of maintaining intense interaction and close relationships between academic staff and advanced students in organizational settings that grow larger and more bureaucratic. Effective systems are composed of thousands of small worlds of laboratories and seminars for which such descriptive terms as craft and apprenticeship are still appropriate. What the best macro frameworks of system, bureaucracy, and profession do is to generate and support the best micro settings. The multiplication and grand diffusion of these small worlds becomes the heart of the problem.

Any country can have advanced higher education that has little or no relation to research activity and training. Numerous master's degree and professional-degree programs exhibit this option. Conversely, countries can have much research activity and even research training accomplished away from the locales of advanced education. Research and research training found in private corporations and state-sponsored laboratories offer this second option. What we explore in detail in this volume are the conditions of the third possibility, the unity option, in which research and research training are carried out in academic locales as an intrinsic part of graduate or advanced education, either simultaneously or in a linked sequence. Research, teaching, and advanced study are thereby so closely interrelated that one informs the others. What does this historic nexus look like in modern dress, after much apparent transformation? Where does it still appear, and with what strength? What conditions serve to maintain it or to diminish it? The descriptions and analyses provided in the following chapters lead us toward informed answers to these fundamental questions.

The second volume of this study explicates in a more fully comparative fashion the basic characteristics of the five systems here explored. Building upon the extensive materials presented in the country chapters of this volume, and adding the findings available in other writings on higher education in these countries, that unified analysis specifies generic and country-specific conditions that separate research from teaching and study and, conversely, serve to keep these activities closely linked. The conditions of integration can be specified at national, institutional, and base unit levels of higher education systems, varying from type and degree of national coordination to the local structure of academic groups in departments and chairs, institutes and seminars. Notably, supportive conditions have changed considerably over time, particularly between the first half and second half of the twentieth century, attendant upon the growth that has followed from movement into mass higher education and the intensification generated by the virtually exponential expansion of specialized knowledge.

Supportive interaction among research, teaching, and study is increasingly difficult to maintain. But in each national system, in the face of varied obstacles, we find connections that have evolved from sustained effort to fuse the production of knowledge with its dissemination, linkages fashioned by those who understand that a certain complementarity must be maintained if science and scholarship are to prosper. In a grand historical sense it is the luck of the draw that the German system offered the best set of conditions throughout the nineteenth century and early twentieth century. And it has been the spontaneous adjustment of universities and their constituent departments and schools more than the direction provided by national plan and consensual action that have led the American graduate school in the last half-century into arrangements that best enable and enact a research-teaching-study nexus, turning the graduate level into the great strength of the American educational system. In the United States and elsewhere, there is much to be gained both in analytical explanation and in balanced public policy by attending to the graduate or advanced level of higher education as much as to the undergraduate or pre-advanced programs. The two volumes of this study together seek to move analysis and popular thought in this direction.

PART ONE

Germany

Introduction

Our five-country analysis begins with Germany, where an early marriage of scientific research and university education first led to the development of research-based universities. Claudius Gellert highlights the original meaning of the Humboldtian ideal of a unity of research, teaching, and study—of education through science—and the subsequent evolution in the nineteenth and twentieth centuries of practices developed in the name of this commanding ideal. Wilhelm von Humboldt placed the subject, not the student, at the center of his conception. In seminars and laboratories, professors and students were to join hands in the pursuit of new knowledge. Whatever the later ideological shifts in this central doctrine, the pragmatic result was a set of universities geared to academic research. By the last half of the nineteenth century, German universities were widely considered the most advanced in the world, attracting students and visiting scholars from other countries who sought to learn the newest methods of inquiry. Here were universities that concentrated on specialized research and the preparation of research specialists. Advanced education received sturdy research foundations.

However, this classic elite system has been buffeted throughout much of the twentieth century. During the first three decades the entrenched power of chairholding professors deepened the rigidities flowing from a closed academic oligarchy, with its small constraining monopolies of power. The Fascist period then brought an immense loss of talent, the denial of academic freedom and institutional autonomy, and, by 1945, a deep crisis of legitimacy for a tainted professoriate. All claims to intellectual preeminence had been lost. And hardly had German officials and scholars partially restored the universities to the ethos and capability they possessed before the rise of Hitler when expansion into mass higher education, beginning in the 1960s, hit with growing force. Gellert reviews in detail the effects of a fivefold expansion between 1960 and the mid-1980s: the development of *Fachhochschulen* as a fast-expanding "nonuniversity" sector favored by government; the extensive overcrowding of students in universities designed for one-third or one-half of actual enrollment; the concomitant shift in professorial duties from research to teaching; and the growing anonymity of the student in the mass university, especially within a historic structure that had only weak curricular organization and that put great store in the capacity of "mature" students to make their own way among courses, programs, and universities.

The drift of research, pure and applied, from universities to other enterprises, for example, the Max Planck institutes, is yet another threat to the unity of research and teaching. If the Humdoldtian legacy is a stubborn one in Germany, much talked about and much praised, the German universities are operationally in a muddle and the old ideal is perhaps more hindrance than help. The system struggles to effect a productive differentiation among and within institutions which will maintain the unity of research, teaching, and study in certain locales even though it is explicitly and fully surrendered in others.

German higher education in the contemporary period is therefore experiencing considerable difficulty in differentiating and supporting an advanced level of university training. But inside and outside the academy, the commitment to research runs deep. The struggle is to find the organizational and funding patterns that will keep that commitment closely related to teaching and advanced study. On this critical matter, the two chapters on Germany prepared by Claudius Gellert have much to say.

ONE

The German Model of Research and Advanced Education

Claudius Gellert

A tradition of a unity of research and teaching has long existed in the German-speaking realm of higher education. *Einheit von Forschung und Lehre* defined the professional role of university academics whereby their teaching would be closely intertwined with and directly based upon their ongoing research. University teachers should always be involved in research, and specific insights and outcomes of their respective research activities should directly become the substance of their teaching. Further, university teachers were obligated to conduct research whose results would be immediately utilized for teaching purposes. To understand how this concept came about, it is necessary to examine the historical situation from which it emerged.[1]

EMERGENCE AND DEVELOPMENT OF THE HUMBOLDTIAN IDEAL

The historical situation of "Germany" at the beginning of the nineteenth century was determined by its relationship with France and indirectly by the political and social consequences of the French Revolution. From 1792 to 1807 most of the German principalities were at war with France. A few of these nearly eighteen hundred sovereign dominions were important European powers, but most were merely independent castles and villages.[2] Several peace treaties constituted only short interruptions of the ongoing wars. Prussia was one of the very few German states that managed to avoid war between 1795 and 1805, but in 1806 she sought to challenge France and was soon defeated.[3] Thus Napoleon was able to realize his plan to create a well-balanced power structure in Middle Europe with several medium-sized sovereign states that would neutralize each other. German polities west of the Rhine were annexed by France; many minute principalities, particularly the "Church-States," large monasteries and dioceses, were merged with the most powerful dynasties. The frontiers were, in some instances, drawn quite arbitrarily. Thus by 1807 the old Habsburg Empire had disappeared, and the development of a unified national state, which in England and France had taken place much earlier, was obstructed for another sixty-four years.

In contrast to that class in England and France, the German bourgeoisie was then still socially weak and politically disorganized.[4] The belated industrialization and slow economic development, the defeats in the Napoleonic wars with the subsequent reorganization of the principalities, and the continuing absolutist reign of the monarchies and the *Junker* aristocracies contributed to a political and cultural atmosphere characterized by constant upheavals, crises, and a lack of national identity. The small and politically powerless, although intellectually awake, middle class remained within a basically feudal framework and sought to find its identity in art, literature, and philosophy.[5] Educated clerics, teachers, higher civil servants, academics, and poets were not willing or able to fight for political emancipation but attempted to become socially assimilated with the nobility and tended to expect reforms from an "enlightened monarch."[6]

While the bourgeois classes created in their literature and philosophy an ideal picture of the bourgeois world,[7] and some liberal, high-ranking Prussian administrators were able to undertake political and social reforms that equipped the rising bourgeoisie with a limited amount of freedom and self-government,[8] the enlightened *Bildungsbürgertum* (educated bourgeoisie) slowly succeeded in implementing a more nationally oriented culture. As Joseph Ben-David and A. Zloczower have noted: "The advocacy of German instead of French culture, unknown before, became now the popular ideology affecting even the French-educated upper class. There was a feeling that the real strength of the Nation was in the realm of spirit and culture."[9]

This political and cultural development had vital repercussions on the future conception of a new German university. Considerable educational progress had been made during the eighteenth century when, T. L. Jarman writes, "under the influence of the courtly humanism of the academies a new spirit had found its way into such modern universities as Halle and Göttingen."[10] Now universities became more attractive places of work for intellectually and politically interested members of the bourgeoisie. At the same time, in many respects most universities were still outmoded. Ben-David describes them as "traditional institutions, dominated by professional faculties of law, theology, and medicine, [which] did not allow real freedom of thought and speech, since they were subject to the control of both the State and the Church."[11] In this context some leading Prussian administrators, preeminently Wilhelm von Humboldt, who had been influenced by political events in France and by German Idealist philosophers, became convinced that a rational development of state and society was possible only with the assistance of rational and knowledgeable citizens.

The philosophy of Idealism stemmed from Kant, but it went beyond him.[12] The Idealists Hegel, Schleiermacher, Johann Fichte, and Friedrich von Schlegel maintained that the world could be deduced from an a priori conceptualization of reality. They believed in a dualism of being and man (object and subject). Theoretical understanding of the world could only be found in universal or "absolute" knowledge; "praxis" was seen as a relative variable. The organization of reality could be deduced from this absolute knowledge.[13] According to the Idealists, the task of philosophy was to discover and to analyze this "truth as such." Consequently, all *Wissenschaft* (academic learning and research) was defined by the idealists as philosophy.[14] They conceptualized Wissenschaft as the moral and practical duty to organize reality according to absolute knowledge; the place where this knowledge would be discovered was the university.

To achieve this aim, the university still had to train students to become civil servants, teachers, and doctors, but this training was to take the form of an apparently purpose-free process of searching for truth.[15] The academic community was defined by Fichte as the paradigm of a rational society and was thus "an ideal community of free thinkers."[16] In contrast to the eighteenth-century system of academies and vocational schools, which were primarily meant to meet the administrative needs of an absolutist bureaucracy, the new conception of the university was to determine its relationship to state and society freely and independently.[17]

Of all the theoreticians and administrators who attempted the task, Wilhelm von Humboldt was the most successful in transforming these ideals into concrete plans for the foundation of a new university. For Humboldt a fundamental difference between a practical, vocational education and a general education based on pure Wissenschaft existed: "These two forms of education are determined by different principles. General education is meant to strengthen, ennoble and direct man himself, the specialist education will only provide him with skills for practical application."[18]

The new university was to be reorganized on the basis of this differentiation, and general education, the "pure idea of science," was to be given primary importance. Thus, according to Humboldt, the universities had to be reformed in such a way that students and professors could pursue this eternal objective—"truth as such"—and consequently be able to reorganize state and society on these rational principles. Humboldt called this educational program *Bildung durch Wissenschaft* (education through science). For Humboldt this also necessitated a different understanding of the role of teachers and students. The traditional relationship of authority between pupil and teacher was to be replaced by the idea of an undirected, free cooperation between students of different levels of knowledge: "The university teacher is not any longer teacher, the student not any more just learning, but the latter researches himself and the professor only directs and supports his research."[19]

When Friedrich Wilhelm III founded a new university for Berlin in 1809, it was based on these Humboldtian conceptions. The subject, not the student, received primary attention. "The relationship between teacher and student. . . is changing," Humboldt wrote. "The former does not exist for the sake of the latter. They are both at the university for the sake of science and scholarship."[20] Since the search for truth was not to be restricted by considerations of time, immediate occupational purposes, or state control, professors as well as students had to be enabled to teach and learn what interested them. This led to the principle of a unity of research and teaching for the professors, since the contents of teaching were to be direct reflections of the continuous search for objective knowledge.[21] A corresponding principle applied to students: "Freedom of learning" allowed them to select freely from what was offered in various disciplines, to change universities whenever they liked, and to take their final exams when they felt ready for them. This principle was later described by Abraham Flexner:

> His credentials [those of the student] being recognized at face value, he can go where he pleases—thus, if he will, overcrowding Berlin, while Tübingen might do better by him. He selects his own teachers; he wanders from one university to another; he may waste his time in fencing or drinking, he may forego vacations in order to work as "Famulus" in a laboratory or clinic. In the professions where a logical order of studies prevails, he may take advice or neglect it at his peril. He is treated like a man from the day he matriculates.[22]

In the following years the other German universities continued to be reformed according to the new principles, and two new foundations, Breslau in 1811 and Bonn in 1818, directly adopted the model of Berlin.[23] The outmoded institutional pattern of the eighteenth century crumbled everywhere. Between 1794 and 1818 twenty universities within the German realm, mainly Catholic foundations, were dissolved. In some cases this was just a formal act, since these universities had not had any students or professors for years.[24] The narrow, denominationally oriented structures of the previous century were replaced by more open, liberal, and scholarly arrangements. Friedrich Paulsen has summarized well the ideal of a new German university as it emerged in the beginning of the century:

> Its principle was to be, not unity and subordination, but freedom and independence. The professors were not to be teaching and examining State officials, but independent scholars. Instruction was to be carried on not according to a prescribed order, but with a view to liberty of teaching and learning. The aim was not encyclopedic information, but genuine scientific culture. The students were not to be regarded as merely preparing for future

service as state officials, but as young men to be trained in independence of thought and in intellectual and moral freedom by means of an untrammelled study of science.[25]

The Ambiguity of Success

The foundation of the university at Berlin in the early years of the nineteenth century shocked the entire system. Essentially medieval universities made all possible haste to modernize themselves accordingly. Prussia took the lead, with its size and number of universities giving it a kind of hegemony.[26]

The actual development of German universities during the nineteenth century in some respects confirmed the intentions of the early reformers and proved their concepts to be successful. Supported by the rapid process of industrialization and a strengthening role of the bourgeoisie, universities adopted new tasks for society and economy that turned them into true research universities.[27] So successful was this conception that the new university structures and practices established in its name did not change substantially during the entire nineteenth century.[28]

The philosophical faculty became the most important of the faculties, since it contained an entire range of scientific disciplines that made enormous progress during the century and that tended toward a high degree of specialization.[29] Equally important, the philosophical faculties became the places for teacher training. In 1810 the *Examen pro facultate docendi* determined that all teachers of secondary schools should pass an academic examination. This was not only the beginning of state exams for many disciplines, but also improved the prestige of schoolteachers.[30] As a result students became oriented toward the final examinations, and clearly defined course programs were developed.[31]

Admission to universities was also regulated at an early stage. Between 1812 and 1837 most of the German states introduced the *Gymnasialabitur* as the final examination of secondary schooling (*Gymnasium*). The *Abitur* soon became a necessary requirement for university admission. The *Gymnasien* were meant to educate universally, but in such depth that every *Abiturient* would be enabled to study any subject at any university. As in France, general education at the Gymnasium consisted of languages, literature, history, mathematics, physics, and some chemistry and biology.[32]

As the modern German university was meant to provide a forum for the common search for truth, seminars were added to lectures as a principal form of learning. The orientation to research and the increasing specialization of disciplines led to the establishment of laboratories and to differentiation among university personnel. The professors were supported by assistants, and the universities were gradually departmentalized into institutes for specialized research. With the introduction of state examinations and

other university degrees, the traditional doctorate no longer carried with it
the medieval *jus ubique docendi* (right to teach everywhere). Between 1816
and 1838 the *Habilitation* was introduced in Berlin and consequently became
the formal qualification for teaching at all universities.[33] As a result, the unpaid *Privatdozent* (private docent) who had passed the Habilitation and was
waiting for a chair, became an important feature of the German university.
Since many Privatdozenten had to teach without ever achieving professorships, this made a university career socially very selective.[34] The institution of the *Privatdozentur* also enlarged the powers of the professors (*Ordinarien*), since the latter decided who achieved the Habilitation and who won
appointments in laboratories and clinics.

The fame and influence of the nineteenth-century German university on
other systems of higher education derived from the success of German
universities in highly specialized scientific and scholarly research. As Ben-
David observed: "Until about the 1870's German universities were virtually the only institutions in the world in which a student could obtain training in how to do scientific or scholarly research."[35] In Eric Ashby's terms:
"The German universities . . . became the envy of the Western world. In
Liebig's laboratory in Giessen, for example, students came to work from all
over Europe. Every student had to find his own way for himself. Liebig and
his disciples were to be found in the laboratory from dawn until far into the
night."[36] There was no guidance or counseling for students, no informal
contacts or extracurricular activities, which might have helped the students
toward broader personal development. Everything was geared toward
academic research.[37] The new ideal was the university as research center.

The evolution of the German system into the forefront of scholarship internationally came at some price. For one example, Humboldt's concept of
an undirected and free pursuit of academic research was severely distorted
during the second half of the century. A narrow intellectualism in the
academic world replaced his humanistic concept of Bildung durch Wissenschaft.[38] The ideal put before the student was no longer the liberal
humanism that had permeated the new university in Berlin. Instead it became a single-minded, almost fanatical commitment to the advancement of
knowledge, one that excluded philosophy, practical applications, and any
idea of education-for-life.[39]

Further, if according to the traditional ideal the philosophical faculty
was meant to provide a basis for an unrestricted and free pursuit of knowledge and a search for truth without state interference, the last one-third of
the nineteenth century was characterized by an ever increasing orientation
of research to military and industrial demands.[40] State expenditure on
military research comprised two-thirds of all Imperial expenditure for scientific purposes after 1871. By the end of the century, private economic
interests were involved in many academic research programs.[41]

Most important, perhaps, the international prestige of the German university toward the end of the nineteenth century disguised the hierarchical structures and the authoritarian character of the institutes in which the professors reigned autocratically. Most professors had not only become defenders of Bismarckian politics and German imperialism but also proclaimed within their disciplines authoritarian and expansionist tendencies. As Hans-Werner Prahl put it, "The German professors of the pre-war period were powerful within the universities (domination of the ordinarien), and outside the universities the majority of them tended to stoop to the ruling elite."[42] Most German professors of the time formed an unofficial alliance with the landowners and the rising industrialists against the aspirations of the working class and the petty bourgeoisie. Under the cover of *Wissenschaftlichkeit*—an attitude of defining everything exclusively in scientific or scholarly terms—many faculty were partisans of the authoritarian state and reacted aggressively against societal movements that would have changed the social and political system. Most political parties were able to send well-known professors into parliament.[43] The culmination of the German professors' support of the existing social and political conditions and of their loyalty to the Wilhelmine regime was reached in 1915, when over thirteen hundred professors and intellectuals signed a manifesto that favored the official aims of war, particularly the military and economic conquest of the neighboring countries in Western and Eastern Europe. Only a small minority of the university teachers opposed these aims.[44]

Thus the humanistic university ideals of Humboldt came to be misrepresented in important respects. The universities had become state institutions in a dual sense: not only were they governed directly by the state, they were by now also loyal supporters of the political regime. The research function of the German university, as it had been idealistically conceived by Humboldt, was distorted toward the end of the century by its orientation to industrial and military needs. The educational intentions of Humboldt (Bildung durch Wissenschaft) had failed to gather momentum. On the contrary, the free pursuit of knowledge and the search for truth that originally were intended to create enlightened and liberal citizens able to contribute to the rational organization of state and society were replaced by the socializing effects of hierarchically structured universities that transmitted a political culture allied with the aims of the Wilhelmine regime.

TWENTIETH-CENTURY TRAVAIL: 1900–1960

The political and cultural heritage also determined the fate of the German university system after World War I. Germany was fundamentally affected by radical social and political changes, including a large drop in economic output, massive unemployment, deep-rooted racist ideologies, embitterment of defeat, and a general lack of democratic values and institutions.[45] With the establishment of the Weimar Republic, the universities also found themselves in a difficult situation. The defeat of the political regime most professors supported should have been sufficient reason for critical reflection. But this intellectual clarification did not occur. The university continued to reproduce authoritarian modes of thinking and hierarchical institutional patterns.

Since the latter part of the nineteenth century, most faculty members in German universities had seen themselves as apolitical.[46] They developed a distinction between the political activities of scholars as private individuals and their role as professors who *ex cathedra* proclaimed the objective truths of Wissenschaft. This did not prevent many of them from taking sides with right-wing political programs.[47] During the Weimar Republic the equation "political equals democratic equals nonobjective and nonacademic" became the instrument that allowed German professors both to support the antidemocratic movements of their time and to explicate their "unpolitical existences." To be "unpolitical" meant, in fact, to acclaim the power of the governing classes in Germany as well as the power of the German *Reich* over other states. This belief in the ideological notion of an apolitical existence was for instance displayed by the renowned novelist Thomas Mann in 1918:

> I confess that I am deeply convinced that the German people will never be able to love democracy, simply because they cannot love politics as such, and that the much defamed authoritarian state (*Obrigkeitsstaat*) is the state form which, for the German people, is the most adequate one, the most beneficial one, and most wanted by them. . . . Away with this foreign and disgusting catch-word 'democratic'![48]

After the war and the abolition of the militarist monarchy, the German universities and their professors did not attempt to examine the reasons that led to political disaster. The university regularly celebrated the founding of the German Reich, which occurred on January 18, 1871. Kurt Sontheimer points out that speeches made at these celebrations usually included three major topics: a comparison of the glorious past of the Empire with the sad appearance of the Republic, the desire for the reconstruction of the old glory and power of the Reich, and an appeal to the students to regain this lost greatness.[49]

Such activities certainly encouraged students to hate the Weimar governments and the Social Democratic movement. Traditional modes of thinking and antidemocratic prejudices that many students, mostly upper middle-class, had already adopted at home were reinforced by their professors. The *Deutsche Studentenschaft* (German Student Union), founded in 1920, was basically nationalistic and anti-Semitic. The *Korporationen*, reactionary student associations that primarily engaged in beer drinking and fencing, had a strong influence on the general behavior of students. In the mid-1920s their members often discriminated against and persecuted Jewish university teachers.[50] By 1931 half of the Deutsche Studentenschaft supported the National Socialists. The National Socialist German Students Association (NSDStB) took over the organizational lead.[51] After the National Socialist German Workers' Party (NSDAP) had gained power, the students organized a general meeting under the slogan *Aufbruch des deutschen Geistes* (emergence of the German mind) at all German universities.

The NSDAP, heavily supported by industrialists and the conservative upper class, continuously gained power and parliamentary representation in the early 1930s. They openly propagated their antidemocratic, antisocialist, imperialistic, and racist slogans. Hitler's *Mein Kampf* was sold by millions of copies. Thus there could be but little doubt about the political intentions of the emerging regime. Hitler's political slogans, including his racial ideas, were also accepted by the universities. After Hitler gained power in 1933, it did not take the universities long to adapt to the new situation. In 1937 a speech made at the University of Göttingen revealed a new understanding of science and learning:

> We renounce international science. We renounce the international republic of learning. We renounce research for its own sake. We teach and learn medicine not to increase the number of microbes, but to keep the German people strong and healthy. We teach and learn history not to say how things actually happened, but to instruct the German people about the past. We teach and learn the sciences not to discover abstract laws, but to sharpen the implements of the German people in competition with other peoples.[52]

The university in Nazi Germany had ceased to be a *universitas* in the original sense. The universities degenerated into institutions of propaganda for the official ideology. Truth, for the National Socialists, was defined by the *Herrenvolk*, the "master race." As Arnold Nash puts it: "The sole criterion of truth of an idea is whether it will serve the German race, or rather the Nazi Party, in its unquenchable and avid thirst for power and yet more power."[53] Consequently, the truth of any set of ideas, according to the National Socialist view, was not to be seen in objective facts but was embodied by the führer.

Since the universities, like any other institution, were affected in every aspect by National Socialist ideology, nonacademic principles determined university life. On the administrative level the adoption of the Leadership Principle (*Führerprinzip*) meant the complete elimination of the governing power of both professors and students. Professors and students were organized respectively into a "teaching-corps" and a "student-corps," each with a "leader-spokesman." They in their turn were directly responsible to the

Rector as "the *Führer* of the University." None of the officials was elected but rather was appointed by the minister of education.[54] As early as March 1935, the universities were forced to participate in the National Socialists' military program; they were instructed to help indoctrinate their members with the idea of "defense-mindedness" (*Wehrhaftigkeit*). The curriculum was reorganized to give "defense science" (*Wehrwissenschaft*) priority over all other disciplines.

It is probably wrong to assume that a majority of the German academics supported the National Socialists before 1933. However, the "apolitical" universities were to a large extent responsible for the emphatic acceptance by a majority of students of not only anti-Marxist but also generally anti-democratic thinking, which later turned into open terror . Despite the expulsion of many of their colleagues for political and racist reasons, many professors soon identified themselves with the new situation.[55] Fascinated by the national "revolution," they saw their hopes for a quick resurrection of German imperialism and a fast liquidation of democracy and socialist movements fulfilled.[56] This identification was not abolished before the total breakdown of the Third Reich.

German universities became victims of National Socialism, in part because their uncritical and chauvinistic values legitimized nearly every policy proclaimed to destroy the Weimar party system and to restore Germany's strength internally and externally. This institution, which in the early ninteenth century was to have engaged in the free discovery of truth based on the humanistic principles of Idealist philosophy, had fallen victim to the illusion that a fanatical devotion to research (accompanied by neglect of general liberal values as a vital guiding function of such an institution) could preserve the principles and ideals of its founders.

University Reform after World War II

The reestablishment of the German university after 1945 was characterized by a specific set of structural and normative problems.[57] One of these consisted in the intended reinstallment of an independent research function, that is, the prevention of political intervention. Another major issue was the political and moral failure of universities and their members during the interwar period. A third question, related to the second, was the degree of specialization of Wissenschaft, which in the past seemed to have led the universities to neglect fundamental concerns, such as the provision of adequate professional training and a humanistic, politically enlightening *Allgemeinbildung* (general education). As a consequence the postwar university debate concentrated on this humanistic and political Allgemeinbildung of future graduates.[58]

The initial reform movement after World War II ought to be placed in that context. The basic intentions of this movement were summarized under the slogan *studium generale* directed against a *studium speciale*, which was regarded as dangerous. Specialists, it was realized, who are well informed within the narrow limits of their subjects but are not able to integrate their knowledge into the broader societal framework and its ethical and political necessities, were the products of traditional university training. Instead, it was argued, society needed the truly and generally educated graduate as envisaged by Humboldt. The studium generale movement, therefore, led to the creation of collegiate homes for students, in which positive social behavior was to be brought about, and it initiated curricula that contained broad and fundamental courses in sociology and political science.[59]

But the studium generale movement has neither succeeded in producing improved forms of communication and interaction in the universities nor has it ever lead to serious reflections on structural reforms. This movement, instead of revealing the oppressive and undemocratic nature of the organization of teaching and research in the history of German universities, diverted attention from the crucial topics. Jürgen Habermas summarized the situation as follows: "At that time the university was inserted into democratic society with a certain political extension of its traditional self-understanding, *but otherwise just as it was.*"[60]

Professors at German universities had always been completely in charge of all teaching and research within their subject areas. They were personally responsible for research funds allocated to their respective departments (in Germany called institutes), and thus they not only decided about the academic development of a particular part of the university but also authoritatively reigned over all other members of that institute. This monocratic system of institutes created problematic dependences and led, as Max Weber put it, to *proletarische Existenzen* (proletarian existences).[61] Weber was mainly referring to the *Assistenten*, junior faculty members who were, often for decades, organizationally as well as personally dependent on a professor.

This state of affairs basically remained unchanged and was one of the reasons for the student unrest and related political events of the late 1960s. Along with the reproach of political conservativism, students and younger academics began to put forward demands for intrauniversity democracy and participation in all university affairs.[62] But it was a long time before some new universities took the lead and implemented such schemes. On a national level it was not until 1976 that more democratic decison-making processes were introduced by the *Hochschulrahmengesetz* (Federal Framework Law for Higher Education).

ADVANCED TRAINING IN GERMAN UNIVERSITIES

During the last quarter century hardly any other institution within the Western industrial societies has experienced such a comprehensive and rapid transformation as tertiary education. The number of pupils in upper secondary schools and the transfer rate into tertiary education have risen dramatically almost everywhere. In most European systems, however, the proportion of the age group that completes secondary schooling and the share that enters higher education are considerably smaller than in the nations that have moved more fully into universal secondary and mass higher education. Thus analyses of expansion rates always have to take into account the overall degree of participation. Higher education systems like that of the Federal Republic of Germany, which have expanded most during the last decade or two, have in absolute terms considerably lower participation rates than those of Japan and the United States. After enormous expansion in the Federal Republic, about 20 percent of each age cohort at the end of the 1980s entered higher education.

This strong expansion of educational opportunities was made possible by a sound and flourishing economy. During the 1960s and early 1970s, the Federal Republic, like most Western industrial societies, developed at a steady rate, with exceptionally high economic growth and simultaneous improvement of the overall standard of living. Inflation and unemployment remained at a comfortably low level. A permanently growing gross national product, trade surpluses, and other positive aspects of the economy enabled the government to support a speedy enlargement of tertiary education. Under such circumstances early calls by educators, industry representatives, and politicians for a considerable expansion of educational opportunities at all levels were rapidly translated into national educational policies, enabling increasingly larger proportions of the population to participate in higher education.

The arguments underlying these initiatives rested on two main political considerations. A manpower approach was rooted in the conviction of employers and policymakers that the national pool of highly qualified manpower had to grow if the country was to compete successfully in the world market in times of rapidly changing technology. A second consideration, the social demand approach, found widespread support among those who maintained that the traditional education system had primarily served small societal elites, and that many gifted young people never had the opportunity to develop their talents. Postcompulsory education became regarded as a general civil right.

As a consequence, public authorities developed a series of measures aimed at extending compulsory education and developing a wider range of programs at the secondary and postsecondary levels, moves that would allow the educational system to draw on a wider pool of educational talent and meet the aspirations of new groups. The authorities introduced or improved comprehensive systems of means-tested grants for pupils and students. At the higher educational level, resources were deployed to develop a more diversified institutional framework and thereby to reduce the homogeneity of the system and its domination by the university sector. A more practical, vocationally oriented sector, the *Fachhochschulen*, emerged and began to constitute a major counterweight to the traditional universities. The general trend now is away from the traditional predominance of the university sector, with a shift toward other organizational patterns and educational emphases. Disappointment with the inertia displayed by the traditional universities has been a significant reason for these changes. The universities, in any case, are hard pressed to adapt to the increasingly rapid economic and technological changes that most industrialized societies have experienced in recent years.

Aided by these moves, especially the institutional differentiation, enrollment expanded five times between 1960 and 1989, from under 300,000 to more than 1.5 million. The university increase was over fourfold, while attendance outside the university sector (primarily at the Fachhochschulen) rose eight times (see table 1-1). Academic staff in universities and other institutions, which included teacher training colleges and arts academies, also increased considerably, quadrupling in those years. In recent years the number of teaching staff has continued to rise but at a pace that trails the earlier and more sustained boom in student numbers (see table 1-2).

Basic Features of Advanced Training

Teaching at German universities remains characterized and somewhat burdened by the traditional Humboldtian idea of a unity of research and teaching, particularly the expectation that university teachers use the results of their research directly for teaching purposes. This has led to a certain unwillingness on behalf of the professoriate, especially in the past, to participate in the planning and implementation of clear curricular patterns. It also has profound effects on the nature of "graduate education." Compared with the United States, virtually no graduate education exists in Germany in terms of a well-organized system of advanced coursework beyond the level of first degrees. Almost all teaching (and learning) is considered advanced in the German tradition. First-degree students are expected to master fully their subjects and in the end to be qualified to engage in research. The type of thesis required for a master's degree in England or the United States is also expected from most of those finishing the first degree at German universities.

Nevertheless, different kinds of students can be distinguished according to the level of their advancement. In most subjects universities now have in-

TABLE 1-1   Students, by Kind of Institution, Federal Republic of Germany,
1960–1989 (In Thousands)

Year	All Students		Universities	Art Academies	Fachhochschulen
1960	291,1	4.3%ª	238,4	8,5	44,2
1965	384,4	6.6	299,7	8,7	76,0
1970	510,5	9.5	410,1	10,9	89,5
1975	840,8	14.1	680,2	15,4	145,2
1979	983,6	15.3	784,2	17,0	182,4
1983	1273,2	17.8	976,6	20,4	276,1
1985	1338,0	18.1	1015,1	21,7	301,3
1987	1410,8	19.1	1060,0	22,2	328,6
1989	1509,0	21.5	1128,3	23,4	357,3
Year	New Entrants				
1960	79,4	7.9%ᵇ	60,0	2,6	16,8
1965	85,7	13.3	61,3	2,5	21,9
1970	125,7	15.4	91,6	3,4	30,5
1975	166,6	19.5	119,9	2,8	43,8
1979	177,7	18.2	125,2	3,0	49,6
1983	233,0	21.5	160,1	2,9	69,9
1985	207,7	19.5	141,3	3,0	63,4
1987	229,7	22.9	155,7	2,7	71,3
1989	252,6	29.1	171,9	2,9	77,8

SOURCE: Bundesminister für Bildung und Wissenschaft, 1990, 138–139.
ª Percentage of 19–25-year-olds
ᵇ Percentage of 19–21-year-olds

termediary examinations after two or three years, the so-called *Vordiplom* or *Zwischenprüfung*. Since the exact formalities vary from university to university and from discipline to discipline, it is not possible to compare these exams with degree levels in England or the United States. Most important, these early examinations do not enable those who have passed them to leave the university to work in the respective fields. They are not publicly recognized as professional qualifications.

At the highest level, doctorates do of course exist. But the work toward a Ph.D. is not combined with a specifically organized degree program. In many subjects, so-called *Oberseminare*, special seminars for advanced students, are offered. These are not only for Ph.D. candidates but also for students near the completion of the first major degree. Many Ph.D. candidates, at least in the social sciences and the humanities, have little contact

TABLE 1-2 Personnel, by Kind of Institution and Subject Area, Federal Republic of Germany, 1972–1988

Year	Total	Humanities, Sports	Law, Economics, Social Sciences	Mathematics, Sciences	Engineering	Agricultural Sciences	Medicine	Arts
Universities and art academies								
1972	57,978	13,235	5,132	12,297	6,487	1,637	15,064	2,014
1976	68,201	13,297	6,923	14,695	8,321	1,786	17,775	2,406
1980	76,013	13,282	7,796	17,035	10,276	1,984	18,658	2,425
1984	81,169	14,510	7,822	19,839	10,893	1,952	20,149	2,416
1986	85,618	14,371	8,175	21,157	11,585	2,108	21,103	2,459
1988	91,446	14,398	8,590	23,134	12,714	2,293	22,388	2,692
Fachhochschulen								
1972	7,825	132	1,499	292	5,122	141	—	496
1976	8,492	119	2,140	482	4,947	196	—	462
1980	9,221	107	3,076	439	4,626	335	—	516
1984	10,204	152	3,562	553	4,836	373	—	537
1986	10,436	187	3,633	592	4,912	376	—	549
1988	10,611	177	3,785	752	4,788	400	—	529
All institutions								
1972	65,803	13,367	6,631	12,589	11,609	1,778	15,064	2,510
1976	76,693	13,416	9,063	15,177	13,268	1,982	17,775	2,868
1980	85,234	13,389	10,872	17,474	14,902	2,229	18,658	2,941
1984	91,373	14,662	11,384	20,392	15,729	2,325	20,149	2,953
1986	96,054	14,558	11,808	21,749	16,497	2,484	21,103	3,008
1988	102,056	14,575	12,375	23,886	17,502	2,693	22,388	3,221

SOURCE: Bundesminister für Bildung und Wissenschaft, 1990, 220.

with universities or their supervisors; they mostly work at home. Therefore this academic activity beyond the first degree is not comparable with graduate work in other university systems. Several universities now offer programs in further or continuing education, but the extent of these provisions is very limited and the qualifications and certificates gained from such programs are also generally not equivalent to academic degrees.

The lack of a formally organized level of graduate teaching is also bound up with other primary features of German higher education. For one, the German university system does not distinguish between academic and professional training. All degree programs, those for professional qualifications in such fields as medicine, law, and architecture as well as those for primarily academic purposes, are on the same level and finish with degrees after approximately seven years. There are no separate graduate schools for business, law, or medicine. The university degree in the subject is both an academic qualification—it supposedly enables the graduate to engage in research—as well as a professional qualification, which is required for practical and applied occupational activities. Students in physics may finish with a state examination that certifies them for a teaching job at secondary schools, or they may take a diploma examination that opens employment opportunities in industries. For the former, the examination is handled by government authorities; for the latter, it is given by the university following requirements defined by field-related government ministries.

The specific problem of the relationship between research and teaching is particularly significant at the advanced level within the first-degree programs. (These programs now last about seven years on the average; the students themselves determine the time of their examinations.) It is primarily during the second half of most programs that the topical research activities of the faculty play an important role in teaching. At this level professors conduct seminars in which they present and discuss theory and recent empirical findings in their respective fields. To be accepted into these seminars, students must usually have passed a number of lower qualifications, for instance, by having attended lectures or lower seminars. In many cases they must have passed the preliminary examination that occurs about halfway in the program. It seems reasonable to define those last two or three years of the ordinary degree programs at German universities as equivalent to the early years in graduate programs in Anglo-American universities.

It is almost impossible to distinguish between faculty for undergraduate and graduate students in German universities. Not only does this distinction between categories not exist formally, but even if we differentiate between advanced and other students, the teaching staff cannot be separated along those lines. However, in many subjects junior faculty teach beginners and less-advanced students; they are not called professors but are known by such titles as *wissenschaftliche Mitarbeiter* and *Akademische Räte*. This leaves senior faculty free to train advanced students. In 1988 the number of non-professorial teaching staff was considerably larger than that of the professors: at 47,000 they were almost twice as many as the 24,500 professors.[63] As the number of academic personnel stagnated, the student/teacher ratio increased markedly: from 9 to 1 in 1970, the ratio rose to 15 to 1 in 1987, returning to the level found in 1960.[64]

Faculty in different subject areas have expanded at different rates during the last fifteen years. Although the humanities show hardly any increase between 1972 and 1984, medicine grew by almost one-third, and mathematics, sciences, engineering, and the social sciences increased by nearly 50 percent or more (see table 1-2). In the most recent years both the humanities and the social sciences have seen only small expansion in faculty, even though student numbers in these areas have continued to rise.[65] The social sciences include economics and business studies, areas that increased substantially, but political science and sociology received few additional positions.

It is difficult to distinguish faculty time spent on undergraduate versus graduate teaching. Most professors are required to offer lecture courses that can be attended by all students. The officially required amount of teaching for professors is eight hours per week, with no differences in this respect among *Länder* (states), individual universities, and major subject areas. Junior faculty teaching loads are much lower, usually only four hours per week. Most of their positions last for a limited period of three to six years, and their teaching obligations are kept modest because these faculty members are expected to work toward a Ph.D., or the Habilitation, the higher doctorate, which is the formal precondition for selection to a professorship. A few junior staff have permanent teaching positions; they face a heavier load of eight or sometimes twelve hours per week. Normally not expected to do research, these staff members are hired almost exclusively for teaching or some service function.

Professors are generally employed to teach a specific area within their respective subjects. But differences exist here as well; some professorships are advertised very broadly, covering an entire academic field. Twenty or thirty years ago, this was virtually the rule, but recently universities have tended to hire specialists, particularly in the natural sciences and engineering, but also in the social sciences. Even though junior staff are expected to engage in research and to work toward higher academic qualifications, junior positions are primarily filled to meet departmental teaching requirements. The need in a specific area will usually determine whether a particular candidate is chosen or not.

Historically, the German system guarded against institutional inbreeding. A long-standing tradition required that the first permanent employment of a professor be at a university other than the one from which he or she received the Habilitation. But numerous exceptions to this rule appeared. During rapid expansion in the late 1960s and the 1970s, many universities did not even require the Habilitation as a precondition for a professorship. Many junior faculty members were promoted to the professorial rank from within their departments. During the 1980s, with positions scarce, the old principle of *Hausverbot* ("house or home inhibition") has been reconfirmed, particularly for full professors, although exceptions are still possible.

The principle of Hausverbot leads to a considerable amount of academic mobility within the university system. Compared to most university systems in the English-speaking world, this mobility has not led to much differentiation and hierarchization of the universities in quality and prestige. Whenever particular professors have taught in certain universities, the public has always proclaimed differences in the reputations of individual university departments. If and when prestigious professors left a university, the prestige of that subject in that university also declined. But normally the reputation of the university as a whole was only marginally affected. Systemic features move powerfully in the opposite direction to restrain prestige hierarchy among the institutions. For one, professorial salaries are standardized. Ten or twenty years ago universities or ministries of education of Länder governments were still able to offer special benefits for academics they wanted to attract. But this mechanism of differentiation has been largely abolished. The main possibility of persuading someone to stay (or to come to a position in the first place) now consists of extra money for research assistants and equipment.

Most important, the system of open access to universities has strong equalization effects. Since the secondary-school leavers can freely choose which universities they will attend,[66] and since the universities are obliged to accept all candidates with an Abitur (the degree given by the Gymnasium sector of the secondary system), regardless of available capacities, universities are subjected to a continuous leveling-out process. In this respect universities in the Federal Republic are clearly distinct from those in the United Kingdom and, especially, in the United States.

THE RESEARCH SYSTEM

The Federal Republic spent almost the equivalent of $20 billion dollars on research and development (R&D) in 1985—2.66 percent of the Gross Domestic Product (GDP). This percentage was only surpassed by Japan and the United States with 2.82 percent and 2.83 percent, respectively.[67] Of this amount 38 percent was financed by state and national governments, and 61 percent came from the economic sector. If the governmental contribution in Japan was considerably lower (21 percent), in the United States it was surprisingly high (50 percent).

Funding of Research Sectors

In the Federal Republic 72 percent of research funds was spent in the economic sector, 12 percent was used by government agencies, and 15 percent was spent by higher education institutions. This latter percentage is not high when compared internationally, although in the United States it is, at 13 percent, even lower.[68]

We can distinguish four major research sectors in Germany: universities, nonprofit research organizations, state institutes, and the private sphere. Universities receive most of their research funding from national and state governments. Much of this support is contained in the basic funds for the normal operation of the institutions, in capital expenditure for buildings, equipment, and the like, and for personnel. Most of the salaries are paid by Länder ministries, but half the costs for buildings and large equipment is met by the federal government. Along with these basic funds individual professors or groups of researchers can apply for specific research funds. The *Deutsche Forschungsgemeinschaft* (German Research Foundation), which is governed by university representatives and financed by federal and state governments, is the most important addressee for such applications. But other large, partly private foundations, such as the *Volkswagenstiftung* or the *Stifterverband für die deutsche Wissenschaft*, also play an important role.

Among nonprofit research organizations we can distinguish between those publicly financed and controlled and those privately organized. The latter comprise many mostly small enterprises often created and run to support their founder-managers, but which are not permitted to make profits. The best known of the former, quasi-public research organizations is the Max Planck Society with its roughly sixty research institutes. It was founded in 1948 as a successor to the Kaiser Wilhelm Society, created in 1911. Its main task is the pursuit of undirected, fundamental research in selected, primarily scientific, fields. It receives all its funds from public sources (central government and Länder), is controlled by a public board of governors, and possesses much academic independence. Another important organization with a quasi-public character is the Fraunhofer Society for the Support of Applied Research (*Fraunhofer-Gesellschaft zur Förderung der angewandten Forschung*), with thirty-five institutes that are primarily active in technological fields. For most of these institutes only the core funding is from public sources; 70 percent of it is acquired through contract research.

Two main groups of state institutes can be distinguished. The first consists of thirteen *Grossforschungseinrichtungen*, large government-financed research laboratories, 90 percent of which are funded by the federal government. They were created in the 1950s and 1960s primarily for fundamental and applied research in nuclear energy programs, space technologies, and biological and medical research. Obliged to pursue mission-oriented research, they have little institutional autonomy and are controlled by yearly budgets. The second group consists of institutes in the so-called *Blaue Liste* (blue list), some thirty-five research and thirteen service institutes in a broad range of disciplinary areas, with a considerable representation of the social sciences and humanities. They were created after a 1975 agreement between the federal and Länder governments, and their funds are usually shared between the federal government and the Land in which they are located. Beyond these two main groups exist numerous *Bundesanstalten* (federal organizations) and other research institutes directly financed by and responsible to federal ministries. They supply research results directly relevant for policies of the respective ministry.

Finally, considerable research is done in private profit-making research firms, dependent upon outside funding from public or private sources.

A summary of total expenditure in the Federal Republic on Wissenschaft (including R&D) from 1979 to 1987 is in table 1-3. The figures include sums spent on academic teaching. Government authorities[69] and nonprofit research organizations increased their Wissenschaft contributions during those years from about DM 28 billion to roughly DM 42 billion, a growth rate of approximately 50 percent. The economic sector almost doubled its R&D expenditure, from less than DM 19 billion to more than DM 35 billion, and it has been considerably more willing to support research activities than the German governments.

Because these figures include funds necessary for the general operation of universities, including teaching, they may conceal "hidden" R&D efforts by the state, possibly in the universities. But this interpretation does not hold up. The government has increased its expenditure within its own realm of research activities only by roughly 15 percent, from DM 1.5 billion to DM 1.8 billion, between 1979 and 1987 (see table 1-4). State contributions to the economic sector increased by only one-half as much as funds from industry. In absolute figures the state supported industrial R&D with DM 4.4 billion in 1979 and DM 6.1 billion in 1987, while industrial support rose from DM 18.3 billion to DM 33.5 billion. Even more remarkable is the restriction in governmental support for the universities. During those eight years, support increased only from DM 5 billion to DM 6.6 billion, merely 25 percent, in contrast to about 40 percent in government support of industrial R&D. This may imply a lesser regard of the government for university research. But it probably has less to do with the official perception of differing quality standards in the respective societal areas than with the specific industrial needs that have emerged in recent years as a consequence of rapid technological change. In this respect the universities in the Federal

TABLE 1-3   Wissenschaft Expenditures in the Federal Republic of Germany, 1979–1987, by Financial Sources (In Millions of D-Marks)

Financial Source	1979	1981	1983	1984	1985	1986	1987
Public budgets							
Regional authorities							
Federal Republic	11,096	11,821	13,196	13,495	14,493	14,745	15,693
Länder (states)	16,888	19,745	21,323	22,086	23,873	24,133	25,668
Districts	200	231	229	222	266	266	226
Total	28,184	31,797	34,748	35,803	38,632	39,144	41,627
Nonprofit organizations	422	442	729	907	1,008	1,008	1,008
Total for public budgets	28,606	32,238	35,477	36,710	39,641	40,152	42,634
Percentage of total public budget	6.1	6.0	6.2	6.3	6.6	6.4	6.6
Economic sector							
Industry and trade	18,663	22,082	25,459	26,990	31,093	32,700	34,700
Endowments and donations	325	398	429	430	434	435	435
Total for economic sector	18,988	22,480	25,888	27,420	31,527	33,135	35,135
Total for all sources	47,594	54,718	61,365	64,130	71,168	73,287	77,769
Percentage of gross national product (GNP)	3.4	3.5	3.7	3.6	3.9	3.8	3.8

SOURCE: Bundesminister für Forschung und Technologie, 1988, 349.
NOTES: Wissenschaft expenditures include the sums spent on academic teaching as well as on research and development (R&D) outlays. The non-profit organizations are primarily state financed.

TABLE 1-4 R&D Expenditure in the Federal Republic of Germany, by Sectors and Sources, 1965–1987
(In Millions of D-Marks)

		Expenditure in the Economic Sector			Sources		Expenditure in the State Sector		Sources	
Year	Total R&D Expenditure	Total	State	Economy	Nonprofit Organizations	Foreign Countries	Total	State	Economy and Nonprofit Organizations	Foreign Countries
1965	7,910	4,570	560	3,970	30	10	430	400	30	—
1969	12,250	7,320	1,040	6,222	28	30	660	630	30	—
1973	20,460	12,020	2,340	9,448	15	217	1,040	1,020	20	—
1977	27,735	17,360	2,890	13,849	15	606	1,300	1,260	40	—
1979	34,477	23,341	4,430	18,349	48	514	1,578	1,508	38	31
1981	39,345	26,610	4,835	21,407	58	311	1,709	1,565	129	15
1983	43,942	30,462	5,255	24,702	81	424	1,756	1,692	47	17
1985	51,598	36,640	5,973	30,108	55	504	1,843	1,767	55	21
1987	56,860	40,280	6,155	33,550	65	510	1,860	1,777	61	22

TABLE 1-4 (cont.)

	Expenditure in Nonprofit Organizations		Sources		Expenditure in Universities and Colleges		Sources
Year	Total of Expenditure	State	Trade + Industry + private Institutions	Foreign Countries	Total of Expenditure	State	Trade and Industry
1965	1,000	916	84	—	1,450	1,430	20
1969	1,310	1,154	156	—	2,250	2,200	50
1973	2,480	2,190	287	3	4,270	4,200	70
1977	3,115	2,704	311	100	5,065	4,961	104
1979	3,465	3,310	87	68	5,154	5,044	110
1981	4,085	3,745	303	37	5,874	5,759	115
1983	4,237	4,077	119	41	6,256	5,907	349
1985	4,946	4,741	147	58	6,696	6,302	394
1987	5,820	5,578	174	68	7,110	6,660	450

SOURCE: Bundesminister für Forschung und Technologie, 1988, 352, 353.

Republic may indeed be regarded by public authorities as less flexible and less responsive than other research sites.

This impression is enhanced if we compare the rates of expenditure by the government in the university sector with its contributions to nonprofit research organizations. Although R&D funding at universities grew by only about 25 percent, R&D expenditure at nonprofit research organizations increased by roughly 70 percent (from DM 3.3 billion to DM 5.6 billion). Total government research spending inside and outside the universities has reached about the same level. Thus it appears that the research conditions outside the universities were generally looked upon more favorably by government for both practically oriented research in the economic sector and basic research in the nonprofit research organizations.

If we look closely at the expenditure of funds inside universities and outside of that sector, a possible explanation of this pattern emerges (see table 1-5). An enormous difference exists in the way universities and nonprofit research organizations use their available funds. If the former spent almost two-thirds on personnel (more than DM 14 billion out of DM 22.8 billion in 1985), the nonprofit research organizations spent less than one-quarter (nearly DM 4 billion out of DM 16.7 billion). The main reasons for this difference are the teaching costs in the university sector and secondarily the costs of large clinical and medical provisions. Nonprofit research organizations utilize funds much more directly for research purposes than do the universities. When student numbers increase, additional resources for the universities are even less likely to be used for research than are funds given to research projects outside them. Clearly, the trend is away from research support at universities in favor of increased expenditure at extramural research institutes.

Public Wissenschaft expenditures fall into three broad categories: institutional support, project support, and international cooperation. The distribution of funds was almost equal in the first two areas—about DM 7 billion each—and much lower in the third.[70] In institutional support (expenditures for buildings and equipment), the amounts given to universities were fairly low, less than DM 1.2 billion in 1988,[71] while the large nonprofit research organizations, for example, the Max Planck institutes, and the state-run research institutions, such as the Grossforschungseinrichtungen, received considerably more. Sites of pure research use more money for equipment in the sciences and engineering than do universities.

Among the research and scholarly institutions outside the universities, the greatest spenders are the large research laboratories—Grossforschungseinrichtungen—(more than DM 3.3 billion in 1987) followed by such state institutes as the Bundesanstalten (almost DM 1.4 billion).[72] The Grossforschungseinrichtungen spent most of their funds on scientific projects (more than DM 2.7 billion), followed by engineering research

TABLE 1-5 Public Science Expenditure by Areas and Kind of Expenditure, Federal Republic of Germany, 1979–1987
(In Millions of D-Marks)

Area of Activity	Year	Total Direct Expenditure	Personnel Costs	Other Current Expenditure	Expenses for Buildings	Other Investments
Universities and colleges, clinics included	1979	16,508	10,327	3,793	1,396	990
	1981	19,179	12,076	4,411	1,670	1,021
	1983	20,993	13,122	4,963	1,777	1,130
	1985	22,825	14,083	5,827	1,457	1,456
	1987	24,217				
Science and research outside universities and colleges	1979	12,122	2,786	6,865	355	2,114
	1981	13,295	3,301	6,918	508	2,566
	1983	14,655	3,598	7,864	589	2,602
	1985	16,758	3,993	9,213	671	2,879
	1987	18,350				
Total public science expenditure	1979	28,630	13,113	10,659	1,752	3,105
	1981	32,474	15,378	11,329	2,178	3,588
	1983	35,648	16,721	12,828	2,366	3,732
	1985	39,583	18,077	15,040	2,129	4,336
	1987	42,567				

SOURCE: Bundesminister für Forschung und Technologie, 1988, 355.

(DM 472 million), and medical investigation (DM 131 million). State institutes also spend most of their funds in these three areas, but they spend a considerable amount in agriculture and minor amounts in the social sciences and humanities. Of the more autonomous nonprofit research organizations, the Max Planck institutes alone (which are also primarily engaged in the natural sciences, secondarily in medicine, and in a minor way in the humanities and social sciences, and very little in engineering) spent just over DM 1 billion in 1987.[73] The Fraunhofer institutes, the fourth largest group of research organizations outside the university sector, primarily do research in engineering fields, spending a small amount in the natural sciences, and less than 5 percent in the humanities and social sciences.[74]

In 1985 research personnel in the universities totaled about 30,000: approximately 9,000 in scientific fields, 6,000 in engineering, 3,500 in medical fields, 1,400 in agriculture, and over 9,400 in the humanities and social sciences (table 1-6). Technical personnel totaled 14,000 (with almost four-fifths in the first three subject areas), and there were more than 25,000 "other personnel," namely secretarial and other administrative staff.

In research organizations outside the university sector, there is an even larger concentration of R&D personnel in the natural sciences than in the universities.[75] Almost half, 27,000 out of 55,000, are working in scientific fields. Personnel in engineering are also comparatively high, totaling almost 10,000. In contrast, research personnel in the humanities and social sciences consisted of only about 7,800 people, slightly more than 14 percent of the total. Most of the latter are found in libraries, archives, and museums.

Further evidence that the universities have been treated badly by the government in recent years is seen in the comparative support offered to the main alternative sector of higher education, the Fachhochschulen. Although the financial expenditure for faculty in absolute terms is lower at the Fachhochschulen than at the universities (DM 16,000 compared to DM 26,000 in 1985), the increases in support per faculty member in the former were larger than in the university sector during the last few years. The Fachhochschulen saw an increase of 24 percent between 1980 and 1985; the universities had to be satisfied with only 1.5 percent.[76]

Universities have clearly experienced rough weather. They have had to cope with stagnating general funds in a time of rapidly rising student numbers. They have had to accept that the other major sector of higher education has been judged more relevant to employment and the needs of the economy. Most important, the university sector is in danger of losing its traditional reputation as the leading research institution in society. More public and private funds for research have increasingly been spent outside the universities, either in industries or in nonprofit research organizations. This drift of research to outside research-centered organizations further

TABLE 1-6 R&D Personnel at Institutions of Higher Education by Kind of Personnel and Discipline, Federal Republic of Germany, 1985

Personnel	Total	Natural Sciences	Engineering	Medicine	Agricultural Sciences	Humanities and Sociology
R&D personnel at universities and colleges	69,007	20,219	12,150	16,934	4,372	15,332
Researchers	29,438	9,199	5,918	3,536	1,381	9,404
Technical	14,216	4,781	2,566	3,925	1,113	1,831
Other	25,353	6,239	3,666	9,473	1,878	4,097
Researchers in Institutions outside universities (1987)	54,906	26,831	9,646	5,581	4,912	7,834

SOURCE: Bundesminister für Forschung Technologie, 1988, 405, 411.

attenuates the traditional Humboldtian ideal of a unity of research and teaching.

Research and Advanced Training

In accordance with criteria developed by the Organisation for Economic Co-operation and Development (OECD), the West German government calculated in a 1988 report the percentage of time spent by faculty on R&D activities at institutions of higher education.[77] Within the university sector there are no large differences among the major subject areas: in the humanities and applied arts, about 30 percent; in law and the social sciences, including economics, about 35 percent; and in all the remaining disciplinary areas about 45 percent.[78]

The small time differences as stated by the government are based on considerable uncertainty, an acknowledgment made in a report stating that actual research activities in higher education "can hardly be accounted for without large-scale empirical surveys."[79] Such surveys do not exist. The disciplinary differences in the amount of time spent on research are undoubtedly larger. In the natural sciences the time necessary to keep up with recent developments in one's field and to contribute to its development is considerably longer than the time required in many disciplines in the humanities and social sciences in which the subject contents do not change as rapidly. The requirements of teaching also vary greatly; the curricular core essential for well-informed teaching changes faster in the sciences than in the arts and social sciences (see chapter 2).

That some faculty members hardly engage in research or publishing at all has much to do with the overall institutional framework of the university system. Compared with the American and British systems, the university sector in the Federal Republic hardly contains any institutional incentives and control mechanisms based on competition and quality comparisons between universities and within them.[80] Lacking autonomy from state intervention, the universities are not, for example, free to select their students or to offer salary differentials to their faculty.[81] The professors also have civil service status, which gives them employment security and leaves them considerably free as individuals to do as they like—in research or in teaching.

To understand the relationship between research and advanced training in German universities, other broad features of the higher education system (explored in more detail in chapter 2) have to be taken into account. First, as pointed out earlier, there is virtually no separate level of graduate education. Most academic programs last more than six years, and degrees in different fields, including professional areas, are approximately on the same level. Clear patterns of course work toward doctoral programs hardly exist.[82] Nevertheless, many candidates who work toward a doctorate take part in research activities in their departments by means of part-time employment as research or teaching assistants.

Second, the tradition still holds that in principle students should reach the theoretical and methodological boundaries of their respective disciplines by the time they take their first degree. They are required as part of the final examinations to write theses comparable to master's theses elsewhere. German universities also expect their students to pass intermediary exams after two or three years. Then, during the second half of their studies, students are confronted in seminars and lectures with topical research results from professors' work.[83]

Third, many of the more able, or more visible, students get drawn into the research activities of the faculty during the last part of their studies. These involvements range from assistantships in small empirical surveys to minor tasks in laboratories and computer centers to part-time jobs in research projects. Some advanced students thereby have an opportunity to gain firsthand research experience. However, these possibilities are limited.

Fourth, a major additional area of possible research influence on the teaching process is the overlapping employment of professors inside and outside the university. Virtually all directors of Max Planck institutes are simultaneously professors at universities. The same duality applies also to many other senior researchers in nonprofit research organizations and state institutes. Results from this outside research work no doubt influence what is taught in universities. Curricular conditions that are often criticized as too unstable and heterogeneous may in fact be advantageous; they enable professors to incorporate into their teaching aspects of topical research that in a more rigid curricular structure would be left out.

These features suggest that research and teaching may be fairly well integrated in the university sector of the Federal Republic. But counterforces loom large. For one, the overwhelming majority of first-degree students are more or less left to themselves during the course of their studies. They often have difficulty in getting to know their professors or participating in research activities. Students also have significant problems of orientation in a system that has little curricular organization, thereby still following the Humboldtian principles of freedom of teaching and freedom of learning. A disorganized curricular pattern, resulting in part from overloading courses and programs with new and recent research orientations of professors, has contributed to excessively long periods of study. Neither systematic guidance of undergraduate teaching nor clear and purposeful research orientation exists. Students who have to earn their living while at the university not only extend the time spent on taking courses but also concentrate on the minimum examination requirements. They are generally not in a position to evolve a serious research interest. This unfavorable position of many

students was worsened in 1983 when a system of student grants was transformed into a repayable loan scheme. In the late 1980s the minister of
education in Bonn modified this scheme so that only about one-half of the
financial support had to be paid back.[84]

Another negative pull away from integrated research and teaching is
that the amount of actual research involvement of students is very small.
The exact figures are difficult to determine, but overall fewer than 10 percent of all first-degree students get such a chance. No organizational division exists between "ordinary" students and those who want to develop a
particular research interest: basically they are treated similarly up to their
final examinations. Recently, demands have increased to shorten the normal course length by limiting it and to add a graduate level of training for
those who are specially interested in, and can qualify for, an academic
career. Such suggestions have had little effect. Some universities, in a
limited way, have begun to take up organizational recommendations of the
Wissenchaftsrat (Academic Council) to introduce so-called *Graduiertenkollegs*,
special doctoral programs that also include a clearly structured course
pattern.[85]

CONCLUSION

To understand the present German research system and its relationship to
academic training we have to recall the origin and evolution of the Humboldtian university. This concept emerged under the influence of Idealist
philosophers and liberal Prussian administrators at the beginning of the
nineteenth century. Influenced by the goals of the French Revolution, they
hoped to create an enlightened population that would participate in the
creation of a rationally organized society. Toward this end, teachers and
students were to be given a maximum amount of freedom to teach and to
learn whatever they wished. Teachers were expected to follow the Idealist
notion of a permanent search for "truth as such," that is, to do research and
to utilize the results of their own research directly in their teaching. Students were seen as almost equal partners of professors in the search for
objective knowledge. These expectations together constituted the call of the
Humboldtian principle of a unity of research and teaching.

The actual development of the German university system during the
nineteenth and twentieth centuries did not follow these idealistic notions,
even though most observers and participants have been inclined to think so
until recently. The new research emphasis was indeed successful in its own
terms. The strict concern with fundamental research led to a new type of
university institute with a hierarchical structure of control that, particularly
in the sciences, broadened the frontiers of knowledge. This "research university" model has had considerable impact on universities abroad. But

despite Humboldt's idea of a purpose-free pursuit of pure knowledge, the German universities continued primarily to train for the professions. And the new orientation adopted a narrow conception of the production of knowledge that did not include broad humanistic concern. With its positivistic and apolitical definition of research and scholarship, it also paved the way for an extremely conservative role for the professoriate and the student population. It proved to be open for abuse in the research itself: much of the topical research toward the end of the century was done for economic and even military purposes. In contrast, the English and the American models, while incorporating the research concept, continued to maintain a commitment to humanistic concerns in the form of liberal education and character development.

The ways in which the idea of a "unity of research and teaching" developed in English and American universities is an indication that the German ideal has by no means become a universal principle. In England a strong tradition of orienting university education to the student's personal development rather than to disciplinary requirements prevailed. Although the old ideal of character formation was transformed into the concept of "liberal education," which put considerable emphasis on scientific and academic training, the intellectual aspect of learning always remained embedded in the broader function of improving a person's personality.[86] English universities were able to do both: to define clear areas of established knowledge, which were organized as binding curricula, and to encourage their academics to engage in research as part of their defined duties. The latter might or might not coincide with what teachers did in their teaching. There was no obligatory link between the two. Research became an important professional characteristic of university teachers, but the research results did not have to be directly utilized for teaching purposes. This insured that academics became and remained acquainted with research activities, and it seemed to be a sufficient proviso to guarantee high intellectual standards in teaching.[87]

In the United States, the German research example was adopted toward the end of the nineteenth century. But in contrast to England, the consequences for the organization of university teaching and research were more radical. Apart from a complex process of differentiation in the overall system of higher education, which was related to diverging interests, purposes, and functions in tertiary education,[88] the sector comparable to the European universities—the "research universities"—was characterized by a gradual process of internal differentiation.[89] The three major functions of the leading American universities developed in three ways: liberal education, in some respects similar to its British counterpart, is almost exclusively reserved for the undergraduate level;[90] professional training is placed in specialized professional graduate schools; and the research function is exercised mainly within the academic graduate school of arts and science. Thus, compared with the German university tradition, the American universities considerably segment teaching and research. Of course, the professors are often the same, whether they teach undergraduates or graduates, whether they deal with Ph.D. candidates or with aspiring professionals. But a close connection between ongoing research and teaching mainly exists in the graduate schools of arts and sciences. This is the sector within the American research universities that has preserved and developed the German heritage.

The expansion of the university system in Germany after World War II has led to an awkward structural and functional muddle. The transformation of the system into loci of mass higher education, with about five times more students now than in the early sixties, has jeopardized the traditional balance between the tasks of academic inquiry and the advanced training of students. The old ideal of a unity of research and teaching is still part of the official frame of reference at universities. But in recent decades friction occurred in this system because of an increasing discrepancy between the traditional research orientation of university faculty and their actual involvement in training large numbers of students.

This tension threatened to break up the conventional institutional framework, either by external differentiation (the introduction of comprehensive universities and Fachhochschulen), or by internal functional separation (attempts to distinguish professional from research programs). But despite several decades of reform discussions, the contemporary German university is still characterized by structural features that obstruct fundamental reform: the constitutionally guaranteed open access to all universities for anybody with a certain secondary degree; the students' ability (with only a few *numerus clausus* restrictions) to freely choose subjects, universities, and time of examination, and their freedom to leave and reenter the system as they wish; the professorial freedom to teach whatever they prefer. All these features are sanctioned by the Humboldtian principle of the freedom of teaching and learning; the overloading of programs and courses according to individual research interests of professors; the lack of guidance by teachers, so that many students find it difficult to get organized; the widely criticized length of studies in most subject areas,[91] and the bureaucratic and state control of organizational matters, including the civil service status of the professoriate.

In the contemporary period of emerging mass higher education the Humboldtian formulation has therefore become increasingly inadequate. The challenges and requirements of advanced manpower training on a massive scale have largely proved to be incompatible with the old ideas and structures. Course work averaging seven years for a first degree is a clear indication of the failure of the attempts at reform.

Despite the rapid expansion of the German system of higher education during the last quarter century, stringencies and restrictive policies have caused the support for universities to stagnate and the conditions for research and teaching to deteriorate considerably. Because student numbers continued to rise but expenditures on staff remained almost the same, most universities have become enormously overcrowded. Professors and other teaching staff find it difficult to cope with the sheer volume of teaching, let alone to organize meaningful research programs. Under these circumstances many observers feel that the training of advanced students is in jeopardy; they often do not receive the individual attention they need to develop research interests and skills.

Several structural features of the German system also make it difficult to produce advanced scholars and to maintain high standards. There is no clear separation between undergraduate and graduate studies. Apart from doctoral students there are virtually no graduate students. Doctoral students are not part of a special program, but usually work on their own, if they are not, as in some scientific fields, bound into an ongoing research enterprise. The German system, moreover, hardly distinguishes between professional and academic degrees. Thus all students, even though most have no such intention, are expected to acquire the skills and knowledge that will enable them to participate in research activities. This emphasis on research training appears during the last two or three years of the first-degree effort. It is usually limited to theoretical training in seminars and lectures.

Research funding in the Federal Republic has been surpassed only by Japan and the United States in the recent past. Increased support has been given primarily in the economic sector, by industry and commerce, while support by the German government has trailed. Moreover, within the comparatively low R&D budget of the German government, there is a clear trend of offering less research money for universities and more for industrial laboratories and nonprofit research organizations. It is unclear whether this trend is caused primarily by a governmental conception of decreasing research efficiency at the universities, perhaps as a consequence of overcrowding, or by a heightened concern about industrial R&D needs. But the possible repercussions and dangers for universities are manifold. If this trend of an exodus of research from universities to outside research sites should continue, one of the basic pillars of the system, the unity of research and teaching, may be further undermined.

Despite these developments, general research support for a broad variety of research institutions functions fairly smoothly. And to the extent that there is considerable overlap between senior academic personnel of universities and outside research institutions of the Max Planck type, a relatively new pattern of research training is strengthened. Ph.D. students and even some advanced students about to take their first degrees are absorbed into research projects located as much or more in nonprofit research organizations as in universities. Although the numbers are not yet large, such specific, highly advanced research activities centered considerably outside universities may be particularly valuable for aspiring young scholars. At the end of the 1980s reform discussions continue to swirl in and around the historic German model of the modern research university. For the overall system, with Anglo-American models much in mind, demands increase for an enforced differentiation in quality, prestige, and type of institution. Many academics, politicians, and committees press to shorten substantially the first-degree programs and to introduce a clearly demarcated graduate level. But the Humboldtian structures are old and resistant, and the vested interests of the main actors within the system are strong.

NOTES

1. See Gellert, *Society, Politics and Universities.*
2. Mann, *Deutsche Geschichte,* p. 23.
3. Stein, *Grosse Kulturfahrplan,* pp. 868–876.
4. Prahl, *Sozialgeschichte des Hochschulwesens,* pp. 181–186.
5. Plessner, *Verspätete Nation.*
6. Goethe, for instance, expressed this view when he pointed out that "revolutions are entirely impossible, as long as governments are constantly just and awake, so that they meet them (revolutions) with adequate (social) improvements and do not prevent them for too long, so that the most necessary alterations might be enforced from below." This paternalistic attitude encouraged the political hierarchy to undertake reforms from above. Quoted from H. Böhme, *Prolegomena zu einer Sozial- und Wirtschaftsgeschichte Deutschlands,* pp. 23–24. See also Ben-David, *Centers of Learning,* p. 14.
7. Mehring, *Deutsche Geschichte vom Ausgang des Mittelalters,* pp. 104–112.
8. Böhme, *Prolegomena zu einer Sozial- und Wirtschaftsgeschichte Deutschlands,* pp. 27–40.
9. Ben-David and Zloczower, "Universities and Academic Systems in Modern Societies," p. 52.
10. Jarman, *Landmarks in the History of Education,* p. 214.
11. Ben-David, *Centers of Learning,* p. 14.
12. Erdmann, *Philosophie der Neuzeit,* Vol. VI, pp. 7–30.
13. Ibid., pp. 48–64; and Vol. VII, pp. 7–17 and 35–45.
14. In the following we use the German term *Wissenschaft* to refer to research and scholarship in a broad sense (the natural sciences, the humanities, and the social sciences).
15. According to Schleiermacher, this could be realized only when equal and autonomous individuals freely communicate. Such conditions required more independence for universities from state interference. "It is easy to see that the natural direction of the universities is such that the dominating influence of the state should again be brought back to its natural frontiers." Schleiermacher, "Gelegentliche Gedanken der Universitäten im deutschen Sinn," pp. 533–642.

16. Fichte, *Sämtliche Werke*, Vol. VIII, p. 203; König, *Vom Wesen der deutschen Universität*, p. 115; Conze, "Das Spannungsverhältnis von Staat und Gesellschaft im Vormärz," pp. 207–269.

17. Offe, "Historische Aspekte der Funktion und Struktur der deutschen Universität," pp. 20–31.

18. Humboldt, *Schriften zur Politik*, pp. 257–258.

19. Humboldt, *Gesammelte Schriften*, p. 261.

20. Humboldt, *Schriften zur Politik*, p. 256.

21. Nitsch, et al., *Hochschule in der Demokratie*, p. 21.

22. Flexner, *Universities*, p. 320.

23. Prahl, *Sozialgeschichte des Hochschulwesens*, p. 201.

24. Ibid., pp. 199–200.

25. Paulsen, *German Universities*, p. 52.

26. Flexner, *Universities*, p. 316. For a detailed account of the foundation of the University of Berlin, see König, *Vom Wesen der deutschen Universität*, pp. 160–167.

27. The actual economic and sociopolitical changes cannot be dealt with here. A good account of the political weakness of liberalism and the bourgeoisie, as well as the consequential alliance between aristocracy and industrialists (particularly the role of Bismarck), is given by Barraclough in *Origins of Modern Germany*.

28. Paulsen, *German Universities*, p. 61.

29. Riese, *Hochschule*, pp. 62–65; Ben-David, *Centers of Learning*, pp. 93–100.

30. Fricke, *Beiträge zur Oberlehrerfrage*.

31. Prahl, *Sozialgeschichte des Hochschulwesens*, pp. 242–244.

32. Ben-David, *Centers of Learning*, p. 73; Flexner, *Universities*, pp. 306–311.

33. Prahl, *Sozialgechichte des Hochschulwesens*, p. 245.

34. Busch, *Geschichte des Privatdozenten*.

35. Ben-David, *Centers of Learning*, p. 22. Ben-David also points out that this superiority in research was not accompanied by equal superiority in training for professional practice or in general education, since "excellence in professional practice, or in education for its own sake, was much more difficult to measure than excellence in research."

36. Ashby, "Nineteenth Century Idea of a University," p. 3.

37. According to Ashby, the German graduate was the product of a "university cult" (with attributes such as "meticulous accuracy," and "earnest dedication to labour"; moreover, he was "intense, dogmatic, his mind stocked with footnotes"). However, the English graduate, the "reasonable man whose motto was 'in nothing too much'; impregnated with the traditions . . . ; suspicious of intellect disengaged from character" must also be seen as a product of a "university cult." Ashby, *Universities*, p. 7.

38. König, *Vom Wesen der deutschen Universität*, pp. 154–160.

39. Ashby, *Technology and the Academics*, p. 25.

40. Jarman, *Landmarks in the History of Education*, pp. 213–214.

41. Pfetsch, *Zur Entwicklung der Wissenschaftspolitik in Deutschland*, pp. 179–180.

42. Prahl, *Sozialgeschichte des Hochschulwesens*, p. 208; see also Jens, *Eine deutsche Universität*, pp. 302–323.

43. Andernach, *Einfluss der Parteien auf das Hochschulwesen in Preussen*.

44. Prahl, *Sozialgeschichte des Hochschulwesens*, p. 291.

45. Landes, *Unbound Prometheus*, p. 398.

46. Jens, *Eine deutsche Universität*, pp. 302–323; for a general account of the German universities around the turn of the century, see Ringer, *Decline of the German Mandarins*.

47. Abendroth, "Das Unpolitische als Wesensmerkmal der deutschen Universität," p. 191. Max Weber's support of the principle of a separation of politics and the academic profession has, however, often been misunderstood as an attempt to legitimize the proclamation of right-wing political convictions within the universities. (See Prahl, *Sozialgeschichte des Hochschulwesens*, p. 290.) In fact, his intentions were quite opposite, since he was convinced that only by the implementation of this principle would the political abuse of professorial positions be prevented. Weber, *Wissenschaft als Beruf*, pp. 582–613.

48. Mann, *Betrachtungen eines Unpolitischen*, pp. 194–196.

49. Sontheimer, "Haltung der deutschen Universitäten zur Weimarer Republik," pp. 30–31.

50. Pross, *Vor und nach Hitler*, p. 70.

51. Giles, "University Government in Nazi Germany."

52. Quoted from Nash, *University and the Modern World*, p. 114.

53. Ibid., p. 117.

54. Ibid., p. 118.

55. Jens, *Eine deutsche Universität*, pp. 324–348.

56. Hartshorne, *German Universities and National Socialism*.

57. The terms "German" and "Germany" will be used synonymously for "West German" and "Federal Republic of Germany."

58. Flitner, "Universität—Berufsschule oder Bildungsstätte?", pp. 13–14; for a comprehensive account of the development of German universities after World War II, see Kloss, "University Reform in West Germany," pp. 323–343.

59. Habermas, "Universität in der Demokratie," p. 120.

60. Habermas, *Toward a Rational Society*, p. 5 (emphasis by Habermas).

61. Weber, *Wissenschaft als Beruf*; see also Busch, *Geschichte des Privatdozenten*.

62. See, for instance, Bergmann, *Rebellion der Studenten*.

63. This is only the faculty with regular teaching positions and does not include extra personnel hired primarily for research purposes. Bundesminister für Bildung und Wissenschaft, *Grund- und Strukturdaten 1986/87*, pp. 196–197.

64. Ibid. See also Thoma, "Früchte der Bildungs-expansion," p. 33.

65. Bundesminister für Bildung und Wissenschaft, *Grund- und Strukturdaten 1986/87*, p. 212.

66. Only the places in a few subjects, such as medicine and pharmacy, are restricted; they are distributed by a federal agency on the basis of a complicated system of credits, with some use of a lottery mechanism.

67. Bundesminister für Forschung und Technologie, *Bundesbericht Forschung 1988*, p. 391.

68. The highest percentage spent in the university sector was in the Netherlands (24 percent), closely followed by Canada (23) and Japan (20). Bundesminister für Forschung und Technologie, *Bundesbericht Forschung 1988*, p. 391.

69. The federal government, the Länder (states), and the communities. The largest contribution came from the Länder, with roughly 60 percent, followed by the federal government, with over one-third, leaving the communities with less than 1 percent.

70. The expenditure here only comprises federal resources. Bundesminister für Forschung und Technologie, *Bundesbericht Forschung 1988*, p. 362.

71. This is less than the average spending on the universities during the previous five years. Bundesminister für Forschung und Technologie, *Bundesbericht Forschung 1988*, p. 362.

72. Ibid., pp. 381–383.

73. Ibid.

74. The total expenditure of the Fraunhofer Institutes was DM 439 million in 1985. Bundesminister für Forschung und Technologie, *Bundesbericht Forschung 1988*, p. 381.

75. Ibid., pp. 410–411; see also table 1-6.

76. Wissenschaftsrat, *Erhebung der laufenden Mittel für Lehre und Forschung 1986*, p. 44.

77. Bundesminister für Forschung und Technologie, *Bundesbericht Forschung 1988*, p. 346.

78. In teacher training colleges, theological colleges, and arts academies, the respective amount is 15 percent, in the *Fachhochschulen* only 5 percent. The latter figure is most certainly too conservative. The Fachhochschulen contribution to applied research, particularly for projects in technology transfer, has rapidly expanded in recent years.

79. Bundesminister für Forschung und Technologie, *Bundesbericht Forschung 1988*, p. 346.

80. For the United States, see Gellert, *Wettbewerb und Leistungsorientierung im amerikanischen Universitätssystem*.

81. Gellert, "State Interventionism and Institutional Autonomy."

82. Teichler, *Higher Education*, pp. 150–151.

83. During the so-called *Hauptstudium*—the "main program"—in contrast to the "basic program" before the intermediate examination.

84. Gellert, "Politics and Higher Education," pp. 217–232.

85. Wissenschaftsrat, *Empfehlung zur Förderung von Graduiertenkollegs*.

86. Gellert, *Vergleich des Studiums*, pp. 27–31.

87. One indiction of the growing importance of research in British universities was the introduction of the Ph.D. in 1917. See Simpson, *How the Ph.D. Came to Britain*.

88. Riesman, *On Higher Education*.

89. There are roughly two hundred doctorate-granting institutions in the United States. These are called "research universities" here. In other classifications the term refers to the approximately one hundred universities that produce the largest number of Ph.D.'s and have the largest funds for research. See the Carnegie Commission on Higher Education, *Classification of Institutions of Higher Education*.

90. The American "liberal arts" concept is, however, characterized by a stronger interdisciplinary emphasis; in England the "single honours degree," a specialized training in one subject, is still prevalent.

91. In contrast to Germany, the organizational features of the leading sector within the higher education system of the United States are well-ordered and transparent. The traditional principle of a "unity of research and teaching" is no comprehensive attribute of the overall system of research universities in the United States. The strong research orientation and its support stem from factors that in many re-

spects have little to do with the requirements of teaching. See Gellert, "Wettbewerb und institutionelle Differenzierung." For a detailed analysis of present-day American universities, see Clark, *Academic Life*, and Clark, ed., *Academic Profession*.

BIBLIOGRAPHY

Abendroth, Wolfgang. "Das Unpolitische als Wesensmerkmal der deutschen Universität." In *Universitätstage 1966. National-Sozialismus und die deutsche Universität*, by H. Herzfeld et al. Berlin: Freie Universität Berlin, 1966. Pp. 191–205.

Andernach, Norbert. *Der Einfluss der Parteien auf das Hochschulwesen in Preussen 1848–1918*. Göttingen: Vandenhoek & Ruprecht, 1972.

Ashby, Eric. *Technology and the Academics*. London: Macmillan, 1958.

————. *Universities: British, Indian, African: A Study in the Ecology of Higher Education*. London: Weidenfeld & Nicolson, 1966.

————. "The Future of the Nineteenth Century Idea of a University." *Minerva* 6, no. 1 (Autumn 1967): 3–17.

Barraclough, Geoffrey. *The Origins of Modern Germany*. Oxford: Blackwell, 1966.

Ben-David, Joseph. *Centers of Learning: Britain, France, Germany, United States*. New York: McGraw-Hill, 1977.

Ben-David, Joseph, and A. Zloczower. "Universities and Academic Systems in Modern Societies." *Archives Européennes de Sociologie* 3 (1962): 45–84.

Bergmann, Uwe, et al. *Rebellion der Studenten oder Die neue Opposition*. Reinbek: Rowohlt, 1968.

Böhme, Helmut. *Prolegomena zu einer Sozial- und Wirtschaftsgeschichte Deutschlands im 19. und 20. Jahrhundert*. Frankfurt: Suhrkamp, 1972.

Bundesminister für Bildung und Wissenschaft, ed. *Grund- und Strukturdaten 1986/87*. Bonn, 1986.

Bundesminister für Forschung und Technologie. *Bundesbericht Forschung 1988*. Bonn, 1988.

Busch, Alexander. *Die Geschichte des Privatdozenten. Eine soziologische Studie zur grosbetrieblichen Entwicklung der deutschen Universität*. Stuttgart: F. Enke, 1959.

The Carnegie Commission on Higher Education. *A Classification of Institutions of Higher Education*. Berkeley: Carnegie Commission on Higher Education, 1973.

Clark, Burton R. *The Higher Education System: Academic Organization in Cross-National Perspective*. Berkeley, Los Angeles, London: University of California Press, 1983.

————. *Academic Life in America: Small Worlds, Different Worlds*. Princeton, N.J.: Carnegie Foundation for the Advancement of Teaching, 1987.

————, ed. *The Academic Profession: National, Disciplinary, and Institutional Settings*. Berkeley, Los Angeles, London: University of California Press, 1987.

Conze, Werner. "Das Spannungsverhältnis von Staat und Gesellschaft im Vormärz." In *Staat und Gesellschaft im deutschen Vormärz, 1815–1842*, ed. W. Conze. Stuttgart: Klett, 1962. Pp. 207–269.

Erdmann, Johann E. *Philosophie der Neuzeit*. Vols. VI and VII. Hamburg: Rowohlt, 1971.

Fichte, Johann G. *Sämtliche Werke*. Vol. VIII. Berlin: Veit, 1845/46.

Flexner, Abraham. *Universities, American, English, German.* New York: Oxford University Press, 1968 (first 1930).

Flitner, Andreas. "Universität—Berufsschule oder Bildungsstätte?" In *Was wird aus der Universität? Standpunkte zur Hochschulreform,* ed. G. Schulz, 9–25. Tübingen: Wunderlich, 1969.

Fricke, K., and F. Eulenburg. *Beiträge zur Oberlehrerfrage. Die geschichtliche Entwicklung des Lehramtes an den Höheren Schulen.* Leipzig: Teubner, 1903.

Gellert, Claudius. "Politics and Higher Education in the Federal Republic of Germany." *European Journal of Education* 19, no. 2 (1984): 217–232.

———. "State Interventionism and Institutional Autonomy." *Oxford Review of Education* 11, no. 3 (1985): 283–293.

———. *Vergleich des Studiums an englischen und deutschen Universitäten.* 2d ed. Munich: Lang, 1988.

———. "Wettbewerb und institutionelle Differenzierung—Anmerkungen zur universitären Leistungsbewertung in den USA." *Beiträge zur Hochschulforschung* 4 (1988): 467–496.

———. *Alternatives to Universities.* Paris: OECD, 1991.

———. *Society, Politics and Universities in England and Germany* (forthcoming).

———. *Wettbewerb und Leistungsorientierung im amerikanischen Universitätssystem.* Frankfurt, New York: Lang (forthcoming).

Gieseke, Ludwig. "Die Diversifikation des tertiären Bildungsbereiches in der Bundesrepublik Deutschland." *Wissenschaftspolitik* 27 (1982): 42–56.

Giles, Geoffrey J. "University Government in Nazi Germany: The Example of Hamburg." Working paper. Institution for Social and Policy Studies, Yale University, 1976.

Habermas, Jürgen. "Universität in der Demokratie—Demokratisierung der Universität." In *Protestbewegung und Hochschulreform,* 108–133. Frankfurt: Suhrkamp, 1969.

———. *Toward a Rational Society. Student Protest, Science, and Politics.* London: Heinemann, 1971.

Hartshorne, Edward Y. *The German Universities and National Socialism.* Cambridge: Harvard University Press, 1937.

Humboldt, Wilhelm V. *Gesammelte Schriften.* Vol. XIII. Berlin: Behr, 1920.

———. *Schriften zur Politik und zum Bildungswesen. Werke.* Vol. IV. Stuttgart: Cotta, 1964.

Jarman, T.L. *Landmarks in the History of Education.* London: Murray, 1963 (first 1951).

Jens, Walter. *Eine deutsche Universität.* Munich: Kindler, 1977.

Kloss, Günter. "University Reform in West Germany—The Burden of Tradition." *Minerva* 6, no. 3 (Spring 1968): 323–343.

König, René. *Vom Wesen der deutschen Universität.* Darmstadt: Wissenschaftliche Buchgesellschaft, 1970 (first 1935).

Landes, David S. *The Unbound Prometheus.* London: Cambridge University Press, 1969.

Maassen, Peter, and F. van Vught, eds. *Dutch Higher Education in Transition.* Culemborg: Lemma, 1989.

Mann, Golo. *Deutsche Geschichte des 19. und 20. Jahrhunderts.* Frankfurt: Fischer, 1960.

Mann, Thomas. *Betrachtungen eines Unpolitischen.* Berlin, 1918.

Mehring, Franz. *Deutsche Geschichte vom Ausgang des Mittelalters.* Düsseldorf: Wande, 1946.

Nash, Arnold S. *The University and the Modern World: An Essay in the Philosophy of University Education.* New York: Macmillan, 1943.

Nitsch, Wolfgang, et al. *Hochschule in der Demokratie.* Neuwied: Luchterhand, 1965.

Offe, Claus. "Historische Aspekte der Funktion und Struktur der deutschen Universität." In *Faktoren und Zielvorstellungen der Hochschulreform in der Bundesrepublik,* ed. UNESCO-Institut für Pädagogik, 20–31. Hamburg, 1969.

Organisation for Economic Co-operation and Development (OECD). *Post-Graduate Education in the 1980s.* Paris, 1987.

———. *Alternatives to Universities in Higher Education.* Paris, 1990.

Paulsen, Friedrich. *The German Universities and University Studies.* London: Longmans, Green, 1906.

Pfetsch, Frank R. *Zur Entwicklung der Wissenschaftspolitik in Deutschland 1750–1914.* Berlin: Duncker & Humblot, 1974.

Plessner, Helmut. *Die verspätete Nation.* Frankfurt: Suhrkamp, 1974.

Prahl, Hans-Werner. *Sozialgeschichte des Hochschulwesens.* Munich: Kösel, 1978.

Pross, Harry. *Vor und nach Hitler. Zur deutschen Sozialpathologie.* Freiburg: Olten, 1962.

Riese, Reinhard. *Die Hochschule auf dem Weg zum wissenschaftlichen Grossbetrieb.* Stuttgart: Klett-Cotta, 1977.

Riesman, David. *On Higher Education: The Academic Enterprise in an Era of Rising Student Consumerism.* San Francisco: Jossey-Bass, 1981.

Ringer, Fritz K. *The Decline of the German Mandarins.* Cambridge: Harvard University Press, 1969.

Schleiermacher, Friedrich. "Gelegentliche Gedanken der Universitäten im deutschen Sinn." In *Werke,* F. Schleiermacher, Aalen: Scientia Verlay, 1981 (first published 1808). Pp. 533–642.

Simpson, Renate. *How the Ph.D. Came to Britain.* Guildford: Society for Research into Higher Education, 1983.

Sontheimer, Kurt. "Die Haltung der deutschen Universitäten zur Weimarer Republik." In *Universitätstage 1966. National-Sozialismus und die deutsche Universität,* H. Herzfeld et al. Berlin: Freie Universität Berlin, 1966. Pp. 26–35.

Stein, Werner. *Der grosse Kulturfahrplan.* Munich: Herbig, 1978.

Teichler, Ulrich. *Higher Education in the Federal Republic of Germany.* New York: Center for European Studies, Graduate School of the City University of New York, 1986.

Thoma, F. "Früchte der Bildungsexpansion. Das Studium dauert zu lange und ist zu spezialisiert." *Süddeutsche Zeitung,* June 30, 1988.

Weber, Max. "Wissenschaft als Beruf." In *Gesammelte Aufsätze zur Wissenschaftslehre,* M. Weber. Tübingen: Mohr, 1968. Pp. 582–613.

Wissenschaftsrat. *Erhebung der laufenden Mittel für Lehre und Forschung 1986.* Cologne: Wissenschaftsrat, 1987.

———. *Empfehlung zur Förderung von Graduiertenkollegs.* Cologne: Wissenschaftsrat, 1988.

TWO

The Conditions of Research Training in Contemporary German Universities

Claudius Gellert

The German university system, as described in chapter 1, is characterized by structural features that affect both its operations and the education of future scholars. Higher education in the Federal Republic of Germany has changed from an elite system of advanced learning for a select few to a massive enterprise for professional training. This shift, begun in the late 1960s, has been accompanied by institutional differentiation that has introduced new forms of higher learning. Economic, political, and social forces have also put additional pressures on the traditional university system. Labor market expectations for highly skilled manpower, political pressures toward more accountability and intramural democratization, and social demands for increased open access and enhanced educational opportunity have placed universities under great strain to legitimize their tasks and organizational patterns.[1]

Drawing upon chapter 1, we begin with a brief review of the general changing context of university life in Germany as a framework for the microlevel analysis that follows. Four features are central: expansion, differentiation, the Humboldtian tradition, and patterns of research funding.

THE CHANGING CONTEXT OF UNIVERSITY ORIENTATION

The most important precursor to change in the structure and orientation of higher education in industrialized societies has been overall quantitative expansion. Between 1960 and 1989 in West Germany, as we have seen, the number of new entrants more than quadrupled and the number of students increased more than fivefold. The percentage of students among the nineteen- to twenty-six-year-old population also increased more than fourfold during that time, from 4.3 to 21.5 percent. Since the mid-eighties, and contrary to many predictions, student enrollment has continued to increase.[2] That the total number of students continued to grow has partly been due to lengthening study periods, which in itself is somewhat a reflection of the declining opportunities in the labor market in recent years. Moreover, many secondary school leavers now look first for some practical training (an apprenticeship, for instance) before embarking on a course in higher education some time later.

This strong expansion of higher education was not possible without a considerable increase in academic personnel. But the growth rate did not keep up with student numbers. During the 1980s few new academic positions were created, and vacancies were also rare in recent years, since the rapid expansion in the late 1960s and 1970s resulted in a large group of academic personnel who will not retire before the mid- and late 1990s. In this important respect the conditions for training advanced scholars have not been favorable.

Accompanied by a long, protracted reform process, differentiation has been an important feature in West German higher education. With the emergence of the *Fachhochschulen* (vocationally oriented institutions), partly through the transformation of engineering schools and advanced vocational schools (*höhere Fachschulen*) that concentrated on economics, social work, and agriculture,[3] a rapidly growing alternative to the university sector was established. Compared to the universities, these new institutions were characterized by distinctively new features: greater responsiveness to industrial needs and expectations from the labor market; disciplinary concentration in areas such as engineering, business studies, and social work; more practically oriented teaching; support of increased educational opportunities through offerings to mature students and formally disadvantaged social groups; shorter study periods; greater teaching loads for professors; fewer research activities and principally in applied areas; and no graduate training or doctoral programs.

Most of these characteristics also appeared in an important German experiment in higher education, the model of the *Gesamthochschulen* (comprehensive universities). Created in a few *Länder* (states) in the early 1970s, these institutions were meant to combine traditional university programs with the more applied courses of the Fachhochschulen; they were also open for nontraditional secondary school leavers.[4] However, the Gesamthochschulen did not prove successful, primarily because students overwhelmingly choose the longer university courses instead of the short, more applied Fachhochschul programs. The model consequently became abolished as a leading concept for higher education reform in Germany in the 1985 revision of the Federal Framework Law in Higher Education (*Hochschulrahmengesetz*). But the Fachhochschulen have prospered as a powerful alternative sector. Traditional universities are now often challenged to demonstrate that their long study periods and sometimes disorganized curricula can match the stringent, tightly structured course programs of the Fachhochschulen. A comparative framework for the assessment of the conditions for student training at preadvanced levels now exists.

At the same time, the traditional Humboldtian conception of a research university continues to dominate debates about university life today. Many academics, administrators, and politicians still believe that the prevailing ideals of the early nineteenth century should continue to be the guidelines for the organization of German universities. Chapter 1 described these ideals as centered on the aim of educating an enlightened population who would then be able to participate in shaping a humane and democratic society. In the process professors and students would be enabled to discover and disseminate "objective truths" in an environment undisturbed by immediate considerations of vocational purposes or state intervention. Two enduring beliefs have followed and are still guides to behavior: "freedom of teaching and learning," the notion that professors should be absolutely free to teach whatever they think necessary and that students should be unrestricted in their inclinations to study where, what, and how long they deem desirable; and "unity of research and teaching," where the content of teaching should be a direct result of the research process. These two ideals led to certain behavioral outcomes that still prevail. Professors have an unusually high degree of independence because they are negligibly bound by obligations to contribute to curricular coherence or to student counseling. In turn, students can choose and change universities at will: universities must admit applicants who have passed the *Abitur*, with the exception of a small number of subjects that have a *numerus clausus*.

Finally, changing patterns of research funding are potentially encouraging a radical departure from core elements of the traditional university paradigm. Government and private institutional support of research is slowly moving away from universities, toward nonprofit research organizations and other extramural research units. This trend, if it continues, will pose a real threat to the old dogma of a unity of research and teaching, since the interdependence of the two constituent parts is in jeopardy if one of them is threatened. With the gradual slipping away of a traditionally essential structural component, a continuation of this trend would also necessitate a fundamental revision of the overall definition of universities.

RESEARCH ORGANIZATION AND SCHOLARLY TRAINING

What are the consequences of the Humboldtian heritage and the present modifications for the organization of research programs and the training of advanced students? In-depth interviews with academics and students help us understand how those actively participating in the system perceive and evaluate developments. Interviews were carried out in the three disciplines of physics, economics, and history at six universities in three German Lander (Bavaria, Berlin, and Hamburg) and at Max Planck institutes outside Munich.[5] The three universities of Munich, Hamburg, and Berlin are among the largest institutions in the country, with more than 50,000 students at Munich and Berlin and almost that number at Hamburg. The Technical University of Berlin is also a large institution; the Bavarian regional universities of Augsburg and Regensburg are considerably smaller, with about 15,000 students each. The professors approached in Hamburg and Berlin were more cooperative and willing to answer questions than their colleagues in the southern universities of Munich, Augsburg, and Regensburg. When our interviews took place in early 1989, universities were in a turbulent state. Some professors therefore initially associated our project with ongoing student unrest; it was only after explaining that this study was part of an international project that they agreed to cooperate.

Physics and history in Germany are unified disciplines even though they consist of many specialties. This is not the case with economics. "*Okonomie*" is found only in a few universities. In most institutions there is a separation between *Volkswirtschaftslehre* (VWL) and *Betriebswirtschaftslehre* (BLW): the former corresponds to what in the Anglo-American context is called economics, the latter approximates business studies. The comparison between BWL and business studies is not exact, because to some extent students of BWL also have elements of VWL in their course programs. Apart from that, BWL as well as VWL is a normal undergraduate degree and recipients are awarded the same kind of diploma and take a similar examination. For employment purposes, the two subjects are largely compatible. If BWL is more practically oriented than VWL, graduates of the latter nevertheless often enter the business world. German students generally also take one or two minor subjects: for the two wings of *Ökonomie*, the minors are likely to be law, statistics, or sociology, fields that prepare graduates in more generalized subject matter suitable for a broad range of professional areas.

In our interviews we concentrated on five topics:

- departmental research conditions, including funding and personnel support
- the effect of faculty research activities on teaching
- the active involvement of advanced students in research enterprises
- the status of aspiring academics, particularly doctoral students
- the Humboldtian concept of a unity of research and teaching in relation to recent university developments.

Changing Research Conditions

The departmental framework for pursuing research projects is quite different from discipline to discipline. A physics professor at Hamburg University described the situation as follows:

In our institute we are dealing with experimental physics (*Festkörper-Physik*). Theory plays only a marginal role; the theoreticians work relatively isolated within the institute. Research is carried out in five research groups. They each consist on average of two professors, fifteen students, some auxiliary personnel, and a few assistants each. The assistants are people with Ph.D.'s who are employed on a half-time basis and are expected to work, besides their teaching, toward a higher doctorate (*Habilitation*). These Ph.D. positions are mostly financed through external sources, roughly two-thirds of them. Without those external sources from funding agencies, research could not work at all in our institute. These external funds normally have to be reapplied for every two years. The actual duration of projects is usually hardly less than four years. Those who participate in these projects in order to gain a qualification usually do not overspecialize in a problematic manner. Despite a (inner-university) *numerus clausus* the number of students in our department has tripled during the last ten years. The institute funding, which had been on a constant level over the last ten years, has now been cut by 10 percent, since the university has to save ten million DM in personnel expenditure.

Another physicist, in theoretical physics at the Technical University in Berlin, considers himself to be in a special situation compared with his experimentally oriented colleagues. His research depends less on big research equipment and laboratories, and he is not involved in large-scale projects. Rather, his interests lie in the development of fundamental theoretical issues. Since his working instruments are mainly "paper and pen," all he needs in addition is a powerful computer. He is satisfied with his research conditions, since through his involvement in a *Sonderforschungsbereich* (a special research project lasting several years, occasionally involving academics from different institutions and from several disciplinary backgrounds), he can rely on sufficient funding from the Deutsche Forschungsgemeinschaft (DFG, the German Research Foundation).

Another physics professor, an astrophysicist at a Max Planck institute, also had little to complain about regarding research conditions, since his work was also mostly theoretically oriented; all he needed was loose cooperation among working groups. Because of the sound financial basis of the Max Planck organization, he did not feel he had to compete with other researchers for funding. However, international competition in scientific achievement was an important source of motivation for his work.

In business studies (BWL), the situation at Regensburg University is described by a professor:

At our department ["*Institut*"] there exist several research projects, primarily funded from outside. The institute has eight professorships, twenty-five positions for assistants, and ten for research associates, which also are financed from external sources. While the assistantships are civil-service positions for a specific number of years (usually between three and six years), the research associate positions are dependent on the duration of projects. The research at my Chair is financed one-third through regular university budgets, another third through state funds from outside, and finally one-third from private sources. There exist several cooperative projects [in the area of marketing] with private companies. The chance to get such projects going with private industries depends to a large extent on the reputation of the individual professors.

This business studies professor pointed out that the numbers of new entrants in his department are sharply up. With almost 800 freshmen appearing in the *winter* semester of 1988–89, each professor had approximately 100 more students. Like his colleagues, he considered this to be the paramount interference with research.

According to the information provided by a professor of economics (VWL) at Munich University, no research projects are financed from private industry in his department, but a number of research activities are funded by the DFG or the Volkswagen Foundation. Research pursued at the department is mostly of a theoretical nature, but some of it is used for applications in economic policy making. Some empirical research is done on regional topics. In the distribution of available time, he reported that 30 to 40 percent was used for research, 40 to 50 percent for teaching, and 10 to 20 percent for administration. In addition to the rapid rise in student numbers (primarily in BWL, but also in VWL, since many of the former study the latter subject as a minor), he was worried about the deterioration of library funds. This, he felt, had serious consequences for the type of theoretical research pursued in his department.

An economics professor (*Sozialökonomie*) at Hamburg University complained about the rather isolated work of individuals in his department. He said that funding and work space were bad and equipment had partly been purchased by staff members. Cooperation was low. Institute activities emphasized teaching, which together with administration comprised 80 to 90 percent of time and capacity. Often, therefore, research was conducted in his "free time," that is, outside the department. Since most of his research consisted of "intentional reading" and the preparation of publications, very little research was financed by third parties. His chair had three half-time research assistant positions occupied by doctoral students. These positions were not considered very attractive since they paid badly and did not offer promising career prospects; it was therefore difficult to place good candidates in such posts.

Although the professor at Hamburg University considered the supervision of diploma theses to be part of his teaching activities, an economics professor at Regensburg University counted this thesis work as part of his research. Nevertheless, his distribution of time and energy still leaned toward teaching, with 70 percent expended on teaching, 10 percent on administration, and only 20 percent on research. But this distribution varied somewhat from semester to semester. Sometimes he has to deal more with beginners and younger students who are in their *Grundstudium*; the teaching burden is then about double that of other semesters when he is dealing with advanced students. He pointed out that matriculation figures had continually risen, and the number of new entrants doubled during the last semester. At the same time the positions for academics remained the same.

In history the situation is more similar to economics than to physics (and therefore similar to the more theoretically oriented VWL than to BWL). As a professor from Munich University pointed out, research financed by third parties occurs only when some department members have contracts with publishers or are invited to give papers at conferences. *Akademische Räte* (lecturers in English terminology) employed in tenured positions are not supposed to engage much in research, and they would in any case find little time for it because of their heavy involvement in teaching. Assistants with doctoral degrees, however, have very limited teaching duties but are expected to work toward a higher doctorate. The distribution of time for tenured lecturers was estimated to be 75 to 80 percent allotted to teaching, none for administration, and 20 to 25 percent for research. The assistants who were expected to do a higher doctorate, in contrast, spent about 30 to 40 percent of their time in teaching, 10 to 20 percent in administration, and 50 percent in research.

Here, as elsewhere, conditions for research have been heavily influenced by the rise in student numbers; during the last ten to fifteen years a professor's teaching obligations have doubled, including the supervision of advanced students for diploma theses. Another major problem was seen in the decreased quality of secondary school leavers. After the upper-secondary reform of 1976, pupils could specialize in three or four subjects, which, in one interviewee's opinion, negatively affected their study capabilities.

A history professor in Hamburg pointed out that most research was highly individualized in his department. Technical requirements were minimal. Some projects were financed by the DFG, but there was little institutional provision for interdisciplinary cooperation. Student numbers had increased moderately during the last few years. Since the beginning of the 1980s, Hamburg has implemented a *numerus clausus*. As a result the teaching load had risen "only" by about 25 percent. If it should rise any further, our informant believed that the quality of education could not be guaranteed. He also saw the decreased funding of libraries as a major problem.

The evaluation of research conditions, as we have seen, varies considerably from discipline to discipline. In experimental physics, representatives from applied fields occasionally complained that the expensive and highly sophisticated equipment they needed was partly outdated. Their colleagues from theoretical physics, needing only powerful computers, did not have such problems. Generally, most professors thought that the funding base for expensive equipment was satisfactory. Finance of research projects through the largest research council, the German Research Foundation (DFG), and through state support as well as private foundations was usually considered to be functioning well.[6] However, there has been a tendency in recent years for the DFG to treat engineering and science subjects more favorably than the humanities and social sciences.

According to our informants direct research funding from industry or other private commercial sectors did not exist at any meaningful level. But this may have been partly determined by the selection of disciplines. If we had looked at other subjects, particularly engineering and medicine, the private funding would have been more prominent. Moreover, the 1985 revised Framework Law has only slowly been translated into state legislation. One major change in the new law liberalized access to outside research funds for university members. Thus professors from disciplines included in our survey may also have access to private research funds in the future.

Despite sufficient funding (at least in physics) of specific research projects and large equipment, the overall financial situation of institutions of higher education is recognized as being difficult in recent years. Few new permanent positions at the professorial level have been allocated. In periods of rising student numbers this has led to a deterioration of research conditions. Lack of building funds means that most departments and laboratories suffer from extreme space limitations. Library conditions are thought to be catastrophic in such fields as history and economics. Even a professor of physics complained that 90 percent of the library budget at his department was used for keeping the most essential journals; only 10 percent was available for purchasing books. Such limiting conditions, which not only affect the research process but also the ability of pursuing one's studies in an effective manner, have repeatedly led to student demonstrations at several German universities. And in 1989, for the first time in a long while, the federal and state governments saw the need to considerably increase public expenditure for higher education during the next few years.[7]

Surprisingly, most of the interviewed professors were not worried about the quality of research at their institutions. A majority of physics professors, in whose departments the detrimental effects of scarce resources should have been felt most, were convinced that the research quality at German universities internationally enjoyed a high reputation. Several Nobel prizes in physics, won by Germans in recent years, seem to support such claims. On the other hand, several professors believed that the financial situation at universities was going to worsen even further during the next few years. They cited the continuing rise in the number of students as a factor. Another concern was that a considerable number of academics would reach retirement age in the 1990s; politicians may not be prepared to provide sufficient funds at a time when personnel problems of turnover and recruitment are most urgently felt.

Departmental and university administration is another area of discontent. A majority of those questioned complained about large administrative burdens placed on department and university levels, particularly as a consequence of increased student numbers. Many professors also criticized the central university administration as highly inefficient and obstructive in matters of research organization: for example, in personnel decisions and in the channeling of external funds to respective departments.

Apart from such contextual features, the research process itself, according to respondents, has changed over the last twenty to thirty years. Three areas of change seem to have affected professorial self-image and may have repercussions for the training of advanced students.

First, several respondents referred to the consequences of technological progress, particularly to the introduction of modern computers as a more efficient means of academic and scholarly production. The point applies not only to scientists but also to historians and economists, who occasionally remarked that even personal computers had revolutionized knowledge in both quantitative and qualitative respects. For economists they enabled far-reaching calculations for econometric models; for social historians this new technology opened the possibility of building large-scale data banks, particularly for comparative purposes.

Second, a widely noted trend in modern research consists of increasing specialization. Several academics had negative comments about this tendency; they pointed out that often the theoretical interpenetration of their subject areas was threatened and that the teaching process itself was endangered. Since clear-cut, circumscribed curricula are not often offered within the system, the teaching of ever more specialized contents becomes, from the student perspective, less and less relevant for the final examination. This has led on all levels to the declining appeal of many courses.

Third, according to several respondents, the growing specialization in many research fields has had a positive effect in internationalizing the research process and promoting international cooperation. Many professors feel that they now have to travel abroad more often to exchange ideas and to present their research results: in certain areas of expertise fewer and fewer people can be found in Germany. This point was particularly stressed by physicists.

To conclude this overview of research conditions in German university departments, we can summarize that, according to their own assessment, the interviewed academics spent on average about one-half of their time on research, one-third on teaching (including preparation time), and the rest on administration. But we must note some marked differences. One concerns the type of teaching. Introductory teaching is considered to be more time-consuming than teaching on the advanced level of diploma candidates. Inexperienced students obviously need more "spoon feeding," while the advanced ones are expected to work through scholarly materials or scientific problems independently. Moreover, in seminars during the second half of many undergraduate programs students are often asked to present papers and thus themselves to "manage" the teaching situation; this to some extent relieves the instructor of extensive preparations. Also, in such mass disciplines as business studies or (in some universities) physics, the demands on professors are felt to be heavier than in other fields. Then, too, in small universities the pressure of teaching is less, since there are fewer student examination papers to mark.

Finally, some interviewed academics felt that despite government willingness to support expensive scientific equipment in technological areas generally believed to be vital for an export-oriented economy, the research conditions in other areas also had to be improved, in order to uphold a high quality of research within the university system.

Research and Teaching

What then are the consequences of the existing research conditions for the training of advanced students? What are the structural preconditions for research participation of "graduate" students or even undergraduates? At which level of instruction can we speak of purposeful research training for advanced scholars?

Generally, as noted in chapter 1, the macro organization of teaching, learning, and examining in Germany differs significantly from that of Anglo-American systems. In Germany the distinction between undergraduate and postgraduate studies does not really exist. Master's degrees, diplomas, state exams, and the like, which are all first degrees and approximately on the same level, are, apart from doctorates, the only university degrees offered. In the past, even Ph.D.'s were often taken as a first degree. Therefore research training in a taught form, to the extent that it exists at all in a formal way within the German system, occurs mostly within the normal course of studies. The decisive influences occur toward the end of a student's course program. But since there is no clear institutional break between educating professionally oriented students and training students for research, as we observe it in American research universities,[8] the conditions of learning for normal students (undergraduate students in the Anglo-American terminology) are also largely the conditions for the formation of future scholars and researchers.

In this context some professors made a distinction between research and academic activity. Although many contend that most students by the end of their studies have not been involved in any kind of research, they presume that most of them have learned to work academically, that is, to use scientific and scholarly methods, to approach a problem systematically, to use literature and data. For a history professor in Hamburg, even the final M.A. or diploma thesis has little to do with research. And an economics professor at that university who favors the creation of separate graduate level programs (but thinks that is unlikely, for financial reasons) explained that in his department the thesis, written before the final examinations, requires three months for preparation. The thesis topics are decided by lottery. Under these circumstances, he added, it is not likely that an independent and interesting academic piece of work will result. The thesis has more the character of an examination and an academic exercise.

The overall pattern of teaching and learning is therefore one of the keys to understanding the problems of research training. Curricula at German universities, if they exist at all, are often vague and lead to many problems of orientation for students as well as for lecturers. The ideal of a unity of research and teaching is still used by university teachers to excuse lack of participation in the elaboration of even medium-range curricula. The students' traditional freedom to change universities as often as they wish and their freedom in many subjects to choose examination dates also contribute to organizational uncertainties.

Moreover, the German university system puts great store in examinations, mostly written, that are taken at the end of six or seven years of study. Despite intermediate exams, which students in most programs have to pass half-way through their studies, no evaluation of their capabilities in these exams or in seminars counts toward final marks. Since everything depends on the final exam, it becomes a very heavy burden on students. It also has detrimental repercussions on the motivation of highly interested and able students to look at the process of academic training other than in purely instrumental ways.

This examination approach perpetuates the idea that it is possible and adequate to reproduce an entire body of academic knowledge in a few exam sessions after a long period of study.[9] In reality, in most subjects, some kind of prearranged selection of possible examination topics takes place. Notably, many students postpone serious examination preparations until a year or less before the actual event. Many of the activities of previous years are thus deemed superfluous or at least superficial. Some sort of system of continuous and accumulative assessment with a gradual build-up of credits would certainly involve more institutional control and would most likely result in more efforts to master the subject matter. Finally, the heavy pressures of the all-decisive final exams not only contribute to the ongoing extension of the period of study but also put an unfair burden on those who are less able to produce optimally in extreme situations.[10] Under these circumstances it is not surprising that several interviewed students remarked that they saw little sense in participating in certain lectures and seminars that would otherwise have interested them, since they felt preoccupied above all with the threatening prospect of having to cope with the all-decisive examination some time in the future.

Thus, the conditions enabling students to become acquainted with research activities and to develop academic curiosity are hardly ideal. In other countries this familiarization with the adventures of scholarship and research often occurs in the intimate atmosphere of small seminar sessions or well-ordered laboratories. In the Federal Republic no institutional selection of the most able students takes place. Formally, all students are grouped together until the very end of their time at the university. And those who might be particularly interested in more than training for a well-paid job are confronted with the same methods and conditions of teaching and learning as everyone else.

The conditions are anything but intimate. Lectures with several hundred students are no exception, and seminars often contain one hundred or more. The amount of written work is minimal, and the habit of not attending lectures or seminars at all is widespread. Thus the tacit institutional control and supervision that are a structural given in many other systems hardly exist in Germany. Students frequently complained during interviews about the minimal amount of counseling and the individual responsibilities expected of them. They are largely left to themselves, which adds to their orientation difficulties. Universities are often experienced by students as anonymous, uncommunicative, and alienating.[11]

In our interviews students frequently bemoaned the lack of didactic capabilities of instructors; this tends to weaken student motivation and their interest in learning. *Hochschuldidaktik* (staff development) is indeed largely absent at German universities. Professors are chosen exclusively on the basis of publications; their pedagogical abilities are infrequently put to the test. Some students, particularly in the humanities and social sciences, are quite disturbed by this. As one recent graduate said: "During my whole university time I have only come across one male and one female teacher who were really capable of presenting the contents in an optimal way. . . . I do not understand why respective qualifications are not obligatory for university instructors."

These organizational features undoubtedly deter many advanced students from getting involved in more specialized research training as a step toward an academic career. With their motivation dampened, they concentrate their efforts instead on an instrumentalist approach to graduation. A history student stated that he "would not want to work in such an environment later, anyway"—an opinion no doubt endorsed by many of his peers.

A major finding of our survey is therefore the almost unanimous acknowledgment that the average student at German universities is not involved in research. Some universities do, however, experiment in some programs (particularly in the social sciences) with "project-oriented" courses: one of the best-known examples of this is the sociology program at the University of Bielefeld. During one or two semesters a small research project is carried on by instructor and students. But, as one student emphasized, these project-oriented seminars are not popular since they are considered to be very time-consuming, keeping students from other obligatory courses. Participating in such a seminar extends the student's time to completion even further.

Preliminary Research Training

As we have seen, despite the traditional attempt to combine research activities with professional training and to lead graduates to a qualification that consists of both elements, average students during the course of their university studies have little chance to actually get involved in research. For most of their time at the university, students are fairly passive recipients of information transferred in lectures and seminars. And even at advanced seminars where in some cases professors report on their ongoing research, the active involvement of the students themselves is minimal. Where, under these circumstances, is the formation of future scholars and academics then happening? Is it possible to point to developmental levels or to organizational arrangements that give advanced students at least an informal acquaintance with research methods and training to become future scholars?

Many professors pointed out that the closest students come to research is during the last phase of their education, when writing a diploma thesis. Virtually all course programs at German universities require the submission of such a thesis, whether for a diploma (usually in such established professions as architecture and engineering), an M.A. (usually in the humanities), or a state exam, for example, for teachers or lawyers. Here the situation differs considerably among subject areas. The time required for writing such a thesis varies enormously: for example, from about three months typically (sometimes six months) in business studies, to about six months in history, and about one year in physics. However, as students pointed out, these are only the official time periods the universities designate for thesis writing; in reality the interval is often extended by several months. Permission for extension may be readily obtained: a medical certificate often suffices. Significantly, the extent to which academics associate the diploma thesis with research varies. If physicists generally emphasize that work on the thesis is indeed research, professors in business studies deny this completely. Other subjects are viewed as somewhere in between. Volkswirtschaftslehre (general economics) is close to business studies, while history approximates physics in this regard.

One reason for this differing outlook is the type of research done for a thesis and how the topics are decided upon. In physics most of the diploma theses are written as part of an ongoing research project. Examples are those produced under the auspices of Max Planck institutes: all consisted of "commissioned" pieces of established research projects. Contents flow from empirical research, which is naturally considered to be genuine research.

There is, however, a general split between the training of two broad groups of physics students, those who have chosen to become secondary school teachers and are aiming at a state examination at the end of their studies, and those who aspire toward an academic- or research-oriented professional goal, finishing with a diploma. Although the latter are usually doing their diploma theses as part of departmental (or extramural) research projects, the prospective secondary school teachers are mostly not involved in topical research enterprises. The kinds of lectures the two groups attend also differ to some extent. For the group of "diploma-physicists" specialized lectures are given toward the end of their studies that familiarize them with the topical research interests of professors. This helps them to bridge the more general contents of their former studies with the particular concerns of their diploma theses. Finally, diploma candidates are subjected to yet another specific treatment in the form of small-group tutorials and *Praktika* in which they become acquainted with specialized experimental techniques. These tutorials require so much personnel that often additional academic staff are hired with external research funds.

If the range of choices among thesis topics for physics students is rather limited (they are bound to ongoing research projects at the department), this does not mean a subject at the other end of the spectrum, for example, business studies, which rarely puts its students into contact with research during the diploma-thesis, allows its advanced students more freedom in selecting topics. Business studies is also characterized by very little initiative from students in choosing topics. But business students usually do not regard their field as highly academically oriented: its scientific or theoretical elements are thought to be fairly limited. Only a few doctoral theses are written for the purpose of an academic career. The students of history, in contrast, enjoy the greatest choice in selecting their own topics for a thesis, usually within an M.A. program, in part because of the lack of large-scale, department-based research projects in their field. Several of our respondents referred to the research process in history as highly individualistic; this assessment was also shared by many professors of economics for their own field.

History, like other humanities, is also characterized by a related feature that affects the selection and training of researchers. Because this discipline is an individualistic one and because research competency here seems to be difficult to teach—the ability and inclination to theorize about respective academic topics does not require craftsmanlike capacities but a rare talent difficult to detect—the selection and support of the most gifted students appears to be particularly burdensome.[12] As a lecturer in history at Munich University explained, it is almost always the final thesis, in history usually an M.A. dissertation, which reveals qualitative differences between candidates. We should remember that this occurs after almost six years in the program. The informal selection of more qualified and academically interested students thus happens at a late stage, and, as was pointed out by some students, deters many of them from getting involved and interested earlier. The fact that many students remain unknown and have to study in a comparatively anonymous atmosphere is thus not helpful for the selection of future scholars.

There exists, of course, a doctoral level of research training that tells much about the situation of aspiring scholars and young academics in the German system.

The Situation of Aspiring Scholars

Ph.D. "programs" in many disciplines and at most universities are lonely activities. The overall picture from the humanities and social sciences is that university graduates are left largely to themselves. Supervision and other contacts are rare. Special seminars for advanced students, in which they can present their ongoing research, are organized sporadically. The likelihood for a student of history to be selected for one of these advanced seminars, it has been reported, is less than one in ten.[13] One student complained that there was very little guidance and counseling and too little institutional provision for advanced students to report about their ongoing work. The same student, however, was also critical about tendencies to reduce the periods of studies by the introduction of clearer and more binding curricula. He claimed that such attempts would turn universities into schools; apparently he was not aware of the implicit contradiction in his position.

Many of those working toward a Ph.D. in various disciplines are institutionally supported by half-time contracts as research assistants. They are engaged in service activities for professors doing research and part-time teaching and examining. But many respondents thought this concept of half-time employment for doctoral candidates had not proven successful. One reason is that the contracts are often given for nineteen hours, to save on benefit payments that go into effect at twenty, hence depriving the research student of this benefit. A good share of those employed were working more than they were paid for, and most were busy with routine tasks unrelated to their Ph.D. project. Often they were not allowed to teach independent courses but instead had to carry the heavy burden of correcting exam papers. Several professors complained that it was sometimes difficult to fill such posts with able people. A student of economics commented that professors ought not be surprised if they have difficulty in finding students for such jobs, since they themselves were to blame if they overburdened students with time-consuming routine work.

The proportion of intended Ph.D.'s among the investigated subjects is highest in physics. A professor in Berlin reckoned that about one-third of *Diplom-Physiker*, those with a diploma received after six to seven years, intended to write a doctoral thesis. These doctoral candidates are more likely to be employed because external funding is usually available. The period of research required to write a Ph.D. thesis, according to his experience, is roughly five years.

A history professor in Hamburg pointed out that the general training and career situation for young and aspiring scholars is bad. In his field, assistant positions hardly exist. Since those who are able to get half-time employment are heavily engaged in service contributions for their respective professors, many dispense with the prospect of a doctoral program. A history professor at Munich University reported that the career prospects of young historians at his department were minimal. Only five positions for assistants and associates, two of them with tenure and three for contract positions of up to eight years, were possible. Since all were occupied, he did not expect any changes for the next eight years. And outside the department the opportunities for an academic career were even smaller.

Ph.D. candidates in the humanities are generally not involved in departmental activities, but work by themselves at home and in libraries. Most of the history professors who were interviewed did not know precisely how many doctoral students they had. Very often the thesis topic is only informally talked about by graduate student and professor. Critically, the doctoral candidate does not register with the university, as he or she would in the Anglo-American context. Thus the professor often does not know whether a particular theme previously discussed with a student is still being tackled. Under these circumstances the actual number of completed theses is low.

Thus, in Germany, aspiring researchers can acquire necessary skills mainly by participating in research projects pursued by academic personnel. This situation obtains most fully in physics, to a modest degree in economics, and lightly in history. In such cases occasional opportunities exist for able and interested students to become involved in research; they usually do not do their own research but participate in and observe the actual research process in the multiperson project. A few students commented that often only students with sufficient funding from their parents had enough time to engage in such efforts, since a majority of them had to use much time during the semester earning money outside the university.

This type of scholarly training is rather informal: its rules and practices are largely invisible and often opaque. Our respondents reported that selection criteria are highly subjective and dependent on personal impressions gleaned from teaching situations. "Good" students often make an impression on their professors early in their programs. They are then gradually involved in small-scale research tasks. Later many of them stay on to become regularly employed assistants and to work for the Ph.D. Some students evaluated this selection process critically: in their opinion, many advanced students get chosen for small research jobs on the basis of personal rapport with professors, while others who might be equally gifted but shy and less visible often had no opportunity to prove their abilities.

It is primarily in the sciences (here, physics), that quasi-formal patterns of research training exist. According to a physics professor at the Technical University of Berlin, about one-quarter of the *Diplomanden* continues to work for a Ph.D. As he points out: "We have project positions, usually with external funding, that are exclusively meant for the research project, and teaching positions, where the candidates have to share their time between the doctoral thesis and the teaching obligations. For the decision to continue with doctoral research, it is primarily their personal motivation which counts." As he also explained, all the doctoral positions at his department were filled with candidates from within his own realm, that is, with advanced students and graduates whom he had known for a while. This "internal" recruitment and selection is a typical pattern at most German universities: external applications for doctoral programs, which occur in other countries, are fairly unknown.

At the Max Planck institutes a number of advanced students are also engaged in research as part of their diploma thesis or as doctoral students. Formally, one of the professors at an institute, who usually share their time with positions at a university, takes responsibility for the overall supervision of diploma candidates as well as for doctoral students. As a physics professor in an institute near Munich pointed out, he and his colleagues had very positive experiences with diploma candidates, since most of them were highly motivated and could be intensively supervised at the institute. Each member of the institute supervises on average between one and two diploma theses. The results, even on the diploma level, are sometimes published in international journals.

The positions for doctoral candidates in the Max Planck institutes are usually limited to two to three years. Candidates from all over Germany can apply: among thirteen doctoral candidates in one institute, four had taken their diplomas at other universities. However, the possibilities for further employment after doctoral work are minimal. Most employees are employed only for five years. Ten-year positions in pure research in the institutes are very limited. Thus, there is little job security.

Only a few tenured positions are available for nonprofessorial lecturers in the German system. At this level recruitment is largely informal. Even when universities are required by law to advertise junior positions, public advertising is not much more than a formality. At the professorial level a certain amount of prearranged selection also occurs: a senior scientist at a large university reported that five of his seven colleagues had written their Habilitation theses under his supervision.

Hence, within a system that is in most respects rather formalized and oriented to bureaucratic accountability, we find much informal decision making in the selection of doctoral students and in their later advancement into the scholarly ranks—a process that could be deemed highly efficient. Even though most university affairs, from the recruitment of professors to the development of curricula and the formulation of examination rules, are normally regulated by parliaments and ministerial administrators, and though most aspects of university life have to be legally waterproof, the important task of training and recruiting future generations of scientists and scholars is left considerably to individualistic and arbitrary decision making. Does this perhaps imply that a discrepancy exists between fact and fiction in other areas of German universities, that informal arrangements are brought about by requirements of the academic system, regardless of official ideology? The obvious case in question is the Humboldtian conception of a unity of research and teaching.

Humboldt and Present Realities

Many academics whom we interviewed stated that the greatest threat to university operation and the pursuit of research was the continuing expansion of the system. Despite the numerous recent forecasts that predicted a declining student body by the second half of the eighties, no such downturn has occurred. On the contrary, some departments we visited had experienced up to a 60 percent increase in new entrants during the past two years.

This continuing expansion results from a combination of factors, the most important of which is a new willingness to study. If in recent years many school leavers have opted for some practical training, many who had chosen an alternative education came to realize that those with high qualifications are more readily employable, particularly in a tight labor market. But higher education graduates in recent years also encounter risk in finding employment. The Rectors Conference has stressed that while the number of graduates has grown since 1980, as a consequence of the greatly increased number of applicants entitled to enter tertiary education, a disproportionate number of young and middle-aged people are already employed and will not soon create vacancies by retiring from their positions. Also, the relatively low rate of economic growth since the mid-1970s has been accompanied by lower employment, especially in public service, since the late 1970s and the early 1980s.[14]

Naturally, differences in expansion and overcrowding exist among disciplines and between small and large universities. Classes in business studies or, to a lesser extent, physics, are much more overcrowded than, for example, history. History ceased to be a mass subject when it became clear about 1980 that employment opportunities for teachers would decrease dramatically. Small, provincial universities generally have many fewer students per teacher or per available space than the massive urban institutions.

Decreased employment opportunities in the public sector also has had repercussions for the occupational hopes of prospective academics. This surely was one of the most unfortunate developments for the scholarly training and recruitment of young academics in the German university system during the 1980s. But employment opportunities can vary from year to year; more constant are the structural components influencing the training of advanced students. The predictions, based on demographic calculations and the expectation that many professors will retire in the near future, of rapidly increasing opportunities in the academic labor market after about 1995 will not radically improve the process of academic selection and research training, as long as structural conditions at the universities do not change.

The crucial issue is the tight interdependence or even congruence between professional undergraduate and advanced research training within the German system. As described earlier, few interviewees saw much research activity occurring during normal undergraduate teaching and learning. Strangely enough, the same respondents, when asked if they saw any problems with the old conception of a unity of research and teaching, denied this. Most of the interviewed professors seem to interpret this question as referring solely to the faculty. The traditional conception did of course embrace students.

The faculty's positive assessment may lie in the fact that almost all respondents, even if they acknowledged that only a small part of their teaching was directly based on their research activities, considered some kind of teaching to be useful. They believed that teaching could lead to a rounded personality, which in turn would indirectly improve one's research; that during the preparation of lectures and seminars it was possible to discover new aspects of a field which would otherwise remained undetected; that sometimes even seemingly fundamental problems, if looked at more closely, revealed new dimensions closely related to one's specialty.[15]

If we ask, then, to what extent the principle of a unity of research and teaching is a realistic reflection of the research and teaching process at present-day German universities, it appears that we are mostly dealing with a mythological remnant from an earlier historical period. In the early nineteenth century this conception was intended to serve as a political instrument against the suppressive dominance of the absolutist state; today it does not serve any explicit political programs nor any practical curricular measures. In reality the Humboldtian principle has been superseded by a development toward a functional segregation between (in the terminology of the Anglo-American models) undergraduate and graduate teaching. But German universities have difficulty accepting this fact, because the professoriate, through their lobbying organizations (like the Rectors' Conference), insist that the principle of a unity of research and teaching is necessary as a general model for university instruction. In this way they secure for themselves maximum freedom of action and the least possible obligation to engage in such activities as the development of binding curricular patterns.[16] The trend in the day-to-day routines of teaching and learning, as was acknowledged by most respondents, nevertheless does move in the direction of more stable and clearer organizational features. The self-image of the German university is clearly characterized by a considerable cultural lag.

CONCLUSION

The university system of the Federal Republic of Germany is characterized by antagonistic components. For one, the traditional conceptions of a unity of research and teaching and a complete freedom of teaching and learning continue to prevail. Practitioners, however, see little empirical reason to cling to these ideals. Second, the system in many respects is rigidly governed by bureaucratic formalities. But in the crucial task of securing highly qualified young scholars for the next generation of academics, informal decision making almost completely takes over.

After many years of discussion and failed attempts to unite incompatible approaches, those holding positions of responsibility in this university system still struggle to overcome its fundamental contradictions. It should be acknowledged as evident, as many professors have already conceded, that it is counterproductive to maintain that every student can and should be made into a researcher. A more realistic approach would open up opportunities for structural changes, not least in the area of training advanced students to become future researchers. The notion of training itself, together with the concept of education, could then be redefined in a more useful perspective. In Humboldt's formulation, *Bildung* meant above all intellectual training and was thus far away from the corresponding concepts of the Anglo-American tradition, which were directed more to development of the individual than to academic subjects. A redefinition of Bildung would clarify the need for appropriate guidance and supervision during the advanced training of future scientists and scholars. It might also pave the way for a new concept of undergraduate education that would more adequately meet the needs and expectations of both students and prospective employers.

In the ongoing debate about the nature of higher education in Germany, the introduction of separate undergraduate and graduate levels of higher education steadily attracts an increasing number of advocates. Those in favor of separation often attempt to demonstrate the merits of such models elsewhere in the world. The graduate level would include taught courses, however alien to the paradigm of "training by research." But a major formal change does not seem in the offing. Until it occurs, a majority of university professors will continue to cling to Humboldtian conceptions, while pursuing informal, pragmatic means of resolving fundamental contradictions.

NOTES

1. The German unification of 1990 added five new Länder (states) to the eleven in the Federal Republic of Germany. This has not only enlarged the overall system of higher education but may well have consequences for the tasks and definitions of tertiary education. It is too early to see a clear picture emerging. What basically seems to be happening, as of 1991, is a rapid adjustment, largely enforced by the West German authorities, of the former German Democratic Republic (GDR) system to Western paradigms—a difficult and often painful process. Departments and institutions are being dissolved (mainly in the social sciences and humanities), in order to be recreated according to the standards of the (former) West. The future of the strong research component of the old GDR system in the form of research academies is as yet unclear. How long it will take to bring quality standards of teaching and learning as well as organizational aspects of the research process up to the level of the West remains to be seen. Even such basic issues as the reconciliation of the vastly different salary levels between East and West German professors will take some years to resolve. With regard to the provision of future scholars, it seems unlikely in the near future that the former GDR universities will play a major role in recruitment and training.

2. Secretariat of the Standing Conference of the Ministers of Education (KMK), *Report on the Development of Education*, p. 78.

3. Gieseke, *Auf Tradition in die Zukunft*.

4. Pritchard, *End of Elitism?*

5. I would like to thank interviewers Erich Eisenstecken, Werner Frohlich, and Thomas Hinz for their thorough work.

6. The DFG, an independent funding body controlled by representatives of universities and financed by the Federal and Länder governments, is the main agent for the distribution of government research funds. For the system of public research funding, see Bundesminister für Forschung und Technologie, *Faktenbericht 1990 zum Bundesbericht Forschung 1988*, pp. 17–85.

7. The number of faculty positions (without clinics), which remained stable between 1980 and 1988, was roughly 130,000. From 1988 to 1990 an increase occurred for the first time in a decade; the numbers climbed to 134,300 in 1989 and to 135,000 in 1990. Whether this will really change conditions in the dramatically

overcrowded universities remains to be seen. See Wissenschaftsrat, "Stellenausstattung der Hochschulen 1989/90."

8. See Clark, *Academic Life.*

9. Goppel, *Kontinuität und Wandel,* chapter 6.

10. From learning psychology we know that underachievers function with difficulty in stressful situations, such as examinations, but they may, under "normal" conditions, be more efficient and productive than others.

11. See Gellert, "Andere Ziele, andere Zeiten."

12. Binder and Hewel, *Verbindung von Forschung und Lehre,* p. 64.

13. Ibid., p. 68.

14. Bundesminister für Bildung und Wissenschaft, *Hochschulpolitische Zielsetzungen,* p. 14.

15. See also Binder and Hewel, *Verbindung von Forschung und Lehre,* p. 72.

16. See Lämmert, "Wissen ist Ohnmacht."

BIBLIOGRAPHY

Binder, Gisbert, and Petra Hewel. *Die Verbindung von Forschung und Lehre an deutschen Universitäten.* Manuscript. Cologne, 1981.

Bundesminister für Bildung und Wissenschaft (BMBW), ed. *Hochschulpolitische Zielsetzungen der Bundesregierung.* Bonn, 1986.

———. *Grund- und Strukturdaten 1988/89.* Bonn, 1988.

Bundesminister für Forschung und Technologie (BMFT). *Faktenbericht 1990 zum Bundesbericht Forschung 1988.* Bonn, 1990.

Clark, Burton R. *The Academic Life: Small Worlds, Different Worlds.* Princeton, N.J.: Carnegie Foundation for the Advancement of Teaching, 1987.

Gellert, Claudius. "Andere Ziele, andere Zeiten. Der angloamerikanische Mut zur Erziehung wird durch kürzere Studienzeiten belohnt." *Deutsche Universitäts-Zeitung* 19 (1988): 20–23.

Gieseke, Ludwig. *Auf Tradition in die Zukunft. Die Hochschulen in der Bundesrepublik Deutschland. Bildung und Wissenschaft* 1–2 (1987). Special edition.

Goppel, Thomas, ed. *Kontinuität und Wandel. Perspektiven bayerischer Wissenschaftspolitik.* Munich: Oldenbourg, 1991.

Lämmert, Eberhard. "Wissen ist Ohnmacht. Die deutsche Hochschule bestraft die Lehre und fördert die nutzlose Ansammlung von Informationen." *Die Zeit* 24.7.1989: 44.

Pritchard, Rosalind M. O. *The End of Elitism? The Democratization of the West German University System.* New York: Berg, 1990.

Secretariat of the Standing Conference of the Ministers of Education and Cultural Affairs of the Länder in the Federal Republic of Germany (KMK). *Report on the Development of Education in the Federal Republic of Germany 1989–1990.* Bonn, 1990.

Wissenschaftsrat (WR). "Stellenausstattung der Hochschulen 1989/90 wieder in Bewegung." *Pressemitteilung,* Cologne, June 1990.

PART TWO

Britain

Introduction

British higher education presents a fascinating second case in our five-nation comparison. It too is a classic elite model, one smaller in scale than found in West Germany, with close personal relations between professors and students in a system that closely controls access to the universities. The authors of the British papers point to a "craft" tradition, an "apprenticeship model," in which many British *under*graduates still have "personal tutors." Before World War II, Mary Henkel and Maurice Kogan report in chapter 3, Britain also exhibited a high absolute and relative level of governmental sponsorship of scientific research. This support included a strong commitment to mission-directed research, much of it carried on in state-owned laboratories. In and outside the academy, science prospered. Early on, British professors expected to do research, even to involve their undergraduates in research activities. Thus, higher education in this particular international center of learning offered an integration of research and teaching, research and study, in the small undergraduate worlds of the universities—and in the preparation of a few advanced "research students." And quality always took precedence over quantity—"a thin, clear stream of excellence," in one British phrase—with the orientations of Oxford and Cambridge providing considerable indirect steerage in the system as a whole.

But the years since World War II have not been kind to Britain—"the British disease" has been a prevalent description of an ailing economy—and the growing heavy dependence of British higher education on a single patron, the national government, has taken its toll. That patron has turned restrictive, even hostile and punitive. During the quarter-century since the merger of two ministries into the modern Department of Education and Science (DES) in 1964, the central government has steadily developed an elaborate set of national policy bodies, some inside the central political machinery and governmental bureaucracies and some directly outside, but funded by the government, to steer science and to guide higher education. The trend toward *dirigiste* control came to a head in the 1980s in the form of massive budget cuts attended by selective reductions among institutions and disciplines.

In a national system that has remained highly selective in university undergraduate work, postgraduate enrollments have remained quite small. Small universities and small departments have treated graduate students mainly as individual research students. Typically, there are not enough of them to justify "taught courses" and systematic training, especially at the doctoral level. The intense fiscal restraint of the 1980s has exacerbated this problem. Master's level degrees have become more used as endpoints. In chapter 4 Tony Becher examines in detail the strains and problematic nature of master's and doctoral work, and their underpinnings in research, at a time when international competition demands broad coverage of disciplines and specialties and enlarged outputs of scientists and engineers. These demands press hard against the limits of a system rooted in small numbers and close interaction between faculty and students. The craft tradition is seemingly not enough; more systematic preparation at the advanced level, for much larger numbers of students, is apparently needed. A distinctively British version of the problem of graduate education is clearly evident.

THREE

Research Training and Graduate Education
The British Macro Structure

Mary Henkel and Maurice Kogan

Research training and graduate education (often called "postgraduate education") in the United Kingdom should be viewed against the background of radical changes in British higher education and science policy since the end of the Second World War. In this chapter we show how policies for graduate education are changing indecisively at a time when the British government is making determined efforts to change science policy.

Both graduate education and science policy must be viewed in light of the peculiarities of preparation at the pregraduate levels. The majority of British pupils attend comprehensive secondary rather than selective schools, and they leave at the age of sixteen. The latter stages of secondary education provide for the substantial minority of sixteen to nineteen year olds who stay beyond the compulsory age limit. Despite some recent broadening, this is a period of specialization leading to academic examinations. Those who then go on to higher education usually follow highly specialized three-year courses leading to a bachelor's degree. Work for the first degree is thus considered a basis for research degrees, where knowledge and academic skills on entry are to some extent taken for granted. In spite of substantive connections, however, the graduate and undergraduate stages are sharply distinct, though they are usually both passed in the same academic departments.

British higher education, in common with most systems, has moved from being highly selective, catering to about 3 percent of school leavers in 1945, to wider access, sustaining a proportion of about 15 percent since the early 1970s. Several new universities were established in the 1960s, as was a wholly new sector of higher education, led by thirty polytechnics, which, if not well-funded for these purposes, were not excluded from participation in graduate training and certain forms of research. All universities were

71

deemed to be research institutions by virtue of their favorable funding, the contracts of their teaching staff, and the highly selective range of students (the top 6 or 7 percent) whom they recruited.

This postwar system was subjected to changes of policy in the 1980s. Research activities were to be allocated to universities selectively, at the same time as the system was asked to begin to double the age participation rate of its undergraduates. Government set up machinery, beyond the reach of the invisible colleges of academics, which attempted to induce movement from the traditional academic objective of the disinterested pursuit of knowledge toward strategic research devoted to economically useful ends.

Historically, the links between research activity and graduate education have been strong in Britain. Selectivity in research funding will probably lead to a further concentration of graduate training. But two reservations must be placed against that expectation. First, much of Britain's expansion in graduate education is in programs based mainly on systematically taught courses, which characteristically lead to a master of arts or master of science (M.A., M.Sc.) rather than to a master of philosophy (M.Phil.) or doctor of philosophy (Ph.D.). The latter are largely awarded on the production of a thesis. These taught courses have grown throughout the system, appear in a wide range of subjects ranging from the most academic to the most applied, in polytechnics no less than in universities, and will largely escape the thrust toward concentration. Second, while the government and its appointed bodies have made determined attempts to change the objectives and machinery of research policy, they have been less systematic in tackling the consequences for graduate education. Its distribution, objectives, and links with such functions as the recruitment of teachers for a changed and expanded system remain an underregarded area of public policy. The evolving research policy thus forms the essential framework for a discussion of graduate education policies.

THE ACADEMIC RESEARCH SYSTEM

Although the histories of graduate education and research policy in the United Kingdom are linked, the connections between them have been weak. Research policy has remained contestable and to some extent confused. But it has always been a likely subject for political thinking on the grand scale, and in the 1980s research policy underwent substantial review and change. By contrast, very little policy thinking about graduate studies is evident; the main disciplinary groups, not the government nor the funding bodies, have concerned themselves, albeit in fragmentary fashion, with its objectives and organization.

The history of research policy has largely been that of policies for science and technology. In the past little attention was paid to the humanities. A short-lived policy interest in the social sciences emerged in the 1960s when the recommendations of the Heyworth Report in 1965 led to the creation of the Social Science Research Council. But even in science policy, a perceptive commentator has observed how "time and time again . . . there was resistance to the idea that governmental programs in science and technology should be coordinated in any but the minimal sense of avoiding undue duplication" so that "the idea of a deliberate 'science policy' was explicitly rejected."[1] The United Kingdom has not been backward in scientific development or, indeed, in investment, but this has been advanced more through the power and commitment of its many academic centers and individuals working within a free and benign environment than through the purposive intervention of the state, as was to a larger extent the case in some of the other European systems.

There were anxieties in the nineteenth century about science's contribution to industry and commerce, particularly when comparison was made with foreign competitors. This growth of science received passive official acquiescence and deference was paid to the scientific establishment, particularly the Royal Society. But the scientific community felt inhibited from asking for much money. Grants were given for pure research to individuals or through the Royal Society for the funding of expeditions or specific pieces of research. Funds were available for such expensive utilitarian research as that conducted by the Geological Survey and the Ordnance Survey, and for research done for technical branches of the Local Government Board or on explosives for the Home Office or on lighthouses for the Board of Trade, and this tradition of mission-directed research was to remain strong in different forms in the twentieth century.[2]

At the turn of the century, in 1899, the National Physical Laboratory was founded to bring scientific knowledge to bear upon everyday industrial and commercial practice. It opened the way to substantial state support for scientific research and particularly for research to be conducted in state-owned laboratories. This organizational tradition is carried on to the present day through funding by both government departments and research councils. The First World War strengthened the link between science and technology and government and saw the establishment of an Advisory Council on Scientific and Industrial Research in 1915 and its associated Department of Scientific and Industrial Research (DSIR) the following year. The DSIR created its own laboratories, which eventually numbered fifteen. It administered an industrial research association scheme to set up, cooperatively, research laboratories to be partly funded by industry. And it awarded research grants to postgraduate students and university staff. In 1918 a committee under the chairmanship of Lord Haldane asserted strongly the need for intelligence and research that could support the activities of government. Haldane advocated, however, that research ought not be in the hands of departmental ministers; the Haldane principle of research council autonomy was thus born.

In the period between the two world wars, governmental support for research and departmental research capacities grew; the budget was tripled between 1920 and 1939; expenditure was high by contemporary international standards. The Second World War, however, was the great turning point in government-science relations. Elite scientists had debated the relationship between science and society and the extent to which science should be coordinated governmentally. Various bodies were set up by different governments, culminating in the creation of the Office of the Minister for Science in 1959.

Meanwhile, after the First World War, research councils were created, a process that continued until the 1960s: the Medical Research Council (MRC) in 1920, the Agricultural Research Council (ARC) in 1931, the Nature Conservancy in 1949, which became the National Environment Research Council (NERC) in 1964. The Science Research Council (SRC) as well as the NERC were created through the transfer of some of the DSIR's functions in 1964. They emerged at the same time as large changes in the machinery of government occurred. In 1964 the Office of the Minister of Science was merged with the Ministry of Education to form the Department of Education and Science (DES). This was plainly intended to insure that higher education and science policy should march in step with each other. Anecdotal evidence suggests, however, that the two most senior officials responsible for these two blocks of policy had hardly encountered each other within twelve months of the merger of the two institutions. By 1980 the two commands had been amalgamated into one role.

The growth of R&D was substantial by 1964. Both civil and military R&D cost less than £10 million in 1939; industry was spending over half that figure. The total expenditure of government grew from £30 million in 1950–1951 to £115 million in 1963–1964. The number of economically active qualified scientists and engineers grew by about 50 percent between 1956 and 1965 to a total of over three hundred thousand. Most worked in industry. Education took second place and government third.[3]

Steady R&D growth occurred because government allowed public expenditures to increase. Its mechanisms for control and policy were in place, but it did not seek to enforce a coherent set of objectives and priorities. Much depended on the inclinations of researchers whose numbers grew less as a by-product of research policy and more as a second-order effect of the large-scale expansion of higher education, which was to quadruple by the early 1970s and thus provide tenurial places for teachers who were also supposed to be researchers.

The history of science and research policy in the United Kingdom in the

1960s and 1970s displays some contradictory trends. There was certainly substantial growth in public investment. A report of the Organisation for Economic Co-operation and Development (OECD) maintained that in the OECD countries until the 1960s the public had faith in the efficacy of science, and scientists had high political prestige.[4] But clear lines of policy were not discernable in the United Kingdom because government largely responded to the demands of academics. It was still a period of optimism based on assumptions of a direct relationship between investment in higher education, including its research component, and economic growth. Governments were moving from euphoria, however, toward a concern about the rational allocation of resources and a questioning of the role of science and technology in economic growth. Economists and systems analysts were becoming significant influences upon science policy. According to the OECD, a mood of disenchantment set in in the late 1960s; budgets became tighter and scientists lost some of their influence and credibility in government and with the public.

However, that OECD version is contestable in Britain. Three characteristics seem to emerge from the British scene. First, rational planning was certainly emphasized in research policy from the 1970s on. The British Rothschild Report (1971) exemplified the emphasis now placed upon the explicit planning of development within the area of the science budget. Yet research budgets expanded from £767 million to £2,151 million between 1964 and 1975.[5] In health and social services research, for example, the Department of Health and Social Security (DHSS) established thirty-eight mainly six-year rolling contracts at the beginning of the 1970s. In this golden age the U.K. government seemed confident, even in the uncertain areas of social policy, that science could be enlisted to solve policy problems.

With that confidence went a desire for more certainty, and the 1970s were marked by increased demands for rationality in research commissioning.[6] Government would commission research as would a customer making a contract with researchers. Chief scientists would insure that research was both competent and useful. Government would take proportions of research council monies into departments' direct control, in recognition of the applied nature of their work. This new framework was an optimistic child of its time. A 1972 Government White Paper following the Rothschild Report stated: "The new framework provides a partnership within which science will have more influence on the government's central policy making activities than before and which will contribute more directly and effectively to the task of making the best use of science and technology for the needs of the community as a whole."[7] Toward the end of the 1970s, however, optimism faded and the economic difficulties induced by the oil crisis made it more difficult to sustain an unchallenged place for science. With the return of a Conservative administration in 1979, the scrutiny became even more critical. Over the last decade more directive policies have emerged and several strands of them can now be adumbrated.

In the 1980s, and particularly toward the end of the decade, the overriding trend was the transfer of power over research and science policy from leading academics (within the protection of their institutions), the funding bodies, and research councils to government. Government, in turn, placed greater emphasis on the role of industry and employment in the determination of research and science policies.

In shifting the locus of decision making from the academy to government and industry, the authorities were supported by parliamentary pressure. The House of Commons Public Accounts Committee maintained in 1988 that ministers ought to involve themselves in determining the topics to be financed by research councils; the Committee attacked the arm's-length relationship that existed between the DES and the research councils.

After a century or so of indeterminate policies the U.K. government had now entered upon a period of determined rationalization in which the objectives were to be predominantly set by government and what it regarded as the needs of the economy. To some extent it was supported by the science and technology elite who shared its views about the need to concentrate research and advanced teaching.

Characteristics of the Current Research System

Governing Mechanisms. Ministerial responsibility for both science and higher education rests with the secretary of state for education and science and the related department, the DES. The DES appoints the Advisory Board for Research Councils (ABRC), whose secretariat it provides and whose chairman it appoints. The Advisory Board coordinates and directs the overall policies for the five research councils (to the four identified earlier, a social science research council, later renamed Economic and Social Research Council (ESRC), was added in 1965). The DES provides policy directives for the main institutional sponsoring bodies, the Universities Funding Council (UFC)—the 1989 successor to the famous University Grants Committee—and the Polytechnics and Colleges Funding Council (PCFC). This DES system responds to central structures associated with the Cabinet Office and the Treasury, which put pressure on the DES and the Advisory Board in setting research objectives, assessing performance, and controlling budgets.

Central government's mechanisms for controlling science and research have been an issue since the 1918 Haldane Report. One question, which has recently reemerged, is whether there ought to be a single minister responsible for science and technology across the board. This extended realm has been divided between the secretary of state for education and science, the minister for technology, and various elements of the cabinet office structure. The British government's most recent pronouncement was that "there is no call for the creation of a separate and all-embracing science and technology ministry."[8]

The government declared in 1987 that it had "begun to undertake a searching review of R&D priorities across government, defence as well as civil, with a view to increasing the contribution of government funded R and D to the efficiency, competitiveness and innovative capacity of the United Kingdom economy." It decided to create a strengthened central structure that would establish collective ministerial consideration of science and technology priorities under the prime minister's leadership with the assistance of an expanded independent advisory body—the Advisory Council on Science and Technology (ACOST)—which could advise across "the whole of scientific and technological endeavour, international as well as British." ACOST would thus advise on priorities for science and technology, their application to both the public and private sectors in accordance with national needs, the coordination of science and technology activities, and participation in international collaboration.

ACOST was created to establish working arrangements with departmental advisory bodies including the Advisory Board for the Research Councils (ABRC). Its secretariat is located in the Cabinet Office and reports to the chief scientific adviser. A Science and Technology Assessment Office helps departments, the research councils, and the UFC to assess their R&D expenditures and evaluate the results. The ambition is to establish clear objectives for expenditure and to develop systematic criteria for assessing and managing research. ACOST will be responsible for insuring that all bodies involved in public R&D pay attention to the economic impact and commercial exploitation of the work supported as well as to other national benefits. The Assessment Office will build up a picture of the relative contribution of the different R&D expenditures to the U.K. economy; it will contribute advice on these matters to the new, strengthened central structure.

These arrangements display two principal features of current British government policy: the continued belief in the power of government to assert and insist on objectives of publicly financed research, and the determination to refer to industrial and other economic objectives at every level of the research commissioning and implementation system.

These features are reflected in the coordinating board of the research councils. The Advisory Board for Research Councils consists of the heads of the councils, chief scientists from government departments, and eminent persons chosen by ministers to represent both the academic and the nonacademic world. Research Councils submit corporate plans for ABRC comment. The ABRC recommends how much should be allocated to the councils for research funding, studentships, and particular initiatives. It vets their plans and estimates and has recently made efforts to appraise the performance of the councils. The ABRC has attempted in the last three years to create selective research strategies that would tend to concentrate research, and research training, in far fewer institutions.[9]

In spite of these attempts to be more directive, close observers have not thought the board to be particularly strong at policy analysis or implementation:

> There have been two ABRC enquiries on graduate studies but no action has ensued. . . . Only the political vulnerability of ESRC [the research council for the social sciences], and the PAC [Public Accounts Committee of the House of Commons] enquiry, have put pressure on the Council and even these have had no effect on it. The ABRC is toothless. It is not prepared to use its clout to redistribute funds between the research councils. . . . It is not geared to make policy decisions . . . there would be great difficulty in reaching consensus . . . [and] it has no effective analytic capacity.[10]

But these defects may be remedied by decisions reported in the press in January 1990 to give ABRC more executive powers.

Machinery for Setting Research Objectives. The structure for policy making as described above represents a substantial shift from the period of relative trust in researchers to set the agenda for publicly funded research. Not only are such central funding bodies as the ABRC and the UFC setting the policies and priorities for research but they, too, are coming under the hand of far more determined policy directions from the inner circle of government, namely, the prime minister's office, the cabinet office (in which sits the government's chief scientific adviser), and the cabinet office–based structure ACOST.

The increasing power of the central mechanisms is accompanied by the values, language, and operational techniques associated with management rather than academic philosophies. The devices through which the system attempts to ensure the setting of objectives are: corporate plans written by the five research councils upon which they are interrogated by the ABRC; the application of performance measurement by the ABRC to the research councils and by the funding councils of the universities and the polytechnics and colleges to research institutions; and the restructuring of the research councils themselves to place a stronger premium on planning and evaluative machinery at the expense of discipline-led decision-making groups. Following a report by an ABRC committee chaired by one of its industrialist members, the government was even invited in 1989 to consider a proposal for a supercouncil to replace the five research councils. This initiative fell within the tendency to aim at overarching research objectives at the expense of a system in which there was responsive sponsoring of research proposals put up by the academics. Objections were lodged by, among others, the two research councils for social sciences and science and engineering, on the grounds that a large and monolithic structure was likely to be counterproductive, particularly at a time when the research councils were being asked to be flexible and responsive to change, and irrelevant to the continuing problems faced by the science base; "the interface problems were exaggerated."[11] The social science council had reaffirmed its commitment to fund proposals arising spontaneously from the social science community, "recognising that a significant proportion of original and innovative work comes from this source.[12] Like other research councils it planned to set aside about thirty-five per cent of its research budget for such grants.

Within the new overarching research policies set by government and its advisory bodies, some division of labor is taking shape. The research councils are seen as defining priority areas of national interest, as well as funding reactively in response to applications submitted by academics. Reciprocally, the universities' funding body sees itself not so much as defining possible areas of research as strengthening the growing research centers in universities, through allocating funds on the basis of regular assessments.[13] The setting of objectives for research has been accompanied by similar exercises for research training, to which we refer later.

The Institutional Base and Its Funding. The DES negotiates research budgets with the treasury and these form the bases upon which the ABRC makes its recommendation on distributions to the five research councils. The DES also secures the funds reaching universities and other higher education institutions, including those imputed for research, through the UFC and PCFC. The total science budget, which makes up 80 percent of research council funds (other elements coming from commercially commissioned research or from individual government departments), is divided as follows: 26 percent for research grants; 13 percent for postgraduate awards; 34 percent for the support of institutes and research units. The remaining 26 percent covers international subscriptions (12 percent), capital (8 percent) and administration (6 percent).[14]

Departments other than the DES contribute about 45 percent of the total government expenditure on civil research and development. Of this, about 75 percent is applied, 20 percent "strategic," and 5 percent basic research. The United Kingdom spends a lower proportion of its gross domestic product on civil R&D than does France, the Federal Republic of Germany, Japan, or the United States.[15] Policy on "sectoral" funding by government departments changed in the 1980s. If many departments continued to directly commission research themselves, they were more restrictive in both the amount of research they sponsored and in the objectives for which support is given. One result has been to replace long-term projects, in which students might receive training, and eventually employment, by ad hoc and short-term projects.[16]

The institutions through which research and development are carried out include: higher education, principally the universities but also some of the public-sector polytechnics; private-sector industry; centers or units funded directly by the research councils; and the research, development, and advisory units of government departments.

In 1965 the government made an important policy determination affecting the future of research when it decided to organize higher education into a binary system; higher education's contribution to research traditionally came from the university side of that divide. The universities were expected to advance research and scholarship over the entire range of studies, from fundamental and theoretical advances to applications, and were funded to do so through the so-called dual system. The duality rested in the fact that university core funding, and the resources for buildings and equipment, allow for research, and thereby constitute a first money stream. About one-third of teaching time was later imputed to nonteaching activities. Universities also had a second line in that they were considered eligible to compete for research grants and contracts from the five research councils. By contrast, the "public sector," led by thirty polytechnics, would concentrate largely on applied research and development, and thus contribute more closely to the economic and social life of their regions and areas. Hardly any of their core funds were imputed to research, and their unit costs were correspondingly lower. They too could compete for research council funds and studentships, but given their relative lack of resources for research they started with heavy disadvantages.

More recently the binary division became confused by two developments. The first was the growing encouragement of research in public-sector institutions. Their central funding body created a research fund of £2.5 million, a trivial sum that the House of Lords Select Committee believed to be insufficient, but the policy was thought successful because it raised morale, improved teaching quality, retained good staff, and generated private income.[17] All eighty-four public sector institutions will probably receive some resources from the new funds the Polytechnics and Colleges Funding Council will reserve for research. The Further Education Act of 1985 also allowed polytechnics to sell research and consultancy services and retain the proceeds for their own uses. Then, under the Education Reform Act of 1988, polytechnics and other institutions offering advanced further education became incorporated as independent bodies and thus presumably able to develop their research and research training functions with even less inhibition. Public sector institutions have already produced 3000

TABLE 3-1   Research Funding of British Universities, 1982–1988
(In Millions of Pounds)

Source of Funds	1987–1988	1982–1983	
		Actual	At 1987–1988 Prices
Research councils	185	118	150
Other U.K. government bodies	90	51	65
U.K. industry	69	27	34
U.K.–based charities	108 ⎫		
Overseas sources	42 ⎬	63	80
Other sources	32 ⎭		
Total	526	259	329

SOURCE: UFC Circular Letter 22/89.

research graduates. These developments clearly fly in the face of the general policy of concentrating effort in research.

The second blurring of the binary division may result from the attempts to stratify the already selective universities and thus produce concentrations of research.[18] The distinction between a university largely devoted to teaching and a polytechnic striving to establish its research profile may become difficult to detect.

The three research councils for the natural environment, agriculture and food, and medical research have relied heavily on their own institutes or funded units with a university base for the pursuit of their objectives. For example, NERC has spent two-thirds of its research monies on institutes, and the AFRC expenditure has been at least proportionally as much. But both councils are now committed to a policy of increased support to universities and polytechnics and a reduction of their own staff within the institutes. NERC support to universities increased from 12.5 percent of total budget in 1984–1985 to 21.5 percent in 1989–1990. At the same time it reduced 16 percent of its own manpower between 1983 and 1987. The AFRC made similar reductions but remains committed to strengthening the role of the institute in fundamental and strategic research.

The funding base of university research is given in table 3-1. These figures must be added to the £760 million received from UFC grant and home student fees in 1987.

Publicly funded research through higher education institutions and research council centers and units is not the only way in which public money enters the research system. Multifunding from both private and public sources is thought to strengthen the freedom and autonomy of university research, particularly in respect to "individualistic thinkers."[19] From Victorian times the government has financed its own research centers and many still exist either within government departments or as institutions directly funded by government departments. Recently the government has attempted to divest itself of those facilities for which the private sector might take financial responsibility. It has also attempted to persuade industry to fund a higher proportion of the research undertaken within treasury-supported higher education institutions. A government response to a House of Lords Select Committee noted in 1987 that according to OECD figures less than 66 percent of the total R&D carried out by industry in 1985 was funded from industry's own resources in the United Kingdom, compared with higher figures in other countries, notably 98 percent in Japan in 1984.[20] Moreover, much little-acknowledged research, mainly of an applied kind, was taking place in public authorities outside central government, including the National Health Service and local authorities.

Current Policies and Priorities

Throughout the latter half of the 1980s the system was strengthened to identify and pursue centrally conditioned objectives. The following priorities emerged: strategic research; research relating to economic concerns; concentrated research activity in centers where both economy and excellence could be pursued; and a determined pursuit of similar objectives in graduate education. The international dimensions of research involving greater access to and knowledge of research in other countries has also been of interest.[21]

In the 1970s policy decisions on the organization of research and its funding separated basic research, concerned with the advancement of knowledge, and applied research, directed toward specific practical aims and objectives.[22] Increasingly policymakers[23] identified the importance of "strategic research," a concept introduced into the policy arena in the early 1970s.[24] It is distinguished from basic research, which is "curiosity-driven" and has unpredictable results in both time and field, although the results may be wealth creating. Strategic research is not targeted as specific wealth creation but lies in areas in which the emergence of application may be expected though not predicted.[25] This conceptualization enabled some accommodation between the demands of scientists and the perceived needs of government and the economy. The intention was, to some extent, to override the traditional conflict between the endorsement of basic and applied research. To support strategic research would be to support that basic research which would ultimately lend itself to application and to the economy. Basic and strategic research together accounted for 65 percent of publicly funded civil research and development in 1986. They were predominantly the responsibility of universities and research councils.

From the mid-1980s the research councils produced corporate plans that reflected an increasing orientation to strategic research and the potential benefits to the economy and society of research outputs. The engineering board of the Science and Engineering Research Council, for example, described itself as *dirigiste* in its approach to policy "in order to supply industry with the knowledge base necessary to sustain and introduce advanced technology."[26] Its science board, maintaining that the bulk of their funds went to unsolicited application, devoted 30 percent of its funds to multidisciplinary research relating to identified initiatives. At the beginning of 1989 the SERC stated its intention to endorse strategic as opposed to basic research to the point of 60 percent of their funds. The social science research council devoted nearly two-thirds of its research funds to existing and approved development programs and centers as opposed to research grants. Until recently, in contrast, 20 percent of research commissioned by government was categorized as strategic.

Research and the Economy. Government policies are saturated by a desire that economic concerns ought to stimulate research. The government has exhorted industry to play a stronger role and has told higher education institutions that those responding to the needs of business would be rewarded.[27] It has also become government policy to move its own funding for civil R&D away from "near-market" research toward basic and strategic research. The government hopes it can reduce its own contribution to research finance and persuade industry to enlarge the scale of its support. The reaction from industry has not been encouraging: at least one multinational conglomerate has declined to accept a shift from government to user funding on the grounds that industry makes its contribution through taxes. Government's enthusiasm for industry to play a dominant role in the determination of research, either through sharing decision making or through a larger contribution to its funding, has thus far greatly outstripped industry's eagerness to assume that role.

The 1989 House of Lords Select Committee maintained that government's policy is weakened by a failure to define "near-market" research and is seriously flawed if carried too far. The committee observed that just because research is near the market, the public interest does not necessarily cease. It argued earlier, in 1986, that government support for research should rise, not fall. While the main responsibility for development should rest with industry, even there some public support is essential if there is to be competition on even terms with overseas companies supported by their own governments. In spite of this parliamentary dissent, however, the government made several attempts to persuade industry to take more responsibility for the financing of research and to strengthen the links between higher education and employment.

Policy movements have somewhat reflected the changes in scale and expense of science in, for example, nuclear physics. The British contribution to the Conseil Européen pour Recherche Nucléaire (CERN) and the inclusion of a nuclear structure facility at Daresbury within the SERC core program were evidence of the SERC's determination to sustain a British place in international "big science," despite its commitment to a 20 percent reduction over five years in resources devoted to particle physics. (A decision has since been taken to close Daresbury.) The scale and expense of science were also reflected in new policy emphases on collaboration between different centers internationally and the creation of large-scale interdisciplinary research centers.

Concentration of Research. The moves toward selectivity and concentration began in 1981 when the University Grants Committee was required to reduce the sums distributed to universities. It made judgments about the quality of the individual universities, including their research capacity, which led to considerable discrimination in the distribution of funds. The same process was taken further in 1986 when the UGC graded universities on their research standing. Eventually, 14 percent of funds reaching the universities was to be distributed on judgments of research quality. In 1988 both the UGC and the ABRC began a series of policy debates about whether universities ought to be graded according to their capacity to perform research and to offer advanced research or specialist "honours" courses at the undergraduate levels. The process began with a report of a committee led by Professor R. Oxburgh on earth sciences.[28] It suggested there should be three tiers of university departments in this field, ranging from Level 1 with around thirty staff to Level 3, which would offer only service teaching. This report would have led to the closure of twelve departments out of thirty-two.

The Oxburgh Report was soon followed by two others with similar conclusions. The Edwards Report on physics shared with the Stone Report on chemistry the belief that science departments needed a full-time funded staff of at least twenty faculty if they were to provide single honors courses and undertake competent research. Although the Stone Report noted that chemistry in the small project mode could be effective, it nonetheless cited the benefits of concentration: "There would also be clear educational advantages from research workers at all levels who would carry out their research against a wider scientific background containing experts in several areas and with visiting speakers and academics from overseas." More effective use of equipment, a wider range of specialist technical and support staff with properly equipped workshops, well-stocked libraries, and up-to-date information systems would be available.

The strongest evidence of an evolving policy of concentration and selectivity was a proposal to create Interdisciplinary Research Centres. In 1989 the Science and Engineering Research Council stated its intention to quadruple by 1991 the number of such centers it sponsored.[29] The ABRC planned to create a further twenty in addition to the eight it already sanctioned. However, these plans were brought to a halt by ministers who expressed doubts about the selection of subjects for IRCs and their management.

The trend toward concentration was, however, significant. In its 1989 Corporate Plan, for example, the SERC announced that it had raised the threshold for grant applications during the five previous years, so that the average grant size rose from £52,000 to £75,000 between 1984 and 1988, and the percentage of renewable grants doubled. The total number of grants awarded then fell from a peak of 2,500 to 1,800. But enthusiasm for these policies varied across the range of disciplines. On the face of it, the natural sciences, and particularly physics, were the subject areas that most obviously justified concentration. But the multidisciplinary theme in IRCs also appealed to some social scientists; the Economic and Social Research Council was successful in creating two of them and planned further initiatives in this field.

The science policy background to graduate education in the United Kingdom was thus subject to determined changes in the 1980s. Government was intent on concentrating research and in funding it selectively. Interdisciplinary work was somewhat encouraged also; this was likely to take research resources away from established disciplinary centers. A leading policy motive was to insure that publicly funded science would lead to economically beneficial outcomes. While the power to determine academic objectives remained in the last resort at least with academics themselves, the framework established by central government organizations, which recruited industrialists to monitor scientific endeavors, became tougher and more prescriptive.

The effects on graduate education and research training began to percolate through the research councils and into the institutions only toward the end of the 1980s. As science policy became increasingly *dirigiste*, policymakers were only beginning to consider the consequences for graduate training and for the associated policy question of how the academic system might be restructured in the next decade and century.

GRADUATE STUDIES

Even though the government has struggled with science policy and reached conclusions, whether practicable or not, no similar policy debate about graduate studies has taken place. Only recently has there been any attempt, and that not a systematic one, to elucidate objectives and organization across the board. Policymakers have lately also begun to think about problems of replenishing future higher education staffs. The arguments about the nature and direction of graduate studies have remained mainly within the academic community.

The history of graduate studies in Britain starts from a position of almost total disregard until the nineteenth century, when, after considerable struggle, the English and Scottish universities inaugurated higher doctorates awarded on the strength of a distinguished corpus of scholarship rather than on an examined thesis. Then in 1895, a watershed year, Oxford instituted lower graduate degrees, the bachelor of letters (B.Litt.) and bachelor of science (B.Sc.); Cambridge admitted its first research students; and all four Scottish universities adopted the doctor of science (D.Sc.), doctor of letters (D.Litt.), and doctor of philosophy (D.Phil.) as five-year research degrees. It was not until 1917 that the first British university introduced the lower doctorate, the Ph.D., awarded on the strength of a thesis (or the D.Phil. at Oxford established in 1919). The stimulus for the establishment of the Ph.D. came in part from an American initiative that was itself a reaction to German developments. In 1913 the Association of American Universities compiled a list of U.S. institutions deemed to offer a bachelor's degree of sufficient standard for entry to advanced study abroad; in 1916 the same list was sent to all British universities, again as a guide to acceptabilty for entry to graduate studies. As Simpson noted: "The impact of this communication at a time when. . . the British government and universities were at last becoming aware of the urgent need to organize such studies on a much larger scale than hitherto was remarkable."[30] The American document brought to the fore that Americans could enter doctoral studies in other countries, but not in the United Kingdom.

The Ph.D. took off immediately and attracted enthusiastic support in some quarters. "The Ph.D. . . . will be a real and very great departure in English education—the greatest revolution, in my opinion, of modern times" (Ernest Rutherford 1918).[31] Within three years it was established in almost all departments of all British universities and with virtually identical regulations. Within five years nearly eight hundred had been awarded. In the majority of institutions and subjects it became a sine qua non for teaching in higher education and for research in all areas of academic study, although, as we shall see, its adoption as an employment qualification varies widely among occupations. In midcentury, between 1950 and 1965, it even outnumbered master's degrees. Then master's degrees, based usually on systematically taught courses and a minor dissertation ("taught master's," to distinguish them from M.Phil.'s awarded largely for a dissertation) came on stream.

The doctoral degree still remains the principal qualification for entry to the academic profession. Its growth in the several decades following the Second World War coincided with the quadrupled recruitment of undergraduate students to the higher education system that provided the academic positions to which those with graduate qualifications could aspire. The number of full-time students working on taught master's in universities increased by 75 percent between 1966–1967 and 1974–1975. The comparable increase for research degrees, Ph.D.'s and M.Phil.'s, was 31 percent.[32] The system continued to grow in the 1980s: between 1982–1983 and 1987–1988, the number of full-time research students in universities increased by 24 percent and those on taught master's courses by 19 percent with only some small slackening off in 1987–1988. Part-time postgraduate research students in the universities increased markedly during those years. Part-time students enrolled in taught courses increased by no less than 51 percent in the universities over the six years. But although the supply of places was maintained and they were filled, there were roughly only 1.7 applicants for each place in scientific postgraduate training.[33]

By the end of the 1980s policies for the funding and development of graduate studies were beginning to come under stronger public scrutiny, but national policies were not much clearer than in previous years. Uncertainties about purposes and resources were reflected in a spate of uncoordinated but significant assaults on different aspects of policy. The discussion concerned academic content as much as planning of places and staff. British universities took on the need to supervise and examine students' reading for research degrees more carefully.[34] Discussion about the desirability of taught doctorates reached a negative conclusion,[35] although a committee concerned with research organization in physics[36] emphasized the need for taught elements in doctoral studies, a practice that had begun to spread in other disciplines too. The research council for the social sciences took, and then abandoned, an initiative in promoting taught doctorates, but later proposed in the 1989 Green Paper that social science doctorates should include a core curriculum in research training.[37] The most important policy statements failed to mention the training of research students, but the distribution of research training among institutions was implied in the contested attempt to stratify institutions in terms of their research qualities, which we have already noted, and in the research councils' efforts to reduce the number of outlets for research awards.[38]

By the end of the 1980s graduate studies were subject to various pressures from outside the institutions. In the past they had been a virtually spontaneous outgrowth from the activities of teaching and research. Now, the five research councils were beginning to assume positions on graduate studies, albeit not of the same kind in different disciplinary areas. Some remodeling of graduate studies followed in the wake of attempts to coordinate and stratify research work. At the same time graduate studies seemed well able to survive as a result of student demand, particularly in the dramatic growth areas of taught master's courses, both full-time and part-time.

Characteristics of Graduate Studies

Government and the Funding Base. The central authorities for graduate education are largely the same as those described above for the research system. The DES determines the balance between first degree and graduate studies in the two sectors of higher education, the universities, assumed to be "private," and the polytechnics, until recently owned by local authorities and other institutions which constitute the "public" sector. Both sectors receive most of their recurrent money from central government. More detailed control over the number of places at each institution is undertaken by the two principal funding bodies, the Universities Funding Council and the Polytechnics and Colleges Funding Council. The research councils cannot determine the scale of the provision except that graduate studies are nourished by research they fund and by studentship awards to individual institutions and students. In the humanities studentships are made available by the British Academy, which receives money for these purposes from the DES.

In the public sector, a further dimension of central influence is maintained through the Council for National Academic Awards (CNAA), again appointed by the DES, which validates study leading to advanced degrees in this sector.

As with research provision, research council funding of graduate students is coordinated and guided by their advisory board, which vets corporate plans and budgets and general objectives. In the latter part of the 1980s research councils began to make more manifest what they regarded as the objectives of graduate study within their subject areas. However, neither the objectives for graduate education nor the forms of its funding nor even an adequate collation of data about it have been made explicit or comprehensible by the policy machine. Institutions still determine what is developed in graduate studies, but they may be encouraged or otherwise by central funding or by policy statements. Critical comments made from the field suggest that when policy statements are made, and related initiatives launched, they seem to lack continuous momentum or stability or any convincing policy framework within which institutions can confidently plan and work.

Funding for graduate studies takes two forms: the two funding councils and, in some subject areas, the research councils, which provide funds for teaching and research staff, buildings, and equipment; the other is support to students for the payment of fees and living costs.

The five research councils and the British Academy supported, in 1985–1986, nearly four thousand research studentships and about the same number of other postgraduate awards; over half of these awards were given by the Science and Engineering Research Council. But only 35 percent of all doctoral candidates are thereby supported. Although the picture is not clear, it is obvious that many students are supported by their own funds, employers, and some private foundations. Some are employed as assistants in research programs. The majority of SERC research studentships went to the sciences; the majority of their other postgraduate awards, allowing for taught master's, went to engineering studies, particularly information technology. The research councils tended to respond to the initiatives of institutions that promoted their own taught courses and then sought recognition for the award of student support. Contrary to more general policies that relied upon some kind of lead from employer wishes, research councils have tended to regard institutional ambitions as a better indication of need and demand than the statements of employers. They have felt that employers might have relied too long upon established reputations; their statements of needs are also difficult to articulate and aggregate.

These public sources of funding apply almost wholly to full-time students. Part-time students are expected to receive money from employers or from local education authorities (who are almost never able to provide it) or to fund themselves. The research councils may prime the pump for an experimental part-time course but not on a continuing basis. Some leading members of research councils are suggesting that some of the monies be shifted toward part-time studentships.

It remains for individual institutions to determine how to use the resources received from the funding bodies. Within the general expectations of the funding bodies they still exercise their own preferences on the balance to be struck between undergraduate and graduate studies. Individual institutions, therefore, follow their own assumptions about the weightings allowed for different levels of study. A characteristic allocation of resources by a university to its constituent departments would allow an undergraduate full-time equivalent to be assigned the value of 1.0, a taught master's student 1.3, and a research student 3.0. Enhancement of resources to departments that recruit overseas graduate students is also becoming commonplace.

The Institutional Base. The fifty-three universities (fifty-one in Great Britain, two in Northern Ireland) remain the main providers of postgraduate education. In 1986 the proportion of postgraduate to undergraduate students in the universities was approximately 1:4; in the public sector institutions it was approximately 1:10. In the university sector postgraduate studies expanded by over 21 percent between 1982–1983 and 1987–1988 while overall undergraduate numbers remained more or less the same.[39] (The growth of postgraduate numbers between 1966–1967 and 1987–1988 is shown in table 3-2.) In 1987, 68 percent of postgraduate *awards* (26,567) in universities were on courses leading to higher degrees as opposed to the less prestigious postgraduate diploma courses (11,973). The corresponding figures for the public sector were 2,327 and 6,726.

Under strong guidance from the recently disbanded National Advisory Body for public sector higher education, which determined their finance, and the Council for National Academic Awards, their source of validation, public sector institutional participation in graduate education is growing. In 1988–1989, 4,700 students were registered for CNAA research degrees. The CNAA extended its policy of internal validation, so that twenty-four institutions had by this time established their own research degree committees and, of these, thirteen had powers to register students for Ph.D.'s. The proportion of students taking higher taught degrees to those registered for research degrees was 4.5 to 1 in the public sector compared with the university ratio of 1.5 to 1. This diffusion of research training among a larger number of institutions grew at the same time as the total number of students reading for research degrees decreased. Against this trend toward diffusion, research councils and other funding bodies were contemplating concentration.

Despite the growth of graduate studies in the United Kingdom—unlike in the United States—they have not been strongly institutionalized and are even marginalized. (See chapter 4 for an elaboration of this point.) Most graduate students are not trained within the protection of graduate schools but only within the same departments as undergraduates. Graduate schools in the basic disciplines hardly exist, although there are some autonomous business schools, and in some professions, for example, architecture, separate institutions may offer training. Graduate studies hover unhappily between structures mainly devoted to undergraduate education and units concerned with the performance and furtherance of research. A description of graduate study at Oxford could pass as a description of graduate studies in Britain as a whole:

> The reality of graduate study arrangements at Oxford is organic and varied, the outcome of piecemeal and haphazard change; at any moment there are different parts of the university engaged to different degrees and efforts to improve performance. . . . [There are] well publicised expressions of dissatisfaction felt by some graduate students with various aspects of the present arrangements and with what is seen, even after 50 years expansion, as unwillingness on the part of some senior members to recognise that graduate studies are now a major concern of the university.[40]

Selection and Assessment of Students. The criteria for student selection vary according to the studies they pursue. The quality of the British first degree is sharply defined within a stated system of classifications ranging from first-class honors to third-class honors and pass degrees. The proportion receiving each class of degree varies considerably between subjects and institutions. Candidates for research degrees are usually, but not universally, required to have obtained first- or upper second-class honors; in some institutions and in some disciplines students may not be recruited without a first-class degree. Student awards, which are made by the research councils and the British Academy (for humanities), constitute a powerful system for asserting academic standards for the recruitment of research students. The British Academy almost exclusively makes its awards to first-class honors students. The National Environmental Research Council recruits one-third of its awardees taking up Ph.D.'s from those with first-class honors, and the proportion has gone up recently; the great majority have upper seconds. The Agriculture and Food Research Council recruits students for specific projects and is thus less likely to recruit first-class candidates, but the standard has recently improved. The Economic and Social Research Council allows institutions (it calls them "outlets" for research awards) to offer places to students with either first or upper second degrees. It has also recently been asking institutions to differentiate between different grades of upper second-class degrees in order that candidates who can finance themselves but have lower rather than upper second degrees may be recruited for research degrees. However, the norm is to recruit from the best.

Those entering taught master's degrees must also possess an upper second-class honors degree if they are to compete for a research council award. But the student population is recruited from a wider range of qualifications than in the case of research degrees. Institutions vary more widely in the threshold they maintain for recruitment. In some universities and other institutions it is possible to enter a taught master's course without a first degree if other forms of relevant experience and high general ability are demonstrated.

Student Enrollment Patterns. Students in taught courses outnumber research students in both universities and the public sector (table 3-2). Although full-time students outnumbered part-time students in universities at the end of the 1980s by a ratio of approximately 5 to 3, the trend was otherwise: there were more new part-time students than full-time. Over one-third of the part-time postgraduate university population studied either business, finance and management (BFM) or education, predominantly in taught courses. In both universities and the public sector, taught master's courses in these two subjects were the major growth areas.

In public sector institutions, the numbers of students studying science remained higher than in other subject fields, although only courses in computing and data processing grew. Electronic and electrical engineering were the only growth areas in engineering. In both the university and the public sector, the number of students in the arts, humanities, and social sciences was declining.

Among new full-time graduate students in 1987–1988, men outnumbered women in the universities by nearly two to one, but among part-time

TABLE 3-2   Number of Postgraduate Students in U.K. Higher Education, 1966–1988

| | Research Training | | | | |
| | University Sector | | Public Sector | | |
	Full-time	Part-time	Full-time	Part-time	Total
1966–1967	18,409[a]	—	317[d]	—	
1977–1978	24,291[b]	14,247[b]	2,557[d]	—	
1987–1988	26,305[b]	16,772[b]	2,640[d]	1,550[d]	47,267

| | Taught Courses (Master's, Etc.) | | | | |
| | University Sector | | Public Sector | | |
	Full-time	Part-time	Full-time	Part-time	Total
1966–1967	13,564[a]	—	—	—	
1977–1978	25,382[b]	10,263[b]	9,648[d]	—	
1987–1988	29,812[b]	19,363[b]	6,823[c]	13,485[c]	69,483

SOURCES: [a] Expenditure Committee of the House of Commons, *Government Observations on the Report, Department of Education and Science,* Command 6611, 1976.
[b] UGC, *University Statistics, 1987/88,* Vol. I, Universities Statistical Record, 1989.
[c] Council for National Academic Awards, *Annual Report 1987–88.*
[d] Estimated figures provided by Council for National Academic Awards. The ratio of full- to part-time is estimated at roughly 60 percent to 40 percent.

students the difference was much smaller. Overall, women made up 38 percent of postgraduate students originating from the United Kingdom. Gender differences in the level of qualifications sought were evident. Men taking full-time university courses were more likely to be registered for research degrees, while women registered full-time were more likely to take taught courses. In the public sector in 1987–1988 more than twice as many men as women were awarded master's degrees. Excluding the Diploma in Management Studies courses, where men outnumbered women by more than three to one, more postgraduate diploma awards went to women. Women had not participated strongly in the growth areas of BFM and information technology in either the public sector or in universities.

Overseas Students. Overseas students outnumber U.K. students in four subject areas: veterinary science, agriculture and related studies, business and financial studies, and engineering and technology, with civil engineering the most popular engineering course. Electronic engineering attracts most U.K.-domiciled engineering students, but in this subject, too, overseas students outnumber them. Overall, as many as 39 percent of postgraduate students are from overseas, in spite of a sharp increase in their fees; the largest numbers appeared in the late 1980s. Two countries (Hong Kong and the United States) each provided over four thousand students. But in the latter part of the 1980s the number of new entrants from European countries rose much more rapidly than those from elsewhere, and students from countries of the European Community were eligible for tuition fees at the U.K. rates.

The internationalization of graduate studies in the United Kingdom raises policy issues. Some programs, usually taught master's, are fashioned deliberately to meet the needs of overseas students from countries still strengthening their higher education systems. But other courses that might be expected to meet direct U.K. employment needs are not viable without overseas students. Matching demands from overseas and home raises problems of course planning. With the increase in students from other EC countries, policies for reciprocal arrangements are being developed. But EC students pay home tuition fees and not enhanced overseas rates, so that departments, now enjoined to increase their earnings, gain no financial advantage or even lose. A ceiling may be placed on EC admissions for this reason.

The Range and Nature of Provision. The range of postgraduate programs in the university and the public sector is substantially the same although the emphases differ. Both sectors offer research degrees at the doctoral and master's levels, as well as taught master's degrees, postgraduate diplomas, and certificates, of which the Postgraduate Certificate in Education is most popular. Postexperience or continuing education courses across the spectrum of subjects are also listed. In public sector institutions the Diploma in Management Studies caters to the largest number of mature students.

The Ph.D. (known as the D.Phil. at a minority of universities) provides the framework for individual pieces of research, normally carried out under supervision for three years full-time, at the end of which students submit a thesis. It may be completed in an equivalent amount of part-time study, but the full-time degree remains the norm. Ph.D. students, generally based in university departments, are spread across many institutions of different categories, sizes, and reputations, including polytechnics and colleges in the public sector. Some are employed in industrial establishments or hold awards in institutes funded by research councils and private foundations.[41]

Doctoral students may work on a prespecified individually funded project or be attached to a research group working on a large project within which they can identify a piece of work for themselves, or they may work individually on a self-generated topic, perhaps as the only Ph.D. student in the department to which they are attached. The pattern varies greatly according to subject. Their program may be entirely based on their own research or, increasingly, it may have a taught component: the place of the taught elements of Ph.D. programs varies widely.

Many more science and technology students than those in humanities and social science were registered for Ph.D.'s in departments or institutes that involved them in teams engaged in research programs or in large-scale projects, a significant difference between them and their peers in other subjects. The Winfield Report (1983) recommended extending the recently established linked award schemes, in which students funded by the social sciences council were linked to existing research projects.[42] However, this linkage was advocated in the name of enhancing student contributions to knowledge rather than their training. The scheme has, in fact, come to an end.[43]

M.Phil.'s are predominantly research degrees—in effect, Ph.D.'s in miniature, involving some course work and the submission of a dissertation. They may also be awarded as a consolation for failure to achieve a Ph.D.

Taught master's (M.A.'s, M.Sc.'s, M.B.A.'s, M.S.W.'s, and others) are the heaviest growth area in British graduate studies. In the 1970s the UGC and the research councils actively encouraged the expansion of postgraduate taught courses (programs) relative to research studies (including the introduction of taught course elements in Ph.D. programs).[44] They also encouraged collaboration by employers in specifying content and contributing to teaching and in supervising courses designed to meet specific training needs. The growth of full-time taught-course students in universities between 1966–1967 and 1974–1975 was from over 13,000 to nearly 24,000, an increase of 85 percent; from 1982–1983 to 1987–1988 they increased from 25,000 to nearly 29,000, an increase of 19 percent.[45] In the public sector, in 1987 more than 20,000 students were registered on CNAA master's, postgraduate diploma, and Diploma in Management Studies courses. More than seventy new CNAA (Council for National Academic Awards) postgraduate and postexperience courses were validated in 1987–1988.[46]

Master's programs involve systematic study mainly through course work at an advanced level, but also such programs usually include a minor research or equivalent exercise. They have multiple purposes. They may be a prerequisite of study for a Ph.D. in such subjects as economics and mathematics, where the development of knowledge of the subject is progressive. Since the mid-1970s the concept of prerequisite training has begun to spread to other subjects. Master's degrees may be the first level at which a degree is offered, as in demography or socio-legal studies, and may therefore constitute initial training. They may cover new study areas, or highly specific areas of work, or an area of future specific employment. Taught master's are often offered on a part-time basis: they may occupy a year of full-time study or its part-time equivalent. The lack of funding for doctoral-level study has probably persuaded more students to take a master's as a second best. These degrees have helped departments to earn income from fees because, unlike undergraduate fees, they are not subject to limits imposed by the funding councils.

Although they fall outside our study of graduate education, postgraduate qualifications that lead, not to a degree, but to a diploma or graduate certificate, occupy an important position. These may be awarded at the end of courses in subjects too specific for the award of a master's degree, for example, photography, film, and television, or they may be a less-advanced version of a master's and not require the submission of a dissertation. Sometimes they are awarded to those with insufficient qualifications for admission to a master's degree. Higher education institutions vary in their standards that differentiate master's from diplomas. Some diplomas, however, have achieved high status and enable those students who want them to proceed to higher degrees.

In the United Kingdom, professional education and training has differed from the United States in two major respects. Almost all of the major professions admit students to training and education at the undergraduate level but require students to continue after taking a bachelor's degree, or the equivalent, in a combination of supervised practice and further qualification. This is true of law, medicine, accountancy, architecture, and engineering. In social work, pharmacy, and education, the first degree is also a qualification to practice. In social work and education it is possible to take a first degree in a subject other than the professional area and go on to add to the professional qualification in a postgraduate sequence. In some professions it is still possible to enter what is virtually an apprenticeship system and to qualify through instruction and assessment at the same time as practical experience is gained; this remains true of law and accountancy. In law, accountancy, engineering, social work, and nursing, full professional qualifications can still be achieved without the award of a first or a graduate degree. Increasingly, however, these areas are being colonized by courses leading to qualifications of graduate status.

Research has not occupied a dominant position in any of these professional areas, including medicine, until recently. In medicine the most esteemed clinicians have not been the leading researchers, although this position is changing rapidly. In all the other professions a process of academicization is taking place. Six chairs exist now in social work; in 1960 there was none. Chairs in nursing studies have been established. Accountancy and associated areas such as business and management studies have grown substantially within higher education and with them the number of academic posts and research activities.

Research councils (the social science council is an exception) have taken some action to develop postdoctoral work, thus demonstrating concern that the replenishment of the academic system requires institutional support. Their schemes are small, however, and the use of the postdoctoral period of research as a recruitment period for higher education teaching is not clearly defined; it varies, too, among subject areas. Two factors are leading toward a stronger emphasis on postdoctorals. First, the surplus of able Ph.D.'s, who previously would have moved directly to an academic appointment, can be retained as postdoctoral students and workers. A second factor derives from the changing structure of the Ph.D. itself. If some subjects are beginning to require a year of preparation, perhaps in a master's or M.Phil. course, under the present funding arrangements doctoral students will have only two years of studentship in which to continue with their doctorates. This might mean that preparation for the doctorate will be more restricted than under earlier, more generous assumptions; hence the students will be less adequate for entry to a full research and teaching career. In some areas the subject of doctoral studies is deliberately restricted to make it an exercise feasible within the three-year period during which grants are available. These factors might make for an increased emphasis on postdoctoral studies, although funding for them hardly appears on the policy scene. Almost all the graduate studies funding bodies have minimal provision for postdoctorals.

Staffing. Because graduate training in Britain is offered by the same departments as is undergraduate training, it is difficult to determine the number of faculty members involved, except as a crude proportion based upon the number of student places allocated to the different levels of degrees.

The full-time teaching and research staff numbered nearly 30,000 in 1987–1988, in universities paid wholly from general funds (see table 3-3). A slight majority are involved in the professional and vocational areas of study. Also, the universities employ large numbers of part-time teaching and research staff who contribute to graduate studies teaching, as do many full-time staff who are not wholly university financed: the latter numbered over 16,000 in 1987–1988. The total number of full-time teaching and research staff in universities was then over 46,000. The number not wholly financed has continued to rise steadily, presumably in response to government pressure on universities to seek outside funding. Nearly 10 percent of the staff were in professorial or equivalent grades, 20 percent at reader or senior lecturer levels, nearly 60 percent at lecturer or equivalent, and 11 percent in other grades. Seventeen percent were women.

The average age of wholly financed full-time staff increased from 43.7 in 1985–1986 to 44.6 in 1987–1988. In the latter year 15 percent were under thirty-five and 16 percent were fifty-five and over. The age of staff in different disciplinary areas varied considerably. Mineral engineering, metallurgy, and architecture had the highest proportion of staff over thirty-five

TABLE 3-3 Full-time Teaching and Research Staff in British Universities Paid Wholly from General Funds, by Major Subject Areas (1987–1988)

Major Subject Areas ("Cost Centers")	Number of Academic Staff
Administration, business, and social studies	5,951
Medicine, dentistry, and health	4,364
Engineering and technology	4,173
Physical sciences	3,307
Languages, literature, and area studies	3,127
Mathematical sciences	2,393
Other arts	2,357
Biological sciences	2,180
Education	1,350
Agriculture, forestry, and veterinary science	654
Other cost centers	24
Total	29,880

SOURCE: UGC, *University Statistics 1986/87*, vol. 1, Students and Staff, published by Universities Statistical Record, 1987.

years. The highest proportion of young academics are found in computer studies, law, electrical and electronic engineering, and veterinary studies. In most subjects, however, young academics are not being recruited, and the average age of faculty has gone up a year for every year since the end of the 1970s.

Figures for the public sector are not available in equivalent form. In January 1987 the polytechnics employed over 16,000 full-time equivalent teachers.[47] Within the public sector the polytechnics undertake the bulk of research and graduate training, but colleges and institutes of higher education offer some taught master's work. The proportion of staff time spent in all public institutions on these activities is less than that devoted to them in the universities.

The "graying" of the academic staff has prompted efforts to change the age balance. Reasonably attractive retirement schemes have made it possible for tenured staff over fifty years old to be "bought out" in both sectors. Such a scheme was inaugurated in 1981 and revived in 1987. On a lesser scale, "new blood" schemes have also enabled the University Grants Committee to allocate posts, mainly but not wholly in shortage subjects, which can be filled by younger academics. The earlier scheme was planned centrally on somewhat restrictive conditions. A scheme started in 1988, supported by a sum of £70 million, enabled universities to identify posts likely to fall vacant by 1994 and recruit full-time staff before the vacancy occurred. A "new blood" scheme administered by the Royal Society also helped to modify the age balance.

At the end of the 1980s academics, especially, are growing anxious about the capacity of the research and teaching systems to reproduce themselves. Fewer academics have been full-time permanent academic staff members since the early 1980s. Other considerations adversely affecting recruitment have been a lag in salaries from the levels sustained by other public-sector employees, the passing into law of provisions for the abolition of academic tenure, a feeling of undervaluation, and a resulting general demoralization among academic staff.

Government and the Setting of Objectives. Until recently, academics virtually alone set the objectives for graduate study. To a large extent they still do, and it is their capacity to attract students to the very wide range of provision described earlier which largely determines the courses offered and the objectives underlying them. The motives impelling both students and staff to engage in graduate studies are various. Much still depends upon individual student interest in the subjects; for example, since only a small minority of those taking advanced degrees in history obtain academic appointments and since job opportunities outside academia are few, historical studies must be pursued largely for their own sake. Other courses are offered because the academic staff wish to teach in their special areas of interest. The proliferation of master's courses is also encouraged by the prospect of attracting fees that the students bring with them, which are not controlled by either the DES or the funding councils.

The links between these motives and the range of objectives that can be analyzed from public statements or from the views expressed in the interviews undertaken in this study are not easily made. The Universities Funding Council has noted a continuing debate about whether the primary purpose of providing research studentships was to train researchers or to produce research; also, that the DES and research council advisory board thought the former, but in the humanities the production of research was considered the primary purpose. The official statements of objectives have not changed since 1974, when the government commented on the *Third Report* of the Expenditure Committee of the House of Commons (PAC), 1973–1974. The broad objectives of postgraduate education were: to meet the nation's future manpower needs; to provide further training for qualified, suitable, and keen students; and to contribute to the advancement of knowledge. In 1987 when the House of Commons Committee of Public Accounts reported on postgraduate awards on the basis, again, of examination of evidence from the DES and some of the research councils, the Committee noted precisely the same objectives as those recited in 1974.[48] Both reports, over a distance of fifteen years, noted that "meeting the need for trained manpower is the primary aim." The PAC accepted that matching manpower supply and demand could only be a broad aim and acknowledged the overlap between the manpower objective and the wider education objectives of the awards program. It also noted an assurance from the DES "that all the research councils regularly review their policies and practices on postgraduate awards." It accepted the science council emphasis of meeting manpower needs by directing awards to perceived shortages in particular areas and believed this goal should continue to be a major determinant in making future awards, which other awarding bodies should adopt.

Such statements of predominantly instrumental objectives do not command universal support among either higher education teachers or their students and seem to conflict with an official contribution to an OECD exercise reported in 1987 which suggested that "British universities see themselves as maintaining their traditional functions and their traditional academic excellence during the rest of the century."[49] The OECD analysis did not take account of the considerable growth, noted earlier, in the numbers of taught master's degrees, many taken part-time. Some of these degree programs have different objectives from those of maintaining academic excellence (except inasmuch as it is implied, or hoped for, in all academic activities). The same OECD report noted that postgraduate degrees in business studies and accounting were increasing by over 10 percent a year, but it did not remark on universities' shifts toward money-seeking research activities. Nor could it predict the newfound commitment to continuing education and to such externally promoted developments as the Enterprise Scheme advanced by the government's Training Agency (offering large cash rewards to institutions attempting to "inbed" enterprise into the curriculum). Any statement of the purposes of graduate studies would also have to take account of the greater part played by nonuniversity institutions.

Research Councils and the Objectives of Graduate Studies. The purposes of research council funding of graduate studies vary across subject areas. The councils differ in the extent to which they attempt to direct institutions in the purposes of graduate studies. Their funding of research studentships generally has reflected caution in defining students' research too closely.

At one end of the spectrum the British Academy, which funds research training in the humanities, has historically followed the philosophy of the famous Robbins Report of 1963. The objectives have been to support study for the sake of individual fulfillment, to sustain a number of people pursuing scholarship in the humanities as a contribution to civilized society, and to insure continuity of scholarship. The academy also sees its function as helping to replenish the academic community and contributing indirectly to teaching in schools. Its policies are thus demand-led and can be contrasted with the five research councils. More recently, however, the British Academy has been considering whether it ought to combine the demand-led approach with a somewhat more directive style. This might, for example, lead to more awards for modern languages or oriental languages or European Community law.[50] The academy sees the development of taught master's courses as encouraging the growth of these relatively under-provided subjects, but it holds that students should not go directly from undergraduate degrees to doctorates because they are often not ready to frame research projects while still taking their first degrees. It has set up a pilot system offering twenty awards at the master's level in the hope that these students will additionally then be able to apply for a three-year re-search degree.

The Medical Research Council has traditionally been cautious about directing research students. It awards 150 research studentships to univer-sities each year but only 50 to its six research units. It also participates in the award, as assessors, of 200 research studentships a year in the biological sciences made by the science council. Its interest in funding postgraduate studies is in part concerned with replenishing the academic profession in clinical medicine and in such basic disciplines as biomedical research. But this concern is inextricably connected with other outcomes from postgradu-ate study. Postgraduate students, and particularly postdoctoral students, make a significant contribution to the advancement of knowledge. The council found it difficult in the past to interest clinicians in research because it might divert them from a successful medical career. But the importance of sustaining research interests because of their connection with clinical work in such areas as cellular and molecular biology is now recognized. A coincidence of interest ensues: future leaders of the medical profession will have an academic background different from those currently in such posi-tions, who often have no research training.

The Science and Engineering Research Council (SERC) is the main pro-vider of awards and other forms of funding for the whole range of scientific and engineering research. The Council assumes that the Ph.D. ought to en-able students to get thorough research training, although they might also contribute to knowledge by completing a piece of research. It also, like the Natural Environment Research Council (NERC), believes that industry needs more trained researchers and that it is its duty to help provide them.[51]

Both SERC and NERC have created Collaborative Awards in Science and Engineering (CASE), together with a modest provision for Ph.D.'s in Total Technology. Although the relatively low take-up by students of these research awards suggests that students concur with the preference of senior academics not to confine the subjects of research too closely, SERC has been contemplating a more substantial experimental scheme for engineering Ph.D.'s based on two years of research in a higher education institution and a further two-year period in a Teaching Company style of experience. Its advanced course studentships are seen as a way of providing trained manpower for the private sector of the economy. SERC is developing its commitment to younger graduates already in industry through its Integrated Graduate Development Scheme. It is moving toward work for older graduates in service through two schemes promoted cooperatively with the Open University. But the council's overall policies for continuing education are totally undeveloped. SERC looks to industry to fund the schemes on the scale required.

The Agricultural and Food Research Council also evinces dual interests in advancing the scientific base and in contributing toward the economy. It plans to provide a base for a competitive agriculture and food industry in the United Kingdom. Its studentships are thus awarded within predefined policy objectives. The AFRC institutes, in which much of the relevant research and research training take place, look after industry's needs; at the same time, however, they make a feature of advancing the cause of basic science in their field through research programs and the training of researchers for them.

The social science research council (ESRC) has been explicit about its training objectives.[52] It aims to develop and maintain "a first class national research capacity in the social sciences." The council will provide support for advanced training for the best students in both social science disciplines and appropriate professional subjects in the most appropriate research and educational environments. It offers short courses, workshops and conferences for training-related activities, and a research program to develop ideas for improvements in training. Established researchers can help develop their research by means of its special schemes. In all those arrangements it seeks to create knowledgeable and skilled researchers; research by postgraduate students, which will contribute to knowledge and understanding; and trained social scientists who will "act as catalysts in improving expertise and performance in their employment."

The ESRC has yet to develop a comprehensive policy. Several measures have been tried to insure that its graduate training policies are relevant through a range of schemes such as collaborative awards to link academic study with employment and various targeted efforts in such subjects as industrial relations and management education. Important gaps in research and advanced training remain for students in public administration and in social research.[53] Concern about the use of graduate studies in public administration is not equal to that expressed in favor of connections with industry. Certain initiatives, however, have been taken in health services research and training by the Medical Research Council and ESRC and in planning and public administration by the ESRC. In 1989 the ESRC returned to an earlier theme when it proposed a stronger methodological core for doctoral studies.[54]

Current Policy Issues and Proposals for Change

Although policy making for graduate studies is relatively unstructured, several issues present themselves to the system at large and to the institutions; questions of purpose and content are widely discussed, and policies relating to the concentration of graduate studies, recruitment for the staffing of higher education, and manpower planning have emerged.

Objectives of Graduate Study. The balance of objectives between the advancement of knowledge and of training—of orientation between individual originality and the acquisition of skills general to the discipline and to research—does not have general consensus. One point of view stresses "a positive contribution to knowledge and creativity" in the disciplines.[55] But the Ph.D. is also intended to provide training in research methods to equip individuals to become researchers and scholars at the highest level; this implies a command of technique beyond that required for one piece of research. The 1982 report of the Advisory Board for Research Councils assumed that training was the prime purpose of the degree; others have laid more emphasis on its importance for the advancement of knowledge.[56] The latter objective was strongly supported by all historians whom we interviewed; physicists were more likely to emphasize training as primary; the economists, as befits their station midway between science and the arts, held a variety of views.

Purpose is linked with substantive content. The Ph.D. was increasingly sought when continuing growth in the academic natural sciences could be assumed. Now that science departments are at best in a steady state, and the number of academics in most disciplines is reduced, the nature of the Ph.D. for those aiming to pursue an academic career is questioned. Some academic leaders think it might be appropriate for Ph.D. programs to offer broad-based research training rather than the opportunity to do a highly specialized piece of work.[57] Inquiries undertaken in conjunction with later 1980s reviews by the Advisory Board for Research Councils and the social science research council demonstrated widespread support for the introduction of taught components into the British Ph.D. and for the concept of the doctoral program.[58] Some changes had been introduced, but haphazardly rather than centrally led, without a clear pattern.

The more radical step of converting the Ph.D. into a predominantly taught degree was judged by a committee of the Committee of Vice-Chancellors and Principals to have negligible support.[59] This issue is linked to that discussed above: the conflict between sustaining the research objectives of the Ph.D. and its function of supporting originality and contributions to knowledge and increasing demands for competence and the advancement of technical requirements in some areas. In economics, for example, the requirement will increasingly be for an M.A. or an M.Phil. after one year before a two-year full-time period of research training. (But this will be affected by a recent ESRC decision to allow for a three-year full-time period of research training.) In history there are uncoordinated movements toward preliminary training in specialist techniques appropriate to the pursued dissertation, which might then be followed by a full three years' study. Most academics agree that the scope of dissertations must be reduced if the three-year norm is to be achieved. In economics some institutions have followed the American example and experimented with accepting three articles in a linked research area in place of a full-blown dissertation.

The Vice-Chancellors' committee scrutinized the methods of supervising and assessing graduate students in 1986.[60] Its guidelines included proposals for a regular system by which students were to be informed of their obligations and those of their supervisors for the submission of work, an annual review of progress, and individual tutorial supervision.

The growth of master's courses is considered a healthy development in British higher education, to judge by the encouragement given by the two main funding councils. These courses meet a wide range of specific needs. Students are able to advance in academic and professional status as the result of a one-year full-time course or two-year part-time course. At the same time, the master's courses have status problems. Doubts about standards were strongly expressed in an interview with a leading historian. There is something of a trade-off in some courses between academic standards and the need to respond to market demands and to increase fee earnings.

Policy Pressures on Academics. Issues of purpose and content might largely originate from the academy itself, but system managers are increasingly pressing policies on it. These policies are not wholly thought through, but they typically insist on efficiency, as in the concern with doctoral completion rates, on scientific effectiveness, as in the policy of concentration, and on a larger and more tentative concern with manpower planning and academic recruitment.

Both institutions and students have been pressed to insure that Ph.D. dissertations will be submitted for examination within three, or at most, four years. Throughout the history of the Ph.D. in Britain the ratios of completion ("submission rates") have caused greater anxiety in the arts, humanities, and social sciences than in science and technology.[61] The issue first came to a head in 1979 in a report from the comptroller and auditor general that highlighted the exceptionally low completion rate of social science Ph.D.'s, and in the subsequent appearance of the chairman of the then Social Science Research Council before the Public Accounts Committee of the House of Commons. In 1982 the Advisory Board of the research councils criticized the indefensibly low submission rate for social science Ph.D.'s. A 1983 study of six universities showed a four-year submission rate in the social sciences varying from 6.6 percent to 30.5 percent.[62] The Advisory Board then made some general recommendations, including the limiting of student awards to departments providing high quality supervision and to institutions with acceptable rates of completion within four years. The submission rate improved in the late 1980s, but this policy continues to be administered by the social science research council amid much contention and distress in the institutions.[63] They maintain it curbs good work in the more diffuse areas of history that require time for exploration, and in such areas as developmental economics, where students take time to gain access to developing countries. The policy also conflicts with students' needs to gain teaching experience in their research centers to make them effective members of academic institutions once they qualify.

A principal theme of the late 1980s was the concentration of graduate studies implicit in the research funding policies and explicit in the patterns of student grants. The assumption made by both ministers and the academics who helped them administer the graduate training systems was that the quality and productivity of the Ph.D., or of any other research-related activity, were most likely to be achieved through concentration in a small number of institutions and the introduction of more structured programs with a greater emphasis on training. The policy of concentration was first explicitly followed by the Medical Research Council and the Agriculture and Food Research Council, partly in the name of achieving higher quality or more targeted contributions to knowledge. The AFRC in particular claimed an exceptionally high submission rate.

Planning. Alongside these somewhat intuitively derived policies is uncertain confidence in the efficacy of manpower planning. The argument against it holds that the system will respond to needs as they present themselves and that market reaction is better than long-range plans, which are almost always falsified by events.[64] The 1987 DES White Paper announced a review of qualified manpower, but by the end of 1989 none had emerged, and it was not certain that the review would cover graduate training. Individual research councils have attempted to change the balance between research training and the funding of research projects in order to fund enough projects to absorb those trained. This somewhat laconic approach is applied to the specific issue of how the system will recruit its future staff. Some participants predict a sufficient surplus of Ph.D.'s in most areas to meet foreseeable needs, and that the transference of resources from undergraduate to graduate training is relatively easy.[65] The House of Lords Select

Committee on Science and Technology warned, however, in 1989 that manpower shortages could put U.K. plans for civil R&D at risk. "The rewards offered to scientists and engineers and those who train them are still abysmally low."[66] The chairman of the research council supporting the social sciences (ESRC) also warned that social sciences would simply not exist in the 1990s unless more graduate students were trained in the subject.[67] The ESRC current level of 250 training studentships a year was "scandalously low"; the council was preparing a series of measures to expand research training.[68] Among its proposals were a higher proportion of Ph.D.'s instead of advanced training courses, support for part-time Ph.D. fees, and the encouragement of training in research methods.

Reports on the future of university chemistry and physics prepared in the late 1980s referred to the need for "new blood schemes" to insure proper balance of staff in physics departments and to the "distorted age distribution of academics in chemistry," notably the concentration of staff in the thirty-five to fifty-five age bracket.[69] The Stone Report on chemistry suggested that a significant fraction of restructuring money ought to be devoted to the appointment of new staff below thirty-five years of age with a consequent adjustment of the numbers in the middle age group. It also remarked that further provisions will be necessary after the restructuring period if the system is to move to an even age distribution.

Past experience has evoked skepticism about the efficacy of planning. One research council expressed the difficulty:

> Predicting manpower needs in particular disciplines is not easy. This arises from the long term constants involved in the educational process compared with the often rapid fluctuation of the demand for particular skills that can take place in the labour market including the science base. The general response of the research councils to the problem has been . . . to maintain the level of overall numbers at a time when society itself is becoming increasingly in need of scientific, managerial and technological skills.[70]

Overscrupulous prediction of needs may not be helpful, but some attempt to anticipate changing demands cannot be avoided. It is impossible to find a central point in the policy and awarding system where a coherent view is taken of higher education staffing needs.

The problems of staffing higher education are both quantitative and qualitative. Beyond the serious age imbalance lies the matter of a large-scale exodus of faculty in the 1990s. The effects of mass retirements will be accentuated by the fact that academics have been allowed to retire from the age of fifty on quite advantageous early severance terms. Thinning out of the senior ranks will not be effectively offset by schemes to recruit new blood—younger faculty members to whom no permanent appointments may be offered. And even if the flow of able candidates for faculty positions is secured into the 1990s when the first mass retirements occur, the system faces the question of what constitutes appropriate graduate training for its teachers. Higher education at present assumes that most students will be well qualified school leavers capable of taking "honours" degree courses with a high degree of specialization and initial competence. They ought to be taught by faculty with full research training because much of the teaching in the final stages of the British undergraduate course depends upon recent research developments and, in some subjects, students are required to undertake a modicum of research themselves. If, however, the age participation rate increases from about 15 percent to 30 percent, as intended by government, large areas of higher education will change. Not all undergraduates will need to be taught by academics whose primary pursuits are research and scholarship. Recruitment might be better drawn from those who have pursued more systematic training in their subject at the master's level or by those who take doctorates where the taught elements overweigh those of original research. These issues have hardly begun to be discussed within British higher education.

POLICY IMPLICATIONS

British policies in higher education have moved from a system in which the institutions' determination of their own academic profiles and the motivations of individual students were the driving force toward one in which policymakers are striving toward new policy frameworks. Funding bodies state objectives and policies for research and training which they incorporate into corporate plans for scrutiny by the Advisory Board for Research Councils, the DES, and, from time to time, committees of Parliament. Nonetheless, as almost all of our interviews testify, these stated objectives and overarching plans are not converted into a coherent national policy for U.K. graduate studies. As in other OECD countries, graduate education in the United Kingdom remains "less the result of policy initiatives than of the aggregation of innumerable individual decisions."[71] Such policy shifts as can be noted have been imposed by the pursuit of other goals, such as general policies about higher education, overseas students' fees, research funding, and the labor market for research-trained personnel. Government has encouraged interventions by its intermediary bodies in areas perceived to be short of graduate training, but these have varied over time in response to changing assumptions about manpower needs.[72]

Yet if there are some generic concerns that have not yet emerged, other issues have been subjected to drastic policy changes without sufficient attention to the enterprise that is to be developed. Many concern both research and graduate studies policy, and we summarize them as follows:

- Recent history demonstrates that the British government has decided to concentrate the power for making policy decisions for research and graduate studies. This is demonstrated by the development in the Cabinet Office of an assessment unit and by the appointment of ACOST, which will coordinate the work of government, the ABRC, and the funding councils. In doing so, the government has appointed senior industrialists to key positions from which there will be oversight of research and graduate education. The intention to concentrate power in the system is exemplified in the 1989 proposal, now abandoned, produced by a working party of the ABRC, but voiced by other powerful groups too, to create a super-research council, with specialist divisions to some extent corresponding to the existing five research councils, which will in some way ensure coherent decision making and priority setting.
- Associated with this determination to find unitary objectives and to create strong coordinative machinery is a reduction of the traditional, arguably essential, pluralism of both science and higher education and their autonomous capacity for self-development.
- As a particular consequence of the rejection of scientific and organizational pluralism, the government has asserted its own priorities, in particular by giving power to representatives of industry and business in decisions about academic research and science priorities. This is exemplified by the appointment of nonacademics to the chairs of ACOST and the two principal higher education funding councils. The contrast can be made with those countries where chairs of research councils are appointed through election by academics, and with the many U.S. systems for evaluating higher education in which the key actors are not appointed by government but are the academics themselves. Instrumental steerage by industrial and business executives becomes the issue.
- The British government could have been criticized in much of its recent history for making a timid analysis of its policy options in research and graduate education. It has now chosen to be bold. But it has based its choices on an essentially political analysis largely arrived at through the exercise of intuition in which it attributes gross faults to the present system. Strong efforts have been made to introduce performance measurement into both research and higher education on the basis of judgments made in advance of methods of measurement that would operate conjointly with adequate peer review.
- The political judgment of the day is that the higher education research and development system is poor at developing the results of scientific inquiry for purposes of the economy. The analysis made by the British government in the early 1980s was unlike that of the

United States and Japan in that the U.K. authorities failed to note how potential contributions to the economy must rest upon the encouragement of fundamental research. The government has, however, with the support of the advisory board of the research councils, reached the compromise formula of "strategic research," which recognizes the importance of fundamental research within a setting of economic application and relevance. The issue is the depth of commitment to basic research.

• The exercise of government preferences is almost wholly directed toward the economy in its industrial, commercial, and service sectors. It has virtually ignored the needs of the public sector in its efforts to plan research and graduate education, although local government, the health service, and central government have been subjected to drastic reforms requiring advanced training and associated research and development for their proper assimilation.

• Until very recently graduate studies have been largely neglected as a policy question. They have not been effectively institutionalized, so that both their funding and distribution and key issues of curriculum and organization remain largely internal to the academic system. It is an issue only recently considered by the ABRC and hitherto has only been taken up by those involved with specific subject areas in the research councils, funding councils, and elsewhere. Studies to be launched by the DES and the ESRC in 1990 may lead to policies based on analysis.

• The government has advocated a concentration of research (and graduate studies) on the assumptions of the importance of backing excellence and of rationalizing potentially expensive provision. These policies have been criticized from many perspectives. It is a conceptualization that mainly addresses the economic issues involved in "big science."

• Concentrating research also concentrates graduate studies through the restriction of the "outlets" for awards to graduate students. In some areas where costly laboratories and equipment are involved, policies of concentration, whether in interdisciplinary research centers or through the award of large rather than small grants, have the same effect.

• Associated with concentration has been tightened control. Control has been concerned with attacking such obvious indicators as low submission rates of dissertations in certain areas. These policies do not take systematic account of the key structural issues. These include: the changing nature of the undergraduate sequence preceding graduate study; the extent to which those with three-year studentships find it difficult to complete on time, either because of the nature of the subject area or because of the pressure to find teaching experience or employment early within their graduate life; and the need to identify those areas of research training that belong more properly to the post-doctoral period.

• There is universal, and realistic, skepticism about the ability of the authorities to engage in successful manpower planning. Perhaps the system will be able to turn itself around sufficiently to deal with the quantitative aspects of the large number of retirements expected from the 1990s onward in the academic system or the needs of particular new occupations and changing zones of the economy. But among the qualitative issues affecting the research and teaching staff in higher education, certain matters ought to be tackled now. The government intends to extend the recruitment of undergraduates into a far higher proportion of the age group than is now happening; it also plans to bring more segments of the population into higher education; the teachers of some of the students, particularly the ones with weaker academic qualifications whose higher education is more experiential, will be trained less appropriately through traditional doctoral research studies. They might be better equipped through systematic work at the master's level or in doctorates that contain a higher degree of disciplinary training than at present. The planners are not anticipating the expanded and changed staffing needs of higher education, starting with the changing teaching patterns.

A further policy implication should be noted. In compiling this report we have been struck, as have others, by the paucity of simple data about postgraduate students.[73] The sources of funding for the majority of students are a matter of conjecture. The numbers of staff and students in the different categories of graduate studies are not collated, so that the researcher or policy analyst must go to several sources to build up composite pictures of the entire graduate system, but then cannot easily compare like with like over time and between the university and public sectors. The destinations of graduate students are a matter of informed impression rather than of systematic inquiry. The new machinery for assessment at the center of British government is primarily directed at research. Studies of the uses to which different forms of graduate training are put in different sectors of employment should surely contribute toward a more rational form of policy making. Investigations just beginning in the early 1990s may remedy these faults.

The lack of concern about the future of the academic system itself is troubling. The training and recruitment of future researchers and teachers of researchers may well be met by short-term changes in the balance of undergraduate and graduate education. But short-term planning will not make it possible for future recruitment to be well matched to the changing higher education scene in the United Kingdom. Even more important, the nature of the official discourse about graduate education is remarkably narrow in a country that rightly lays claim to having made massive contributions to world culture and science. Higher education remains short of a knowledgeable constituency able to advance its claims against the narrow and selective instrumentalism advanced by politicians, administrators, and too many of the academic elite itself.

A shift in institutional arrangements for research and graduate study is implicit in our description of changes in the U.K. system. Research training has taken place mostly in the same university departments (the polytechnics still occupy a relatively minor role) that undertake research and scholarship and offer undergraduate teaching. Selective funding of research and research training, and the specific identification of research resources in university funding, are likely to lead to some divorce of research and graduate study. Some university departments and their teachers will receive resources and time only for research that supports their teaching. Stratification of a hitherto unitary professoriat into teachers and researchers might thus emerge.

NOTES

This chapter is based upon a study of contemporary policy documents and other secondary sources and two sets of interviews. The first set of interviews was conducted in the national government, the research council system and the British Academy and Royal Society, and the national "intermediary" bodies—the University Grants Committee (UGC); the National Advisory Board for Public Sector Higher Education (NAB); their successor bodies, the University Funding Council (UFC) and the Polytechnic and Colleges Funding Council (PCFC); and the Council for National Academic Awards (CNAA). A second set of interviews was conducted with university academics in economics, history, and physics; we also interviewed students reading for advanced degrees in these areas. These latter interviews contributed mainly to chapter 4, in which we discuss graduate studies in the disciplines, but they were also a primary source for this chapter.

1. Much of the following account is based on Gummett, *Scientists in Whitehall*.
2. Poole and Andrews, *Government of Science in Britain* (quoted by Gummett).
3. Gummett, *Scientists in Whitehall*.
4. Organisation for Economic Co-operation and Development, *Science, Government and Society*.
5. Gummett, *Scientists in Whitehall*.
6. Kogan and Henkel, *Government and Research*.
7. *Framework for Government Research and Development*.
8. *Civil Research and Development*.
9. Advisory Board for Research Councils, *Strategy for Research*.
10. Interview with senior policymaker, 1988.

11. Economic and Social Research Council, *Social Sciences. News from ESRC* (July 1989); and Science and Engineering Research Council, *Bulletin* (Autumn 1989).

12. Economic and Social Research Council, *Corporate Plan 1988-1993.*

13. Universities Funding Council, *Council's Research Policy.*

14. House of Commons, *Seventeenth Report from the Committee of Public Accounts.*

15. Ibid.

16. *Civil Research and Development.*

17. House of Lords, Select Committee on Science and Technology, *Civil Research and Development.*

18. In 1986 the UGC mounted a research grading exercise upon which differentiated funding has since been based. Similar policies were advocated in the Advisory Board for Research Councils, *Strategy for Research.*

19. Universities Funding Council, *Council's Research Policy.*

20. For example, House of Lords, *Civil Research and Development.*

21. Ibid.

22. *Organisation and Management of Government R and D.*

23. Advisory Council for Applied Research and Development and Advisory Board for Research Councils, *Science Base in Industry.*

24. *Report of a Study on the Support of Scientific Research in the Universities.* Dainton Report.

25. Science and Engineering Research Council, *Corporate Plan.*

26. Science and Engineering Research Council, *Report for the Year 1986-87.*

27. Department of Education and Science, *Higher Education.*

28. University Grants Committee, *Strengthening University Earth Sciences.* Oxburgh Report.

29. Science and Engineering Research Council, *Corporate Plan.*

30. Quoted in Simpson, *How the PhD Came to Britain*, p. 155.

31. Ibid., p. 21.

32. Expenditure Committee of the House of Commons, *Government Observations on the Third Report Session 1973-74.*

33. Blume and Amsterdamska, *Post-Graduate Education in the 1980s.*

34. Committee of Vice-Chancellors and Principals, *Academic Standards in the Universities.* (Reynolds Report).

35. Ibid., *The British Ph.D.*

36. *Future of University Physics.*

37. Economic and Social Research Council, *Discussion Paper on Research Training for the 1990s.*

38. Advisory Board for Research Councils, *Strategy for Research.*

39. University Statistical Record, *University Statistics 1987-88.*

40. Oxford University, *Report of the Committee of Enquiry into Provision for Graduate Students.*

41. Science and Engineering Research Council, *Corporate Plan.*

42. Economic and Social Research Council. *Social Science Ph.D.*

43. Ibid., *Annual Report 1987-88.*

44. Expenditure Committee of the House of Commons, *Government Observations on the Third Report Session 1973-74: Postgraduate Education.*

45. University Statistical Record, *University Statistics 1987-88.*

46. Council for National Academic Awards (CNAA), *Annual Report 1986–87*.

47. Department of Education and Science, *Teachers in Service and Teacher Vacancies 1986–87, Statistics Bulletin* 9/88, table 4.

48. National Audit Office, *Report by the Comptroller and Auditor General*.

49. Blume and Amsterdamska, *Post-Graduate Education in the 1980s*.

50. Interviews with members of the British Academy, 1988.

51. Interviews with members of the Science and Engineering Research Council (SERC), 1988.

52. Economic and Social Research Council, *Corporate Plan, 1988–1993*.

53. Social Research Association, *State of Training in Social Research*, and *Report on the Future of Training in Social Research*.

54. Economic and Social Research Council, *Discussion Paper on Research Training for the 1990s*.

55. Science and Engineering Research Council, *Corporate Plan*.

56. *Report of the Working Party on Postgraduate Education*.

57. Economic and Social Research Council, *Social Science Ph.D.*

58. Young, et al., *Management of Doctoral Studies in the Social Sciences*; Economic and Social Research Council, *The Social Science Ph.D.*; Advisory Board for Research Councils, *Strategy for Research*.

59. Committee of Vice-Chancellors and Principals, *British Ph.D.* Ash Report.

60. Committee of Vice-Chancellors and Principals, *Academic Standards in the Universities*. Reynolds Report.

61. Rudd with Hatch, *Graduate Study and After* and *Highest Education*; Blume and Amsterdamska, *Post-Graduate Education in the 1980s*; and Economic and Social Research Council, *Social Science Ph.D.*

62. Economic and Social Research Council. *Social Science Ph.D.*

63. Ibid., *Annual Report 1987–88*.

64. Interview with a senior policymaker and with members of a research council.

65. Interview with senior policymaker.

66. House of Lords, *Third Report of the Select Committee on Science and Technology*.

67. Report of speech, *Times Higher Education Supplement*, 31 March 1989.

68. Economic and Social Research Council, *Annual Report 1987–88*.

69. University Grants Committee, *University Chemistry*.

70. Interview with research council officials, 1988.

71. Blume and Amsterdamska, *Post-Graduate Education in the 1980s*.

72. Ibid.

73. Blume and Amsterdamska; *Post-Graduate Education in the 1980s*; Economic and Social Research Council, *Social Science Ph.D.*

BIBLIOGRAPHY

Advisory Board for Research Councils. *Strategy for Research*. London, 1982, 1987.

Advisory Council for Applied Research and Development and Advisory Board for Research Councils. *The Science Base in Industry*. London, 1986.

Blume, S., and O. Amsterdamska. *Post-Graduate Education in the 1980s*. Paris: Organisation for Economic Co-operation and Development, 1987.

Civil Research and Development. Government White Paper. Response to the First Report of the House of Lords Select Committee on Science and Technology. Session 1986–87. Cmnd 185. London: HMSO, 1987.

Committee of Vice-Chancellors and Principals. *Academic Standards in the Universities.* Reynolds Report. London, 1986.

———. *The British Ph.D.* Ash Report. London, 1988.

Council for National Academic Awards (CNAA). *Annual Report 1986–87.* London, 1988.

Department of Education and Science. *Higher Education. Meeting the Challenge.* Cm 114. London: HMSO, 1987.

———. *Teachers in Service and Teacher Vacancies 1986–87. DES Statistics Bulletin 9/88.* London, 1988.

Economic and Social Research Council. *The Social Science Ph.D.: The ESRC Enquiry on Submission Rates.* Winfield Report. London: School Governing Publishing, 1983.

———. *Annual Report 1987–88.* London, 1988.

———. *Corporate Plan 1988–1993.* London, 1988.

———. *Discussion Paper on Research Training for the 1990s.* London, 1989.

———. *Social Sciences. News from ESRC.* London, July 1989.

Expenditure Committee of the House of Commons. *Government Observations on the Third Report Session 1973–74: Postgraduate Education.* Cmnd 6611. London: HMSO, 1976.

A Framework for Government Research and Development. Government White Paper. Cmnd 5406. London: HMSO, 1972.

Future of University Physics. Edwards Report. 1988.

Gummett, Philip. *Scientists in Whitehall.* Manchester: Manchester University Press, 1980.

Higher Education. Robbins Report. Cmnd 2154. London: HMSO, 1963.

House of Commons. *Seventeenth Report from the Committee of Public Accounts.* Session 1987–88, Postgraduate Awards, HC 166. London: HMSO, 1987.

House of Lords. Select Committee on Science and Technology. *Science and Government 1981–82.* First Report, vol. 1. HL 20/1. London: HMSO, 1981.

———. Select Committee on Science and Technology. *Civil Research and Development,* Vol. I: *Report.* Session 1986/87. First Report (HL20/I). London: HMSO, 1987.

———. *Civil Research and Development.* Government Reponse to the First Report of the House of Lords Select Committee on Science and Technology. Cmnd 185. London: HMSO, July 1987.

———. *Third Report of the Select Committee on Science and Technology,* HL 24. London: HMSO, 1989.

Kogan, Maurice, and Mary Henkel. *Government and Research: The Rothschild Experiment in a Government Department.* London: Heinemann, 1983.

National Audit Office. *Report by the Comptroller and Auditor General. Department of Education and Science: Postgraduate Awards HC 368.* London: HMSO, 1987.

The Organisation and Management of Government R and D. Rothschild Report. Cmnd 4814. London: HMSO, 1971.

Organisation for Economic Co-operation and Development. *Science, Government and Society.* Paris, 1971.

Oxford University. *Report of the Committee of Enquiry into Provision for Graduate Students.* Oxford, 1987.

Poole, J. B., and Kay Andrews, eds. *The Government of Science in Britain*. London: Weidenfeld & Nicolson, 1972.

Report of a Study on the Support of Scientific Research in the Universities. Dainton Report. Cmnd 4798. London: HMSO, 1971.

Report of the Working Party on Postgraduate Education. Swinnerton-Dyer Report. London: HMSO, 1982.

Rudd, E., with S. Hatch. *Graduate Study and After*. London: Weidenfeld & Nicolson, 1968.

————. *The Highest Education*. London: Routledge & Kegan Paul, 1975.

Science and Engineering Research Council. *Bulletin*. London, Autumn 1989.

————. *Corporate Plan*. London, 1986, 1989.

————. *Report for the Year 1986–87*. London, 1987.

————. *SERC Bulletin*. London, 1988.

Simpson, Renate. *How the PhD Came to Britain: A Century of Struggle for Postgraduate Education*. Guildford: Society for Research into Higher Education, 1983.

Social Research Association. *The State of Training in Social Research*. Report of an SRA Subcommittee. London, 1985.

————. *Report on the Future of Training in Social Research*. London, forthcoming.

Universities Funding Council. *The Council's Research Policy*. London, 1989.

University Grants Committee. *The Future of University Physics*. Edwards Report. London: HMSO, 1988.

————. *Strengthening University Earth Sciences*. Oxburgh Report. London, 1987.

————. *University Chemistry—The Way Forward*. Stone Report. London: HMSO, 1988.

University Statistical Record. *University Statistics 1987–88*, vol. 1. London, 1989.

Young, J., M. P. Foggarty, and S. McRae. *The Management of Doctoral Studies in the Social Sciences*. London: Policy Studies Institute, 1987.

FOUR

Graduate Education in Britain
The View from the Ground

Tony Becher

An understanding of the practicalities of graduate education in Britain may be enhanced by bearing in mind four particular characteristics of the educational system described in chapter 3.

First, the curriculum in secondary and undergraduate education is more highly specialized than in most other countries. At present, although major changes are underway, students in their final years at secondary school concentrate on a narrow range of three or four subjects. Accordingly, many entering undergraduate courses already have a reasonably advanced understanding of their major field. The norm is still to study for a bachelor's degree in a single discipline. This makes possible a comparatively short, three-year program for the first degree. It also means that those embarking on postgraduate work (" graduate education" in American terms) may be somewhat ahead of their counterparts in some other countries. The possibility of a one-year master's and a three-year doctoral program arises in large part from these considerations.

Second, and reinforcing the effects of specialization, the system remains an elite one in the main institutions providing doctoral programs. Access to undergraduate places in these institutions, particularly the universities of Oxford and Cambridge and the leading London University colleges, is strongly competitive. The demands at first-degree level are correspondingly high. At the same time, there is considerably less overall diversity of standards across universities than in, say, the United States or Japan. Despite signs of a possible change in policy, recruitment to degree courses has so far been confined to a small proportion of the total relevant population (the age participation rate is about 6 to 7 percent for universities and about 15 percent for the system as a whole). The size of the postgraduate community varies considerably between universities, but the expectations for levels

115

of academic achievement, particularly for the doctorate, are reasonably comparable.

A third closely related feature is the relatively small scale of individual universities.[1] The smallest university (Keele) has not much more than 3,000 students in all; Oxford and Cambridge, which are the largest, leaving aside the federal universities of London and Wales, have under 15,000 each. As will be seen later, this places significant constraints on economies of scale in postgraduate teaching.

Finally, graduate education remains marginal to a system traditionally and strongly geared to first-degree provision. As noted in chapter 3, despite the steady growth over the years in postgraduate numbers, neither individual institutions nor the system as a whole have made the structural and organizational adjustments necessary to take this growth adequately into account. Graduate students are the poor relations of the university community, rather than—as in the United States—its principal source of pride.

Other, more specific, features of U.K. higher education which differentiate it from that of other countries will be mentioned where they are most relevant.

THE DISCIPLINARY SETTINGS

Academic disciplines are in their nature international, rather than parochial.[2] Nonetheless, the cultural and economic context affects the overall pattern of research in significant ways, and gives rise to distinctive national profiles in each field. The common feature shared by economics, history, and physics in the United Kingdom during the decade of the 1980s was an adverse financial climate that has resulted in cutbacks in provision and limited growth in terms of new development. Each discipline has been affected somewhat differently from the others.[3]

Physics has in some universities failed to survive as an autonomous discipline.[4] Even the most secure departments have lost research assistants and suffered cuts in technicians and equipment. Many worthwhile research proposals remain unfunded. The more costly areas, especially high energy physics, are under continuous critical scrutiny. A move toward selectivity in the funding of research is raising problems for departments engaged in small-scale, often commercially oriented research. Interdisciplinary programs in newly developing areas enjoy some preferential support. As noted in chapter 3, government research funding priorities favor strategic research and applied work, as against those frontier topics that tend to attract the ablest researchers and to earn the greatest professional recognition.

In economics there has been a move away from large-scale research on macroeconomic topics, reflecting the reduced public confidence in such work after the 1970s oil crisis.[5] Within the central core of the subject research has thus tended to become more individualized. The overall standing of the discipline remains high, but there has been a shift of emphasis in two main directions, reflecting trends elsewhere. First, the mathematical basis of the subject has become increasingly sophisticated, resulting in more highly theoretical approaches and a relative devaluing of traditional topics in political economy. Second, economists have played an active part in the rapid growth of managerial and business studies, in part at the expense of their own discipline (though theoretical economists are thought to have relatively little to offer in these fields).

History has always been in Britain a strongly individualistic subject with no overall research structure of the kind to be found in physics and very little in the way of collaborative funded activity. Because of its lack of direct vocational relevance, it has found itself on the defensive in the current, strongly instrumental, climate. Staffing provision has been reduced in many universities and some departments (especially of social, economic, and political history) have suffered closure or amalgamation. Nonetheless, the disciplinary community itself remains vigorous, since its survival is not strongly dependent on external research funding.

Given the differences in the three disciplines under review, it is not surprising that the opportunities for research training differ markedly from one field to another. As noted in the other national studies in this volume, physics offers considerable scope for doctoral candidates to become part of the disciplinary research organization by serving as junior members of a collective program. Those studying for doctorates in history, in contrast, must expect to work largely on their own, carving out highly personal research careers on the same pattern as their mentors. Economics lies somewhere between the two extremes, with some degree of commonality and interdependence of research activity but little of the large-scale, well-organized pattern prevalent in some of the key areas of physics.

These variations are overlaid by others deriving from the characteristics of the institution in which research training is offered. In all three subject areas the settings for graduate education range from reasonably substantial departments with fifty or more academic staff (or nearly one hundred in one case in physics) to much smaller units able to accommodate only a handful of doctoral students.[6] Clearly, the opportunities for choice of topic, collaborative research, variety of supervisory and other support, and extent of available resources will vary substantially from one end of the spectrum to the other.

Within each discipline, moreover, the potential research issues that a graduate student might reasonably be expected to tackle vary considerably in their degree of complexity. Some subdisciplines offer reasonably "tidy" problems which, although intellectually demanding, lend themselves to neat, clear-cut solutions. In such areas (theoretical physics, mathematical economics, and intellectual history would be cases in point) able students might be expected to complete the work on their dissertation (itself relatively brief and self-contained) within a three-year period. But other specialisms within the same fields are characterized by "messy" problems, often demanding a sizeable body of data collection and analysis, together with the acquisition of specialized skills (instances include a number of areas in applied physics, labor economics, and most areas of history, especially those concerned with an unfamiliar cultural and linguistic setting).

These sources of variety in the pattern of doctoral programs contribute to a richly complex and varied set of arrangements for graduate education and research training. But despite this variety, as will be seen in the following discussion, a number of salient common issues emerge.

THE STRUCTURE OF GRADUATE EDUCATION

Forms of Purpose and Provision

The forms of graduate education in Britain, as in many other countries, are superficially straightforward. A clear distinction can be made between master's degrees and doctoral study, although the nomenclature varies considerably with the former. Part-time enrollments are a small but growing minority, their growth consequent to some extent on an increasing intake of mature students already in employment.

Master's courses ("programs" in American terms) show the greatest variation in type, purpose, and standard. Some of them serve, among other functions, as a preparatory stage for a doctoral program (particularly in economics, where some options are specifically designed with that possibility in view). Others appear to cater primarily to the advancement of a personal interest in a particular field (such as medieval history). Still others offer a marketable skill or a vocational qualification (examples include applied optics, health economics, or international relations). Many owe their existence to the identification, by an entrepreneurial department, of a viable market whose clients may be attracted for quite diverse reasons.

The size of the degree course (program), too, may span a wide range, from half a dozen or so students to forty or more. The smaller, less viable courses will normally depend to a significant extent on individual study and tutorial work; the taught element in the larger courses may in contrast be fairly substantial. More doubts were expressed by respondents to the study about consistency in the standards of master's degrees than about those of either doctoral or undergraduate provision.

In some institutions the Master of Philosophy (M.Phil.) degree stands apart from other master's awards (such as Master of Arts, Master of Science, Master of Education) in being offered to those who submit doctoral dissertations somewhat below the minimum required standard. In others it exists as a qualification in its own right. The M.Phil. has a higher status than other master's awards, and those who elect to register for it are normally expected to work over a two-year time span and to submit a reasonably substantial dissertation.

If other master's courses offer some limited experience of research activity, as against a more narrow training in techniques, it is only through doctoral work that any significant emphasis is given to developing originality in research. But even here, there is no clear consensus as to purpose.[7] Some interviewees contended that the function of the Ph.D. should be no more than to provide advanced training, allowing the full-blooded pursuit of new knowledge to come later, at the postdoctoral stage. In contrast, others maintained that any doctoral thesis must comprise an identifiably original contribution to its field. The former argument was advanced by a minority of both academic physicists and economists in the interview sample, but by no historians: the latter view was dominant across all three fields.

The divergence here led to questions about the emphasis to be given to formal teaching in the doctoral program. The general view holds that, apart from students working in areas already well covered in the undergraduate course, the majority would need some systematic training in their chosen specialism. But many of those interviewed also underlined the further need for "hands on" practical research experience, whether working in a group, as in some physics and economics fields, or individually, as in history. In practice both training and practical experience currently remain in place, even though the relative incidence of each varies across disciplines and departments. An attempt by the Economic and Social Research Council in the mid-1980s to establish "taught Ph.D." programs on a pilot basis was abandoned shortly after its inception.

Overall, then, graduate education in Britain embraces many different types of activity, from an interest in developing the capabilities of high-flying research academics to the provision of part-time master's courses in topics, such as local history, with a strong amateur interest. Between the two, a number of master's courses are designed to match particular labor market requirements.

The Pattern of Training

Where formal research training courses are provided in postgraduate programs, these normally run throughout the period of a one-year full-time master's degree, although the commitment is often reduced in the final term to allow for individual work on a short dissertation. In doctoral work, training is understandably concentrated in the early stages. Beyond the first year taught courses give way to less formal (and in many cases optional) graduate seminars and workshops.

But the nature of doctoral training, and the emphasis given to it, varies considerably across disciplines and institutions, for two main, partly interconnected, reasons. The first is a lack of commonality in students' training requirements. This is particularly evident in history, where the subject matter spans an enormously wide range. There are seldom enough takers in any given specialism to allow a close focus on particular needs: a training program in paleographic techniques might have to cover the whole time span from A.D. 500 to 1500, so large parts will be irrelevant to each class member. Consequently many students have to take their own initiative in mastering, often by independent or guided study, the techniques essential to their own topic. In economics, in contrast, the demand for common technical skills, especially those related to mathematics, appears to be on the increase. In two of the three departments visited, a substantial training element was institutionalized in the form of a requirement for doctoral students, with a few exceptions, to complete a preliminary master's course before embarking actively on their own research. Physics provision lay between these two. There was no across-the-board requirement for initial training; each specialist group set its own norms, and in most cases students were expected to follow a tailor-made introductory program with some element of formal assessment.

The second reason for the differing emphases on formal training relates to a feature of the British system mentioned in the introductory remarks, namely, the generally small scale of postgraduate work. Except in a few of the largest departments, there is not a sufficient critical mass of doctoral students in any one subject area to allow for a suitable range of viable taught courses to be mounted. In the smaller centers, therefore, essential training may have to be provided on an individual or small group basis, rather than in a graduate class. One particularly effective way around this problem, in the case of history, is found in the Institute of Historical Research. Although formally a part of the University of London, the Institute runs several graduate courses on key topics which are also available to students from other associated universities. No other instances were identified of this type of interinstitutional consortium for advanced training and other collective activities, but it appears to offer a possible model for history departments in other geographical areas and possibly for other subject fields as well.

What seems quite clear is that no possibility currently exists in Britain to move toward a pattern comparable with that of the large American graduate schools, many of them providing a substantial element of organized coursework as part of the overall doctoral program.

The Time Span of the Doctorate

The U.K. higher education system is unusual in the range and scale of its public funding support for both undergraduates and postgraduates, stemming from the postwar welfare state tradition, which saw education as a public rather than as a consumer good. Until very recently, the majority of British students could expect to receive fully subsidized fees and means-tested grants sufficient to allow them to complete their courses without the need for outside earnings. Any move toward a partial loans system for postgraduates would change this pattern, but the long-standing expectation has been that of a free subsidy. Borrowing money to complete a higher degree on the pattern common in the United States and some other countries is not part of the prevailing national culture.

As noted in chapter 3, only about one in three postgraduates is grant-aided. But for those who are, doctoral study makes demands on the public purse, and the period for which grant funding is available is therefore rigidly circumscribed. The norm is for a three-year award for doctoral research, with rare and special exceptions running to four years. The amount of grant aid is not at present differentiated (as, for instance in the United States or Japan) across the subject range. Where students enjoy other sources of financial support (from industrially sponsored awards, or in the case of overseas students from their own governments or international agencies), the tendency is also to favor a three-year norm.

The recent governmental concern, noted in chapter 3, about low completion rates among doctoral candidates,[8] especially in the social sciences,[9] has led to a further set of pressures for rapid submission of the doctoral thesis. The expectation has been that the program should be completed within three years, although university regulations normally allow for a four-year period. For students funded by the Economic and Social Research Council, institutions have had recognition withdrawn if any department has failed to meet completion rate targets. The sanctions have been seen as unreasonable and unfair in their operation and have been widely resented by the academic body, in part at least because they have penalized whole institutions rather than individual graduate programs.

In practice the national three-year time span is relatively rarely achieved in any of the three subject fields under review. Some academics accordingly tend to argue for a reduction in the requirements for the doctorate (one powerful elder statesman in physics is known to have advocated that the Ph.D. should be defined as the level of work a reasonably industrious postgraduate student could achieve within three years). Others maintain that a proper combination of breadth and depth, professional competence and intellectual originality, can seldom be achieved in under four years. The question of international standards is also commonly invoked as an argument against further debasing the currency. But even allowing for doctrinal differences, no respondent in our interviews wished to advocate a normal term of less than three years or more than four. A system of incentives to departments, allowing them to use savings (based on a four-year funding norm) from students completing in a shorter period to subsidize additional research awards was strongly favored and considered likely to result in better completion rates than a system based on penalties.

1991 saw an important development. The Economic and Social Research Council, which had previously exacted the heaviest penalties for noncompletion within three years, reversed its previous policy. It began to allow a four-year completion period, including preliminary (one-year) master's training. This brings its practice in line with what the majority of academics interviewed in our study would consider a reasonable period for completion.

The Nature of the Thesis

Stipulations about completion rates are in any case somewhat arbitrary, since, as noted earlier, doctoral topics come in a wide variety of shapes and sizes. The nature of the particular research issue, as well as of the subject field, is reflected in the form and extent of the final thesis.

As might be expected, in neat, self-contained problems the thesis itself may be relatively brief (in theoretical physics, for example, it may be considerably less than one hundred pages). In many areas of history, where the data base may be extensive and the analysis of it highly detailed, some departments have found it essential to impose an upper limit of 80,000 to 100,000 words to keep the exercise within reasonable bounds.

Expectations about the form the thesis should take are broadly related to the normal mode of research output of the discipline concerned. The most prized products of historical research emerge in book form, reflecting the concern within the discipline to tackle significant problems in all their complexity: it is understandable that those aspiring to become professional historians should follow this model. In many areas of economics, however, the trend is toward journal article publication: many leading economics departments will now accept a thesis in the form of three or more article-length contributions, not necessarily very closely linked, of publishable standard.

However, few physicists—who almost universally write up their findings in brief journal contributions—seem comfortable with such a notion, and their ideal is for the doctoral candidate to produce a reasonably coherent, examinable account of his or her work in continuous prose.[10] This ideal has to be modified in fields such as high energy and space physics, where the long lead times for experiments make it impossible for a student to see a single project through from beginning to end. Here, the typical thesis might involve data collection from one setting, experimental design from another, and data analysis from yet a third. Again, in specialisms with relatively short lead times (optics, say, or superconductivity) a student may necessarily have to bring together two or more distinct (but preferably interrelated) pieces of work.

PROCESSES WITHIN THE PROGRAM

Recruitment and Selection

As in many other countries, the growth of higher education in Britain slowed down substantially after the mid-1970s. The many new academic posts created during the previous rapid expansion had been filled by relatively young candidates: few vacancies could therefore be created by retirement. The result was an acute shortage of new appointments, and a strongly competitive climate for aspiring academics.

This dearth of academic job opportunities, in all except a few growth areas such as finance and business studies, was accompanied by a relative decline in academic pay and a general deterioration in working conditions. Both factors have served in recent years as a disincentive to those who might otherwise have wished to embark on a teaching or research career in higher education. In addition, starting salaries for graduates in industry and commerce have risen substantially, while the levels of graduate student grants have not kept up with inflation. The financial difference between entering the general labor market after a first degree and going on with full-time study is now very marked.

Graduate student recruitment levels were therefore reported to have declined in recent years in each of the subject areas under review in each of the institutions visited. Despite this, few of those concerned with recruitment considered there to have been any serious deterioration in the quality of students admitted. In current circumstances only students strongly committed to further study would contemplate applying for a graduate program. Earlier, some young people who enjoyed student life postponed entry into the outside labor market by registering for a higher degree: often, the motivation of such students was not particularly strong. Nowadays there are few such applicants; those who are admitted are already largely self-selected.

The decline in recruitment to graduate programs has been ameliorated in two main ways (see chapter 3). First, the number and range of master's courses has substantially increased. The aim has been to attract students who wish to continue with academic work for a variety of reasons, but who do not wish to undertake the major commitment of a doctoral program. Second, there has been a determined recruitment drive by many departments and institutions to attract students from overseas. The incentive to do so is strong, since the fees charged to students outside the European Community are set at a high enough level to bring tangible benefits to the departments concerned.

These strategies operate differentially for history, physics, and economics. Some history departments have benefited more from initiating new M.A. courses (including, in some cases, part-time ones) than from overseas recruitment. The field tends to be more culturally specific than physics or economics, and the majority of overseas applicants are accordingly from Australia or North America. Both physics and economics, as disciplines, have developed strong international communities and both have been able to draw on overseas connections to build up graduate recruitment. In economics, where many completing a first degree are attracted by high salaries into the financial world, the overseas graduate students in some departments outnumber their British counterparts.

"Infilling" of graduate programs by overseas recruitment was recognized by some respondents to be a risky strategy, depending on a politically and economically volatile market. However, although the quality of applicants could in some cases be hard to assess, the general view was that the careful selection of overseas students insured that they were an asset rather than a liability to their recruiting departments.

Practices for selecting graduate students from among those who apply for places will necessarily differ, depending on the pressure of numbers. But few departments, whether in economics, history, or physics, now face a high ratio of applicants to places available in graduate programs. Moreover, given that most such applicants are also strongly motivated, less emphasis would appear to be accorded to selection procedures than was the case in previous years.

A general consideration deserves mention here. Under a widely-held principle, graduate students, and particularly doctoral candidates, ought to move from their initial undergraduate department to one in another university for further study. Physicists maintain that this gives the graduate students access to a wider range of ideas and techniques. Economists contend that it exposes them to a different range of value assumptions. Historians typically take a somewhat different line, arguing that a doctoral candidate should choose the supervisor likely to be most knowledgeable about his or her topic, wherever that supervisor might be. But the general effect is to discourage inbreeding by urging good candidates to move on elsewhere.

Since a relative shortage of applicants exists today, each department is strongly tempted to hold on to its own best students. Good arguments favor this: the candidate's strengths and weaknesses are already known; the candidate already "knows the ropes" and does not have to spend valuable time adjusting to a new environment; and for doctoral candidates, matching student with supervisor is less unpredictable than with two strangers. In any event we found more cases of students continuing as graduates in their own institutions than might have been expected if the general arguments against inbreeding had been taken seriously.

Selection of internal applicants presents relatively few problems, since there is already ample evidence to serve as a basis for judgment. The selection of candidates from other U.K. universities tends to follow a more or less formal procedure usually involving an applicant's interview with the member of staff concerned with graduate admissions, if not with the putative supervisor as well, together with the provision of documentation about the first-degree course and tutorial references. Often, particularly for Ph.D. applications, this procedure may be supplemented by informal contact between an applicant's previous undergraduate tutor and a member of the recruiting department. Overseas admissions are necessarily less personal and subject to more elaborately bureaucratic safeguards.

In most instances, however, there has already been a measure of preselection, related to the availability of grant funds. Because of the limited number of graduate student awards, only those with good first-degree results are offered them. Those with less good degrees are not in a position to apply unless they have independent sources of funding. The same is true of many overseas students qualifying for grants from their own governments.

The department needs to satisfy itself when selecting doctoral (as against master's) students that a suitable supervisor is available in the field in which the candidate wishes to work. The initial, if tentative, matching of student to supervisor is usually carried out at this stage. For inside candidates this is seldom more than a matter of mutual agreement between two people who already know each other. The matching process for outsiders varies from subject to subject and department to department: clearly, the smaller the department the less room there is for choice. Often an applicant may come with a recommended supervisor in view (particularly in history, where reputations tend to be quite closely identified with topics). Where this type of matching is not possible, the department must make the best choice it can (although scope is almost invariably allowed for subsequent changes in the case of evident mismatch). All respondents were emphatic that, in the absence of clearly adequate supervision, a candidate should be advised to apply elsewhere.

One incidental point regarding selection procedures illustrates the constraints imposed by tight completion deadlines. Departments are hesitant to consider recruiting evidently able but unorthodox doctoral candidates who wish to embark on a relatively high-risk project because they may possibly overrun the required period. Conformity and dependability are at a higher premium as selection criteria than they might otherwise be.

Choice of Thesis Topic

Usually, anyone wishing to go on from a first to a higher degree will expect to become more specialized and will have decided which broad direction the specialism will take. For master's candidates the choice of program may be expected to reflect that decision. In undertaking doctoral work, however, a further stage has to be reached, where the precise topic for the thesis becomes clearly defined.

The extent to which a doctoral candidate is able to determine his or her topic varies with circumstance. Where the arrangements are related to a piece of contract research, or based on the requirements of an outside sponsor, the subject matter will normally be quite strongly predetermined. What expectations are reasonable within a three- to four-year period of full-time work may be negotiable, and some choice may be open on methods of approach, but the nature of the problem to be tackled will not be on the agenda for discussion.

The options are less constrained in the case of students with no predetermined contract. However, if they wish—as is typically the case in physics—to attach themselves to an existing research group, this imposes an immediate limitation on the scope of their work, since they must then fit in with the requirements of other individuals and of the program as a whole. Doctoral supervisors in physics generally take the view that newcomers have insufficient knowledge of the specialism to identify what topics are feasible and worth pursuing. Once a student is accepted into a research program, in most cases a suitable topic is identified by the supervisor (in consultation with the leader of the group, if they are not one and the same) and allocated to the student. Negotiation and discussion are not necessarily precluded, but seldom does the student take the lead in the matter of choice of topic, even though the student was earlier relatively free to decide on the general research field.

A directly contrary set of considerations normally operates in history. No institutional factors constrain choice, and most historians believe that, since research is a highly personal process, its subject matter must be such as to demand close commitment on the part of the researcher. The best way to insure that commitment is to allow the topic to be decided by the person who will have to work on it. (This will quite commonly derive from an earlier interest at the undergraduate stage, often already explored as a final year special subject). But with that said, some qualifications need to be made. A candidate may be given an opportunity to work with a leading specialist in a particular field and may decide to trim the topic to derive full benefit from the attachment. It may turn out that unrealistic assumptions are being made about the availability of relevant sources. Supervisors may have other good reasons for suggesting changes in, or modifications to, doctoral topics. But, in general, their guiding role is exercised after, rather than before, the initial choice has been made on the student's own initiative.

Historians, then, are clearly uncomfortable in laying down a topic for a doctoral candidate, where physicists view this as natural and unproblematic. The difference clearly stems both from the working patterns and the knowledge structures of the two disciplines. As might be expected, economists occupy an intermediate position, in a discipline in which knowledge is less tightly structured than in physics but more closely so than in history, and in which some measure of collaborative and interdependent work exists alongside more individualistic approaches.

A crucial interrelationship exists between allocation to a supervisor and identification of a topic, especially in the British system, where doctoral work depends strongly on the supervisor's role. Besides the opportunity to change supervisors, which was noted earlier, there is also corresponding scope—at least in those contexts which allow student choice—to amend or modify the thesis topic. But such freedom carries the penalty of losing valuable time, and it is accordingly discouraged after the first few months except in cases where something has gone drastically wrong.

The Supervisor's Role

British doctoral programs differ from those in most other systems in the central importance given to supervision. This becomes easier to understand if one recalls the initial observations that the present higher education system is relatively specialized, selective, and small in scale. Student groupings are seldom very large, even at the undergraduate level, and opportunities are available in most subjects for small group work. The long-established tradition of tutorial teaching at Oxford and Cambridge (where many British academics received their own undergraduate education) has had an influence on the rest of the system. A residual legacy of what might be described as an apprenticeship model still remains. Students, rather than being trained through standardized procedures, learn what their discipline is about by being attached to a master craftsman and seeing him or her at work.

This notion of apprenticeship survives in some of the individual work undertaken at master's level, where a student is usually allocated a supervisor to offer advice if a dissertation is involved. At the doctoral level it becomes a key element in the process, since, as noted earlier, the element of systematic collective training is limited by the absence in most cases of a substantial number of students in the same or closely related fields.

A brief review of disciplinary differences will help to elaborate the point. In economics, and especially in those departments where initial doctoral training is concentrated into a prior master's program, it may be possible to identify enough common ground, in terms of techniques at least, to justify treating doctoral students as a group. Here, the department becomes established as a recognizable organizing unit for doctoral work, even though its influence will necessarily diminish in favor of the supervisor as the program proceeds. In physics it is likely to be the laboratory that takes on this function, since the pattern of training depends on the subdiscipline and is commonly identified in relation to the team to which the doctoral student is attached. In history the responsibility for deciding what are the student's training needs has to be taken directly by the supervisor, since such needs will depend heavily on the detailed nature of the topic. And in many cases in this discipline no suitable collective program will be on hand, so that the student will have to make up the deficiency himself or herself with such help as the supervisor can afford. A rough spectrum of dependency prevails, with history at one end and economics at the other, but in every case, once the initial training program has been completed the supervisor occupies the center of the stage.

The number of doctoral students a supervisor may be allocated depends on several factors including, most obviously, how many students his or her specialist field attracts. But it was interesting to note that some academics believed that they could not do justice to more than two or three students at any one time (this seemed to be particularly the case in theoretical physics, where contact may on occasion become intense), whereas others were prepared to take on as many as a dozen supervisees. A particular phenomenon in history, which has something of a counterpart in economics, is the "research stable." Here, an academic with a well-established reputation in a particular subject area is able to attract a group of up to, say, a dozen doctoral students in all (perhaps three or so each year) to work on individual topics within that same area. Such an arrangement might be seen as an approximate counterpart, in a very different disciplinary field, to a laboratory group in physics. Where such research stables exist, they are able to fulfill important functions, to which we will return later. But in both history and economics they are the exception rather than rule.

Styles of supervision largely reflect the personal characteristics of the supervisor. Some are strongly subject-centered (a characteristic that physicists are liable to ascribe to themselves, acknowledging a discomfort in dealing with personal issues); others are heavily student-centered, giving considerable emphasis to motivation and personal support.[11] Some are laissez-faire, leaving it to the students to make contact when they wish to do so; others more directive, insisting on regular contact. It was noticeable how often those interviewed justified their practice by reference to their own doctoral experience, modeling it on that of their original mentors, suggesting a craft tradition that operates in the absence of any formal training for the supervisor's role.

One of the supervisor's crucial responsibilities, in the early stages, is to insure that the student's topic is not only well-defined but manageable. The time available for such initial negotiation is normally quite limited, and, in history in particular, the tendency to put off key decisions for more than a term or two must be avoided. Boundaries have to be placed round themes that are not intrinsically easy to delimit: thus, for example, supervisors may suggest choosing aspects where the evidence is readily available, narrowing the coverage in time or space, or reducing the range of sources to be consulted. Besides sharpening the definition of the topic itself a good supervisor will help in the initial decision about investigational strategies.

The pattern of contact between supervisor and student varies across subjects and over time. In physics, especially where the thesis derives from collective, laboratory-based activity, the interaction is likely to be quite close, involving perhaps even daily informal encounters and weekly more formal ones. In "big science" fields the supervisor or the student may have to be away at an external experimental site for part of the time, but even when this is so, most supervisors would expect to keep in regular touch. The pattern of interaction will tend to be reasonably constant throughout the program, with perhaps high points at the beginning and end.

The nature of the work flow tends to be somewhat different in many areas of history and economics, and the student-supervisor interaction reflects these differences. Often, there will be much data for the student to collect, assimilate, and analyze when the research gets fully under way, and the data sources will frequently be located outside the student's university base. It is a common pattern for the second year to be largely occupied by fieldwork, the first spent in preparatory planning and training, and the third and any subsequent years in writing up.

Although the actual practice varies, a typical pattern for historians and economists is for the supervisor to see students between once a week and once every three weeks in the first term or so, when key decisions have to be made about defining the topic and initiating any necessary special training, and then somewhat less frequently as they begin to read themselves into the subject area. Contact in the second year will be relatively sparse, especially if the main data base is located elsewhere. Sometimes a student working abroad may be offered additional supervisory help from an academic colleague in the foreign country: whether or not this is so, some degree of regular correspondence will normally be maintained. After this phase the student may or may not elect to return to the university base, but he or she will in any event be expected to meet the supervisor regularly to schedule the task of writing up and to review material in draft as it becomes available.

Supplements to Supervision

The importance of achieving a good match between supervisor and student, and establishing an effective working relationship, will be evident already. Some persons interviewed used the analogy of a marriage or spoke in terms of a close familial relationship. As in such cases, there can be problems that, if unresolved, may lead ultimately to a breakdown and estrangement. A brief review of the strategies for coping with this eventuality will give some further insights into the differing processes of graduate education in the three disciplines.

Two economics departments we visited attempted to offset, to some degree at least, the close dependence of students on their supervisors. A thesis advisory group for each student was identified. Meeting at intervals, the main supervisor was supplemented by two colleagues (one usually a personal tutor or senior departmental officeholder, and the other having a related subject expertise). But this was acknowledged to be a device costly in staff time, and more useful in problem cases. Moreover, this practice would seem easier to implement in a large department than in a small one, with fewer available specialists in any one field.

Those history departments that considered a similar strategy rejected it on the grounds that ideological clashes between the specialists could be detrimental to the student caught between them. Here, the need for coherence of approach, linked to the concern for a unified and holistic treatment of the subject matter, came out strongly. The preference was to allow a change of supervisor, rather than to supplement an unsatisfactory relationship, even at a fairly late stage in the proceedings.

In physics the type of supplementary backup sought by the economists' thesis advisory group was not seen to be necessary because it already existed within the laboratory setting. Busy supervisors may already have delegated some of their responsibilities to more junior research assistants or even to advanced doctoral students. Because the context would normally be a collective rather than a personal one, most students could expect to draw on the resources of the rest of the group to supplement those available from the supervisor.

To a more limited extent doctoral students in economics and history were also able to turn to others when they found it impossible to disengage themselves from an unsatisfactory relationship with their supervisors. One of those interviewed had, in some desperation, sought help from other academics in the department: from a research assistant, from a lecturer in computing, and from a previous undergraduate tutor in another university.

Although we do not claim that ours was a typical sample of students, we acknowledge that the cases of breakdown in supervisor-student relationships were seen as exceptional. Departments generally take good care to insure that the initial allocation is carefully made; this is all the easier when the doctoral candidate is one of their own former undergraduates.

Other Forms of Interaction

The discussion of the component elements in graduate education has so far concentrated on the ones intended to contribute directly to the award of a higher degree. In master's programs, these mainly comprise taught courses or, where the numbers are too small to make them viable, closely focused tutorial and seminar sessions in conjunction with self-study. A similar general pattern obtains for the training elements in doctoral programs. The same provision serves for both the master's and the doctorate in some fields, particularly in economics, and the first may even be a prerequisite for the second. Doctoral students also have access to a supervisor, who is expected to provide a substantial degree of personal support: where super-vision arrangements also exist for master's students, they are minimal in comparison.

Important additional activities may be provided for the doctoral student which are not specifically related to the production of the thesis, although some have an indirect relevance to it. Many of these activities contribute to a wider preparation of those destined for academic careers, or as a develop-ment of more general skills for those who will move on elsewhere. The ex-tent and range of such broader elements in the program will depend on the size of the doctoral population concerned.

Outside of supervision and basic research training, doctoral students are most commonly involved in graduate seminars or workshops. These are de-signed to bring together scholars working in the same general field, and to promote an interchange and broadening of ideas through the contribution by members, or outside guests, or both, of papers reporting on work in progress. Sessions are often held once a fortnight during term time, on the basis of a preplanned program.

Considerable variations exist between one department and another, as well as between one discipline and another. The largest departments are in a position to offer a much wider range of seminars than the smallest: and indeed, some of the latter may find it difficult to run viable programs even when these are extended to include all staff and master's students as well. In physics, and to a lesser extent in economics, the coverage may need to be quite specialized to attract those working in a particular field: the interests of the historians tend to be less compartmental.

Within the same broad framework, different categories of grouping can be distinguished. At the most formal end, research seminars may be pre-dominantly intended for staff, with students allowed to sit in. Invited speak-ers will typically read prepared, one-hour papers: subsequent discussion will be technical, and the atmosphere often highly competitive. At the other extreme, graduate student workshops will be based on informal interest groups, often meeting outside an academic environment, with an emphasis on short introductory papers, a more impromptu program, and open, unin-hibited discussion. Most of the students interviewed expressed a strong pref-erence for the latter type of activity, although noting that it was difficult to sustain because it depended on a collective commitment that not all their fellow students were prepared to make. Pressure is placed on doctoral stu-dents in some departments to attend one or more formal seminar series, and it is common to require each student to contribute at least one paper to the program. Even where this is the case, attendance may be very variable, and there may be little sense of progression or development of ideas.

As earlier noted, research stables are found in some institutions, where leading scholars in history and economics gather round them a group of up to a dozen students at various stages of progress. Here, as in comparable laboratory groups in physics, the research seminar may be given a more clearly focused form, serving as a useful means of developing and furthering a shared understanding of a particular field of inquiry by a fairly close-knit group. This is perhaps the ideal pattern for graduate seminar work, but it clearly depends on special conditions not often possible to fulfill: generally, the population of doctoral students is too widely scattered to allow for convenient clustering along such lines. Along with research training courses, an exception is provided by the Institute of Historical Studies, which, operating as a regional consortium for several history departments, is able to provide a relatively high degree of coherence and continuity in some of the graduate seminar series it offers.

Becoming part of the "invisible college" in one's own field is an important requirement for those doctoral students who will subsequently take up an academic career. Research seminars of the kind described, when they involve outside speakers who are leaders in the field, offer an opportunity, usually somewhat limited, to get to know key people outside the department. Some supervisors, however, deliberately attempt to give their students wider opportunities for "getting in on the network" by encouraging them to meet or contact colleagues elsewhere and by sponsoring them to attend relevant professional conferences. The latter, in particular, are seen by students as a more valuable experience than the often somewhat constrained environment of a formal graduate seminar, giving an insight into the nature of real-life academic debate in their field.

Another means of beginning to establish a presence in the research community is through publication in specialist journals. Again, some supervisors are active in encouraging students to write up and try to publish parts of their findings independently of the thesis itself. Such a possibility is relatively easy to achieve in those economics departments which accept a thesis in the form of a collection of publishable papers. In physics a paper submitted for publication may also be incorporated into the overall argument of the thesis, although not presented as standing alone. Historians expect a well-integrated, book-length product; the writing of articles has to be seen as a separate (even if related) exercise.

These relatively unsystematic and informal ways of preparing students for continuing work as a researcher tend often to be confined to those who have already shown themselves to be set on an academic career. For the others, involvement in seminars may be justified in terms of offering a useful experience in presenting and debating ideas. A similarly broad justification may be put forward in relation to the opportunities given to doctoral students to contribute to undergraduate teaching, although this also has evidently vocational implications for the aspiring academic.

There is a marked contrast between Britain and many other countries—

the United States in particular—in the policy adopted toward giving graduate students opportunities to teach. In contexts in which students have for the most part to pay their own way through the graduate program, teaching undergraduate classes is a convenient and accepted way of augmenting other sources of earnings. However, as has been noted, the common expectation still is for British doctoral students to be grant-aided, and thus not to be significantly dependent on outside money-earning activities for the first three years. During this period relatively few are offered teaching responsibilities, which are in any case limited in range.

In physics selected students may take on laboratory classes; in economics and history first-year undergraduate seminars and tutorials are the typical offering. It would be very rare for a graduate student to give a lecture course. Few teach more than six hours a week. Only in their fourth or subsequent years, when there may be strong financial pressures for them to do so, are chosen students sometimes enabled to take on heavier teaching loads. Teaching opportunities are often confined to the institution's own graduates, since outsiders are not expected to have a close enough knowledge of the undergraduate curriculum. For the most part, no specific training is given for this responsibility, a fact that concerned a number of students in the interview sample.

Teaching responsibilities are not thus an established part of the pattern of graduate student life, and there can be no automatic expectation that they will be available.[12] Those who are allowed to do some teaching, to judge by the students we interviewed, find the experience enjoyable and rewarding in a sense not primarily financial. Several students commented that having to teach is a broadening experience, forcing one to look outside the confines of one's own particular specialism, and giving one a usefully wider perspective on the thesis topic.

Monitoring and Assessment

Given the strong pressure now exerted throughout the British system for the rapid completion of doctoral work, it might be expected that departments would operate systematic monitoring procedures designed to keep a regular check on the progress toward completion of the work by their doctoral students. This indeed seems to be the case in relation to the early stages of the doctoral program.

Leaving aside whether a student has chosen or has been required to complete a prior master's course, or whether he or she has been accepted for direct entry to a doctorate, the standard practice is to defer formal registration for the Ph.D. until a further procedure has been completed. This will typically take the form of requiring the student to submit, somewhere toward the end of the first year of doctoral study, a substantial piece of written work (preferably a draft chapter of the thesis itself, such as the introductory review of the literature) together with an outline plan of future activity. In many departments the material is then referred for adjudication to a suitably qualified member of staff other than the supervisor; in some this is followed by a critical discussion in which the supervisor may also be involved. The arrangements tend to be more casual in smaller departments with few students; registration nonetheless depends on some form of scrutiny of progress over the initial phase of the research.

However, monitoring from that point onward is left largely to the supervisor, except in cases where an active thesis advisory group exists. This, at least, was the clear impression given in the departments that collaborated in the study, even though there had been an earlier undertaking among all universities to introduce a greater degree of formality into the oversight of doctoral programs.[13] Even those academics who showed a strong concern to keep doctoral work within close time limits and to streamline programs as far as possible tended to argue against further pressure of this kind on doctoral candidates. The general view was that preparation for annual reviews would deflect students' energies from the main task in hand and be liable to undermine their confidence and motivation. It would also add to the already quite substantial burden of bureaucracy imposed by existing demands for departmental accountability for graduate students.[14] There was, interestingly, some evidence of a contrary view from the students themselves. Most of them found the initial review procedure helpful and reassuring and considered that a comparable, if perhaps somewhat less formal, exercise at a later stage would help to focus their activities and provide an incentive for subsequent work.

The steps taken to evaluate students' performance on their way to a doctorate, however informal, have as one of their aims to identify at an early stage those who seem unlikely to achieve work of the required standard. The earlier discussion of recruitment and selection implied that there would be relatively few people in this category, but there are nevertheless some instances in which a person is persuaded to withdraw or advised to proceed to the less demanding qualification of an M.Phil.

For the majority who remain in the program the final hurdle comes shortly after the submission of the completed thesis. This, the viva voce examination, takes a more or less standard form in every subject area and every institution. It has certain features that distinguish it from doctoral assessment procedures in countries other than Britain and will accordingly be described in some detail.

The relative uniformity of standards across British higher education has earlier been remarked. This is sustained and reinforced by an external examiner system that relates to both initial and higher degrees. In every program, it is a requirement that one of the assessors should be a suitably qualified expert drawn from another institution. This external examiner has a key role in ensuring that the same considerations should as far as possible apply in evaluating student performance across the system as a whole. In master's courses the external examiner will see the work of a selected number of students and have full access to the whole body of relevant material. His or her views will be strongly influential in the discussions of individual results.

Doctoral candidates will normally have two examiners (three in some exceptional instances), one external to the institution and one internal. Formally, these examiners are appointed by the university on the recommendation of the department concerned. In practice the supervisor chooses the names after full consultation with the candidate. This helps to ensure that in areas where conflicting schools of thought exist, a doctoral student is not penalized by an examiner with a hostile view. The examination is held in private and not, as in France and a number of other countries, as a public event. In some but not all institutions the supervisor is allowed to sit in as an observer. The two examiners are expected to subject the candidate to rigorous questioning based on the thesis topic and subsequently to come to a shared view on whether the work is acceptable as it stands, whether it should be resubmitted after more or less extensive revision, or whether it is not (and is unlikely to become) up to the required standard. In the last instance the examiners may decide to recommend the award of an M.Phil. Unless the supervisor has failed in his or her other responsibilities, or unless the candidate has ignored his or her advice, it is relatively rare for a thesis to be failed, though demands for revision and resubmission are quite common.

The variety of attempts made to reduce what some regard as an unrealistically high expectation for a doctorate that should notionally take three years to complete have been noted earlier. One central part of any such strategy must be to persuade the examiners themselves to accept more limited and less ambitious theses. Some of those we interviewed considered the attitudes of external examiners to be a continuing problem, but the general view was that a steady change in this direction was taking place throughout the system. Originality in research was still at a premium, but the canvas on which that originality was displayed had necessarily to become narrower.

THE STUDENT PERSPECTIVE

The View from the Ground

Statistics about graduate education and descriptions of broad organizational and policy structures serve to provide an essential overview of the system as a whole. But without some complementary insights into the day-to-day activities that go to make up that system, it is not easy to move beyond an externalist perspective that leaves unanswered important questions about cause and effect. Nor can a fully intelligible picture be obtained without some consideration of the motivations, values, and beliefs that underlie the actions of the people involved. Policy changes are likely to be more effective if they are designed with some sense of the cultural context in which they are expected to operate. Those with a concern to improve the efficiency of the system, as well as those with the more limited wish to understand how it functions, may do well to attend to the views of the graduate students it is designed to serve.

The following discussion explores some of the central issues raised by doctoral students in reporting the nature of their experience. The concerns of master's students are not taken into account, except by implication, because their situation is less complicated. They work in a communal environment, their programs are in general closely structured, the expectations placed upon them are reasonably clear, and the total investment of their time is much more limited than that of candidates for a doctorate. Even if everything goes badly wrong for them, they have lost only a year. But for doctoral students in Britain the ever-present sense of time pressure makes it essential that potential pitfalls should be foreseen and, where possible, evaded. All the students interviewed were acutely conscious of the difficulties they were likely to face if they did not complete their work by the date at which their grants ran out. Few, however, were optimistic that they would meet the deadline, in spite of working long hours.[15] Financial problems did not appear to loom large, since grants were considered just sufficient to manage on without serious discomfort.

The adjustment from undergraduate to postgraduate work patterns and expectations is a difficult one for some students, although it may be eased by the inclusion of some taught elements in the early stages of the doctoral program. But it is the automatic expectation by staff that students should be self-sufficient, self-motivated, and independent-minded (not "spoon fed" as undergraduates are often held to be) that causes the main initial problem for many doctoral candidates. Especially in physics there is also the difficult realization that answers to many questions are not "out there" in the textbooks, or in the minds of the teachers, but are simply not known and have to be found out. In the early stages some students experience "culture shock" in a new and unfamiliar institution; overseas students have a still greater cultural adjustment to make.

These initial anxieties and other comparable worries that may arise during the doctorate period are by no means irrelevant to the successful completion of the program; they may seriously deflect energies that might otherwise be spent on research. Some students commented on the absence of personal counseling or help in the resolution of problems of living accommodations and the like; others commended their department for its "caring attitude" as contrasted with the "sink or swim" policies experienced by students elsewhere. Among the personal, as against more directly work-related, issues that concern students, by far the most pervasive is the sense of isolation engendered by doctoral work. This is sufficiently significant to deserve separate consideration.

Loneliness in Research

There is an isolation inherent in doing one's own particular piece of research. It is perhaps seen in its most extreme form in history, where the graduate student may have little contact with those sharing similar intellectual interests, except perhaps during fieldwork in the libraries, record offices, and other locations where archival material is housed. Even those historians who lead an active social life (and it is not perhaps the most gregarious people who are attracted to historical research) may have few professional interests in common with other doctoral students in their own department. In economics the shared process of initial research training may help to provide a supportive group of fellow students. But the subsequent lack of colleagues engaged on similar problems, given the relatively small scale of research in any particular subfield in any particular institution, may be exacerbated by the large numbers of nonnative students, who often form their own national cliques. The relatively few groups based on research stables run by leading scholars are in a more favorable situation: their intellectual environment is more comparable with that of the physics students working together in a laboratory program. But even in this latter case, the individual may experience some sense of isolation. Often the laboratory groups themselves are very self-contained, offering little contact with other staff or students within the department. And at the end of the day, as one student observed, "you are on your own": nobody else can take the responsibility for producing your dissertation.

That the loneliness is to some extent self-induced emerges from the limited use of graduate student societies and communal facilities. For example, in one department the economics club, run by and for graduates, had collapsed despite two attempts at resuscitation. A similar fate had befallen the graduate history society in another institution.

The overall level of the facilities provided by universities specifically for graduate students reflects the marginality of those students in the system. Housing arrangements, common rooms, food services, and opportunities for social and recreational activities tend to be less adequate than those available for undergraduates, where such facilities and services are separately provided. Perhaps partly in consequence, many graduate students consider themselves to be only rather loosely affiliated to their parent institution—and indeed to their own department. Many have good reasons for working away from base in their second year, and where university regulations do not require more than a single year of residence, a significant number of them do not subsequently return.

The situation of British doctoral students in this respect is therefore intermediate between those of their counterparts in the United States (whose close identity with their institution, and particularly its graduate school, is evident from chapters 7 and 8) and those of the almost completely independent doctoral candidates in France and Japan.

Motivation and Morale

The people who survive the solitariness of the graduate student's life-style do so because they are strongly motivated, though the levels of morale, commitment, and confidence may fluctuate from one point to another in the program. In history and economics a way has to be found to sustain enthusiasm, especially during a long, arduous, and sometimes mechanical and routine process of sifting through the research material. Many respondents pinpointed this as a central issue, giving rise to the need for regular encouragement from a sympathetic and supportive supervisor. The importance of adopting a steady pace of progress was stressed, and of being determined not to give in.

The workload in most physics doctoral programs is generally very heavy, often with particularly exacting requirements in the first and final years. A nine-to-five working pattern is rare. Many students work a ten-hour day and often weekends as well. Those with substantial computing requirements sometimes continue on into the night, when computer access is easier and cheaper. The demanding pace calls for a strong sense of dedication. As one academic remarked: "It's not enough just to have great thoughts; you have to cope with the harsh realities and enjoy the humdrum day-to-day activity of being a physicist."

Students come into a doctoral program for a variety of reasons. A rough-and-ready distinction between three main types of initial motivation can be described. Those who enjoy the student life-style may stay on after graduation, though without any very intense commitment to a long-term future in academia. Others, whose concerns are more instrumental, see a higher degree primarily as a passport to improved employment opportunities. And third are the students who have developed a strong personal investment in their chosen area of study and who see its pursuit as an end in itself.

To make these broad divisions is not to suggest that every doctoral applicant fits neatly into one of the three categories, nor is it to claim that motivations will remain constant over the period of doctoral study. However, the academics interviewed found this a reasonably useful way of classifying the students they had known. They confirmed that members of the first group were the most prone to drop out of the program at an early stage when they discovered the extent of the demands it was likely to make on them. This group is now very few, given all the initial disincentives in the way of enrolling for a doctorate. The more instrumentally motivated students, in general, were prepared to stay the course, although readily tempted away from it if other interesting job opportunities happened to come their way. The students in the third category seemed best fitted to survive the rigors of the program, and from their ranks the university teachers and researchers of the future were most likely to be drawn. In support of this view, some of the students themselves remarked that they drew considerable strength from the fact that their motivation was intrinsic rather than extrinsic. A deep commitment to the discipline was held to be more resilient in adversity than career considerations or the prospect of subsequent financial reward.

Work-Related Issues

Many of the difficulties students identified in discussing their progress through the doctoral program related to aspects of their working environment. One common problem, tied to some extent to more intangible motivational issues, concerned an uncertainty about the quality of work they should be aiming to achieve. As one academic noted: "Supervisors tend to take it for granted that students know what they are doing, and often fail to appreciate the importance of keeping up their morale." A similar point was made by a student: "It's hard to know what is expected of you when you're doing a Ph.D. You can sort out your academic problems with your supervisor and other people who are around, but you still don't know if your work is good enough."

This point relates to the earlier discussion of monitoring procedures. The general view of students was that there should be more explicit appraisals of progress, especially in the second year, and a more conscious attempt to spell out what would be required of a successful candidate. The latter stipulation might be more difficult to achieve than the former, given the variety of expectations and assumptions among academics about the purpose of the doctorate.

Some comments singled out aspects of the working milieu. Among the physicists, one or two students felt that they were being exploited by their research group, treated as "dogsbodies" and given routine and unrewarding chores. Economists and historians spoke about the impact on doctoral student morale of a fragmented disciplinary environment, and of conflict within the faculty. Most students were aware of the growing demands made on academics, many of whom they saw as seriously overworked. They accepted as a consequence that the time devoted to individual supervision must diminish. But the commonest concern was with a lack of structure rather than a lack of attention. Only a minority were critical of their supervisors: indeed, one senior academic contended that they were not critical enough.

Generally, library facilities were considered to be satisfactory, especially since these could be supplemented by outside loans and visits to other major collections. Computing resources provided communally tended to be heavily in demand; there were also some concerns about other resources such as photocopying. The main deficiency identified by both economics and history students, however, was in the provision of satisfactory working space in the department. The available rooms were generally criticized as noisy, crowded, and ill-lighted. Students preferred to work at home as a result, particularly if they had acquired personal computing and word-processing facilities. This further contributed to a sense of isolation.

The particular hazards associated with doctoral topics differ from one discipline to another. Research in experimental physics is particularly vulnerable to accident. A doctoral student might be subject to delays in apparatus being delivered, or may have to cope with faults in its design. The technique adopted may be unsuited to the task and may belatedly have to be modified or scrapped. And across the field in general, there is always the risk of being "beaten to the post" by someone else publishing the same findings first. In economics theoretical topics are considered potentially risky since it is not always easy to foresee if they will yield any satisfactory outcome. In other fields also a line of inquiry in which time has been invested may prove unproductive, prolonging the period needed for completion. Occasionally a student may (usually with insufficient vigilance from a supervisor) embark on an ill-defined or overambitious proposal.

Fewer problems of this kind confront doctoral researchers in history, provided that the initial topic has been clearly enough identified and the sources limited to a manageable level. Given the scattered nature of the subject, there is less likelihood than in physics or theoretical economics of anyone else being engaged on exactly the same problem. A rival researcher would be easily tracked down, because he or she would probably be using the same archival sources: and even if a strong overlap of interest occurred there would still be room for wide differences of interpretation and approach. Nor are there such high chances that a research issue might prove too intractable, since historians are not in the business of posing and solving problems in the scientific mode: their challenge is to make the best possible sense of the data which are available. A more common problem, to which economists working in qualitative, nonmathematical fields are also prone, is the incidence of a writer's block. Sometimes the very qualities of persistence and obsessionalism needed to complete a doctorate get in the way of progress.

THE PRODUCTIVITY OF THE SYSTEM

These glimpses into the working lives of doctoral candidates make it possible to put in context the general overviews in chapter 3 of completion rates for the doctorate; they also help us understand some of the reasons why students drop out of, fail, or prove unable to complete their programs.

Dropout, Failure, and Noncompletion

The term "dropout" refers to students who embark on a doctorate but who withdraw their registration before the end of the four-year period allowed for submission of the thesis. "Noncompletion" relates to the students who have not withdrawn, but who have not been in a position to submit their thesis within four years. Some of these subsequently complete the program; others eventually give up. "Failure" denotes cases in which a thesis has been submitted but found not to be acceptable, even allowing for further modification.

Figures for dropouts were not easy to obtain from the departments visited. Such information is sensitive; the question is not clear-cut, since many decisions about withdrawal are taken either before the formal review procedures leading to doctoral registration or in consequence of them. The incidence would appear to be relatively small, in that few people apply for doctoral work who are not already highly motivated. Those who turn out not to be intellectually strong enough may be advised to withdraw at an early stage; alternatively, the registration procedures may require them to aim instead for an M.Phil. Neither case would technically constitute a dropout from the Ph.D. program as such.

A cause of some attrition in the initial months is the growing awareness of the demands made by the research life style, particularly in history. Students spoke of friends who had found the loneliness insupportable; some of them had themselves come near to giving up. Women respondents were notably articulate on this issue, as on the problems of survival in a competitive, strongly male-dominated environment. Most academics were under the impression that women are more liable to drop out than men, often for domestic or other personal reasons. But some evidence indicates that the women students who do survive have a significantly better completion record than their male counterparts.

Most dropouts, then, whether on academic or personal grounds, withdraw before any final commitment has been made to submit for the doctorate. A common cause of withdrawal later in the program is an attractive job offer from an outside employer. Understandably this would appear to be less common in history than in physics, particularly when the research topic has an industrial relevance, and in economics, where the student concerned may have made a number of contacts in the commercial world.

For a student to fail is also rare, for reasons already noted. Few supervisors are not vigilant enough to recognize, well before the time comes to submit, that their students' work is likely to be considered below standard: their own reputations would not be helped by allowing examiners to see a thesis that is clearly unacceptable. At worst the award of an M.Phil. is likely to be given, so that the eventual outcome is not technically a failure. The few cases that are failed outright are commonly the result of a student's deciding to override the supervisor's advice against submission.

But if dropouts and failures are not an important element in the overall statistics of performance, noncompletion certainly is. Despite all the steps taken in recent years, an obdurately and uncomfortably large number of candidates in economics, history, and physics as in other disciplines fail to complete their theses within a four-year period. Primary among the reasons has been the three-year limit on student grants.

Doctoral students are in general academically competent, dedicated, and hard working. There is no incentive for them to prolong their research period beyond what is necessary to produce an acceptable thesis. To do so would be to penalize themselves financially and to defer still longer the prospects of regular employment. Added to this, their supervisors and departments now show an unremitting concern that they finish their research in as short a time as possible. Nor is there any evidence of significant slack in the system. It could be argued that some supervisors are not directive enough in the initial stages, and that in certain cases an earlier start might have been made. But even those we interviewed who were prepared to adopt a quite strongly interventionist line, and who put considerable store in helping their students to achieve a rapid pace of work, considered that it would be very difficult to come down to a three-year norm.

All the indications seem to point to a realistic target of completion somewhere between three and four years of full-time work—unless the requirements for a doctoral degree are to be reduced below those which now seem generally acceptable, and which themselves represent a drawing back from previously higher levels of expectation. Such a target would not appear unreasonable, even allowing for the relatively specialized base from which most doctoral work begins, when the British system is compared with that in the other countries described in this volume. The case will become even more convincing as school curricula become broader and undergraduate intakes less narrowly focused in ability range.

If it is granted, as the majority academic view contends, that three to four years is the appropriate figure, the three-year funding system seems to have been finely tuned to promote a high rate of noncompletion. Most doctoral students' grants come to an end just as they are engaged in the difficult business of writing up their findings. Unless they have other resources to draw on, they are compelled to find part-time or full-time work, with the inevitable outcome that completion will take longer. Rather than finishing, as they almost certainly otherwise would, within a further year at most, their submission date will often be postponed into a fifth year or beyond.

There is no further entitlement to supervision after the fourth year. Often people have given up without ever finishing the work. For some, the jobs they have taken begin to occupy their main energies and attention. For others, achievement of a doctorate no longer seems so relevant. For others again, the topic begins to go stale after so lengthy an engagment with it.

In policy terms such a situation is clearly wasteful. The change, mentioned earlier, by the Economic and Social Research Council to a four-year period of funding sets a welcome precedent for other research councils to follow. As things have stood so far, only a few students in all three disciplines under review have been so highly committed, hard working, and fortunate in their choice of topics and supervisors that they were able to submit within three years. A larger number, by dint of ingenuity, found enough time in their fourth year to complete the writing up. But even in the best-regulated departments, a significant proportion submitted their theses—if they did so at all—beyond the limit, and contributed to the statistics on noncompletion.

Destinations of Graduate Students

Many of those who embark on doctorates do so in the hope of finding an academic job. Even though all of them have strong credentials, very few will achieve this ambition. For the remainder, distinctive patterns of career opportunities may be identified for each subject field.

In economics some of those who are not prepared to relinquish their hopes for an academic post may keep going on a short-term basis as research fellows, research assistants, or in other postdoctoral positions either with a department or in a free-standing research unit. Some may take up jobs in research consultancy on the margins of academia or in quasi-academic governmental and independent organizations. Others may find teaching appointments in polytechnics, colleges of further and higher education, or secondary schools in the private or public sector. Those prepared to emigrate may look for job opportunities in universities in the United States, Australia, and elsewhere. Many who decide to move out of the academic environment find their way into national and local government, or are employed in a variety of managerial and professional organizations. A sizeable number end up in the City, or in banking, or in general commerce. But in none of these careers does their doctorate give them a significant edge over those with a master's, or even perhaps a bachelor's degree, in economics.

The openings for postdoctoral work for historians are very limited. Since collective, team-based inquiry is a minority activity, there are few funded research assistantships. In the past few years, however, the British Academy—which is responsible for research awards in the humanities—has provided a limited number of three-year postdoctoral awards. Some universities and individual Oxford and Cambridge colleges offer research fellowships for which historians are eligible. The few available short-term university teaching appointments hold only a distant promise of a subsequent permanency. Research-related openings may be found in major historical libraries, record offices, archive collections, or museums (although they may also require a further professional qualification). Some higher graduates may make a career in bodies that cater to the growing public interest in historic sites and buildings. Though not on the same scale as in France or Japan, teaching careers in secondary schools are also a major career option for those with doctorates as well as those with lesser qualifications.

For other careers history has few claims to direct vocational relevance. Common alternative forms of employment include the civil service, university administration, publishing, and the media. Some higher graduates have followed successful careers in the financial world and, with further training, in accountancy, law, and other professions. But most have to take up such posts on terms similar to those available when they first got bachelor's degrees, with the added handicap of a delayed age of entry.

The difficulties of finding a permanent livelihood in academic life are no less in physics than they are in history or economics. Although there are more opportunities for postdoctoral research, most specialisms demand a substantial further apprenticeship before a realistic application can be made for a permanent post. Even at that stage, many long-serving research assistants and research associates can be expected to fall by the wayside. Alternative research openings, however, may be found in industry or in the scientific civil service. Besides those who find opportunities to work in research and development, a significant number of people with higher degrees in physics take up jobs in administration, finance, and other commercial activities. As computing has become an integral part of physics research, there are also openings in fields such as information technology and software development. Few of the students interviewed expected to have any difficulty in finding employment after completing their doctorates, but they were aware that their options might be limited by their specialized professional abilities.

Taking these considerations as a whole, the award of a doctorate has a discernible value in a range of activities outside academic life that call on relevant research skills. But one of the prime purposes of the Ph.D., the preparation of the further generation of academics, is largely frustrated by the limited number of vacancies currently available: one respondent referred to "a lost generation" of potentially creative researchers. And

outside the research context, the Ph.D. does not appear, in Britain, to enhance job prospects. Employers are likely to be more impressed with the
promise of all-round capability of a master's degree holder than with the
implications of more narrowly focused competence attached to a doctoral
qualification.

RESEARCH AND GRADUATE EDUCATION

The general observations in chapter 3 on the relationship between the research system and graduate education can now be elaborated and extended
by reference to the case studies of economics, history, and physics.

Master's courses in general make no significant contribution to the production of academic researchers, since they are not geared toward independent and creative investigation. Their main value lies in promoting the
advanced study of a particular field, and in some cases in the development of specialized practical technique. They may make a contribution to
applied inquiry outside the academic setting, and are accordingly valued
by employers as providing a vocational qualification.

We need to direct our attention to the doctoral degree in considering
how the researchers of the future are prepared. In one straightforward sense
doctoral programs in Britain are well geared to research needs. The linkage
rests on the practice of close personal supervision by an experienced researcher of each doctoral candidate. The importance of research training,
although recognized and acknowledged, becomes subsidiary to the process
of engaging in research under informed guidance. In this respect the British
scene differs from those in which advanced inquiry has to be carried out
with a considerably greater degree of independence—where, one might say,
learning to be a researcher has to be done to a large extent by the light of
nature. It also differs from those—such as the U.S. system—which place a
heavy emphasis on systematic preliminary training, and which offer relatively less support for the research process itself.

But on closer scrutiny, potential problems emerge from the weight
placed on the student-supervisor relationship. Training provision may be
limited and perhaps inadequate because viable-sized groups are lacking.
Consortium arrangements can help, but they usually involve crossing established institutional boundaries and are not easy to organize. A policy of
concentration, requiring all doctoral training to be confined to large centers, would fit in with the research requirements of the more expensive scientific specialisms, but would be hard to justify in subjects such as history,
which involve little collective research activity. At least in part, the training
element therefore remains problematic: in some cases, there would seem to
be no alternative to ad hoc processes of independent individual study.

The heavy reliance on supervision assumes a competence on the supervisor's part which cannot always be taken for granted. Variation in quality is perhaps inevitable when supervisors receive no formal training for the task and when they are often selected for their expert knowledge of the field rather than for their interpersonal skills. Nonetheless, there is usually a tacit recognition within a department of who the best supervisors are and a collective concern to avoid those who are likely to prove unsatisfactory.

The student's dependence on the supervisor may to some extent be offset by the opportunity of working in a collaborative environment. This possibility is most easily achieved in physics, where the laboratory can provide a supportive research community. It also offers a realistic setting in that it models the milieu in which future professional research will be conducted. But here the danger to be guarded against lies in giving research students routine tasks rather than offering them the opportunity to engage in more creative inquiry.

In economics limited opportunities exist for participation in group research. Such opportunities did not appear to be fully exploited in the departments studied, however, where funded research units were often separated from their parent departments and thus not regarded as a central part of the research training provision. The emphasis on allowing students to choose their own topics also tended to militate against a more extensive use of collective projects as a research student base. But those who had worked in such contexts (usually students sponsored by outside agencies) considered the benefits to have outweighed the absence of a greater say in defining their programs.

History provides little scope for doctoral students to work alongside others, except insofar as a few clusters of like-minded researchers may form around a leading figure. This type of organization can be rewarding, but its existence cannot be legislated; and, given the dispersed nature of the subject field, its incidence is relatively rare. Perhaps the best that can be achieved by way of general supplementary support to that of the supervisor is to increase the extent of student involvement with relevant specialist networks. Attendance at professional conferences, for example, was rated more highly by the students interviewed than the more contrived art form of departmental research seminars.

Even if opportunities were taken to link doctoral students more directly to the professional research community, thus reinforcing the pivotal connection currently provided by the supervisor, other problems about the general relationship of graduate education to research would remain to be answered. Questions are raised about whether the system is unduly wasteful; despite a significant tightening up of procedures in recent years, a substantial number of students fail to complete the doctoral program. Reference has already been made to the suggestion that a four-year full-time norm would be likely to reduce the numbers failing to submit and would therefore constitute a more effective use of resources. For the rest, it could be argued that any program as demanding as the ones in question must inevitably have its casualties. There is no clear case for suggesting that current selection procedures are faulty, especially as they are reinforced by a further test of suitability before the end of the first year. It could be, however, that more systematic monitoring in the second and any subsequent years could help to detect incipient problems over completion and enable early remedial action to be taken.

Another critical observation concerns the destinations of those who complete the doctorate. The research system clearly depends on this source for its survival. We can infer that the students are adequately prepared to carry out research—with the proviso that in some specialized fields, particularly in physics, a further stage of postdoctoral experience may be called for. But the numbers trained at this advanced level are far in excess of the demand for them: is it not, accordingly, wasteful to create such an oversupply of what is necessarily a costly resource?

It is the demography of the academic profession in Britain that has created the problem, rather than the policy for graduate education as such. Indeed, as is the case in other countries in the present study, a critical shortage of recruits to the academic profession may be expected in the next decade, so that a reserve cadre of suitably qualified people is likely to be a necessity rather than a luxury. But quite apart from that, many of the people with doctorates who fail to get academic jobs contribute their research skills in other settings. This is as true in history as it is in economics and physics, as the earlier review of student destinations made plain. And as for those who end up in employment unrelated to their qualifications, it can be suggested that they knew at the outset that this might have to be the case and were prepared to take the risk; that their personal qualities and general skills will have been enhanced by the doctoral experience; and that a cultural vindication can be offered for advanced higher education even in cases where its costs may not be straightforwardly justified in monetary terms.

It would be possible in principle to achieve a closer match than the present one between the requirements of the research system and the output of graduate education. Considerations of maximum efficiency would call for a rigorous policy of research selectivity, ensuring that no department below a stipulated size should train doctoral students and that intakes should be tightly controlled. They would also demand the direction of research labor, insuring that groups were recruited in areas of known need. Research students would no longer be allowed an unrestricted choice of subject field, nor would they be given an opportunity to determine the topic of their research. But a directive approach of this kind would be subject to all the disadvantages that attend overcentralized planning. It would certainly play down the element of creativity which the present system, with all its faults, appears to foster. And if creativity were not the central goal, it must be asked whether research would amount to anything more than the exercise of routine professional competence.

APPENDIX
METHODS OF INQUIRY

Our field data derived from in-depth, semistructured interviews lasting between one-half hour and one hour and a half in three contrasting departments in each subject. Details of the departments and the number of interviews held in each subject are set out below, in the context of a brief note on the overall teaching provision.

Economics

A recent study by Towse and Blaug (1989) discovered a total of 2,236 economists employed in higher education, 72 percent of whom were in economics departments of universities or polytechnics. Of the remainder, 14 percent were in research units and 15 percent in teaching or research posts in other departments. The average teaching department in universities and polytechnics consisted of seventeen academic staff.

Postgraduate studies are widely dispersed, at least across universities: thirty-five offer taught master's courses and 90 percent of university departments of economics have Ph.D. students, ranging from one to seventy. Twelve master's programs have fewer than fourteen students in them. Such courses are presumably underpinned by relatively flourishing undergraduate programs.

Three university departments of economics were chosen as the focus of this case study. They were all larger than the average department quoted by Towse and Blaug but were differently organized, had different balances of teachers and researchers and different disciplinary identities. Interviews were held with fourteen academics, six Ph.D. students, and three taught master's students in all. One academic was also editor of an internationally prestigious economics journal. An honorary officer of the Royal Economic Society was also interviewed.

Department A is large, with a historic and prestigious tradition. It has a staff of over sixty, including seven professors. Staff include researchers working in a large, long-established applied economics research unit, many of whom undertake undergraduate and postgraduate teaching. It has three taught master's programs (a fourth is planned) with a total annual intake of seventy students. In addition, about twenty students embark on a research degree each year. The total number of graduate students at any one time is approximately one hundred fifty.

Department B is a medium-sized department in a large (by British standards) university. It has some twenty teaching staff, but the department is one of four employing economists at the university. Unusually, econometrics and statistics are located in a separate department from economics. One of the professors is codirector of a multidisciplinary research unit that employs some economists—the only research unit associated with the postgraduate diploma courses. The total annual intake of taught master's students is approximately thirty-five, and about ten students each year embark on a research degree. Currently about sixty graduate students are in the department.

Department C is relatively new, but has grown rapidly. There are over thirty teaching staff in all, and approximately thirty research staff based in a research institute comprising a number of research units. The majority are employed in an applied economics research unit that receives its core funding from the Economic and Social Research Council and from a government department. It does a substantial amount of contract research with the public sector. A linked consortium has also been set up in collaboration with the relevant public sector service to do short-term consultancy work. The department runs four taught master's programs, one of which is closely associated with the research unit and heavily subsidized by a government department. The annual intake of taught master's students is forty-five and between six and ten research students register each year, all initially for the M.Phil., although most go on to a Ph.D. The total number of graduate students is approximately eighty.

History

No readily available national statistics relating specifically to graduate training in history exist. Even the information about current doctoral students in individual departments is often difficult to track down. They are typically held in a central registry outside the department and are agglomerated with records for other disciplines. It is therefore difficult to offer any clear picture of the existing provision, beyond a very tentative estimate that there are in the order of one thousand students reading for doctorates in history throughout the country, including a substantial proportion from overseas.

Three university departments were selected to form the basis of the present study. None of them was at the smaller end of the scale, where British graduate students are few and far between. Each was somewhat differently organized, reflecting a diversity of specialist emphasis and a different balance between teachers, master's students, and doctoral candidates. Interviews were held with fourteen academics and six Ph.D. students in all. Additional interviews involved the editor of a leading scholarly journal and the director of a major research institute.

Department A is one of the largest in the country—technically a faculty rather than a department with a staffing complement of over fifty posts. It recruits some thirty to forty doctoral students each year, slightly over half being British nationals (the large majority of the others come from the United States, Canada, Australia, and New Zealand). Women candidates account for about 20 percent of the annual intake. One long-established master's degree recruits about fifty students per annum, in a field that attracts many overseas students, and another more specialist offering attracts between ten and twenty. Another master's course began in 1989– 1990, with a target intake of a dozen students; initiation of one or two further programs in future years is proposed. No provision is made for part-time registration.

Department B has a complement of twenty-plus academic staff and a total graduate student population of some twenty-five full-time and twenty part-time doctoral researchers and around half a dozen master's candidates a year. The majority of the students are from the United Kingdom, and all are full-time. The proportion of doctoral students completing in the required four-year period is considered to be higher than the national average (but see the point made above about the absence of either comparative or global statistics).

Department C is in a medium-sized university. It is, in formal terms, composed of three separate history departments. The first is concerned with mainstream history (ten to fifteen staff), and the second with economic and social history (under ten staff); and the third is a small all-graduate department with under five full-time equivalent staff catering to a specialist area of history enjoying considerable lay interest.

There are two existing master's courses, one full-time and one part-time, recruiting some twenty-five home students between them. Two further master's courses were, at the time of the research, due to be initiated (one full-time, aiming mainly at overseas students, and one part-time, catering primarily for home students). A large proportion of the twenty or so currently registered doctoral students are part-time, mature, and home-based, although overseas students are more numerous in one subsection.

Physics

In 1985–1986 all except one of the fifty-odd U.K. universities had a separate department of physics, as did a majority of the polytechnics (twenty-four departments in all). Four university departments have since been closed and at least another dozen or so are expected to disappear soon, by closure or merger with neighboring subject groups. The U.K. universities cover a spectrum from the ancient collegiate and long-established "Redbrick" universities, typically offering an academic physics education, to the technological universities with predominantly applied and vocationally oriented programs and the "new" (post 1960) universities where the physics courses may include aspects of contextual and interdisciplinary study. In the polytechnics the physicists may be located in combined departments and offer full-time and "sandwich" applied courses, often on a modular or joint degree pattern. Polytechnics engage in some research and provide a limited number of opportunities for research students, although they are not specifically funded to do so.

The sizes of the physics departments range from nearly one hundred full-time tenured faculty to under ten. The larger departments usually aim to cover the whole span of research and teaching within the discipline; the smaller ones may specialize in only one or two limited areas.

The three departments selected for the purposes of the present study were chosen to reflect some of these contrasts. In all, sixteen academics and seven Ph.D. students were interviewed; an additional interview was held with the honorary secretary of a professional institution.

Department A is large by U.K. standards, with ninety plus permanent academic staff and over one hundred fifty research students (some one hundred thirty home-based). It has high international standing in both pure and applied research. Much responsibility is devolved to individual specialist groups (currently around ten in number) within the department: these differ considerably in their approaches to research training. Although not immune to financial constraints, the department is likely to profit from current selectivity policies, which favor large units and "research excellence."

Department B is of medium size (thirty-three academic staff, over fifty home and some ten overseas postgraduates), with a long-established international reputation in certain pure research fields. In contrast with Department A, research students are admitted, and their programs overseen, by the department rather than by its five constituent subgroups. Despite its relatively high prestige, the department has already suffered the effects of research selectivity by losing two recent bids for nationally funded research units to larger contenders.

Department C is a small department (sixteen academic staff, under twenty-five doctoral students, some two-thirds of them U.K.-based), with extensive industrial links, in a technological university. The modest size of its postgraduate population results in a less systematic, less formal approach to postgraduate training than is (perhaps necessarily) adopted in Department A. The research emphasis of most of the six subgroups is on collaborative work with industry and with other relatively small university physics departments having complementary expertise.

NOTES

The author, though responsible for this report, was significantly helped in the process of data collection and analysis by three colleagues. Mary Henkel undertook a substantial share of the fieldwork on economics, Maurice Kogan on history, and Penny Youll on physics. His debt to each of them is considerable.

1. The focus of the discussion is on universities, not on polytechnics and colleges, since doctoral programs and advanced research training are mainly confined to universities. However, the nonuniversity institutions now provide a growing share of master's courses, alongside a modest involvement in doctoral work.

2. Clark, *Higher Education System*.

3. An overall view of the development of each of the three disciplines can be found in chapter 2 (Maurice Kogan), chapter 4 (Penny Youll), and chapter 6 (John Brennan and Mary Henkel) in Boys et al., *Higher Education and the Preparation for Work*. More detailed studies of the disciplinary cultures of history and physics are offered in Becher, "Historians on History," and Becher, "Physicists on Physics," respectively.

4. The pattern of provision is reviewed in University Grants Committee, "Future of University Physics," and Institute of Physics, *Physics in Higher Education*.

5. Towse and Blaug, *Current State of the British Economics Profession*.

6. A note on the departments forming the basis of this study in each discipline is provided in the appendix.

7. Committee of Vice-Chancellors and Principals, *British Ph.D.*

8. Advisory Board for Research Councils, *Report of the Working Party on Postgraduate Education*.

9. Economic and Social Research Council, *Social Science Ph.D.*

10. By way of corroboration, the Advisory Board for Research Council's Report observes that "the ability to write a connected exposition of 150–200 pages . . . will be needed in almost every job (whether in higher education or outside) to which a course of research training should lead."

11. Some supervisors find themselves attempting to combine their academic responsibilities with those of a pastoral kind. Our inquiries suggest that both roles should be recognized but separately dealt with: ideally, each graduate student should have a personal tutor, as undergraduates in many British universities now do.

12. Note the contrast here with the United States, where undergraduate teaching is less strongly valued by faculty than graduate work, and where much of the elementary teaching is delegated to nontenured assistants (see chapters 7 and 8).

13. Committee of Vice-Chancellors and Principals, *Academic Standards in Universities* (see chapter 3).

14. The informal obligation for students to contribute a paper to a graduate seminar series could be seen as something of a compromise between systematic interim assessment and the absence of any intermediate monitoring at all.

15. Particularly in history, students embarking on research for no other obvious motive than a strong interest in the subject tend to set themselves high expectations of achievement. The temptation to perfect and polish a doctoral dissertation, rather than to relinquish it when minimum acceptable standards have been reached, remains strong.

BIBLIOGRAPHY

Advisory Board for Research Councils. *Report of the Working Party on Postgraduate Education.* Swinnerton-Dyer Report. Cmnd 8537. London: HMSO, 1982.

Becher, Tony. "Historians on History." *Studies in Higher Education* 14, no. 3 (1988): 263–278.

————. "Physicists on Physics." *Studies in Higher Education* 15, no. 1 (1989): 3–201.

Boys, Christopher J., John Brennan, Mary Henkel, John Kirkland, Maurice Kogan, and Penny Youll. *Higher Education and the Preparation for Work.* London: Jessica Kingsley, 1988.

Clark, Burton R. *The Higher Education System: Academic Organization in Cross-National Perspective.* Berkeley, Los Angeles, London: University of California Press, 1983.

Committee of Vice-Chancellors and Principals. *Academic Standards in Universities.* Reynolds Report. London, 1986.

————. *The British Ph.D.* Ash Report. London, 1988.

Economic and Social Research Council. *The Social Science Ph.D.: The ESRC Enquiry on Submission Rates.* Winfield Report. London, 1987.

Institute of Physics. *Physics in Higher Education.* London, 1988.

Towse, Ruth, and Mark Blaug. *The Current State of the British Economics Profession.* London: Royal Economic Society, 1988.

University Grants Committee. *The Future of University Physics: Report of the Physics Review.* Edwards Report. London: HMSO, 1988.

PART THREE

France

Introduction

In France, Guy Neave and Richard Edelstein remind us, everything is different. If the Humboldtian ideal is found at all, it is hidden somewhere in the special and intricate features of the French structure of higher education and research. Throughout the nineteenth and twentieth centuries, specialized advanced schools—the *grandes écoles*—have taken over the elite selection, training, and placement normally exercised in other systems by leading universities. The universities have become second-best in status and relatively poor in financial support compared to universities in other advanced nations as well as to the grandes écoles. Even more important for our purposes, research has long found a government-funded home outside the universities, in such organized domains as the very large and complex National Center for Scientific Research (CNRS). French uniqueness in the Western world, then, consists particularly of a separate domain for research activity alongside the education and training domains of grandes écoles, universities, and, recently, university institutes of technology (IUTs). And the whole arrangement falls under the support and supervision of a centralized, unitary state that is unabashedly *dirigiste*. In France, when the minister of education speaks, people listen. Rare is the minister of education who does not feel it is his or her duty to reform the research system, improve the universities, and otherwise leave a lasting mark on French culture.

The research foundations of advanced education in this context depend considerably on relations between CNRS laboratories and the universities. Here, as Neave describes in chapter 5, the structure is Byzantine. CNRS laboratories of varying formal status and resource levels operate on as well as off university grounds. University professors serve in the CNRS units, but those organizations do not fall under university control. The labs bring prestige to the universities, not the other way around. And students who seek training to become researchers have to climb over imposing curricular and degree hurdles and to battle for sponsorship if they are to gain access to laboratory training and later laboratory posts.

Neave and Edelstein also clarify a series of central decisions whose unintended effects have widened the divorce between research and training in much of French higher education. As elsewhere, a thorough investment in mass higher education cannot be carried out within the limits of old models of research, teaching, and study. Reforms have added new degrees, pathways, institutional linkages, and examination hurdles. Although many more young people now than in the past enter higher education, only a few progress all the way through to the degree levels and advanced sponsorship that offer substantial research foundations for training and career advancement. And all through the years since the crisis of 1968, there has been a steady undercurrent of reform and drift toward lessening the bureaucratic rigidities of centralized control and increasing the differentiation of programs and talent among the universities. Even in this highly centralized system, there is a struggle toward "the market" in which the fate of advanced education and academic science is entwined.

FIVE

Séparation de Corps
The Training of Advanced Students and the Organization of Research in France

Guy Neave

Governments in Western Europe turned their attention toward both advanced student training and the organization of research in the 1980s. Such attention was in part a reflection of the drive to reinforce government (or public) control over three overlapping areas: efficiency, evaluation, and accountability. This approach, beginning in the United Kingdom around the start of the decade, rapidly spread to the Netherlands, Sweden, the Federal Republic of Germany, and Italy.[1] Just as the issues had some degree of similarity, so too did the questions governments posed to their civil servants, university presidents, and academic staff. At the very least, how many researchers are necessary to insure the nation's competitive position in technological development? Which disciplines ought to be accorded priority? Who should do research? Which types of institutions should continue to undertake research? What ought to be the criteria determining "research viability" at the institutional level?

Though the rise of the so-called Evaluative State is a phenomenon broadly shared across Western European countries, the structural, institutional, and governmental context into which it is inserted is not.[2] The differences between systems of higher education are not limited to what, in Anglo-American terminology, would be termed "undergraduate studies." They go beyond this stage. The way research and the training system for advanced students is organized in France is the product of a different evolutionary pattern than that which pertains in Britain or the United States. The existence of a corps of full-time researchers, with different career trajectories, conditions of service, and criteria for promotion may appear both striking and singular to those whose systems of higher education were heavily influenced by the Humboldtian philosophy, which emphasized the symbiotic linkage of teaching, training for research, and research itself within the same institution.[3] The way these elements are organized in France may stand as a species of counter model. But the model is far from limited to France alone. Many Eastern bloc countries have a broadly similar pattern based sometimes on specialized research establishments standing parallel to the university. In other cases the arrangement takes the national academy form—whether of science, engineering, or pedagogy. If the French system of advanced training and research is of interest per se, it is equally worth our attention because it represents an organizational model usually left aside in the comparative studies of higher education.

Close attention to the French arrangements is justified by another rationale. Major changes in the relationship between university and industry are becoming apparent and, following on this, changes in the institutional location of basic research. The rise of industry-based fundamental research, especially in computer science and biotechnology, has, in certain instances, led to the development of a research training system beyond the walls of academe.[4] How far this trend will continue, what its ultimate repercussions will be for the research and research training systems hitherto located in higher education, remains to be seen. But already evident is a breakdown of the monopoly of research training as exercised by the university. Whether this development points to a revision in the Humboldtian paradigm remains unclear. But it suggests that the particular French version of segmented but conjoined research and training systems may not be irrelevant even for systems grounded upon different assumptions of the proper relationship between research and training for research. As a recent report from the Organisation pour la Coopération et Développement Economiques (OCDE) noted: "The role of universities in fundamental and strategic research is threatened . . . by the growing tendency to create self-standing research institutions which are not regulated by the limitations imposed by the traditional statute of university teachers and by the rules of tenure."[5] Thus, contemporary developments taking place inside research systems founded on the Anglo-American interpretation of the Humboldtian model may be clarified by an understanding of a major alternative pattern, as presented in the French tradition.

HISTORICAL DEVELOPMENT

It would be erroneous to believe that the development of research and research training in France was uninfluenced by the rise of nineteenth-century German scholarship. On the contrary, French authorities were well aware of it. But research in France grew out of an earlier, native pattern of organization based on the establishment of specialized bodies outside the university. This species of institutional accretion has a weighty history, reaching back to the sixteenth century when, in 1529, François I set up the

Collège de France, perhaps the first example in the history of the European university of an institute for advanced study. The following century saw the founding of the forerunner of the *Musée d'Histoire Naturelle* in the form of the *Jardin Royal des Plantes Médicinales*. The Enlightenment continued and strengthened this process. Under the aegis of the statesman Turgot, the first of what was later to form the *grandes écoles*—specialized establishments for the training of high-level manpower for the service of the nation—was initiated with the *Ecole des Ponts et Chaussées* in 1775. Nor was this tradition broken with the Revolution of 1789. The revolutionary period saw the creation of the *Ecole Polytechnique* (1793–1794) and the *Ecole des Mines* in the same year. The former trained artillery officers and military engineers, the latter provided civil engineers, chemists, and, to use an anachronism, physicists. The nineteenth century did not depart from this pattern. The *Ecole Pratique des Hautes Etudes* (1868) and the *Institut Pasteur* (1887) both fulfilled a research training and a research function, but outside the purlieu of the university.[6]

There are two elements to note in this policy of building up establishments outside the university; first, it was the result of central initiative taken at the highest level; second, it gave rise to a dual system of training and scholarship of which only part was associated with the university.

The French adaptation of the Humboldtian philosophy was thus inserted into an institutional universe very different from the one where it had first taken root. And although French scholarship in the nineteenth century did not lack its giants, the effect of the systemic dualism saw them teach and conduct their work in establishments outside the university *stricto sensu*, either in the *Collège de France* or in the more specialized écoles—*Ecole Normale Supérieure, Ecole Polytechnique*, or the *Ecole Pratique des Hautes Etudes*.[7] The university, regarded as a single national and unified body with local and regional components or outposts, exercised a role essentially subaltern in the research sphere. It was not divorced from such a responsibility, but it did not stand on the commanding heights. This strategic position was occupied by the specialized institutes.

The outstanding characteristic in the development of the French research system was that institutional accretion gave rise to institutional segmentation. In turn, segmentation in the higher education system between the university and the more specialized écoles drew a line between training *for* research and the execution *of* research. This distinction took on greater clarity when the development of a national research policy during the 1930s ushered in the proliferation of research funding agencies which, at the same time, also undertook research. Under such an arrangement, the university's task was to train and to prepare for research.[8] Research agencies were to develop the research system atop the research training system in the university.

Government coordination of publicly financed research in France took place swiftly between 1935 and 1939. Earlier, some research funding bodies coexisted: the *Caisse Nationale des Sciences*, the *Caisse Nationale de la Recherche Scientifique*, and the *Centre National des Sciences Appliquées*. The decree of October 19, 1939, merged these agencies to form the *Centre National de la Recherche Scientifique* (CNRS). Today the CNRS is the heart of the French research system.[9] Organizationally separate from both the Ministry of Education and the universities, it is the major single source of both funding and research execution. We will deal with its structure and workings later. Suffice it to note here that the structure of France's present day research organization was in place by 1939.

The Higher Education System

From the standpoint of its structures, French higher education falls into three segments: the grandes écoles, the universities, and what is technically known as short-course higher education, clustered around the *Instituts Universitaires de Technologie* (University Institutes of Technology—IUTs). Some 180 establishments fall into the grandes écoles category; they range from the immensely selective and prestigious *Ecole Polytechnique* and the *Ecole Nationale d'Administration*, which form the heart of French technocracy (the former contributing to the engineering and scientific cadres of top administration, the latter fulfilling a function akin to the British Civil Service Staff College), through establishments specializing in such areas as aeronautical engineering and officer training for the armed forces, to a subsector, privately run, of institutes aligned around business studies and business administration. A most prestigious example of the latter is the *Ecole des Hautes Etudes Commerciales*. Highly specialized, highly selective, and drawing from equally selective grade twelve classes in certain secondary schools, they, not the university, stand as the elite sector in French higher education.[10]

Second in repute stand the seventy-six universities, of which just over one-third were created in the two decades 1958 to 1978.[11] French universities are state-financed, state-controlled establishments, with one or two exceptions such as the Catholic universities of Lyon, Angers, and Lille. Formally speaking, entry to the university sector is open to all those holding the *Baccalauréat*, an upper secondary school-leaving examination, usually sat at age eighteen by some thirty percent of the age cohort. However, certain fields—medicine is one, law another, business studies a third—require a rigorous weeding out during the first year of university work.

The third sector, the University Institutes of Technology, is composed of some fifty-six institutes. They differ from the other two types of establishment in their combination of three characteristics: they are of recent foundation; they are formally selective; and they are based on a curriculum profile that is highly vocational and composed of fields not usually found in universities. Founded in 1966, the two-year IUTs may be seen as symmetrical, though at a less exalted level, to the grandes écoles, both by the degree of their specialization and their selective nature.

Though Paris and Montpellier are among the first European universities, both dating from the early thirteenth century, it is customary to assign the start of France's contemporary higher education system to the foundation of the Imperial University in 1806–1808 during the reign of Napoléon I.[12] The Imperial University was far more than simply the creation of a system of higher education to provide the nation with teachers, lawyers, doctors, and state servants. This umbrella term brought together not only higher but secondary education as well. Legally, individual universities, officially called "Faculties," were part of this overall structure, though they acquired a considerable degree of formal autonomy with the passage of time.

The growth of French higher education throughout the nineteenth and well into the twentieth century, like the research system, rested on a model of institutional accretion. This involved less the creation of new establishments within the university sector than the addition of specialized institutes on its periphery. Examples are the *Ecole Centrale des Arts et Manufactures* in 1829, the *Ecole Libre des Sciences Politiques* in 1872, and later, the *Ecoles Nationales des Sciences de l'Ingénieur* following the *Loi Astier* in 1924. The reform of 1896 put an end to the concept of a national university divided into regional units. It regrouped the various faculties into "faculty bodies," creating thereby a multidisciplinary unit not dissimilar to either the British or American university, but still retaining the term *faculty* to designate it.[13] Only after the upheaval of 1968 did the concept of universities (in the plural) as individual self-standing units emerge from under the shadow of the nationwide university (in the singular) first laid down 160 years previously.

THE SYSTEM OF ADVANCED EDUCATION

If the basic framework of the French research system was in place half a century ago, the same cannot be said of the system of advanced education. As the first major Western European nation to move toward mass higher education, which it attained in the late 1960s, France has been subject to massive tensions that accompanied the transition of elite-based European systems of higher education to this new status. These tensions, in part the result of massive overcrowding and the unwillingness of successive governments to invest in physical plant, in part the result of deteriorating conditions of academic work, affected profoundly both the system and the structure of advanced study. Whether directly or indirectly, they contributed to a remodeling of the advanced education system, the injection of a hefty vocational element, and the reform of the structure of doctoral studies.[14]

When examining the development of advanced education in France, it is important to bear in mind that the reforming impulse is far from lifeless. On the contrary, changes in this sector of higher education take place in the context of a policy that aims at doubling by the year 2000 the total capacity of higher education to around two million students.

From 1960 to 1985 enrollments in all sectors of French higher education rose from 259,000 to 1,166,000. Growth has been particularly marked in law and economic sciences (increasing by more than 6 times) and in the humanities (5.6 times), with lesser but no less marked rises in medicine, dentistry, and pharmacy (3.8 times) and the sciences (2.4 times).[15]

We have already noted the importance incremental segmentation played in the evolution of the French research system. The same rationale also operated within higher education generally: incremental segmentation bore down upon the research system *because* it was the basic procedure for developing the higher education system in general. It comes as no surprise that the way French governments responded to the drive to mass higher education was to refurbish a well-honed instrument in the policymaker's armory and to introduce in 1967 short-course (two-year) higher education in University Institutes of Technology, to develop segmentation to a new height.

Structure of French Higher Education

The structure of French higher education is segmented along two dimensions: by duration of study course, whether short- or long-course institutions, and by access policy, whether selective or open admission. By "open" we mean open to all those holding the Baccalauréat, the upper secondary school-leaving certificate passed around the age of eighteen or nineteen. Within this framework, greatest repute is found in the grandes écoles, which train for leading positions in both the public and private sectors of the economy. Highly selective, they attract the most able students; their courses usually take some five years of study. In the academic year 1985–1986, some 73,000 students were enrolled in the grandes écoles. Short-course selective institutes, whether University Institutes of Technology or Higher Technicians' Sections, offer two-year programs. In the IUTs, studies lead to the *Diplôme Universitaire de Technologie* (DUT).[16] Some 179,000 students followed these courses of study (1985–1986). These establishments offer terminal degrees; formal access to further study is not bestowed. Certain persistent students will go further, however, usually by taking a full first university degree program. Their previous qualification gives them no advantage whatsoever. From the standpoint of linkage with the research system, this is not the role of the IUT.

If the universities fall into a category of long-course nonselective institutions, certain fields are highly selective at entry: medicine, dentistry, and pharmacy are examples. Their programs last longer—upwards of five to six years—compared to the first university degree, which can be earned in two years after the Baccalauréat and results in the *Diplôme d'Etudes Universitaires Générales* (DEUG). Overall, in 1985–1986, some nine hundred thousand students were enrolled in the university sector.

Though routine, this classification of French higher education contains an important paradox when linked with the issue of research training. While the university bears the major responsibility for *initial* research training, it does not at first-degree level draw on those students deemed to be among the nation's best. To be sure, some students whose academic careers brought them into the hallowed precincts of the grandes écoles will transfer across to the university-based research training system later. But it has long been a fact of life that those institutes formally associated with elite education in France have had only an indirect linkage with the research training system. This situation is changing. Since 1981 measures have been taken, primarily through the *Magistère* degree—a program lasting five years after the Baccalauréat—to expand the initial research training system into the grandes écoles themselves. That such initiatives are only now being taken reflects some of the more curious consequences of incremental segmentation.

The University Research Training System: Some Structural Characteristics
Formally speaking, initial research training in French universities has its anchor in the *Diplôme d'Etudes Approfondies* (DEA), which is taken five years after passing the Baccalauréat. Established in 1955, it is highly selective and marks what is termed "third-cycle studies." The DEA stands apart in several respects from the degrees that precede it. Its recruitment tends to be national, even though students in the first two cycles, each two years long, tend to be recruited locally. Also, central government places an upper limit of twenty to thirty-five students admitted to each program. Moreover, each tutor is restricted to no more than five DEA students per year.[17] At this point a rigorous policy of selection operates to control the quality of those admitted to the route that eventually may lead to a research career. Selection is made on the basis of the results obtained by the applicant at the *Maîtrise*, an approximate equivalent to the British master's degree and usually passed four years after the Baccalauréat (Bacc+4), and on a student's portfolio or university record sheet. Also, it is at this level, that is, Bacc+5, that one sees some of the more brilliant and gilded youth whose earlier careers took them through the Ecole Normale Supérieure, Polytechnique, or other grandes écoles, crossing over to join the research training system.

From a structural perspective, advanced or "graduate" training begins with admission to the DEA program. But this raises the issue of the degree and program structure that underpins advanced training in France. Only with the greatest difficulty and the most improbable of mental gymnastics can this be reconciled with what stands in the British or American systems as a clear boundary between undergraduate and (post) graduate study. The terms "preadvanced" and "advanced" have been chosen to describe the French case and to remind readers that categories familiar and valid in their own establishments are not always applicable elsewhere, that it is not always useful to pretend that because two or more countries share the same terminology that it is universally appropriate. Conceptually, few of the assumptions that underlie "undergraduate" study in Britain and the United States find an echo in France. Preadvanced studies are organized into two cycles, each of two years' duration. The first cycle, as has been pointed out, leads to the Diplôme Universitaire de Technologie (DUT) in the IUTs and to the Diplôme d'Etudes Universitaires Générales (DEUG) at the university.[18] Second-cycle studies involve a further two years, terminating in a master's degree. Within this second cycle there is a highly vocational, specialized track leading to such awards as the *Maîtrise en Science et Techniques* and *Maîtrise en Sciences de Gestion*, which are intended to develop immediately usable and relevant skills for industry and commerce. Parallel to them is a "research master's" track that is directly aligned with the DEA; it also includes master's courses that prepare for a career in schoolteaching.[19]

One conceptual difference involves the dividing line between first- and second-cycle studies. It is less hard and fast than the division between under and (post) graduate. First-cycle studies are not self-contained. They tend to lead on automatically to the second. Those entering employment straight from the university first cycle tend to be looked upon as dropouts.[20]

The second difference is at the level of the qualification obtained at the end of the second cycle, assuming for a moment one is uncharitable enough to argue that the end of that cycle is the equivalent of the end of undergraduate study in Britain and the United States. If the duration is the same, the qualification is not. If undergraduate study in the United States ends with the bachelor's degree, the second cycle in France ends with the Maîtrise. In other words, the French preadvanced study overlaps into what in Anglo-American universities would firmly be part of graduate study. Whether the "take off" into advanced work in France is accomplished from a more demanding intellectual base, assuming that the Maîtrise is more demanding, is purely a matter of personal judgment.

A third difference is perhaps more striking from an American than from a British perspective. This is the presence of professionally oriented courses within the first cycle; in the United States these would form part of graduate schools—medicine, law, engineering. Indeed, some 40 percent of first-cycle students are enrolled in courses of a vocational (*professionnel*) or applied nature. The absence of graduate schools is in part a reflection that the liberal arts—or to use a Gallicism, *"culture generale"*—is not part of the undergraduate program but of the upper secondary school curriculum.[21]

The Structure of Doctoral Degrees

The reforms of 1984 introduced a new form of doctorate, the so-called single doctorate (*Doctorat unique*). Previously, study at this level had been crowned with one of four types of doctoral degrees. These ranged from the monumental *Doctorat d'Etat*, first set down in 1820, which in certain humanities fields could take upwards of ten to fifteen years to gather research material, though five years was often thought sufficient.[22] At the other end of the scale was the *Doctorat d'Université*, which, lasting no more than two years, was not a national diploma and was thus bereft of academic *gravitas*. Between them lay the *Doctorat d'Ingénieur*, demanding between one and two years' study and reserved for graduates of engineering schools, and the so-called *Doctorat de Troisième Cycle*. The latter is best rendered as "short-cycle doctorate." It took between one and two years after the DEA and, for many, acted as a preliminary to the Doctorat d'Etat. It served to demonstrate an aptitude for research by contrast with the massive state doctorate, proof final of the ability to make an original contribution to scholarship and research on the basis of sustained effort.

Clearly this structure of multiple doctorates demonstrates that advanced training in France contained two features beyond the usual disciplinary divisions found in Anglo-American university systems. The additional dimensions were both horizontal and vertical; horizontal in setting aside a special award for engineers; vertical in that the shorter, third-cycle doctorate acted as a filtering device for that summmum of academic endeavor and erudition incarnated in the Doctorat d'Etat.

This structure of multiple doctorates was abolished with almost indecent speed by the Law of July 5, 1984.[23] It gave way to a single doctoral degree, earned in three to five years, to be followed later by a *Habilitation*. The latter was to be awarded on the basis of an individual's overall contribution to scholarship over a sustained period and the ability to supervise research. As yet relatively few people have gone through this hurdle. In theory, however, it is intended, like its German namesake, to provide proof of a person's ability to reach the highest levels in the research system.

Governmental initiative to "re-profile" the structure of doctoral-level study in France came as a specific response to the need to forge closer links between the research system on the one hand and the research training system on the other. Though some have argued that the reform is more apparent than real and that the Habilitation simply replaced the Doctorat d'Etat, considerable tensions were generated within academia. In effect the old division between the Doctorat de Troisième Cycle and the Doctorat d'Etat marked an important operational boundary between the system of advanced training and the research system. Before the reform, training *for* research was carried out in the university and was sanctioned by the award of the third-cycle doctorate. The more sustained initiation into "being" a researcher—that is, training by dint of doing research—was the task of the research system and more particularly of the research team, once a person had been granted temporary status as a probationary *attaché de recherche*. The Doctorat d'Etat, at least in the physical and natural sciences, was often defended and taken while employed in a research agency.[24]

The Doctorat de Troisième Cycle thus acted as a boundary post, marking the point where initial training for research ended and where the difficult induction into the world of professional research began. It also marked the limits of that part of the advanced training system over which the university exercised a monopoly separate from that of the research system. The latter, organizationally, remained only partially under the control of the university and, in the physical and the exact sciences, largely came under the aegis of the CNRS. Thus, the duality of doctorates corresponded to a functional duality between advanced training and full-time research systems, which has long been a salient feature of French higher education. Since the issues arising from the 1984 change have direct implications for the interrelationship between the two systems, we will return later to a more detailed analysis.

Student Flows into Advanced Education

Having set out the structure and examined some of the recent reforms in advanced education in France, we now turn our attention to student flows. Is the system of initial training under pressure? If so, in which areas? What trends, if any, has France shared with other European states in pre-advanced and advanced training? From the mid-seventies onward, a time when in many European countries the number of students entering the "zone of initial training" around third-cycle studies was stabilizing or diminishing, France faced pressure from numbers.[25] Between 1976 and 1982, rates of growth for the DEA (Diploma of Advanced Studies, Bacc+5) and its vocational counterpart—the *Diplôme d'Etudes Supérieures Spécialisées*—were around 8 percent per year. Explanations for this development are not, however, homogeneous across different disciplines. In the humanities and social sciences students may have been prolonging study in order to shelter themselves from the economic blizzard raging outside the university, a "push factor" that brought more of them into the zone of initial training. In the fields of management and economics, the student growth rates for the DESS alone from 1978 on were about 12 percent per year. The buoyant demand from industry for students qualified in these fields was one reason given for the increase.[26]

Whatever the explanation, the effect of the economic crisis was to bring more students forward to that part of the preadvanced system that was linked to the research training system. This occurred even though the preadvanced system itself acted as a "cooling out" zone. How intense this pressure was upon the scheme of initial research training can be shown when one examines the output of diplomates. At the level of Bacc+5, the number of diplomates from the DEA and the DESS combined rose from 12,824 in 1976 to 24,381 in 1984. Growth was particularly intense in the humanities which, during the four years from 1976 to 1980, increased by some 88 percent, stabilizing thereafter. A similar growth rate was evident for management and economics students, while those in the exact sciences more than doubled from 3,561 to 8,334.

Unfortunately, the way statistics are gathered does not permit a precise control for different types of doctorate. Nevertheless, taking all doctoral degrees together, third-cycle as well as state doctorate, the output rose from 5,875 in 1975 to 8,304 in 1984, an increase of 41 percent. Given the time required to complete studies at this level, this pattern is likely to be a lagged response to the buildup at the DEA level. Expansion therefore is likely to continue and even accelerate, if some of the measures now being developed by the government to tempt more students into high-level research by financial inducement are effective.

No less interesting is the evidence of the increasing numerical importance of students in the exact sciences as one moves through the three cycles that make up preadvanced and advanced training in France. In 1984, of all first-cycle students (Bacc+2), those awarded diplomas in science accounted for just under one in five; in the second cycle, the corresponding statistic was just under one in four; at the level of Bacc+5 (that is, those holding DESS or DEA diplomas), one in three; and at the doctoral level, more than six out of ten diplomates. Thus, the scientific fields accounted for only a minority of all diplomates at the end of the first cycle but had the largest outflow at the doctoral level.

The reverse is true for the humanities, a field which, in 1984, accounted for 38 percent of all diploma holders at first-cycle level but represented only some 28 percent of all doctoral degrees. Finally, we see an equally tantalizing balance of diplomates in law, economics, and management. One-third of all DEA/DESS diplomates hailed from these fields, but they accounted for less than one in thirteen of all doctoral awards.

This situation can be explained structurally. In law, economics, and management, few students continue into research training because that would leave them open to the charge by employers of being "overqualified." Even so, regarding output, the disciplinary characteristic of the university-based research training system is more similar to the "professional" full-time research system than to either the first or second cycles. While the research training sector inclines heavily toward the exact sciences, the university beneath it tilts toward the social sciences and the humanities. There is a caesura between what we have termed preadvanced studies and advanced education in French universities. And while, as in British or American universities, this break is in part determined by level of study, it is also in the French context influenced by discipline as well.

THE RESEARCH SYSTEM

If the basic structures of France's research system were drawn up immediately prior to World War II, their subsequent development has added a large number of "sectoral" research bodies. Among the most important additions that emerged over the ensuing four decades are: the *Institut National de la Santé et de la Recherche Médicale (INSERM)*, centralizing medical research; the *Organisation de Recherche Scientifique pour les Territoires d'Outre-Mer (ORSTOM)* (Research Organization for Overseas Territories); the *Commission a l'Energie Atomique* (Atomic Energy Commission); the *Office National d'Etudes et de Recherche Aerospatiales (ONERA)* (National Bureau for Aerospace Research); and the *Institut National de Recherche Agronomique* (National Agronomics Research Institute). The Fifth Republic (1958 to the present) brought a further injection of agencies: the *Centre National d'Etudes Spatiales* (National Space Research Center); the *Centre National pour l'Exploitation des Océans*; and the *Centre National de Recherche en Informatique et Automatique.*

The establishment of a permanent cadre of full-time researchers dates from the 1930s. By the early 1950s the research staff with the National Center for Scientific Research (CNRS) numbered 2,000; by 1985, it had grown to 26,000—10,500 full-time researchers; 15,300 engineers, technicians, and support staff.[27] Although it is the largest and most important of the nation's research agencies, the CNRS is not the sole public employer of research personnel. The Atomic Energy Commission employs a further 15,000 research staff; 8,200 come under the responsibility of the National Agronomics Research Institute; 4,500 are under the Medical Research Institute; and around 1,800 are employed by the National Space Research Center. Across all sectors—public, private, national defense, and nonprofit-making organizations—over 300,000 persons are engaged in research.

These five national agencies account for some 18 percent of the nation's research personnel. To this should be added the 45,000 university teachers whose research time is held to be half of their paid activity. In full-time equivalents this represents 22,500 additional researchers or 7 percent of all those engaged in research. To continue this recital across the 215 different public research bodies, the 2,000 or so publicly financed research units (*laboratoires*), and the 1,600 private sector and nonprofit-making organizations also engaged in research would be fastidious and pointless. Suffice it to say that by far the greater part of research personnel in the public sector is to be found outside the universities.[28]

Central Organization

The CNRS is organized along horizontal and vertical axes. Arrayed across the horizontal axis are some forty-nine disciplinary sections ranging from plasma physics to the world of classical antiquity. Each section, termed a commission, brings together in a governing body some twenty-two persons of whom thirteen are elected by a constituency of CNRS researchers and university teachers and a further nine are nominated by the director of the CNRS. Their role, that of a nationally designated, official peer-review group, splits into three separate functions. They evaluate yearly the performance of each researcher employed by the CNRS and pass their assessment on to the director, who has the power to declare the slothful and indolent to be redundant. They evaluate applications for promotion, though formally the decision is made by the director after consultation with a directorial body. Finally, they assess applications from university-based research teams seeking advancement to the status of an "associate laboratory," linked to the CNRS.[29]

Together, these forty-nine horizontal commissions form the *Comité National de la Recherche Scientifique*, which acts as the highest level in the interface between the world of organized research and that of public administration. The Comité National constitutes a vital nexus in the distribution of resources, the determination of advancement, and the disbursement of honors. For this very reason it is also the focus of considerable strife between the representatives of unionized research workers and those senior personages in the academic world, often alluded to as the *Mandarinate*, whose loyalty varies between themselves and the Prince!

The vertical axis brings together a number of interdisciplinary research programs, which in turn unite experts from different specializations. Such a grouping is seen as a counterweight to the discipline-based structure. It includes such programs as energy and basic materials, the environment, and the monitoring and prediction of volcanic eruptions.

This organizational matrix is inserted across some seventeen different directorates whose scientific and administrative responsibilities are of a redoubtable complexity in their interlinkage. In the words of an ex-Minister of Higher Education and Research, these directorates are "reliées par une tuyauterie qui ferait pleurer de jalousie un constructeur de raffinerie de pétrole" (linked up by a series of conduits that would cause a builder of oil refineries to weep with envy).[30] Clearly, the internal organization of the CNRS reflects the high degree of centralization one usually associates with French administration, though in the last five years there has been growing pressure to introduce some degree of decentralization.[31]

Research units linked to the CNRS fall into one of two types: *Laboratoires propres* and *Laboratoires associés*. The former are an integrated part of the CNRS, though often physically located inside a university. In 1986 this type of research unit employed some 3,600 full-time research staff.[32] The latter type are by far the more numerous. They are research units located in universities, engineering schools, or specialist institutes such as the *Ecole des Hautes Etudes en Sciences Sociales.* They bring together both full-time researchers paid on CNRS funds and university colleagues. This system of "associated laboratories" grew up in the course of the 1960s as part of the drive to expand France's research base. Today they number around one thousand and employ approximately 5,000 full-time CNRS researchers.

Both Laboratoires propres and Laboratoires associés are known as B1 research units. They form, however, only a part of institutionalized research in the public sector. Following the reorganization of central government in 1976 and the separation of a Secretariat for Higher Education from the Ministry of Education, a Research Directorate was set up to finance and, for the first time, to assess those residual units not falling into the B1 category. This residual group contains two further categories of laboratory. These are B1* or *Laboratoires recommandés*—recognized research units—and B2 units of which all one can say officially is that they number some two thousand as of 1989.[33] B2 research units cover a multitude of sins. They may well be teams of young researchers who provide the "pool" from which future top research teams are constituted. Equally, they can also be groups of "extinct volcanoes," of scholars whose publication record, even if known (and this is not always the case), is not always impressive. Unsung and very often unevaluated, they are often seen as the poor cousins in the family of research.

These differences in designation are highly significant. Not only are they a public statement of quality and potential, but they also carry with them considerable financial reward or penalty. For instance, B1 laboratories are funded directly from the CNRS. They also receive credits from the Research Directorate of the Ministry of Education. Their multiple funding sources, even within the public sector, give them much independence, though this is not always regarded with joy unbounded by the authorities. By contrast, consider the lot of research units carrying a B1* or B2 label. The former are almost exclusively dependent on the largess of the Research Directorate. The latter live from hand to mouth either on the university's internal research budget or on short-term research contracts with industry.

Evidently, the legal conceit in France that all universities are on equal footing does not extend to the research system.[34] There one finds a clear and formal hierarchy of excellence acknowledged by a formal stratification that emerges in the distinct ways in which different types of laboratory are funded. The most superior gain funds directly from the CNRS while the least reputable rely on the crumbs handed out within a university. It follows that competition to transform B2 research units into B1* and, eventually, to full B1 status is fierce.

Though based on the usual criteria of scholarly performance and peer evaluation, this hierarchy is not evenly distributed across the country. Still less is it evenly spread across different institutions. In part the pattern reflects the concentration of students in and around the Paris basin. Of the 905,000 students in all sectors of higher education in 1985–1986, save the University Institutes of Technology, 32 percent were enrolled in the Paris region. The geographical location of associated research units, which from an organizational perspective have the closest resemblance to the usual university-based research group in the United States and Britain, shows a similar skew; some 37 percent are concentrated in the Paris region. More astounding still is that some 15 percent of all France's associated research units are grouped within *two* establishments within Paris itself, the Universities of Paris VI and Paris VII. This is centralization indeed. Outside Paris, there are five other major poles of concentration which, in descending order, are Lyon (6 percent), Aix-Marseille, Grenoble, Montpellier, and Strasbourg. Together, they accounted in 1987 for just under one-quarter of all associated research units.[35]

Organizational Paradigms

Concentration is one hallmark of the French research system. The other is its organizational science model. The paradigm underpinning the organization of the CNRS is one derived from the physical and natural sciences, rather than from the social sciences or the humanities. Official terminology to describe research units hails directly from the more scientific disciplines. Research units are termed "laboratories," regardless of whether they are engaged in particle physics, economics, or sociology. The science paradigm goes beyond mere name-calling; it extends deeply into the expected form academic work will take.[36] The norm of scholarly work that derives from the laboratory model places stress upon the collective nature of the effort, teamwork structured around a shared paradigm or methodology.

More important, this underlying assumption is reflected in the disciplinary distribution of CNRS researchers. In 1981, 28 percent were working in life sciences, 19 percent in chemistry, 13 percent in mathematics and fundamental physics, 8 percent in engineering physics (*Sciences Physiques pour l'Ingénieur*), 5 percent in nuclear physics, 9 percent in the fields of earth, ocean, atmosphere, and space. Those in the social sciences accounted for 12 percent and those in the humanities 7 percent.[37] Less than one in five full-time CNRS researchers are engaged in the nonscience areas.

Such a disciplinary bias suggests that the role of the CNRS is rather different for the social sciences and humanities, where the nature of the work is more individualistic and disciplinary paradigms less clear.[38] Another dimension of disciplinary bias points to another form of segmentation in French higher education: that between preadvanced study, essentially dominated by the humanities and the social sciences, at least insofar as student numbers are concerned, and the professional research system, set off and dedicated to the sciences. We need to explore how the interface between the two operates and what its consequences are for student induction into research training.

The Professional Research System: Entry and Career Structure

The full-time research system has the salient characteristic of possessing its own conditions of entry and its own career structure. Prior to the creation of the single doctorate (Doctorat unique) in 1984, students completed their third-cycle doctorate at the university and, at an average age of twenty-seven, were recruited on a highly competitive basis into the full-time research system with the rank of attaché de recherche. This was a probationary appointment of some four year's duration, during which the person, particularly in the sciences, was expected to complete the Doctorat d'Etat. In effect, postdoctoral training involving research formed the last hurdle in a long transitionary stage that, beginning with the DEA (Bacc+5), took the student through four selective processes and across the dividing line between advanced training in the university and research in the research system. These filtering processes were selection to a DEA program, selection by the director of a laboratory for research support, presentation of a third-cycle doctorate, and finally selection by the appropriate CNRS disciplinary commission. Between 1976 and 1983, around one applicant in six who appeared before a commission was successful.[39]

Like other state bodies in France, the CNRS is separated into a number of "corps," or ranks, admission to which is formally defined by law in the organization's statutes. Advancement at the lower levels is again laid down by statute and is usually dependent on age and seniority. In the upper ranks promotion is governed by individual assessment of performance carried out by the appropriate subject disciplinary commission inside the CNRS.

Promotion from attaché de recherche to *Chargé de Recherche* was strictly conditioned in the past by the successful completion of the Doctorat d'Etat, or today, the Doctorat unique. Promotion to *Maître de Recherche* depends on demonstrating the ability to direct the work of a research group, or under the new arrangements to have gained the Habilitation, which in effect requires demonstrating the same capacities. To reach the heights of *Directeur de Recherche* one must be capable of assuming the leadership of a laboratory or research group.

A typical career path of a professional researcher means promotion to chargé around the age of thirty-six to thirty-eight and to maître between the forty-fourth and forty-sixth birthday. Of one hundred attachés entering the CNRS, about eighty will advance to chargé, forty-eight attain the rank of maître, and twelve will scale the lonely heights to directorship.[40]

With the Doctorat d'Etat completed, or nowadays the Doctorat unique, the approval of the relevant CNRS disciplinary commission and the security of tenure that this brings are not surprisingly highly attractive, especially when one is trained as a researcher, rarely if ever as a university teacher!

THE FUNDING BASE

From a strictly quantitative standpoint France is one of the major systems of higher education in Western Europe. But expenditures for that system are relatively low. Expressed as a proportion of the gross domestic product (GDP), the higher education budget rarely surpassed 0.5 percent, save in the balmiest of years. In 1960 it represented 0.28 percent; in 1969, 0.57 percent; in 1980, 0.39 percent; and in 1985, 0.43 percent. So severe was the degree of budgetary contraction during the 1970s that the slight upturn over the four years from 1981 to 1985 served only to restore the proportion of GDP assigned to higher education to the level it had enjoyed in 1964–1965. In resources devoted to higher education, France, with 0.43 percent of GDP (1985), badly trailed the Netherlands (1.75 percent) and the United States (1.17 percent). From the perspective of per-student expenditure, France is a high numbers, low-cost system.[41]

This general condition extends partially into the research arena. Evidence is contained in a recent international survey of university research expenditures in the major Western European economies.[42] University research expenditures expressed as a percentage of gross national product (GNP) showed France consistently outpaced by the Federal Republic of Germany, Japan, and the United States over the ten years from 1975 to 1985.

Government funding of university-based research in France, which also includes CNRS-funded teams, also differs from other European countries in support given to different fields. Three general areas stand out as receiving relatively privileged treatment. In 1982 these were the physical sciences (19.3 percent of all government spending on university research compared to a six-country average of 11.7 percent), mathematics and computing (10.4 compared with 2.7 percent), and the life sciences (39.2 percent versus 37.0 percent). Conversely, the proportion set side for engineering and arts and humanities was less than generous.[43]

If this gives us some perspective on the place that French research and its funding occupy in an international setting, it does not provide any insight into the nature of the relationships and linkages that flow from and are dependent upon such funding. The first aspect worthy of note is the central position occupied by the CNRS in the country's total budget for civil R&D. In 1985 the CNRS budget amounted to some Fr 9 billion, just under one-quarter of the total.[44] Second, the funding relationship differs among the different categories of research units. Broadly speaking, this relationship falls into three types. A close relationship is reserved for full CNRS research units (Laboratoires propres) and associate research units (Laboratoires associés). Both are "direct grant" organizations: their support comes directly from the CNRS, without passing through the university administration. To be sure, university presidents may be informed that resources have been attributed to such units of this category as happen to be located in their establishments. But notification is a matter of courtesy, not a right. Effectively, though B1 research units are located in a university setting, they are not dependent on the fortunes of their host. Financially they are unquestioningly the children of the central agency, though they may also seek funding from other sources as well. Top units have multiple funding structures. In 1986 CNRS support, excluding personnel costs, was Fr 550 million for Laboratoires propres and Fr 480 million for associated research units.

A second, looser relationship involves B1* research units. Their funding is derived in the main from the Research Directorate of the Ministry of Education and the Ministry of Research and Technology. Though diversely and externally funded, B1* units are not guaranteed long-term support to the same degree as either full CNRS or associate units. The third pattern of relationship, reserved for B2 units, is almost a mirror image of the first. They are highly dependent on internal institutional funds or on short-term contract work. They cannot apply for CNRS funding.

The flow of funds is not the only dimension in the relationship between center and periphery. There is another resource no less vital: the allocation of human capital. We have seen that the CNRS has its own career structure and recruitment policy. It also allocates its own staff to B1 laboratories. Thus top-flight research units consolidate their position. Financial resources permit B1 units to recruit short-term research and support staff from within the university sector.[45]

The high degree of formal stratification between different types of research units and their relationship to the CNRS emerges as yet another example of organizational differentiation in French higher education. From the standpoint of the type of linkages created with the university, it is curious indeed. The higher the standing of a unit, the greater the opportunities it has to detach itself, both organizationally and financially, from the university. The less fortunate and unrecognized, the more it is dependent on its university environment. If we bear in mind what many see as the gross underfunding of French higher education, then this resource differentiation assumes an even greater significance. Internal institutional resources for support and technical staff, as many government reports have noted, are pitiable in the extreme. Those whose devotion to scholarship is such that they are obliged to employ assistants, and who have neither agreements of association with the CNRS nor contracts with outside bodies, are likely to find themselves paying out of their own pockets.[46]

Finally, just as we saw a concentration of research laboratories around the Paris region, so it is not surprising to find a similar concentration in the research budget. An examination of the spread of institute-based research (*Credits pour la recherche intérieure*) for 1985 reveals that 53 percent of a total outlay, equal to $4 billion (U.S.), was absorbed by the Paris region, with the next highest concentration of 8.5 percent and 7.5 percent appearing in Lyon and Toulouse.

To recapitulate, French higher education in general and the organization of both advanced training and research systems in particular, are grounded upon different structures and repose on models different from those found in Anglo-American universities. The main features of the advanced training system are its comparatively close ties to what we have termed preadvanced study and its high degree of specialization. The two levels, preadvanced and advanced, have in common a vertical differentiation or tracking between professional degree and research-oriented programs. In turn the research system has many outstanding features, beginning with its degree of physical and financial concentration and its heavy disciplinary bias toward the physical and exact sciences, at least in that part of it funded and organized separately from the university. Equally remarkable is the degree of formal stratification in the conditions under which different types of research units operate. So different are the various types of research units in their funding sources and formally attributed status that one may see them as separate elements in a subsystem that links the university in different ways to the research function itself. We need to pay attention to the way the advanced training system and the research system interact.

INTERACTIONS

The University Shapes the Research System

The university primarily shapes the research system in three ways; first, by identifying young talent; second, by providing it with appropriate training; and third, by having jobs available for such talent to take up the challenge of an academic career. All three elements hang together, for there is little that the training system can do to contribute to the quality of the research system if its Ph.D.'s and Docteurs d'Etat are driving taxis or selling vegetables in the local street-corner market.

The growing numbers of students seeking advanced training in the mid- to late-1970s were far from indicative of the system's vigor and vitality. On the contrary, they hid several grave structural weaknesses which, whether taken separately or together, limited drastically the ability of the university-based advanced training system to interact positively with the research system, particularly with that portion located in the university. Two factors account for this breakdown: the drive toward mass higher education ten years earlier and the financial crisis of the mid-1970s.

In common with many other European countries, France had been unable to meet the instructional needs of mass higher education by relying on the output of its advanced training system alone. Expansion in sheer teaching needs at the preadvanced level outstripped the ability of the research training system to meet them. The solution adopted was to recruit large numbers of often inadequately qualified assistants, few of whose earlier careers had brought them even to the outer limits of advanced education. Already by the end of the 1960s, the requirement of having to undergo advanced training as a prior condition of being admitted to academia was partially suspended. In fairness to the governments of the day, the rise of an "instructor class" was not envisaged as a permanent feature in French academia. Nevertheless, under threat of endemic uproar, disturbance, and pressure from the most active and radical assistants' unions, successive governments granted tenure "to them of low degree."[47] By so doing, they confirmed as permanent what previously had been tolerated as a temporary expedient. This meant in effect that for a significant part of university staff the de facto divorce between appointment on the one hand and research training or appropriate research experience on the other was now consummated. And with it went a substantial weakening of the ties between research and teaching.

The conversion of temporary contracts to tenured posts also had dire consequences for recruitment. Coinciding with the post-1973 financial crisis, such a policy froze both recruitment and promotion. More devastating by far, it deprived the university—or, to be more precise, the central administration, since the creation of academic posts and their subsequent allocation to individual universities are among the responsibilities of central bodies—of the opportunity to correct the mediocrity of previous appointments by drawing on the more brilliant products of the advanced training system. This was doubly tragic for, as we have seen, the mid- to late-1970s saw an expansion in the advanced training system, a species of lagged response as the effects of massification worked their way up and through higher education.

The absence of university posts did not pose an immediate threat to the CNRS research system. On the contrary, the absence of employment in the universities gave full-time research an even wider appeal.[48] Thus the segmentation of research between the university and the CNRS research systems appeared to confer a certain degree of immunity on the latter. In the medium term, however, the recruitment freeze appeared to threaten that third element through which the university influences the research system, namely the process of talent identification. This issue caused increasing concern to the authorities from the early 1980s onward and particularly so at the point where preadvanced and advanced education linked up. Such concern led to a series of proposals, few of which were retained, to introduce a fast track for able students within preadvanced education.

Many factors seemed to jeopardize the process of talent identification. Prime among them was the increasing age of those happy and lucky few who embarked on an academic career. The average age of those recruited in 1966 was thirty-two years, and thirty-four years in science; their fellows in 1987 were thirty-eight to forty-one years old. An aging academia, so it was believed, would have less informal contact with young students. No less important, the absence of young academics with research experience deprived able youngsters in preadvanced education of contact with people from a similar age band whose experience in research could fire their imagination. Another factor, blunting the already chipped instrument of university research, was the growing burden of teaching. With academic staff numbers held constant while those of students continued to grow, though less spectacularly than in the 1960s, the teaching load rose. And time devoted to teaching is time lost to research. Government estimates of what ought to be expected in the way of research output from university staff and what effectively they produced, became increasingly defined in terms of a "research deficit."[49] In the view of the authorities, this deficit could be attributed, in part at least, to the persistent burden of mass higher education.

Under normal conditions the university influences its own research system by selecting and training the students who will enter it and who later will renew its cadres. In France mass higher education, by singular perversity of speed and circumstance, broke asunder the process of institutional renewal. If the advanced training system fed into the research system (and, as we shall see, the effect of corporative interests brought about a similar blockage in the CNRS research system), it was largely a one-way flow of trained researchers. The flow rarely fed back to the university. Indeed, the number of those transferring from the CNRS to the university during the late 1970s trickled to a halt.

The Research System Influences the University

If few of those who had exercised responsibilities in the full-time research system crossed back into the world of teaching and research, that does not mean that the research system is without influence on the university. Among other things, the CNRS distributes financial support and human resources in the allocation of its permanent staff to laboratories. It also allocates reputation in a clear and unambiguous manner. Centralization of the major research funding bodies concentrates competition at a national level, and the fewer the number of major agencies, the greater the degree of competition between those seeking funding. And, as we have seen, CNRS influence is pervasive down to the base unit level, particularly in the associated laboratories.

The leverage exercised by the CNRS over the university system is powerful at the institutional level. This is not simply because it acts as a species of academic credit bank where the special coin of exchange, prestige and recognition, is exchanged, bartered over, gained, and lost. There is a historical factor. Prior to the creation in 1984 of the *Comité National d'Evaluation*, which evaluates institutions, the CNRS exercised a virtual monopoly over official peer evaluation. True, the CNRS evaluation procedures applied only to the research domain. They did not extend to teaching, to industry links, and still less to relations with the external community. But the fact that 70 percent of all CNRS workers are physically located in university-based laboratories, and 45 percent in medical research financed by INSERM, gives powerful leverage at the institutional level, whether this is designed or not.[50]

The evaluation of a particular laboratory by the CNRS is often decisive when it comes to choosing whether to develop one specific research orientation within a university as opposed to another. Offically, this is a matter for the scientific council of the individual establishment.[51] But it would be an optimistic or naive council indeed that failed to bear in mind that financial backing and the type of finance available are largely dependent on the assessment of the appropriate CNRS disciplinary commission.

Such leverage emerges in a particularly dramatic manner. By allocating full-time research personnel in addition to funds, the CNRS has the power to determine which establishments are classified as equivalent to "research universities" and which are not. For, in effect, what characterizes a research university in the French setting is the concentration and number of full-time researchers working in it. If we take only senior and tenured staff and set them against the presence of full-time researchers funded by the major research agencies, CNRS included (*organismes de recherche*), we find Strasbourg with 943 academic staff plus 598 full-time research staff; the University of Paris VII with 1,667 and 525; the University of Rennes I in western France with 748 and 109.[52]

One may argue that other indicators are better suited to defining and identifying a research university. Each to his own bent. Either way, a research university is, at base, a concentration of financial and intellectual resources. Since the CNRS is involved in distributing both, it sets the parameters that designate such an establishment. In the academic marketplace it stands as the regulator in the national interest.

Boundary Conflict

In contrast to the universities, the CNRS, even in the difficulties of the mid-1970s, continued to recruit to the tune of 3 percent of its research staff per year. It suffered from overrecruitment during the years 1965–1968. And, like the university, though to a lesser degree, it too came under pressure to grant tenure to junior contract workers (*hors status*) and to emphasize seniority rather than merit as a criterion for advancement. A subsequent slowing down of recruitment had direct repercussions on the articulation between the research system and advanced training. Competition for a place in the full-time research system increased among newly graduated third-cycle doctorands, who now found themselves up against unsuccessful attachés de recherche, fully armed with the Doctorat d'Etat and several articles to their credit. As with the dual career of researcher-teacher in the university, so with full-time researchers: the average age of those recruited rose. In itself it was a trend grave enough, especially in such fields as mathematics and physics where researchers often do their best and most original work when relatively young. But it raised in its wake issues that directly involved the nature of the relationship between the systems of advanced education and research. Should the CNRS recruit young researchers? Or should it admit those whose qualifications—for example, the Doctorat d'Etat—demonstrated proven ability, even if older? If the former, the CNRS would be admitting that one of its functions was the initial training of researchers, a role which, as a professional research body, it had previously eschewed. If the latter, then it risked cutting itself off from young blood. Behind this apparently anodyne issue was a fundamental question of where the boundary between advanced education and the research system was to be drawn. This source of fuzziness became a matter of considerable importance with the arrival to power in 1981 of an administration that had as a priority expanding the nation's scientific and research base.[53]

Expansion of the Research Training Base

The research policy of the French socialist government of 1981 lay in three areas: to give priority to electronics and biomedical research; to strengthen the research training base, especially in engineering; and to redefine the nature of the interface between research, industry, and the university.[54]

This was an extremely radical and ambitious strategy: radical because it sought to forge closer linkages between advanced education and research and between university and industry; ambitious because it sought to give a research base to the engineering grandes écoles, which, by some curious form of historical oversight, had never developed an advanced education system leading on to research.[55] The implications arising from this latter policy were far-reaching. It aimed at linking what many regard as the heart of French elite higher education to research training, which, as noted earlier, was at best an indirect relationship. And it put an end to the monopoly over initial research training, which historically had been vested in the university. The competitive principle that governed the relationship between university and CNRS was thus extended horizontally between the universities and the grandes écoles at the advanced education level (Bacc+5).

Expansion of the horizontal base of advanced education went hand in hand with measures designed, in theory at least, to relocate the marker boundary between advanced education and the professional research system. A key element, noted earlier, was the merging of the four doctoral degrees. Of equal significance, however, was the forging of closer ties between research training and research execution at the DEA level. By dint of ministerial circular, DEA research training was henceforth to be inextricably tied to research teams of solid repute, already associated with the major funding agencies—CNRS, INSERM, etc.[56] The precise implications of this circular are important for several reasons. First, it placed an official responsibility for advanced student training upon accredited research teams that, even if they had already performed this role in fact, had not been formally required to do so. Second, it stipulated that membership of such teams should often be teaching personnel, a requirement that may be interpreted as seeking to restore that link between research training and research execution which policies of the 1970s had sundered. Third, it laid down that research teams in contact with others external to a particular establishment, whether in other universities or in firms, should be involved in advanced education. The latter revealed the clear intent of government to extend the institutional base of advanced student training beyond the university and, where justified, into the private sector itself.

Simultaneously on a different front and against a background of swirling controversy, other measures to restore the research and teaching link were also being undertaken within the university itself. Despite its extremely rough passage, the 1984 Higher Education Guideline Law (*Loi d'Orientation*) sought explicitly to remedy the divorce that had grown up inadvertently during the early 1970s. It did so by creating a new designation for university staff: teacher researchers (*enseignants chercheurs*). In face of railing and scoffing by the more conscientious in academia,[57] this legal instrument, blunt though it was, stood as a serious attempt to redefine academic work and to insure a greater individual commitment to research.

The extension of advanced education laterally into the grandes écoles and vertically beyond the university into industry, and the brutal abolition of the time-honored structure of multiple doctorates, formed part of a strategy launched by an administration bent on harnessing research as the "locomotive" for national recovery. It was also a means of creating a new mobility and interplay between university and research systems, which the combined effects of an overhasty recruitment policy and the financial freeze of the 1970s had brought to a halt. The question such frenetic activity posed was whether the revival of the country's research capacity would extend the power of the CNRS deeper into the system of advanced training. Or would it extend the power of the university over those areas of the research system hitherto coordinated by the CNRS. In short, if more bridges between the university, industry, and the professional research system were to be established, were they to be built up and outward from the university or down and outward from the CNRS? At a time when the university's monopoly over advanced education and training for research had been severely undermined, the issue of coordination was crucial.

Coordination and Conflict

It is now evident that the policy of government rested on top-down coordination, which began to emerge in 1982. Nominations to directorships of CNRS research laboratories, formerly a joint decision by the university president and the director of the CNRS, were brought under the latter's control. More detailed oversight by the center over the activities of CNRS-sponsored laboratories, closer research "steering" from the center, the use of national recruitment competitions to engage researchers whose competencies were in line with government priorities, all gathered momentum as the decade passed. That the Directorate of the CNRS became more proactive in issuing guidelines to both its own and to associated research units was not always welcomed by the scholarly community, however.[58] What was seen by government as a policy of prioritization, rationalization, and coordination appeared in a very different light to the university world. If the CNRS took over increasing responsibility not only for research but, by extending backward advanced education as well, what would remain of the university? The counterattack by the university was an all-out assault not only on the CNRS but also on the research model that agency incarnated. Drawing on foreign examples, principally the United States and Britain, university spokesmen pressed for the breakup of the CNRS, for the integration of its own research units (Laboratoires propres) as autonomous public bodies working within the university, and for the restriction of the CNRS to the status of a research funding council on lines similar to the National Science Foundation or National Institutes of Health in the United States.[59]

This exchange was not a passing expression of exasperation from the university world. That certain sectors of academia should rise against the interference of the professional research system not only shows the differences between them but also raised fundamental issues of control over research training and research. As universities are encouraged to become more independent in seeking outside funding sources, and as the wind of national politics blows strongly in favor of decentralization, of less rigid oversight of a detailed nature by central administration in university affairs, the appeal of other models of research system will continue to exercise its power.[60]

CONCLUSION

Up to 1984 the French research training system rested on a clear though not always efficient distinction between initial training for research and training by research. The former we have designated advanced education or as the initial research training sector. It was, until very recently, a monopoly exercised by the university. This monopoly was removed by the government, largely inspired by the need to expand the research training system as a prior condition of expanding the nation's research base. Research training, at least formally, is being extended into network systems that, based in universities and sometimes in the grandes écoles, are being encouraged to collaborate with and draw upon the world of industry, both private and state supported.[61] We have termed the second part of the research nexus in France the professional research system. It consists of external and sectoral funding agencies that possess their own research units, sign contracts with university-based teams, and have their own financial and legal base. The principal of these is the CNRS.

The particular organizational pattern of the research system gives rise to a further identifying feature of French academia. This is the existence of two types of researchers; the teacher-researcher who as member of a university is expected to devote time to matters of erudition and scholarship, and the professional researcher, whose even-tenored days are taken up with research. For the former, the conditions of employment allocate 50 percent of time to research and 50 percent to teaching. For the latter, if he or she teaches, it is voluntarily. Neither career nor promotion depend on it. They depend on research output. Once granted tenure (*titularisation*) as a civil servant, both types of researchers hold lifetime appointments, guaranteed by the weight of constitutional and administrative law.

Clearly, the nature of academic work is very different for the half-time researcher compared to his full-time fellow. Organizational dualism is then a basic feature of the French research training system. This situation is perhaps better understood as a species of parallelism since, despite the sharing of facilities, despite close collaboration in the task of research and inquiry, the university teacher-researcher and the CNRS researcher exist in different working environments. These environments are characterized by different sources of finance, different bodies for evaluating performance, and, last but not least, differently designated ladder-rank appointments. Two *corps de metier* coexist in the French research training system.

These are not the only features that set the French research training system apart from many of its European neighbors. For one, it is grounded in a physical science paradigm. If this paradigm makes for a relatively unproblematic system of formal evaluation when confined to the sciences, it is more than problematic when it comes to evaluating the social, philosophic or other "value sciences," or the humanities.

A further systemic feature of researcher training in France is the increasing part occupied by the sciences in the output of diplomates as one moves up and into the initial research training system. Why this should be so—the factors that are at play—will be examined in the following chapter. It is an interesting example of the way in which a largely science-based professional research system shapes and molds the training system that feeds it. Organizational and legal separation do not always mean the flow of influence is in one direction.

Another systemic feature, one less surprising to Europeans, is the overwhelmingly public nature of advanced graduate training. Nonstate universities, mainly Catholic, do exist, as do private-sector management schools. But in the former the research base tends to be weak, and the number of students graduating from the latter who move into research training is scarcely visible to the naked eye, let alone to the statistician. Though changes are occurring, especially on the margins of the research system—and we have noted some of them—the pattern has been for research and research training systems in higher education to be public in respect to the establishments feeding them and public in the provenance of their funds. From the time the modern research system was set up fifty years ago, this feature has been scarcely, if at all, altered. Close public control over the research system has long been the norm in the Republic.

The structures of research and research training in France are held together in a state of tension. This tensile structure has its anchor points in the series of successive selective hurdles that are marked by various diplomas and doctorates. Such qualifications fulfill two key functions: they seal off the initial research training system from preadvanced study, which ends at the master's level; they act as avenues of transition and interaction between the two segments of training and professional research. Along the avenues of interaction, new talent is identified, winnowed out, and passed on upward to the world of research. In such a formally segmented system it is important to retain the essentially interactive nature of the relationship between the subsystems. Organizational and formal separation, as this analysis has demonstrated, does not diminish interdependence. Indeed, the interdependent nature of the subsystems emerges in a number of ways. An inability of the research system to absorb the outflow from advanced education risks in the medium term a decline in scientific quality. We have seen that the concern of government over the possible breakdown of the talent identification process in universities which loomed over French higher education in the mid- to late-1970s is a clear demonstration of this interdependence. And the effect of blocked careers upon both university and research system, by weakening the avenues of transition, stands as a further example of interaction.

As elsewhere, recent policies aimed at expanding France's research base have raised fundamental issues. The essential issue is, as perhaps it has always been, at what point does governmental steerage become real control? Is the nature of enhanced state influence itself compatible with the degree of initiative research must display if it is to remain at the cutting edge? French academia is not alone in posing these questions to itself and to its government.

NOTES

1. Kogan and Kogan, *Attack on Higher Education*; Maassen and van Vught, "Janus-Face of Higher Education Policy"; Bauer, "Evaluation in Swedish Higher Education"; Frackmann, "Federal Republic of Germany"; Moscati, "Italy."

2. Neave, "On the Cultivation of Quality, Efficiency and Enterprise," pp. 14, 15.

3. Daalder and Shils, *Universities, Politicians and Bureaucrats*.

4. Declerq, "New Role of the University," pp. 3, 4; Ferné, "Contracting for Sciences in University and Industry," p. 26; Eurich, *Corporate Classrooms*, p. 126.

5. Organisation pour la Coopération et Développement Economiques (OCDE), *Quel Avenir pour les Universitiés?* p. 110 (our translation).

6. Dakin, *Turgot and the Rise of the Physiocrats*; Weisz, *Emergence of Modern Universities*, p. 61.

7. Schwartz, *Pour Sauver l'Université*.

8. Ibid.

9. Comité National d'Evaluation, *Où Va l'Université?* p. 36.

10. One of the major difficulties in comparing education systems arises when the structures of one have no counterpart in another. This is so when dealing with the French *Classes Préparatoires aux Grandes Ecoles* (CPGE). From an American standpoint they would be designated K13–K14. There are some two hundred of these Classes, located in highly prestigious upper secondary schools. Entry to them is determined by the grades earned in the secondary school-leaving examination (Baccalauréat) and by the particular option passed in the exam. There are some thirty-six thousand places in these classes; their curriculum is highly specialized and the level of study so high that it is usually equated with the first two years of university study. The Classes Préparatoires, as their name suggests, prepare students for the various competitive entrance examinations to the grandes écoles. For a more elaborate treatment of this typically French solution to the eternal problem of excellence and democracy, see Neave, "France," p. 15.

11. Neave, "From a Far Flung Field," p. 74.

12. Jilek, *Historical Compendium*, p. 248.

13. Weisz, *Emergence of Modern Universities*, p. 158.

14. Neave, "Strategic Planning, Reforms and Governance"; Neave, "France," pp. 14–15; Organisation for Economic Co-operation and Development (OECD), *Innovation Policy: France*; Bienaymé, "Mésure du Problème Français"; Neave, "Reform of Higher Education."

15. In France these subject areas are studied as they are in Britain and the Federal Republic of Germany, at first-degree level. No professional or graduate schools like the American model exist. Ministère de l'Education Nationale, *Tableau de Bord Edition 1986*, table II-4-1, p. 37.

16. Neave, "France," p. 15. *Sections de Techniciens Supérieurs* are somewhat anomalous in that they are situated atop certain technical upper secondary schools but dispense postsecondary education.

17. Comité National d'Evaluation, *Où Va l'Université?*

18. Doumenc and Gilly, *IUTs*, pp. 50–58.

19. Comité National d'Evaluation, *Où Va l'Université?* p. 108.

20. Lévy-Garboua, "Différenciation des Enseignements Supérieurs."

21. Ben-David, *Centers of Learning*.

22. Ministère de l'Education Nationale, *Demain l'Université: Rapport au Ministere Délégué*; ANDES, *Un An Après La Réforme des Etudes Doctorales*.

23. Bienaymé, "New Reform in French Higher Education," pp. 160–162.

24. Massenet, *Rapport au Premier Ministre*, p. 108.

25. Organisation pour la Coopération et Développement Economiques (OCDE), *Enseignement de Troisième Cycle des Années 1980*, p. 104.

26. Ibid., pp. 20, 73, 20.

27. Devacquet, *Amibe et l'Etudiant*, p. 162.

28. Comité National d'Evaluation, *Où Va l'Université?* p. 133; Massenet, *Rapport au Premier Ministre*, p. 52; Comité National d'Evaluation, *Où Va l'Université?* p. 132.

29. Devacquet, *Amibe et l'Etudiant*, pp. 166–167.

30. Ibid., p. 172.

31. See, for example, "L'Heure de Vérité de la Recherche Universitaire," *Le Monde Campus*, 18 janvier 1990, p. 13.

32. Comité National d'Evaluation, *Où Va l'Université?* p. 131.

33. "Heure de Vérité," p. 13.

34. Massenet, *Rapport au Premier Ministre*, p. 81; Furth, "New Hierarchies," pp. 145ff.

35. Ministère de l'Education Nationale, *Tableau de Bord*, pp. 34–35; "Heure de Vérité."

36. Becher, "Cultural View."

37. "La Recherche," p. 42.

38. Massenet, *Rapport au Premier Ministre*, pp. 28, 47; "La Recherche," p. 15.

39. Massenet, *Rapport au Premier Ministre*, p. 48n; proportion calculated from pp. 37, 44–46.

40. "La Recherche," p. 15.

41. Devacquet, *Amibe et l'Etudiant*, p. 111; Bienaymé, "Deux Millions d'Etudiants en l'An 2.000," p. 10; Jallade, "Expenditure on Higher Education in Europe," p. 43.

42. The differences in definitions are important. Gross national product takes into account all elements of production by nationals in a nation's economic system. The gross domestic product, however, is the total amount of value added by firms and businesses within a particular nation irrespective of their nationality; i.e., it also includes foreign firms. Ministrie van Onderwijs en Wetenschappen, *Dutch Higher Education and Research*, pp. 82, 78, Table 1.2.1.2.

43. Ibid.

44. *Recherche et Universités, Ministère de l'Education Nationale*, p. 10; Rapport Durry, *Condition des Enseignants*, p. 12; "Heure de Vérité."

45. "Heure de Vérité"; Rapport Durry, *Condition des Enseignants*, p. 12.

46. *Recherche Publique, Recherche Publique en 1985*.

47. Devacquet, *Amibe et l'Etudiant*, p. 181; Neave and Rhoades, "Academic Estate," pp. 230–232; Conférence des Recteurs Européens, "European University Systems: Part 1," pp. 64–65.

48. *Recherche et Universités, Ministère de l'Education Nationale*, p. 15.

49. Rapport Durry, *Condition des Enseignants*, p. 32; Comité National d'Evaluation, *Où Va l'Université?* p. 145; Rapport Durry, *Condition des Enseignants*, p. 43; *Recherche et Universités, Ministère de l'Education Nationale*, p. 14.

50. Clark, *Perspectives on Higher Education*, p. 270; *Recherche et Universités, Ministère de l'Education Nationale*, p. 58.

51. *Recherche Publique, Recherche Publique en 1985*, p. 48.

52. Comité National d'Evaluation, *Où Va l'Université?* table pp. 58–59.

53. Ibid., p. 144; Massenet, *Rapport au Premier Ministre, Annex 8*, p. 109; Devacquet, *Amibe et l'Etudiant*, p. 174; Massenet, *Rapport au Premier Ministre*, pp. 52, 31; Republique Française, *France en 1981; Elément Moteur pour Sortir de la Crise*.

54. *Recherche Publique, Recherche Publique en 1985*, p. 49; *Rapport Annexe à la IIe Loi du Plan*.

55. Rapport Annuel, *Rapport Annuel sur l'Evolution de la Politique Nationale*, p. 58.

56. Organisation pour la Coopération et Développement Economiques (OCDE), *Enseignement du Troisième Cycle des Années 1980*, pp. 87–98.

57. Bienaymé, "New Reform in French Higher Education," pp. 160–161.

58. Comité National d'Evaluation, *Où Va l'Université?* p. 141; *Recherche et Universités, Ministère de l'Education Nationale*, pp. 9–10.

59. Milhaud, "Université Est Bureaucratisée."

60. "Heure de Vérité," p. 13.

61. Comité National d'Evaluation, *Presentation du Rapport d'Evaluation: Université Rennes*.

BIBLIOGRAPHY

ANDES. *Un An Après la Réforme des Etudes Doctorales: Debat Organisé par l'ANDES.* Paris: Association des Docteurs des Sciences, 1985.

Bauer, Marianne. "Evaluation in Swedish Higher Education: Some Recent Trends and the Outlines of a Model." *European Journal of Education* 23, nos. 1–2 (1988): 25–36.

Becher, Tony. "The Cultural View." In *Perspectives on Higher Education: Eight Disci-*

plinary and Comparative Views, ed. Burton R. Clark. Berkeley, Los Angeles, London: University of California Press, 1984. Pp. 165–196.

Ben-David, Joseph. *Centers of Learning: Britain, France, Germany, United States.* New York: MacGraw-Hill, 1977.

Bienaymé, Alain. "The New Reform in French Higher Education," *European Journal of Education* 19, no. 2 (1984): 151–164.

———. "Deux Millions d'Etudiants en l'An 2.000: Que Demande la France de l'Enseignement Supérieur?" *Cahiers de l'Université Paris IX Dauphine* 152 (1987).

———. "La Mésure du Problème Français." *Chroniques d'Actualité de la SEDEIS* XXXVI, no. 315 (mars 1987): 102.

Clark, Burton R., ed. *Perspectives on Higher Education: Eight Disciplinary and Comparative Views.* Berkeley, Los Angeles, London: University of California Press, 1984.

Comité National d'Evaluation. *Où Va l'Université? Rapport du Comité National d'Evaluation.* Paris: Gallimard, 1987.

———. *Présentation du Rapport d'Evaluation: Université Rennes.* Paris: Service des Publications du Comité, 1989.

Conférence des Recteurs Européens. "European University Systems: Part 1," *Bulletin de la CRE* 75 (1986): 64–65.

Daalder, Hans, and Edward Shils, eds. *Universities, Politicans and Bureaucrats: Europe and the United States.* Cambridge: Cambridge University Press, 1982.

Dakin, F. W. *Turgot and the Rise of the Physiocrats.* London: George Allen, 1957.

Declerq, Guido. "The New Role of the University in an Information Society: The Transfer of Technology." *Report to the Division of Higher Education and Research Document CCPU* (85) 4. Strasbourg: Council of Europe [photocopy].

Devacquet, Alain. *L'Amibe et l'Etudiant: Université et Recherche: l'Etat d'Urgence.* Paris: Editions Odile Jacob, 1988.

Doumenc, Michel, and Jean-Pierre Gilly. *Les IUTs: Ouverture et Ideologie.* Paris: Editions du Cerf, 1977.

Durand Prinborgne, Claude. "Les Tendances Actuelles de la Politique de l'Enseignement Supérieur en France." *European Journal of Education* 23, nos. 1–2 (1988): 105–123.

Eurich, Nell P. *Corporate Classrooms: The Learning Business.* Princeton, N.J.: Carnegie Foundation for the Advancement of Teaching, 1985.

Ferné, Georges. "Contracting for Sciences in Universities and Industry." *European Journal of Education* 20, no. 1 (1985): 23–30.

Frackmann, Edgar. "Resistance to Change, the Survival of German Higher Education." *European Journal of Education* 25, no. 2 (1990): 187–202.

Furth, Dorothea. "New Hierarchies in Higher Education." *European Higher Education* 17, no. 2 (1982): 145–151.

Haut Comité Education-Economie. *Education-Economie: Qual Système Educatif pour la Société de l'An 2.000? Rapport Presente au Ministre de l'Education Nationale.* Paris: La Documentation Française, 1988.

Jallade, Jean Pierre. "Expenditure on Higher Education in Europe: Past Trends and Future Prospects." *European Journal of Education* 15, no. 1 (1980): 42–43.

Jilek, Lubor. *Historical Compendium of European Universities.* Geneva: Conférence des Recteurs Européens, 1984.

Kogan, Maurice, and Philip Kogan. *The Attack on Higher Education*. London: Kogan Page, 1983.

Lamour, Jean, and Maria Lamour Rentopolou. "France: Un Bilan Intermédiaire." *European Journal of Education* 23, nos. 1–2 (1988): 37–46.

Lévy-Garboua, Louis. "Différenciation des Enseignements Supérieurs Notamment en Premier Cycle." In *Documents Annexes à Demain l'Université: Rapport au Ministre Délégué Chargé de la Recherche et de l'Enseignement Supérieur.* Paris, 1987 [mimeo].

Maassen, Pieter, and Frans van Vught. "The Janus-Face of Higher Education Policy: The Netherlands." *European Journal of Education* 23, no. 2, 1–2 (1988): 65–76.

Massenet, Michel. *Rapport au Premier Ministre sur l'Emploi Scientifique.* Paris: La Documentation Française, 1979.

Milhaud, Gérard. "L'Université Est Bureaucratisée, Politisée et Syndicalisée." *Quotidien de Paris* (March 15, 1986): 6.

Ministère de l'Education Nationale. *Tableau de Bord Edition 1986: Année Scolaire et Universitaire 1985–1986.* Paris: Ministère de l'Education Nationale, 1988.

————. *Demain l'Université: Rapport au Ministre Délégué Chargé de la Recherche et de l'Enseignement Supérieur.* Paris: Ministère de l'Education Nationale, 1988.

Ministrie van Onderwijs et Wetenschappen. *Dutch Higher Education and Research: Major Issues—Facts and Figures.* Zoetermeer: Ministrie van Onderwijs et Wetenschappen, 1988.

Moscati, Roberto. "Italy." In *Prometheus Bound: The Changing Relationship Between Government and Higher Education in Europe*, ed. Guy Neave and Frans van Vught. Oxford: Pergamon Press, 1991. Pp. 91–107.

Neave, Guy. "France." In *The School and the University: An International Perspective*, ed. Burton R. Clark. Berkeley, Los Angeles, London: University of California Press, 1985.

————. "Strategic Planning, Reforms and Governance in French Higher Education." *Studies in Higher Education* 10, no. 1 (1985): 7–20.

————. "On Being Economical with University Autonomy." In *Autonomy in Higher Education*, ed. Malcolm Tight. Milton Keynes, England: Open University Press for SRHE, 1988.

————. "On the Cultivation of Quality, Efficiency and Enterprise: An Overview of Recent Trends in Higher Education in Western Europe, 1986–1988." *European Journal of Education* 23, 1–2 (1988): 7–23.

————. "From a Far Flung Field: Some Considerations of Robbins from a European Perspective." *Oxford Review of Education* 14, no. 1 (1988): 69–80.

————. "The Reform of Higher Education, or the Ox and the Toad: A Fabulous Tale." *Higher Education Quarterly* 42, no. 4 (Autumn 1988): 354–369.

Neave, Guy, and Gary Rhoades. "The Academic Estate in Western Europe." In *The Academic Profession: National, Disciplinary, Institutional Settings*, ed. Burton R. Clark. Berkeley, Los Angeles, London: University of California Press, 1987. Pp. 211–270.

Office of Technology Assessment. *Commercial Bio-technology: An International Analysis.* Report No. OTA-BA, 218. Washington, D.C.: Office of Technology Assessment, 1984.

Organisation for Economic Co-operation and Development (OECD). *Innovation Policy: France.* Paris, 1986.

Organisation pour la Coopération et Développement Economiques (OCDE). *L'Enseignement du Troisième Cycle des Années 1980.* Paris, 1987.

——. *Quel Avenir pour les Universités?* Paris, 1987.

Rapport Annexe à la IIe Loi du Plan. Les Moyens d'Exécution du IXe Plan. Paris: La Documentation Française, 1985.

Rapport Annuel. *Rapport Annuel sur l'Evolution de la Politique Nationale de Recherche et Développement Technologique.* Paris: Conseil Supérieur de la Recherche et de la Technologie, 1986.

Rapport Durry. *La Condition des Enseignants de l'Enseignement Supérieur: Rapport à Monsieur le Ministre Délégué Chargé de la Recherche et de l'Enseignement Supérieur.* Paris, (January) 1988 [mimeo].

"La Recherche: Un Avenir." *Avenirs* 346 (September 1983): 13–17.

Recherche et Universités. Ministère de l'Education Nationale: Comité National d'Evaluation des Etablissements Publics à Caractère Scientifique, Culturel et Professionel. Paris, (October) 1986 [mimeo].

Recherche Publique. *La Recherche Publique en 1985: Rapport Statistique.* Paris: La Documentation Française, 1988.

Republique Française. *La France en 1981 Tome IV l'Enseignement et le Développement Scientifique.* Paris: La Documentation Française, 1981.

——. *Un Elément Moteur pour Sortir de la Crise: Annexé III des Actes du Colloque National: Recherche et Technologie.* Paris: La Documentation Française, 1982.

Schwartz, Laurent. *Pour Sauver l'Université.* Paris: Le Seuil, 1983.

Weisz, George. *The Emergence of Modern Universities in France, 1863–1914.* Princeton, N.J.: Princeton University Press, 1983.

SIX

The Research Training System in France
A Microstudy of Three Academic Disciplines

Guy Neave and Richard Edelstein

The previous chapter examined the two subsystems of research and research training in France, the structures within which they are located, their development, and the interactions between them. The macroperspective revealed several features of prime importance to understanding the differences between the French and other advanced systems of student training, such as the British or American. These differences may be grouped under the two topics of curricular structures and the location of research training and research itself.

In the curricular domain French first degrees (Bacc+2) bear greater similarity to the British system than to those in the United States. They tend to be specialized. The functional equivalent to what in American terminology would be termed a liberal arts curriculum is not found in higher education. It is instead located in upper secondary schooling. Second, French higher education does not share with its British or its American counterparts a clear distinction between undergraduate and (post) graduate work. Rather, the transition is more gradual with advanced work beginning five years after entry with the *Diplôme d'Etudes Approfondies* (DEA). Third, major reforms have been introduced since the mid-seventies in both the orientation of "advanced education" and the structure of doctoral degrees. The former, associated with the reforms of 1976, strengthened a vocational bias that, in common with many other European systems of higher education, is also present at first-degree level. The latter replaced a highly stratified and differentiated series of doctoral degrees with a single *Doctorat unique*, modeled on the Anglo-American Ph.D.

Advanced research training has traditionally been operated as a virtual monopoly by the university, though certain exceptions existed and provided a powerful intellectual input to the research system from establishments such as the *Ecole Normale Supérieure* and the *Ecoles des Hautes Etudes en Sciences Sociales*. The nonuniversity sector did not have a research training mission. Either it provided short-cycle technician-type education or it furnished extremely high-level training for the art of administration, government, and the state technical services, the latter in the shape of the *grandes écoles*. Finally, the location of research as opposed to research training is embedded in an organizational and institutional context very different from that of either the United States or Britain. Put succinctly, the research system is segmented. There is a full-time research system, financed, supported, defined, and evaluated by the *Centre National de la Recherche Scientifique* and a part-time research system whose members are also tenured university teachers.

Against this background, this chapter examines what it means to be a research student in France, using three disciplinary fields—physics, economics, and history—to give a purchase upon such matters as "inculturation" into disciplines and the pathways that students must take and the obstacles they must cope with in their passage from lecture hall to research laboratory. Three universities were chosen: a leading Paris establishment with a reputation of being at the cutting edge in physics and the exact sciences, a large provincial university in Western France, and a relatively small establishment recently founded in the wine-growing area at the head of the Rhône Valley.

THE DISCIPLINARY CONTEXT

The disciplines of physics, economics, and history are indeed international in scope in their scholarly community and in their networks. But they also exist in very specific national settings and are shaped by institutional and organizational characteristics that, in turn, affect the way the individual is inducted into and passes along the path from student to fully fledged researcher. These characteristics provide us with a more nuanced view of the relationship between the training system and the segments of the research system.

Physics more than any other single discipline has served as an organizational paradigm in the structure and nomenclature of the French research system. Although all physics is not big physics, research in this domain often demands heavy investment in equipment, sustained over a long period. The policy of successive governments has concentrated physics research around certain major laboratories in the Universities of Grenoble, Paris VI, Paris VII, and Paris XI Orsay. On their own, these four establishments bring together over half of all CNRS researchers. The cost-intensive nature of nuclear and particle physics has led to the creation of a separate funding and policy-making body with specific national oversight. The *Institut National de la Physique Nucléaire et de la Physique des Particules*

(INNPPP) plays a commanding role. It assigns time on major national facilities (*grands appareils*) to individuals and laboratories. Key decisions lie in the hands of a national commission made up of some twenty-five members.

Centralized decision making and the concentration of resources heavily influence the culture of this domain, which is characterized by fierce competition between laboratories for resources. It also creates a clear hierarchy of academic excellence and an awareness of it among the personnel of competing institutions. For physics, and especially theoretical and fundamental physics, the CNRS is the main reference pole, a feature accentuated by the system of evaluations every four years which has long been part of science policy. As one of our interviewees informed us, "Le CNRS, c'est un signe de famille" (Being with the CNRS means you are one of the family).

Though especially pronounced in nuclear and particle physics, concentration of, and dependence on, centrally allocated resources appears to be less intense in the applied areas of the field, such as microelectronics and solid state physics. In part this situation derives from the policy of strengthening links with regional industry, which has brought in significant third-party resources, a relatively recent development. Naturally, the boundary between the two subdomains of physics is shifting, and never more than at the present. Even so, there are substantial locational differences between the subfields, for while the majority of big science laboratories are managed via the CNRS, the majority of applied physics laboratories are located inside universities.

The major contextual difference that, until two decades ago, operated in economics was its location as part of the Faculty of Law. One explanation for this historically unique pattern is that economics was regarded as part of the sciences of public resource distribution which went hand in hand with planning, with law acting as the means of implementation. Since then, as elsewhere, economics in France has divided into approximately three major subfields: theoretical economics and econometrics; political economy oriented toward sociological, political, or historical issues: and, finally, microeconomics, finance, and economics of the firm (*Economie de l'Entreprise*), fields which, in the United States, would usually fall under the purlieu of business studies. Although the CNRS does act as a reference point in economics, it is by no means exclusively so. Among other bodies to which the economics field looks are the *Institut National de Statistique et d'Etudes Economiques*, a major governmental research agency responsible for the official compilation of national statistics and economic surveys, and the *Commissariat Général du Plan*, which for the past forty years has acted as the national planning agency at an interministerial level. A final characteristic that economics shares with medicine and law is a special national competition, the *agrégation de l'enseignement supérieur*, which stands as the conditio sine qua non for those in the field who seek full professorial status. Candidates were usually assessed on the basis of their portfolio *after* having defended the now-defunct *Doctorat d'Etat*.

CNRS support for economics by funding *laboratoires propres* and *laboratoires associés*, though substantial, is less massive than in physics. By contrast, the backing it gives to history is penurious in the extreme. Of the 20,000 or so full-time CNRS researchers, approximately 100 are historians. Only two history research units have received the title of laboratoire propre, both at Paris: the *Institut de l'Histoire du Temps Présent* and the *Institut de l'Histoire Moderne et Contemporaine*. In many respects the discipline of history stands as the polar opposite to physics in its research and reference network. If certain institutions, namely the *Ecole des Chartes*, the *Ecole d'Athénés*, and the *Ecole Normale Supérieure*, form for some, especially in the area of archaeology and ancient history, the top establishments, history more than the other two disciplines is characterized by substantial political and ideological differences. It is the classic domain of "clusters and patrons": a historian noted that "a top historian is usually someone who has a group of scholars whose work he inspires."

In history both the research training and the research base are located in the university sector, thereby placing it at the opposite end of the continuum to physics where the largest units of the research system remain organizationally separate. There is, however, another characteristic of history unique to France, one that not only deeply affects the processes of inculturation and intellectual socialization but also sets a unique relationship across the boundary between general education and specialist training. A key requirement to prepare for doctoral studies in history is to have successfully sat one of two massively competitive national examinations—the *Certificat d'Aptitude Pedagogique de l'Enseignement Secondaire* (CAPES) or the *Agrégation du Secondaire*. These examinations—the latter of which consists of four papers of seven hours each plus an oral examination!—serve to identify the most talented students for teaching in lower and upper secondary schools. They are not of themselves formal requirements to be able to enter a doctoral program. Rather they provide the financial support via teaching for candidates to undertake the arduous and often extremely lengthy process of preparing a thesis.

Such an arrangement has several consequences that set history off from the other two disciplines. Doctoral students in history tend in greater part to be pursuing a full-time job in addition to their research. This is certainly not true in physics, although some students in economics do support themselves in part-time employment by acting as "classroom minders" (*surveillants, "pions"*). That many of the top historians have taught in secondary school also sets a particular professional commitment to teaching which strongly pervades the value system of the discipline. The fully fledged and newly doctored historian tends to be older than his or her counterpart in the other two fields. Finally, while most trained historians remain inside the education system, they are mainly found not in the university but in the secondary school.

One may make three observations about this pattern: in many respects it is a holdover from an earlier and perhaps more leisured epoch when upper secondary schooling still remained in its elite stage; it constitutes a rare if clear example of the way in which schools directly influence the university;[1] it indicates that the "community" of historical scholarship in France is far from being confined to academe alone.

What emerges clearly from the three disciplines is the very considerable difference in their relationship between research training and the two parts of the segmented research system. In physics the dominant pattern is marked by a duality in which the greater part of research is financed and carried out under the auspices of the CNRS. In economics the commanding heights are less clearly dominated by the professional research system. History is almost totally detached from the CNRS, and firmly located, both in respect of its training and its research, in the education system, though not always in the university.

LOCATION, SIZE, AND THE CONDITIONS
OF ACADEMIC WORK

Two other dimensions operate across academic disciplines in France. One is the predominant role of the nation's capital. The second is the way in which, following the turmoil of 1968, the universities were fractured between different disciplines. In the previous chapter we noted the massive concentration around the metropolitan region (Paris and the Ile de France) of both students and CNRS research units. Parisian universities tend to be larger than their provincial counterparts, and their size is correlated with age of establishment. The majority of the newer universities, founded between 1969 and 1978,[2] were set outside Paris in an effort to provide greater regional equality of access. The newer establishments tend to be not only smaller but also, though there are notable exceptions, less prominent in the research field. Some attempts were made in the course of the 1970s to offset the hegemony of Paris by shifting criteria for financial allocation in favor of smaller, provincial establishments. Visible effects, at best, remain marginal.

No less important because it affects the institutional framework in which disciplines operate was the political decision, taken in the aftermath of 1968, to subdivide certain of the largest establishments. The most prominent example of this process was the metastasis of the University of Paris into thirteen different universities. Nor was the process limited to Paris: it embraced the major provincial universities as well. In those instances where splitting off created two or more separate establishments, the effect has been to create highly specialized universities with a truncated range of *Facultés*. Thus, for example, the University of Rennes I groups together the exact sciences, law, and economics, and the University of Rennes II, the Humanities and Social Sciences. In the universities of Grenoble, which, like Caesar's Gaul *"in tres partes divisae sunt,"* medicine together with the natural and exact sciences were assigned to Grenoble I, the social sciences to Grenoble II, while the humanities and tongues Ancient and Modern dwelt hard by in Grenoble III.[3] This subdivision of the large universities has resulted in a high degree of fragmentation in France's higher education. In 1981 an official government report noted that sixteen universities were multidisciplinary, ten were "in part" multidisciplinary, and forty-one were dominated by one or two faculties.[4]

Irrespective of whether establishments such as these may, within the strict meaning of the term, be called universities at all, since they do not have the full range of disciplines and faculties, size constitutes an additional and very specific dimension in the French setting. Not only does it give rise to highly specialized establishments. It also tends to accentuate the organizational differentiation that naturally exists between large science research teams and the relatively small size of their counterparts in the social sciences and the humanities, particularly when the former, as often tends to be the case, are located in establishments separate from the latter—as, for example, in the Grenoble differentiation. The hiving off of the physical and exact sciences, though often justified on the basis of size and administrative convenience, also reflected a desire on the part of the high paradigm, nonideological sciences to distance themselves from what appeared in the turbulent days of the student revolt as the more politically inspired social sciences and humanities. Opportunistic the motives might have been. Yet, attempts to deal with the issues of size and expansion and to protect the research and research training system provided an organizational underpinning to the expression of cultural differences between the disciplines virtually without parallel in Western Europe.

The breaking out of different disciplines into separate organizational groupings was not simply the older faculties writ large. Each university has its own administration, elects its own president, assigns its own resources, and pursues its own academic way within the limits set down by legislation. Coordination, other than the traditional top-down model exercised by the Ministry of National Education, or nowadays, by the Ministry of Research and Technology as well, is limited. Attempts to increase lateral linkage between universities of the same region are among the major concerns of current policy. In certain specific instances such linkages have occurred: the large science universities of Paris VI and VII have sometimes pooled laboratory resources and permitted personnel from one to work in the research teams of the other. But this is the exception that proves the rule and derives from the fact that both universities not only share a dominant specialism but also stand virtually cheek by jowl on the same site.

Size and disciplinary profile, plus the more conventional distinction drawn by French academics between Paris and the provincial universities, are then important stratifying factors. On this basis universities can be assigned to one of three groupings: the large, specialized universities of the Paris region; the specialized universities in the provinces; and the small "comprehensive" provincial universities that bring together the full range of faculties and disciplines under the formal responsibility of a single *Président d'Université.* Our investigation is based explicitly on this trichotomy.

What are the effects of size on conditions of work both for students and academics? The seventy-six public sector universities in France range in size from the 1,400 students enrolled in the *Université de Corte Pascal Paoli* in Corsica to the over 31,000 brought together in the large establishments of Paris V, VI, and VII. By contrast, enrollment in provincial universities hovers between 13,000 and 15,000 students. Conditions of service for teaching and research personnel in France are set out in nationwide legislation. Formally speaking, time for such activities is the same in Paris as it is in Rennes, Marseille, or Perpignan. But this is offset by the fact that the numbers of research students, irrespective of discipline, tends to be greater in programs located in the metropolitan area than in their provincial equivalents. In part this reflects the numerical predominance of the Paris area. In part it is an echo of that mental set which, in times past, cast the capital's universities as the *summum* of the academic world.

But what from one perspective may be seen as evidence of a flourishing and dynamic intellectual life—large research teams, multitudes of doctoral students—is often purchased at a high price. The smaller but no less flourishing provincial universities can often offer fewer research students per professor, closer attention and supervision, and working conditions sometimes more pleasant and less crowded and certainly less expensive than the capital. As one director of a well-known economics research team remarked, "Nous ne sommes pas comme les Parisiens qui ont parfois jusqu'à quatre-vingts thésards" (We are not like the Parisians who sometimes have as many as eighty doctoral students). There are limits beyond which the theory of critical mass begins to assume negative overtones, especially in the often overcrowded conditions of the Paris region.

Recent developments pose a challenge to the overwhelming hegemony of the Paris universities. The rise of high technology industry has created other specialist poles of excellence to rival the capital: pharmaceuticals and atomic energy generation in the Rhône Valley, aeronautics at Toulouse in the southwest, France's equivalent of the Sun Belt. Nor is this phenomenon limited to the exact sciences, though clearly more visible there. The rise of centers of excellence in economics and the emergence of schools or clusters in history which look to centers and personalities outside Paris, have been an important, though less noted, trend that has gathered momentum over the past ten years. Paradoxically, the smaller numbers of research students in the provincial universities can often be an advantage to both academics and students: for research students, closer personal supervision; for academics, since the weekly time-budget is nationally standardized, more time for research.

FINANCIAL SUPPORT AND SELECTION OF STUDENTS

Before embarking on a more ethnographically oriented account of the conditions, obstacles, and snares that appear to lie in wait for the unwary student bent on pursuing higher learning, there remains one further contextual feature, the ramifications of which influence in no small manner the degree of selectivity, the attractiveness of research, and finally the rate at which trainee researchers complete their theses. This is the financing of students.

From a comparative perspective, the public sector of French higher education is a low-cost enterprise.[5] Students are not charged a "market rate" for enrollment fees. On the contrary, fees at both graduate and undergraduate level are kept deliberately low, if only to avoid the rapidly mobilizable displeasure of the student estate and the consequent high embarrassment of the authorities.[6] In the same spirit student services, welfare, and meal costs are also heavily subsidized. Two consequences flow from this situation. First, it is commonly expected that students or their parents will support such items as living expenses and books. Second, student grants, student fellowships, or internships are rare at the undergraduate level except for those whose parental income is below the national minimum wage level (SMIG).

Notable exceptions exist, but not among university students. They are to be found rather among the gilded denizens of the Ecole Normale Supérieure and the Ecole Polytechnique, who, as the future elite in teaching or as future technocrats, are paid a presalary. This support is continued even if they opt to transfer to research training rather than directly enter government service. In earlier times the use of teaching assistantships was one means by which research students were supported in their studies. This system, however, had several drawbacks. Graduates taken on at the height of expansion during the late 1960s and early 1970s soon found that time taken up by instruction ate into their research. Then, too, the radicalization of the assistant group and its constantly reiterated demands for tenure cast doubts on the suitability of this form of support, with the result that in the early 1980s assistantships were severely reduced in number. Another mechanism that used the school system as a means of employing students at the doctoral level has already been noted in connection with the CAPES and the Agrégation in history.

Curiously, for a system so centralized in other respects, France has no uniform system to support study at the advanced level. On the contrary, student finance at this level is heavily differentiated between disciplines, which in turn reflects evolving national priorities. This apparently anomalous situation raises a number of questions: what is the system of allocating grants or internships? At what point in a student's career is she or he eligible for support? On what criteria are awards made?

Financial support for advanced students in physics is particularly well developed. In practice three major systems are available. Scholarships awarded by the Ministry of Research and Technology (*Allocations de Recherche*) carried a stipend of Fr 7,000 per month (U.S. $1,100) in 1989. Study grants (*Allocations d'Etudes*) awarded by the Ministry of National Education amount to some Fr 16,600 per year (U.S. $2,600). In a recent development, industry-sponsored grants have emerged for joint research ventures between industry and university. At the end of the 1980s the question of student grants and incentives is under review, driven onward by the need both to strengthen the research base in such strategically central disciplines as physics, biology, and engineering, and to encourage more students to move into teaching after finishing research. One such system under review is the so-called *Monitorat d'initiation à l'enseignement supérieur*, grants which will provide up to Fr 9,200 per month (U.S. $1,400).[7]

Although scholarships from the Ministry of Research and Technology are open to students of economics, for example, the impression emerging from interviews is, once again, that even well-reputed university economics laboratories are less generously endowed than their counterparts in physics. Furthermore, Ministry grants are not available to all students. They are reserved for those with the best results in the Diplôme d'Etudes Approfondies (DEA). Publicly financed student support is not broadcast across the student population pursuing research beyond the DEA. Rather, it is a further selective device to help those who have already shown high potential, especially in physics and economics. The most potent instrument for sorting out sheep from goats in history is either the CAPES or the Agrégation. The instruments differ between the disciplines, Agrégation in one, performance in the DEA and subsequent granting of a scholarship in the other. From a functional standpoint the objectives are very much the same. They are to identify and assist a highly performing elite and to draw yet a further line of demarcation between it and the remainder of research students whose theses will be backed by the sweat of their own, or alternatively, their parents' brows!

In Britain and the United States research studentships, internships, and fellowships are made over directly to the student by the appropriate research council, sponsoring body, or university. This is not so in France. Grants from the Ministry of Education and the Ministry of Research and Technology are made over to a particular program or laboratory and are subsequently distributed by the director of the laboratory to the brilliant and needy. Applications for student assistance are filed by the full chairholder to the appropriate disciplinary commission that oversees doctoral programs and validates DEA programs. To be sure, this is a species of national competition. But it is based in the first instance not on student performance or potential so much as the performance of the program from which the request is made. The stronger the program, the more grants it will receive.

A similar mechanism operates inside individual universities for instructorships. Here, a key role is played by the Director of Teaching and Research who, drawn from among full chairholders, fulfills within the university a task not dissimilar to the national disciplinary commissions.

The allocation of student grants for research training has a series of dimensions not present in the same degree elsewhere. The whole process can be seen as a two-layered competition. Competition among programs and chairholders to secure resources forms the first layer. It is all the more bitterly contested, since without such resources chairholders are hard-pressed to nurture their most brilliant students and, by so doing, increase their own attractiveness to possible future applicants to their programs. Thus, in the French context, student grants constitute a particular form of currency of academic exchange,[8] but from the standpoint of the students they operate as a species of "tied grant." Like agricultural laborers in nineteenth-century England, the possession of a grant, like the possession of a cottage, depends on remaining in a patron's employ, the farmer in the one case, the laboratory in the other. In a system where student support is at best parsimonious, gratitude to one's patron is not a minor virtue!

The second layer of the competition is not fought out at the national level by embattled *patrons*. The contest shifts to the individual laboratory or program and to students seeking to bring themselves to the attention of the director of the laboratory, the full professor, or both. Such competition determines who will do his or her research full-time, thereby increasing significantly the chances of a successfully terminated thesis, and who will have to labor in the arid vineyards controlling rowdy schoolchildren or of taking short-term jobs to make ends meet.

To obtain a research grant is a triumph in itself. But such a triumph is the outcome not of sheer intellectual sparkle alone. It is also the outcome of quite massive persistence plus the ability to master and steer one's career across a series of successive hurdles, beginning with the humble *Diplôme d'Etudes Universitaires Génerales* (DEUG), passing beyond the *License* and the

Maîtrise, and making one's mark by an outstanding memoire at the DEA—that is, five years minimum after first entering the university.

The DEA marks an important stage not only for the ambitious student, but also for departments with the ambition for building up their research and research training. For the student in physics and economics the DEA sets the point at which he or she will come into close proximity with the world of research. For historians the DEA is less important. Rather, the function of bringing an individual student to the attention of influential senior staff is served by the Maîtrise which takes place earlier and involves a short thesis, defended publicly before members of the department, and even members of the public if curiosity should get the better of them. The Maîtrise in history is usually presented four years after initial entry to university.

From a departmental perspective and particularly for departments of physics and economics, the DEA is crucial for two reasons: the right to teach the DEA requires Ministry approval; and doctoral programs in a department are dependent on the prior existence of the DEA. No DEA, no doctorate. Furthermore, the Ministry lays down minimum student numbers for DEA programs. Failure to reach them may result in official recognition being withdrawn. For well-established fields and departments in the mainstream of the discipline, this is scarcely a matter of concern. Student selection may be exercised with full republican rigor. But for those still building up or specialized in subfields as yet unperceived as significant by students, the situation is very different. Often a delicate trade-off has to be made between student numbers and student quality.

According to many of our informants, most students opting for research are self-selected. But self-selection, especially in a system where student guidance and counseling, if not absent, are rudimentary, involves considerable acumen and personal career management. In French universities first- and second-cycle studies—"preadvanced study"—are heavily tracked, specialized, and discipline-specific. Changes between disciplines are far from unusual during the first two years.[9] But those who do change are likely already to be facing difficulties.

Essential for any student planning on research is choosing tracks or options recognized as highly selective. These routes are generally known among students. For those setting their sights on physics research, quite important is theoretical physics from the DEUG onward, mathematics, and the *Maîtrise Sciences et Techniques*. For the young aspirant economist, a Maîtrise in economics is a prerequisite. There is, in short, the phenomenon of the "hidden curriculum," in the form of tracks used to select the best students who will later enter DEA programs. The advantages in choosing the correct track for research are as great as those found in secondary education with respect to the various options of the Baccalauréat.[10]

REFORMS IN CURRICULAR PATHWAYS

Making the right choice is no easy matter, and after 1976 it became more difficult. Since that year, successive governments have added to the complexity of the curricular pathways running across years three through five after initial entry. Two waves of reform have profoundly altered the routes that cross from "preadvanced" to "advanced" training. Both reflect changes in policy and both can be seen as correctives to what, at the time, were seen as shortcomings in the curricular orientation of studies at that level. The first wave, in 1976, was triggered partly by the rise of student unemployment and partly by a belated recognition that mass higher education had to cater to rather different student career demands. It involved the development and reinforcement of vocationally oriented degrees. The upshot was a series of vocational tracks that emerged from the second cycle onward at the level of the Maîtrise and later in the specific form of the *Diplôme d'Etudes Supérieures Specialisées*, the vocational counterpart to the DEA. Thus, in parallel to "scholarly" options, there runs a series of vocational degrees, *Maîtrise de Sciences de Gestion* (Management Sciences) and *Maîtrise d'informatique appliquée a la gestion* (Masters in computing applied to Business Studies—MIAGE), which draw from the less dedicated or those given over to the twin contemporary deities of Mammon and Enterprise. Given the rewards and salaries being offered by French industry, particularly for students well qualified in physics and economics, "One has," as one of our informants commented, "to be a little mad to wish to do research."

The second wave of reform broke during the early 1980s. It obeyed a different rationale. The concern of science policy was to increase the number of students coming forward to research and, at the same time, to introduce selective "fast tracks" that would bring forward the "high fliers" by an alternative route to the Licence and Maîtrise. The creation of the Magistère degree was designed to such ends. Three aspects characterize this award. First, since it carries with it particularly favorable financial supports, it is given sparingly by central authority. Universities vie for this program, which is granted only to those that can prove outstanding performance in graduation rates or in setting up joint ventures with industry. Second, it extended the principal of selective admission based on the student's record plus an interview. Third, it introduced into the university world certain features that traditionally have been associated with the elite grandes écoles, selection being one and a highly favorable staff-student ratio another.

The combined effects of these reforms gave rise to a species of vertical differentiation in the curricular pathways linking preadvanced to advanced training. Alongside the long-established License and Maîtrise, which operated largely by student self-selection, they introduced two elite tracks:

the first, a vocational track grouped around such second-cycle degrees as the MIAGE, MST, and MSG, and the second, a fast track to research. Both were distinguished by highly selective admissions carried out at the start of year three. The rise of the mass university was accompanied by the reinforcement of selection, the multiplication of selective programs, and by the establishment of supplementary paths to research.

ASSIMILATION, MOBILITY, AND SPONSORSHIP

As students move beyond the first degree, they are subjected progressively to an anticipatory form of socialization into their future research discipline. The structures marking this process in the French university stand apart from either their British or their American counterparts. The path to the Ph.D. in the United States, and to an increasing extent in the United Kingdom (see chapter 3), proceeds through formal courses, examinations, and submission and defense of one's research proposal. Together, these markers and testing points are designed to ascertain how far the student has both mastered the field in which his or her research is located and also demonstrated his or her degree of assimilation into the disciplinary culture. In the Anglo-Saxon university the rituals of assimilation are conducted inside the department or faculty.

In France the same function takes place at two levels and in very different circumstances. The first level consists of the successive examinations and diplomas, DEUG, and License, Maitrise, and Diplôme d'Etudes Approfondies. They are not merely public examinations, conducted outside the department (*Unité de Formation et de Recherche*). They are also national diplomas. The second level in the ritual of assimilation is internal to the particular department or to the associated research unit where students pursue advanced work. It will, as in American or British universities, be crowned by the defense of the thesis. But in France this is a public occasion before a jury of three to seven members, usually chosen by the thesis supervisor. In theory at least, members of the public have the right to pose questions to the candidate. Thus, the ritual of assimilation, begun in the public domain, strengthened by private induction, is finally confirmed by a public display of the candidate's claim to be member of his disciplinary culture.[11]

But both the structure and the timing of the ritual are determined by disciplinary context. In physics the passage from preadvanced to advanced training, the point of selection, occurs at the moment of entry to the DEA. Most students who are accepted will continue on to doctoral-level research. Between 75 to 95 percent will complete the doctorate. In economics the line of demarcation is less clear-cut and the process of selection more protracted. The winnowing out of future research students continues throughout the full year of the DEA program. Some idea of the pattern of student flow and selection can be gathered from information provided by a major research training program in the Paris region. Of the thirty-five students entering the DEA, twenty-five received this award. Of the twenty-five, some six, four French students and two foreigners, were accepted for doctoral work. In economics marked differences in the doctoral completion rate are also noticeable. They range from around 50 percent in a comprehensive provincial university to virtually all those accepted for a highly prestigious joint-training program involving both universities and grandes écoles in the metropolitan region. A further difference in the disciplines is the usual time needed to complete a doctoral thesis. To revert to our metaphor of rituals of assimilation, the period of initiation varies between disciplinary cultures. The average completion time for a physics thesis is between two to three years; for economics, some four years.

The patterns of assimilation in history set it apart from the other two fields. As noted above, the rites of passage between public and private induction begin earlier, at the public defence of the Maîtrise. Then, of all disciplines, history has tended to demand the most protracted initiation: the now-defunct Doctorat d'Etat could take ten to fifteen years. Today revised regulations have reduced this to some four to five years, to the chagrin of many of the history fraternity.[12] Yet, the period of initiation in history remains among the longest of all disciplines. Finally, the material conditions surrounding disciplinary assimilation in history are often very different from either physics or economics. The majority of physics research students, like those in economics, work full-time on their research. The bulk of history *thésards* are essentially part-timers who have constantly to assert their yet unsubstantiated claims to be "a historian" against the daily wear and tear of their official status as schoolteachers.

Given their other commitments, it comes as no surprise that completion rates in history tend to be low. At a comprehensive university in the provinces we were told that one doctoral student in ten will complete within the new time limit of four years. At one of the larger Paris seminars corresponding figures were cited of between five to ten students out of twenty.

Despite these differences, the three disciplines do share a common trait. Advanced work rarely involves students moving between institutions. The notion that a top French research university should have an active and deliberate policy of head-hunting students from other establishments to lure them away from their alma mater is not indecent—it is unthinkable. A few bold and self-confident souls will make the move. We shall turn to them later. But the typical research student will have passed his earlier degrees at the same establishment where he does his advanced work. Leaving aside the few denizens of certain grandes écoles who opt for research training and are thus obliged to shift across sectors, the practice of moving on to a top research laboratory has far less currency in France than it does in the United States.

Several factors explain this relative immobility. The first is finance. Unlike Britain or the United States, French universities are not residential and dormitories are scarce even for first-year students. It is less expensive to live at home and study at one's local university than to move elsewhere and rent rooms, particularly when additional expense is born either by parents or by part-time work. For the teacher who is also apprentice-historian, the choice of university is often determined by the particular school to which central administration nominates him. In theory, studies at the DEA and beyond draw on a national catchment area (see chapter 5). In reality, the situation is very different.

Finance is not the sole influence at play. A further challenge facing students is best described as the "battle for sponsorship." The backing of gatekeeper personages with the power to advance a student's career has a significant role in a system where finance for advanced study is heavily differentiated by discipline and where distribution is made in the first instance to the research unit and only subsequently to the student. Sponsorship forms a complementary dimension to self-selection. Students seek the support of thesis directors by bringing themselves to their notice. Some may be invited by a particular professor to undertake research. Others, bolder and more enterprising, will seek them out. Some may propose a thesis topic, often based on their DEA or master's work, a pattern of negotiation found particularly in economics and history. Others will have a topic suggested or assigned them, a procedure that appears predominant in physics. Irrespective of who takes the initiative, immobility bears a premium. For individuals to heave themselves above the mass—to know who the professors are, to be aware of the type of research in which they are engaged, to have the opportunity of being supervised for the Maîtrise thesis or DEA memoire—demands time. Especially so in a university system where the staff-student ratio at first-degree level in humanities and social sciences is of the order of 1:32.[13] For the professoriate, too, stability of student presence is important in identifying future talent.

Nevertheless, students do transfer between universities or between different sectors in higher education. Some, as we noted, form part of that elite in the making which ordinarily is destined for the technocracy, central administration, and top teaching positions in the university. By being what they are—*normaliens* and *polytechniciens*, to mention the most visible—they already command considerable sponsorship. In contrast to university students who must employ various stratagems to win a patron's attention, to obtain a short placement in a laboratory, and to make personal contact with those with whom they wish to work in the future—a placement during which students may prepare a short memoire that may later form the basis of the thesis—normaliens or polytechniciens have sponsorship as part of their status. When these students knock, few if any doors will remain closed. One should not conclude, however, that normaliens or polytechniciens are spared the hard and bitter struggle for sponsorship and recognition. But theirs is a battle that takes place earlier in their career trajectory, during the last three years of upper secondary schooling and in the hothouse atmosphere of the *classes préparatoires aux grandes écoles*.[14] The universal sponsorship they enjoy is the fruit of success in an earlier competition.

Sandwiched between the majority of local research students and the occasional elite cosmopolitan who opts for the world of research from "*Normale Sup*" and "*X*" (popular terms for the Ecole Normale Supérieure and Polytechnique) lies a third group, students whose transfer to a university where research is closer to their specialist interests has been advised. Estimates of the size of this group are hazardous. Clearly, they have already acquired a measure of individual sponsorship, for transfer to another university without the personal backing and benediction of one patron not to mention recommendation to a colleague is, at best, delicate. Briefly stated, mobility is an expression of patronage successfully won.

Whether the degree of dependence between research students and their thesis supervisors is greater in France than elsewhere must remain a moot point if only because of the difficulties in making cross-national comparisons of dependence. Yet the quest for sponsorship does not cease with the acceptance of a doctoral thesis. Once past this hurdle, the relationship between ex-student and supervisor will evolve. What starts as sponsorship and dependence mutates into a bond of intellectual allegiance and shared perspectives. In its mature form this relationship becomes the bedrock of that other institution characteristic of French academia, namely, the cluster model of professorial power, authority, and influence.[15] Thus sponsorship is not the happy end to a series of temporary trials which leads to the perfect, if equally temporary, freedom of untrammeled scholarship. It is, rather, the start of an induction first into the values and arcania of the discipline, and later to successive degrees of membership in the cluster, as supplicant or, in fullness of time and the realization of success and ambition, as its patron. Thus does initial servitude hold out the promise of later grandeur!

THE NATURE OF THE RESEARCH EXPERIENCE

Differences in the varying patterns of selection and in competition times and rates are not only discipline related; they also reflect the way in which work is organized within a disciplinary culture. Patterns of work organization vary from large-scale collective research of long duration down to research projects conducted by individual scholars who set their own agendas and are accountable to their peers only through the quality of the resultant publications. The predominant mode in which work is organized has a prime bearing on induction into the discipline and on the relationship between participants as well as on what they expect from each other as colleagues engaged in the same undertaking.

In physics the nodal point of the discipline is the laboratory. In "big science," experiments can last five years or more and be a collective effort. Students taken on board ought to fit in with the research group and have research interests corresponding closely to those of the laboratory. Often the laboratory research agenda determines the student's thesis subject. Certainly, negotiation with the thesis supervisor takes place. But the margin for latitude appears more limited than in economics. Given the collective nature of much physics work, it is desirable for research students to integrate easily and rapidly with the rest of the research team. Some laboratory directors give considerable responsibility to their research students, partly to encourage participation. Others are perceived by their students as mandarins who treat their thésards more as extra hands than as prospective members of the physics community.

Teamwork is the all-pervasive feature of physics and is recognized as such both by thesis directors and students: "On travaille beaucoup en équipe. Je donne beaucoup de responsabilités à mes étudiants" (We do a lot of team work. And I give considerable responsibility to my students). Interdependent though members of the research group are, the nature of that interdependence for students is influenced by the size of the laboratory. The larger the research team, the greater the burden on the student to fit in smoothly, particularly in the large Paris establishments where research units bring together upwards of 150 specialists. Yet, being part of a small unit also creates a form of dependence, though qualitatively different. Such dependence stems from daily contact with the thesis supervisor, though not always to discuss matters related to the student's research topic. For many students this situation is a major departure from the type of work relationship they had with their supervisors earlier in their careers when access to such figures was rare, difficult, and formal. Many are well aware of the privileged position in which they find themselves.

Such privilege is not a matter of gratitude or perception alone. It has solid structural dimensions as well. For if the laboratory stands as the sanctum sanctorum of the physicist—"Un chercheur est quelqu'un qui vit dans le laboratoire" (a researcher lives in the laboratory)—not all DEA students are necessarily located in their supervisor's laboratory. In one provincial university, of twelve students following the DEA program only three were granted this favor. Sponsorship requires confirmation.

The other factor affecting work relationships is the number of doctoral students per thesis supervisor. In some of the larger Paris laboratories the large quantity of doctoral students (twenty-five was one figure mentioned) is often compensated by abundant supervisory staff. A one-to-one ratio is not unusual. Similar figures were cited in smaller provincial establishments. Naturally, such a figure is no indication of the quality of the relationship.

Once admitted to the laboratory and to doctoral work, students find themselves in a relatively free environment. There are no requirements to attend formal courses; seminar attendance varies from student to student, from once a week to once a year. Clearly, in physics the vehicles of inculturation are found less in formally structured occasions than in appearing daily in the laboratory and in contact with those engaged on different parts of the overall project. This presence is particularly significant since it is one of the major points in the research training system where doctorands come into sustained contact with members of the full-time research body. Physics laboratories bring together both CNRS researchers and university teacher-researchers. In such settings the main contribution of the former to the training of advanced students takes place, and at such points the two systems, legally and organizationally separate, act together.

Many features associated with the physics laboratory are also found in economics: the close contact between student and supervisor; the highly favorable staff-student ratio, though the latter tends to show greater variation, ranging from one to one to around one to five. Here again, the organization of work in the discipline shapes the relationship between doctoral students and their supervisors. Certainly, the laboratory paradigm underlines the collective dimensions of research in economics. But emphasis on the collective is not so strong nor so preeminent. Research projects, even when based on a team format, tend to involve smaller numbers, typically two to four persons. Less pronounced is the importance of speedy student meshing with other members of the team. As in physics, fitting in has its advantages: close work with one or two senior researchers; frequent, if not daily, contact with one's supervisor. Yet, openings for individual work and for a more solitary style, relying simply on one's thesis director rather than the collectivity as the agent of initiation, are also possible. Researchers tend to set their own agenda, and the margin of maneuver for students to negotiate a topic seems to be greater than in physics, though obviously the supervisor's approval is essential.

Though induction to research in economics leaves considerable latitude for independent work, such independence is often dearly purchased. Feelings of isolation, of being cut off from one's thesis supervisor, were mentioned by some students interviewed. To this were added feelings of separateness from other students and of being out of touch with other research groups. Whether such angst is simply personal or whether it might indicate that economics is less committed to a single, predominant pattern of work is uncertain. That work is only sometimes located in teams, that these teams are smaller and often shifting as the interests of individuals evolve, may well heighten the sense of fragmentation among certain neophytes. A species of the cooling-out function is present even among DEA and doctoral students. It takes the form of gradual withdrawal from contact with supervisors. Such contact can vary considerably: for good students once a month at least; for poor students once a year is not unknown. Thus even at this level self-selection, if only negative, still operates.

Personal isolation may worry the more sensitive in economics. It is, on the contrary, an integral part of the historian's craft. Both working patterns and, as has been suggested, means of initiation are holdovers from an earlier age. Attempts to introduce new working styles with emphasis on research teams and links into other disciplines, notably the social sciences, have been made, largely by the CNRS itself. But these initiatives are mainly confined to contemporary and Second World War history. Innovative they might be. But they are also the exception that proves the general rule: the predominant working style is highly individualistic, and history is solidly based in the university.

History stands apart from the other two fields in other respects. The first is the relatively large number of students in advanced programs. At a comprehensive university in the provinces, twenty-one doctoral students in history compare most favorably with the fifteen or so enrollments in economics at the same establishment. The second is the accumulation of many doctoral students around leading scholars. To supervise thirty or forty thésards at the same time is by no means immodest for leading historians in the Paris region. Compared to the two other disciplines at the research training level, history's staff-student ratio displays many of the characteristics of mass higher education.

Arguably, quantity is less relevant in a field where inculturation involves primarily the maturation of the student's historical judgment; with being well and widely read; of having the ability to develop new sources; with accumulating breadth in knowledge; and, most desirable of all, with an ability to synthesize. All of these attributes were tested earlier in the CAPES and in the agrégation du secondaire, and, in more settled times, they were confirmed by the traditional Doctorat d'Etat. Not only are these qualities forged and matured in individual endeavor, in the search after and interpretation of new archival material which are the technical aspects in the broad development of the historian's "mentalité." They have been verified by formal competitive examination prior to entry to the doctoral seminar. To acquire this mental set, however, is a function of time, of questioning one's self and one's material, of persistence and finally of winning through in that spectacle that delights the hearts of the gods—the struggle of a strong man in adversity! Given these cultural values, it is scarcely surprising that the training of the French historian should take so long. The passage of time was and remains the very essence of the craft.

Recently and sporadically, history in France has been engaged in revising both research techniques and patterns of work. Collaborative methods with several historians working on the same set of archives have been introduced. The range of analytical techniques has been extended into linguistics and computer usage. As one historian mused in an interview: "The historian's work has changed. There is a new logic of publication which requires more work in groups." More than either physics or economics, history sees itself under considerable pressure from two sources: the government and the physics model. Similar to the forces in Britain that have sought to reduce the duration of doctoral studies, the government is eager to increase student throughput; and, as an allied force, the physics paradigm continues to shape the research system generally. To many historians the creation of the Doctorat unique was a sop to the needs of the exact scientists, faced with international competition. For the historical paradigm, it poses a severe and insidious influence upon training, placing the advanced student in an intellectual equivalent of the procrustean bed, one far too short to permit the comfortable development of historical judgment.

Individualistic though historical work may be, membership in a research group is essential. One meets colleagues and, given the peculiar status of the apprentice-historian as schoolmaster, one restates one's aspirant identity as historian against one's present burden as educationist. From an organizational perspective, the nodal point in this discipline is not the laboratory. It is the cluster in which the main identifying feature is an allegiance to a particular methodology, approach, or interpretation developed by its leader or patron. It permits a further identification of talent. It draws a line between inner and outer circles in its membership, thereby raising in a slightly different context the issues of sponsorship and its confirmation. Finally, the cluster acts as a vehicle for the placement of its members in key and advantageous positions that are both a condition and an indication of its success and standing.

Isolated work and cluster membership are powerful elements in the intellectual fragmentation of the discipline. History in France tends to be highly politicized, reflecting the close links between party political ideologies, the historical events that gave rise to them, and the public role of the historian as analyst of the nation's fortune and disasters.[16] Hence, certain universities are seen as supporting a reactionary view of history. Others enjoy a delicious radicalism. Occasional seismic events—1940, the Liberation, Algeria, and more recently 1968—shake up the historical landscape, summoning forth new radicalisms and assigning older ones to the scrap heap of a new conservatism.

The political, intellectual, and ideological fragmentation of history in France has direct effects on student recruitment and, eventually, on prospects of employment. As stated in an interview: "The professor you work for usually represents a similar ideological position as the student. Thus, [the person] with whom a student chooses to work may affect where you can eventually be nominated." No clearer statement of the rationale for seeking admission to a cluster nor its benefits could be made. Clusters are history's extension to the system of sponsorship. To be sure, conflict between clusters to place their ex-students may often be self-defeating. But it is a bold person indeed who will hazard his or her career by not becoming associated with one of them.

STUDENT FLOWS

Patterns of work, types of behavior, and values to be internalized show immense variation across the three disciplines. What is less clear is the social class composition of those passing through the research training system. From other studies that have focused on such specific institutions as the *Polytechnique*, the *Ecole Nationale d'Administration*, and the *grands corps de l'Etat*, the more selective the sector of the higher education system, the more privileged the social class of students found there.[17] Given our present state of knowledge, what remains unknown is the exact social and economic status of students at the DEA level and beyond, and the probability, controlling for field and social origin, of moving through the successive stages after that point.

Dimensions other than social class are quite revealing of the state of the discipline, whether at the institutional or the national level. In fundamental physics the last five years have seen a rise in the numbers of students entering the research training system. Yet less than five years ago the survival of many smaller departments, particularly those specializing in applied physics, depended on foreign students, mainly from Francophone Africa and the ex-French dependencies. In one physics department of a comprehensive university in the provinces, eight research students out of ten came from overseas. In another, specializing in condensed matter physics (*Physique de la matière condensée*), one-third of the forty to fifty students preparing theses came from abroad, mainly from North Africa. For smaller departments, overseas students, despite their often inadequate qualifications, were the sole means not simply of keeping numbers up but also of preventing the withdrawal of validation for DEA programs and ultimately, the disappearance of doctoral work. Doctoral programs, as noted earlier, are conditional on the existence of a DEA program.

This situation appears to be changing for the better. More French students are coming forward. The physics department in the comprehensive university just mentioned now has a ratio of nine natives to one foreigner and, its academic staff believes, a corresponding rise in selectivity and thus standards. For economics, particularly in the provincial universities, the situation is somewhat different. Research student numbers have fallen over the past decade and even in the major Paris research programs the picture is one of stability rather than growth. The underlying reasons are market-related and will be analyzed in the following section.

A further dimension relating to student background, and one of particular significance in France, involves cross-sector flows, primarily between the grandes écoles and the university-based research training system. Though certain grandes écoles are developing a research capacity (chapter 5), segmentation between university and grandes écoles students who move across to the research world allows these latter students to exercise an influence out of all proportion to their numbers. Though data is not uniformly available across all three disciplines, in physics the highest proportions of grandes écoles graduates are to be found in laboratories at the cutting edge of their field and most especially those in Paris. One third of doctoral students in a laboratory that specialized in high energy and nuclear physics, and two thirds of the thésards in another that specialized in ultrasonics, came from the elite sector. Such figures are certainly exceptional. But they show very clearly that the degree of concentration of talent supports the well-known adage that "excellence begets excellence." A good pointer to the standing of a specific laboratory is the percentage of its thésards who come from the grandes écoles.

In economics the flow from the grandes écoles is present but more diluted. Some economists believe that recent trends have strengthened the tie. They point to an increasing number of polytechniciens moving into the discipline as teachers and as CNRS researchers. Why this occurs remains unanswered. Steps have been taken to consolidate the university–grandes écoles link. The setting up of a joint research program between the Ecole Normale Supérieur, the *Ecole des Hautes Etudes en Sciences Sociales,* and the CNRS is an example. But for the moment it is a pattern still very much the exception.

In history a long-standing tie has always operated at the research training level but has been largely limited to one establishment, the Ecole Normale Supérieure. "Normale Sup" has been a traditional supplier of a small but steady stream of students, many of whom will go on to occupy the topmost posts in the discipline: "Une forte proportion du corps professoral sont des anciens des Grandes Ecoles." Here again, quantitative data is not readily available. However, one interviewee, in a fit of reminiscence, pointed out that of his graduating group of forty, twelve eventually ended up as full professors. The significance of this link is disproportionate to the numbers involved. With their elite background, normaliens enter the field with a distinct advantage, being looked upon as "les poulains des patrons parisiens" (the golden boys of the leading Paris seminars.)

Student cross-sector flows from grande école to university, while by no means massive, exercise a disproportionate influence on the standing of those departments, laboratories, and seminars that receive them. It is largely a self-sustaining process. Only the best laboratories are in a position to attract such talent. Hence, the elite grandes écoles confirm the claims to similar status by particular units in the university. In France the *institutional* origin of students is one of the key elements that contribute to the essential hierarchy of excellence within individual disciplines.

LABOR MARKETS FOR GRADUATES

In chapter 5 we paid some attention to official science and research policy and to the efforts to renew France's research base by injecting more funds, expanding significantly the number of students, revising the structure of the doctorate degree, and developing incentives for the diversification of research and research funding. This planned move toward a French version of "the enterprise culture," one that involves the opening up of laboratories and research units to outside, nongovernmental, third-party contracting, even in history, brings with it a new awareness, sometimes voiced with wholehearted enthusiasm by small units in the provinces specialized in applied physics and microelectronics, sometimes greeted with detached self-interest by economists more ensconced in the development of theory.

Both the university and the research world have been held in thrall to massive recruitments in the 1960s and early 1970s. The situation is about to change under the conjoined effects of three developments: increasing numbers of senior academics will reach retirement age in the course of the 1990s; additional posts are to be created in teaching and research in areas associated with strategic economic change, principally in the exact sciences; and a goal, as yet on paper but nevertheless backed by both Left and Right, is emerging to increase student numbers by 50 percent during the coming decade.[18]

However marked the optimism, the years of blocked promotions have had enduring consequences, though not necessarily negative ones, for all three disciplines. In history lack of posts caused many fully qualified historians to continue to teach in secondary school rather than moving upward to the university. Alternatively, they took jobs in higher education for which they were grossly overqualified. Yet this same situation also obliged clusters of historians who were grouped in the provinces with little prospect of being called to the capital to develop into schools of thought equal in scholarship and originality to Paris. With all the inbuilt advantages of the major national and ministerial archives and libraries that accumulated in the capital of a state centralized for over two hundred years, the hegemony of Paris remains substantial. But it is no longer overwhelming.

Other effects have been less fortunate. Students who might have continued research training had the academic labor market been better, found other outlets. This phenomenon, visible across all three disciplines, was amplified by changes in the general labor market, especially in fields associated with an emerging high technology economy. Over the past five years or so the three labor markets that draw on the output of the research training system—academia, the public sector, and the private sector—have fallen out of phase. Stagnation in academia together with the increasingly attractive terms offered by the private sector drew off substantial numbers of students at the point of linkage between preadvanced and advanced training, with direct implications for research training. By far the largest outflow of students took place not at the end of doctoral programs but before students were firmly embarked upon them.

In physics the major point of hemorrhage occurs after the Maîtrise and involves students reckoned among the most able. The majority of these students move over to the engineering schools (located outside the university as a subsection of the grandes écoles), joining at the second or third year of the program. This development reflects the demand of industry for applied as opposed to fundamental physicists and overlap between applied physics and engineering, especially in the emerging fields of microelectronics.

Most of our interlocutors in the research world lamented this situation but also pointed out that by moving into engineering schools, the students would increase substantially their initial earning level. The extent of this phenomenon is difficult to gauge in the absence of national statistics. In one specialized provincial university roughly half the Maîtrise graduates in an applied physics program specializing in the structures and properties of matter moved over to an engineering school. Clearly, the research training system as it is configured at present is unable to compete with the salaries and conditions of work offered by the private sector, even for the skills that are vital for the continued health of physics research.

The flight away from research appears to affect even normaliens, often seen as the shock troops of France's corps of researchers. Their flight carries them not to the private sector but out of teaching and research and toward government service via the Ecole Nationale d'Administration. Similarly, in economics many students entering the first stage of research training leave for the private sector after completing the DEA. Less than one doctoral student in ten graduating from a comprehensive provincial university found a post either as teacher or researcher in higher education.

Yet among those who do push on to doctoral research, clearly many envisage a career in either research alone or combined with teaching, often in full recognition of and despite the fact that conditions are better outside academia. Private-sector employment, when contemplated by doctoral students, appears as second best, a safety net in the event that their real ambition does not work out. Doctoral students in economics show a slightly different pattern. Banking, insurance, and private-sector consultancies seem to exercise a powerful attraction, in addition to government service in agencies such as the *Commissariat Général du Plan*, the statistics and forecasting branch of the Ministry of Education, and the *Institut National de Statistique et des Etudes Economiques*.

CONCLUSIONS

Two questions sum up the central issue facing the French research training system. Is the hemorrhage of able students a temporary response to an extremely tight academic labor market? Or, given the decline in the status of public-sector employment evident in many European countries, is it part of a deeper-laid, permanent shift toward the private sector? For a higher education system that anticipates expansion, a research system that the government hopes will expand, and a buoyant private-sector industry increasingly reliant on research-trained manpower, this matter is of strategic importance. The ability of higher education to grow in the short term is not in doubt. But will industry's need for manpower at the second-cycle level (Bacc+3 through Bacc+5) continue to draw off students to such a degree that the long-term renewal of the research system is in jeopardy? In short, will industry's appetite for highly trained students eat the research system's seed corn?

The number of DEA students in applied physics and economics opting for a career in private-sector industry was seen by many of our interviewees as a serious loss to research. It also limits the ability of the research training system to anticipate the general growth in higher education during the decade ahead. That industry seeks to attract advanced students at a predoctoral level is caused in part by the relatively small numbers of doctorates procured each year: fifty-six hundred in 1986 (chapter 5). Such recruitment, even though dysfunctional from the standpoint of academia and the research system, is perhaps inevitable if the research training system is unable to meet the increasing quantitative demands placed upon it. These demands are not confined to private-sector industry: indeed, training for the private sector per se scarcely figured historically as a concern of the research training system.

The new governmental intentions to have student numbers grow by one-half by the end of the 1990s may go far to rectify the situation. Assuming that present staffing ratios are maintained, and allowing for the "natural wastage" that comes from retirements, the faculty corps ought to increase by at least 20,000. Yet so long as highly able and qualified students continue to leave prior to research training, only with great difficulty will the research training system be able to meet the traditional role of supplying the university's internal consumption, quite apart from the needs of the permanent research system. The possibility is very real therefore that higher education will be forced to revert to that unhappy expedient, introduced in the 1960s, of basing expansion more on quantity than on quality of academic staff.[19] That policy certainly carried the French university onward to mass higher education. But it also introduced a rare turbulence into the affairs of academe from which it is only today recovering.

Advanced student training and research in France have been shaped by a very specific model of higher education. This model has three parts: the research funding and full-time research system grouped around the CNRS; the training for specialized technical services of the state in the various grandes écoles; and the research training system located traditionally in the university. Such functional differentiation is not without its critics even in France, and more particularly when, as at present, pressure is being brought to bear to increase the numbers of trained researchers. Primary among the strains induced by this differentiation is the organizational and functional division between the research system grouped about the CNRS and its part-time equivalent in universities. Adding greatly to the strain are the demands placed upon the universities by the advent of mass higher education.

As regards the primary division, the nature of the linkage between the university and the full-time research system is heavily mediated by discipline. What emerges clearly from this chapter are the means by which the exact sciences paradigm maintains its supremacy: a high degree of concentration, especially in fundamental and particle physics; an ability to draw together both university-based and full-time researchers; and a high level of financial support for doctoral study. In physics the relationship between university advanced training and the CNRS research system is virtually one of symbiosis. This is not the situation for either economics or history. If the connection is substantial for the former, it is, to say the least, tenuous in the case of the latter. The number of full-time history researchers in the CNRS are minimal. If the institutional location of physics is across the university and the CNRS, if that of economics is mainly in the university with some CNRS-sponsored laboratories, the locale of history is firmly in the university and, as we have noted, in secondary schools.

The French research training and research systems antedated the arrival of mass higher education. Only recently have reforms been introduced into the area of advanced study to accommodate this development, mainly in the form of multiplying vocational programs at the preadvanced stage and in the creation of the single doctorate, introduced in 1986. It is significant that the new doctorate, impelled by international competition, is also seen by certain quarters of French academia as the work of the science lobby and, as such, a reinforcement of the physics paradigm over the research training system.

When examining disciplines as different as physics, economics, and history, one expects differences in inculturation, just as one expects differences in the way both academic work and induction take place. What is striking about the French setting is the manner in which inner disciplinary identity is strengthened by what might be termed "groups of organic cohesiveness"—the laboratory in physics, the cluster in history, with economics exhibiting an uneasy and shifting combination. Certainly these groups fulfill similar functions, even though the work styles of physics and history make each the polar opposite of the other. The laboratory and the cluster select membership. They separate out an inner from an outer circle. And while it is arguable that the laboratory is a modern organizational form of the cluster and that the former grew out of the latter under the impetus of centralized funding and the imperatives of big science, the form taken by these inner groups is highly discipline-specific. Their specificity is such that only with considerable difficulty is a form capable of being transferred from one disciplinary setting to another, as witness the relatively marginal role of the formal laboratory in the training of historians.

Finally, we must highlight the considerable influence that disciplines have had upon the formal organization of universities. In France this development, mediated by the vagaries of history and politics, has given birth to a specialist form of higher education establishment. Although officially designated a university, it is very different from the usual understanding of that term in the English-speaking world. Well over half of French universities are dominated by one or two faculties. That science, medicine, and sometimes law are separated off from the social sciences and humanities is not merely a perverse tribute to the determination of certain high paradigm disciplines to differentiate themselves organizationally from their less paradigmatically strong and more turbulent brethren. It is also an example of certain disciplines seeking to protect the value of their diplomas, and indirectly their identity, by replacing the organizational unity that underpinned the elite model of university by what is virtually a federation of fields, some cognately related, others brought together by the expedient of the moment and frozen into a permanent setting. There can be no more striking monument to the power of certain disciplines to shape their organizational environment than the atomization of the French university which has taken place in the two decades after the initiation of a grand reform in 1968.

NOTES

1. Burton R. Clark, *School and the University*, pp. 292–297.
2. Jilek, *Historical Compendium of European Universities*.
3. Dreyfus, "Ville et la Région de Grenoble," pp. 116–118.
4. Fréville, *Financement des Universités*.
5. Jallade, "Expenditure on Higher Education in Europe."
6. Neave, "Reform of French Higher Education."
7. Courtois, "Création d'un Monitorât pour Attirer les Chercheurs Vers l'Université."
8. Burton R. Clark, *Higher Education System*, p. 270.
9. Neave, "France," pp. 30–31.
10. Ibid.
11. Becher, "Disciplinary Shaping of the Profession." See also chapter 4 in this volume.
12. Martin, "Historien à Temps Partiel," p. 101.
13. Friedberg and Musselin, "Academic Profession in France," p. 107.
14. Lasibille et al., *De l'Inefficacité du Système Français de l'Enseignement Supérieur*. See also chapter 5, note 10.
15. Terry Clark, *Prophets and Patrons*.
16. Dansette, *Religious History of France*.
17. Kościuisko Morizet, *La Mafia Polytechnicienne*; Kessler, *Les Grands Corps de l'Etat*; Bodiguel, *Elèves de l'ENA*; Bourdieu and Passeron, *Héritiers*.
18. Durand Prinborgne, "Evolution et Juridification de l'Enseignement Supérieur Français."
19. Bourricaud, "Réforme Universitaire et Ses Déboires."

BIBLIOGRAPHY

Becher, Tony. "The Disciplinary Shaping of the Profession." In *The Academic Profession: National, Disciplinary and Institutional Settings*, ed. Burton R. Clark. Berkeley, Los Angeles, London: University of California Press, 1987. Pp. 271–303.

Bodiguel, Jean-Luc. *Les Elèves de l'ENA*. Paris: Fondation Nationale des Sciences Politiques, 1986.

Bourdieu, Pierre, and Jean-Claude Passeron. *Les Héritiers: les Elèves et l'Accès a la Culture*. Paris: Editions du Seuil, 1968.

Bourricaud, François. "La Réforme Universitaire et Ses Déboires." *Cahiers de la Fondation Européenne de la Culture*, no. 3, 1978: 1–50.

Clark, Burton R. *The Higher Education System: Academic Organization in Cross-National Perspective*. Berkeley, Los Angeles, London: University of California Press, 1983.

Clark, Burton R., ed. *Perspectives on Higher Education: Eight Disciplinary and Comparative Views*. Berkeley, Los Angeles, London: University of California Press, 1984.

———. *The School and the University: An International Perspective*. Berkeley, Los Angeles, London: University of California Press, 1985.

Clark, Terry N. *Prophets and Patrons: The French University and the Emergence of the Social*

Sciences. Cambridge: Harvard University Press, 1973.

Courtois, Gérard. "Création d'un Monitorât pour Attirer les Chercheurs Vers l'Université." *Le Monde*, 23–24 juillet 1989: 9.

Dansette, André. *The Religious History of France*. London, Edinburgh: Colins, 1964.

Dreyfus, Paul. "La Ville et la Région de Grenoble." *Paedagogica Europaea* XI, no. 2 (1976): 116–118.

Durand Prinborgne, Claude. "Evolution et Juridification de l'Enseignement Supérieur Français." *European Journal of Education* 23, nos. 1–2 (1988): 105–124.

Freville, Yves. *Le Financement des Universités*. Paris: La Documentation Française, 1981.

Friedberg, Erhart, and Christine Musselin. "The Academic Profession in France." In *The Academic Profession: National, Disciplinary and Institutional Settings*, ed. Burton R. Clark. Berkeley, Los Angeles, London: University of California Press, 1987. Pp. 93–102.

Gouldner, Alvin W. "Locals and Cosmopolitans." *Administrative Sciences Quarterly* 1, 1 and 2 (1957): 281–306; 444–480.

Jallade, Jean-Pierre. "Expenditure on Higher Education in Europe: Past Trends and Future Prospects." *European Journal of Education* 15, no. 1 (1980): 33–44.

Jilek, Lubor. *Historical Compendium of European Universities*. Geneva: Conférence des Recteurs Européens, 1984.

Kessler, Marie Christine. *Les Grands Corps de l'Etat*. Paris: Presses de la Fondation Nationale des Sciences Politiques, 1986.

Kosciusko Morizet, E. *La Mafia Polytechnicienne*. Paris: Editions du Seuil, 1974.

Lasibille, G., L. Levy-Garboua, L. Navarro-Gomes, and F. Orivel. *De l'Inefficacité du Système Français de l'Enseignement Supérieur*. Paris, Dijon: CREDOC/IREDU, 1980.

Luttikholt, Harry. "Universities in the Netherlands: In Search of a New Understanding," *European Journal of Education* 22, no. 1 (1986): 57–66.

Martin, Jean-Clément. "Historien à Temps Partiel." *Le Vingtième Siècle: Revue d'Histoire* no. 15 (juillet–septembre 1987): 101–109.

Neave, Guy. "France." In *The School and the University: An International Perspective*, ed. Burton R. Clark. Berkeley, Los Angeles, London: University of California Press, 1985. Pp. 10–44.

———. "The Reform of French Higher Education or, The Ox and the Toad, a Fabulous Tale." *Higher Education Quarterly* 42, no. 4 (1988): 353–369.

Wielemans, Willy. "The Belgian Universities and the Changing Labour Market." *European Journal of Education* 23, nos. 1–2 (1988) 77–90.

PART FOUR

The United States

Introduction

French specialness is exceeded by American exceptionalism. Higher education in the United States is strikingly large, decentralized, diversified, competitive, and entrepreneurial. Over two hundred private and public institutions qualify as doctoral granting universities, of which at least one hundred
are deeply invested in research. Another six hundred institutions, some
known as universities and some as colleges, offer many master's degrees.
Within the first pool of two hundred universities and the larger pool of eight
hundred institutions, great variation exists in the support of research and in
the use of research as the foundation of graduate education.

Within this unplanned "system" in which institutions freely compete,
imitate, and diverge, graduate education early received structural and symbolic distinction in formally demarcated arts and sciences graduate schools
erected as a second tier on top of the historic college, where four years of
study culminated with the bachelor's degree. The graduate school in the
basic disciplines was also distinguished from professional schools more
clearly than on the European continent. The emergence and rapid growth
of universities in the American system in the last quarter of the nineteenth
century made the graduate school a special place for research and research
training.

As Patricia Gumport traces in chapter 7, the habits of mind and heart in
the graduate schools were shaped considerably by the sponsorship of private foundations, particularly during the 1920s and 1930s, before the patronage of science by the federal government took over after World War II.
Federal support of research increased tremendously during the 1950s and
especially the 1960s. But within this support, the federal contribution
varied tremendously across the growing population of universities and the
ever-enlarging population of institutions that offer at least master's level

223

work. And while public and private universities alike have steadily intensified their competition for federal research dollars, they have also turned to
the historic sponsors of the state universities, the individual fifty states, for
faculty subsidy and some research funds, and to the many private sources
that have helped the leading private universities to build institutional resources out of which research infrastructure, research projects, and graduate student support could flow. Institutions steadily diversified the financial
base of their graduate schools, individually drawing upon various private
and public channels of support. Financially and operationally the leading
universities positioned themselves to provide strong research foundations
for graduate education, combining systematic instruction with participation
in the ongoing research of faculty and that required for the doctoral dissertation.

In chapter 8, Gumport highlights the enormous variation in the departmental settings of four disciplines—physics, biology, economics, and
history—in four universities that range along an extended continuum of
differences in research funding and orientation. Professors and graduate
students testify to the import of their settings and to the flow of change induced by institutional ambition as well as by disciplinary advance. Strong
"local organization" follows from departmental and institutional struggle in
a decentralized, competitive system. Campus initiative and departmental
pursuit of prestige become central in the maintenance and quality of a
research-teaching-study nexus.

SEVEN

Graduate Education and Organized Research in the United States

Patricia J. Gumport

National systems of higher education exhibit different histories of efforts to integrate organized research and advanced education. They also reflect different beliefs about the desirability of that ambition and to what extent it has been achieved. At one end of the international continuum, the American arrangements for doctoral education and academic science have become organizationally, politically, and economically so tightly linked that American participants and observers alike have difficulty conceiving of one without the other. As one prominent observer notes, "In American universities the two are done together, in the same places and by the same people."[1]

The American system of graduate education extends beyond the most visible top tier of one hundred doctoral-granting universities into a vast enterprise. Compared to other countries, the scale of operations is awesome, spanning some 800 of the country's 3,400 American higher education institutions, enrolling almost 1.5 million graduate students, and awarding annually about 300,000 master's degrees, 75,000 professional degrees, and 33,000 doctorates.[2] Graduate education programs are embedded within universities as a distinct layer resting atop undergraduate arts and sciences programs, usually drawing on the same faculties and relying on resources derived from an institution's teaching as well as research missions. Reflecting strong local organization, the structural and normative underpinnings of graduate programs reside in academic departments characterized by decentralized faculty authority.

In contrast to the more gradual progression that occurs in the German system, entry to this level of the American higher education system for an advanced degree comes about after a sharp break upon completion of undergraduate education. The majority of incoming graduate students in the letters and science departments have attended comprehensive public schools for their secondary education, usually earning a high school diploma at age seventeen or eighteen, followed by a bachelor's degree from a range of selective institutions, where coursework was a mix of general education and a disciplinary major. Fewer were chosen from the less selective four-year colleges (and the two-year colleges that may lead to them); courses taken here instead often lead to terminal degrees. Selectivity is the key ingredient reinforcing the pivotal role of the graduate school as a site for professional socialization and disciplinary reproduction. As Diana Crane describes the rationale: "The best students are selected by the best graduate schools, the best of these are selected for training by the top scientists, and from this highly selected group come the next generation's most productive scientists."[3]

Retaining the initial Humboldtian imprint from over a century ago, graduate programs reflect a widespread belief, internalized by faculty, administrators, and research sponsors alike, that linking graduate education and organized research produces excellence in both. Accordingly, the basic model for doctoral education has been distinctive: a few years of prescribed course work, followed by examinations for advancement to candidacy, culminating in a dissertation that reflects original research done by the student under the guidance of a faculty committee. Common across fields is an apprenticeship experience intended to integrate teaching and research training.

The linkage of this pattern of doctoral training with sponsored research has historical roots in a national context that has valued these activities for their instrumental contributions to two crucial national tasks—the production of research and the preparation of trained research personnel. To establish and reinforce the research-training fabric, an elaborate, decentralized, competitive funding system has allocated the bulk of basic research resources in individual project grants to university researchers who, as principal investigators, employ graduate student research assistants in campus laboratories. With the exception of a small number of competitive fellowship programs, funding allocations have corresponded to short-term and long-range national priorities, such as economic competitiveness, defense, and health care. Thus, financial support for the integration of graduate education and research has been achieved, for the most part, indirectly and more for its instrumental value rather than for its inherent legitimacy as an ideal. And as research and research training have been transformed into more capital-intensive endeavors, especially in the leading one hundred universities, the stakes have become high for all concerned.

This chapter begins with a historical overview of the development of the American research university. The second and third sections describe the contemporary systems of graduate education and organized research, focusing on policy issues of organization and sponsorship that have prevailed during the last two decades.

HISTORICAL DEVELOPMENT

Modern research universities have become the principal home of graduate education and research in the United States. Although scholars have documented separately the rise of modern American science, the emergence of the American research university, and the emergence of graduate education, little scholarly work has been done at their intersection to examine the factors that account for their interrelationship and for their persistence.[4]

As is true of most social institutions in the United States, the development of research universities has occurred neither linearly nor with centralized planning. Rather, the university research system emerged incrementally through a series of initiatives on the part of universities and a plurality of funding sources, within an economic and political context that increasingly encouraged scientific research.

In contrast to other countries, institutional initiative has been a prominent driving force. Over the past century the expansion of the modern university research system was fueled first and foremost by the ambitions of universities to establish themselves as modern research complexes, either by transforming smaller classical colleges or by establishing new, larger universities. Such ambitions were spurred on by an emerging national system of science that crystallized in the late nineteenth century and a funding system that did not develop formally on a national scale until the mid-twentieth.

The Emergence of Graduate Education

Graduate education achieved a stable American presence during the last two decades of the nineteenth century, when awarding the Ph.D. became a laudable academic goal. The earliest signs of doctoral education in the United States were the granting of the first Ph.D. in 1861 by Yale's Sheffield Scientific School, the second Ph.D. by the University of Pennsylvania in 1871, and the third by Harvard a year later.[5] More significant was the explicit organizational mission of graduate education in the founding of Johns Hopkins University in 1876 and Clark University in 1889. Hopkins especially became known as the "prototype and propagator" of research as a major university function. Coupled with its commitments to scientific research, Hopkins offered merit-based graduate fellowships for full-time study that included state-of-the-art research training.[6]

Both within and immediately surrounding higher education, interest in science had been burgeoning since the mid-nineteenth century, when science was still the individual pursuit of amateurs. Scientists and those seeking advanced study often traveled to Germany for the requisite exposure; work in chemistry even into the 1870s required a trip to Germany.[7] On the American front, after initial resistance to the German idea of studying science for its own sake and after conflicts between self-identified pure and applied scientists, scientific research gradually gained more acceptance, although it took on a distinctive meaning in the American context: American science, Dael Wolfle wrote, would be "a collective enterprise like those in business. Modern science needed labor, capital and management."[8]

Between the founding of Hopkins in 1876 and Clark in 1889, the conceptualization of scientific research had shifted from a personal dream to an exalted vocation. Proclamations at Hopkins reflect this change from what Laurence Veysey called "a rare and peculiar opportunity for study and research, eagerly seized by men who had been hungering and thirsting for such a possibility," to an increasingly more prestigious endeavor, proclaimed by Clark's president as "the very highest vocation of man—research."[9] Science became an increasingly specialized activity that professors could pursue autonomously yet with the security of support, personal advancement, and even prominence, within (and extending beyond the local loyalty to) an academic institution.[10]

Hopkins and Clark were not long to remain isolated experiments dominated by ideals of scientific research and graduate education. Other graduate schools emerged in the 1890s as parts of larger universities whose undergraduate missions and size offered a broad and stable base of support in endowment funds and tuition. Some were established by the founding of a new university soon to offer both undergraduate and graduate instruction, as in Stanford (1891) and Chicago (1892). Others added the graduate school onto an older established private college, as in Harvard and Columbia. Some existing state universities—Wisconsin, Michigan, and Illinois—evolved further from their origins as land grant colleges established with government funds for agriculture and mechanical arts through the Morrill Acts of 1862 and 1890 and the funding of experimental agricultural stations through the Hatch Act of 1887.[11] By 1900 the number of Ph.D.-granting institutions had grown to fourteen, awarding a total of three hundred Ph.D.'s.[12]

In addition to taking on scientific research commitments, Ph.D. programs came to be seen as an attractive feature for expansion and for advancing an institution's competitive position in the growing higher education system. Based on a desire to heighten prestige in their institutions, an increasing number of institutions sought to hire faculty with research interests and to obtain sponsored research funds to build laboratories that would attract eminent scientists. Since faculty increasingly wanted to pursue basic research and to train selectively chosen graduate students, institutions were propelled to provide them with opportunities for research and advanced training, and hence graduate programs, across the disciplines.

The widespread adoption of graduate programs within higher education institutions was enhanced by the development of departmental organization that occurred in the last quarter of the nineteenth century. Departments provided a flexible organizational structure for decentralizing and compartmentalizing graduate instruction. If Ph.D. programs were integrated organizationally as a separate level from the liberal education of undergraduate colleges, they also were made parts of departments responsible for undergraduate instruction in a discipline, a linking arrangement that has been remarkably stable and uniform over time and across campuses. The drive to conform to this structure was so strong that Hopkins and Clark expanded their organizational structures to offer undergraduate as well as graduate programs.

This organizational arrangement permitted control of undergraduate and graduate programs to reside within the same group of faculty.[13] Course work as well as research training could be designed which was appropriate to each discipline and coordinated by each department's faculty. One functional by-product of this arrangement was that graduate programs maintained both faculty and institutional continuity: they allowed faculty to reproduce themselves by training their professional successors, and they promoted cohesion of the university, since the responsibility for graduate students kept faculty attentive to their departments. Graduate programs kept the research and teaching activities interlocked and the institution functionally integrated in spite of increased disciplinary specialization.

Corresponding to established areas of knowledge at the time, departments were able to design different kinds of research apprenticeships that were appropriate to the specialized training in each of the disciplines. The specialization of disciplines mirrored by departments represented professors' vocational aspirations, which were especially apparent in the newly established natural and social science departments whose very existence was justified on the basis of specialized research. Beyond the campus level, as disciplines crystallized into national professional associations, they came to serve as visible external reference groups that would give a semblance of standardization across graduate programs.[14] "Disciplines and departments had powerful reciprocal effects upon one another," Roger Geiger has noted, in reinforcing the authority of departments on campus and the professional judgments of faculty nationally.[15] Thus, the emergence of disciplinary associations further facilitated the development of Ph.D. programs.

Especially during the 1890s, the growing size and complexity of the graduate education and research enterprise encouraged academic management, coordination, and control, which were reflected in the emergent bureaucratic administration on campuses. Even though departments served faculty interests for autonomy over research and instruction, the hierarchies of rank within departments and competition across departments served administrative interests for "productive work" as measured by research output. One observer notes, "Clearly it had become a necessity, from the administrator's point of view, to foster the prestigeful evidences of original inquiry."[16]

The dual tasks of graduate education and research were institutionalized most easily in those institutions that had greater resources, both financial and reputational. Thus at the systemwide level, those who succeeded in the competitive drive for advancement became a leading peer group of institutions. The prominence of this tier in the U.S. system was reflected in their founding of the Association of American Universities in 1900, which marked the culmination of nineteenth-century efforts to establish graduate education and research activities. Ostensibly the AAU was founded to establish uniformity of standards, yet it simultaneously functioned as an exclusive club.[17] The establishment of the AAU signified an implicit systemwide division of labor: a group of institutions differentiated themselves as a sector at the top of a hierarchy of prestige on the basis of their engagement in graduate education and research.[18] Although institutions continued to compete with one another for faculty, graduate students, and philanthropic support, a persistent concentration of fiscal and status resources in this sector became an enduring distinctive feature of the American system, one that amounted to an institutional version of the Matthew effect in which cumulative advantage helps the rich to become richer.[19]

Characterized as "a new epoch of institutional empire-building,"[20] this period of American higher education reflects the surfacing of university concerns for status in an increasingly stratified system. Such concerns were evident in dynamics of academic rivalry such as bidding for faculty and emulating academic programs. Even if the American system is not unique in its inclination toward stratification, the institutional drive for competitive advancement within the research university sector has reflected, according to one American scholar, "almost an obsession."[21]

Thus, the end of the nineteenth century marks the creation of the research university as a new kind of social institution devoted to scientific research as well as to graduate training. The extent of institutional ambition was so pervasive that the developing universities imitated one another in the programs and faculties they sought to develop. On campuses across the country, the homogeneity in the proliferation of graduate programs and faculty positions suggests that universities sought to acquire not only intellectual legitimacy but a new kind of economic and political legitimacy as well.[22]

The Rise of Sponsorship for University Research

The emergence of graduate education in the modern university developed hand in hand with the expansion of a national system of sponsored research. Initially, external resources for academic science were amassed principally from philanthropic foundations, while industry played a minimal role. Not until after World War II were foundations and industry eclipsed by the surge of federal government involvement.

The earliest sources of research sponsorship were wealthy benefactors and their philanthropic foundations. In the 1870s philanthropic contributions to higher education averaged $6 million per year—mainly to individual scientists.[23] By 1890 philanthropic support reflected a more widespread and instrumental orientation, directing funds to the emerging universities for their potential contributions to industrial growth, employment, and commercial endeavors.[24] Philanthropic funds supported a wide array of institutional activities, especially in the applied sciences, including funds for equipment, overall plant expansion, and new professional schools. In some cases the support provided a considerable amount of money, for example, like John D. Rockefeller's $35 million endowment to the University of Chicago.

On a national scale John D. Rockefeller and Andrew Carnegie established the principle of systematic philanthropy. The two largest foundations involved in research were the Rockefeller Foundation, established in 1913 with $182 million, and the Carnegie Corporation, created in 1911 with $125 million. In the early 1920s these foundations favored donations to separate research institutes, such as the Rockefeller Institute of Medicine and the Carnegie Institute of Washington. Universities were uncertain whether foundations would be stable sponsors for academic science.[25] By the 1930s foundations reoriented their giving to become an integral funding base for university research. They allocated project grants and postdoctoral fellowships (the latter preeminently by the Guggenheim Foundation), especially in medical research and the natural sciences, somewhat less so the social sciences. In 1934, for example, the Rockefeller Foundation, which alone provided 35 percent of all foundation giving, gave 64 percent of all foundation funds to social science support and 72 percent of funds made available to the natural sciences.[26]

Although philanthropists may indeed have been "a hidden presence on every American campus,"[27] as put by Frederick Rudolph, their voluntary contributions enabled universities to have essential resources required to institutionalize graduate education and scientific research. Universities and their faculties built their own rationales and adapted organizational structures to expand the scope of their research activities, while training the next generation of knowledge producers. Much of this adaptation to undertake applied research became incorporated into the ideal of service, especially for public universities.

Upholding university autonomy and academic freedom became not only institutional concerns but also issues for individual faculty. Consequently, faculty claimed expert authority in order to establish some distance from the agendas of campus governing boards and the increasingly prominent philanthropists.[28] Professionalization efforts of faculty in this era were, in part, due to the huge presence of external mandates for research, and not merely, as commonly cited, an outgrowth of the explosion of knowledge.

While philanthropic support continued until World War II, private industry had entered the academic scene during the interwar years as an unpredictable supplement.[29] As industry R&D expenditures rose in the 1920s, corporations conducted both applied and basic research in their own industrial labs in the technological areas of electricity, communications, and chemicals. Since industry could also benefit from academic science, corporations needed to demonstrate that business interests were compatible with the university ideal of disinterested inquiry. The success of industrial sponsorship for university research in this era was exemplified by ventures with two prestigious research universities: Massachusetts Institute of Technology (MIT) and the California Institute of Technology (Cal Tech). Nevertheless, corporate R&D funds generally remained in industrial laboratories through the 1930s and thereby continued as a marginal contributor to the support of academic science.

By the late 1930s university research was genuinely flourishing, although it did so primarily in the nation's most visible universities. Evidence for this concentration of research activity is also documented by a similar concentration of research training activity: in 1937 sixteen universities accounted for half of the expenditures on university research and granted 58 percent of the Ph.D.'s.[30] The consolidation of research resources has become linked with doctoral-granting activity, a pattern developed under philanthropic support, which would prove durable and capable of great expansion.

The Surge of Federal Involvement

The national government's sponsorship of research and research training developed incrementally rather than through a coordinating policy on science or on graduate education. Until World War II the federal government played only a minimal role in advancing either scientific research or higher education. The principal exception, noted earlier, was the successful effort in the nineteenth century, with much practical utility in mind, to sponsor agricultural research. But it was many decades later, after two world wars, that the government came to consider universities as a national resource for basic research and training that could assist in economic growth, national security, and health care.

Early signs of federal involvement in academic science began with efforts to designate advisory boards for scientific research. Signifying both the value placed upon modern science and a perceived need to oversee the country's research intentions, the first national organization was the National Academy of Sciences. Founded in 1863 by a congressional charter as "a private, non-profit, self-governing membership corporation of distinguished scholars in science and engineering research," NAS was to "advise the government on scientific and technical matters to further science and technology and their use for the general welfare." Over the next decade, NAS became the site of severe conflicts over membership (limited to fifty) and mission as American scientists from different fields vied for control of the scientific community. It did not develop a powerful relationship to the national government. Instead, Robert V. Bruce has noted that "the federal government remained disinclined to seek the Academy's counsel or even receive it when offered, thus negating the Academy's official reason for being."[31]

A half-century passed before the federal government mandated additional organizational arrangements that were to be more influential in the advancement of scientific research as a national enterprise. In 1919 the National Research Council was established by NAS, essentially to carry out the earlier congressional mandate. As the principal operating agency of both the National Academy of Science and (after 1964) the National Academy of Engineering, the NRC was intended to serve as a bridge between the federal government, the public, and the community of scientists and engineers. Over time the NRC has become a principal organizational base for overseeing national research efforts, including manpower training, and for monitoring how federal funds are channeled into university research.

Rather than actually advising the government, however, the NRC, along with the American Council of Learned Societies (founded in 1919) and the Social Sciences Research Council (founded in 1923), depended upon the resources of philanthropic foundations to assume a prominent role in the promotion of university research. As channels for foundation funds, these organizations provided interested sponsors with access to scientists and scholars as well as administrative assistance in selecting recipients of small research grants and postdoctoral fellowships in the areas of mathematics, physics, and chemistry. By the 1920s, in Geiger's formulation, American science was mobilized under "the guidance of the private elites" who "came together for the purpose of furthering science." The memberships of the National Research Council and the National Academy of Sciences were constituted by "the same group of individuals [who] encountered one another, in slightly different combinations."[32]

The national government's expansion of a large-scale, multiagency funding system to support academic science developed incrementally during and after each world war, culminating in the post–World War II era. In the late 1930s annual federal expenditures for science were estimated at $100 million; most of these funds went to applied research in federal bureaus, especially agriculture, meteorology, geology, and conservation.[33] Some drift in interest toward academia occurred when the expertise of academic researchers became a valued commodity, notably as the federal government called on them to assist in wartime.[34] For example, during World War I, the federal government financed psychologists to construct intelligence tests and encouraged other scientists to follow up on diagnostic physical examinations of close to four million people who were drafted. For such work, universities granted leaves to physical scientists and life scientists as well as to social scientists and historians. The government also began to allocate funds for researchers to work on their home campuses. By 1940 federal funds for university research totaled $31 million. During the 1940s the Office of Naval Research contracted with over two hundred universities to do about twelve hundred research projects involving some 3,000 scientists and 2,500 graduate students.[35] This pattern of mission-agency contracting became the precedent for arrangements made later for the support of relevant research by such agencies as the Atomic Energy Commission (AEC), created in 1946, and the National Aeronautics and Space Administration (NASA), established in 1958. During the war years, 1941–1945, the United States spent $3 billion on research and development (R&D), mostly funded by the federal government, of which one-third was for university research aimed at winning the war and devising "new instruments of destruction and defense."[36]

The expansion of sponsored research in universities was coupled with the expansion of research training. Between 1920 and 1940 institutions awarding doctoral degrees increased from fifty to one hundred. In those two decades doctorates awarded annually increased from 620 to 3,300, a fivefold increase.[37] The caliber of doctoral students also improved significantly. As late as the 1920s the majority of graduate students had been "undistinguished," reflecting "uneven preparation, uncertain motivation and unproven ability."[38] In the 1930s stiffened graduate admissions began seriously to bar unfit students and to seek and aid outstanding ones. To give departments another means of assessing student ability, on a national scale, leading Eastern private universities cooperated in the late 1930s in the development of the Graduate Record Examination (GRE), a durable device used ever more widely during the following half-century.

By the 1950s the federal government had come to look upon research universities as a precious public resource for research and research training, a set of institutions worthy of a "partnership," even during peacetime. The establishment of the National Science Foundation (NSF) in 1952 reflected a growing federal belief that universities were, as Vannevar Bush's 1945 report to President Roosevelt had proclaimed, ideal settings for research that offered "an endless frontier." As the federal research budget grew, the academic research enterprise was solidified in the top tier of institutions. In 1953–1954 the top twenty universities spent 66 percent of federal-sponsored research funds for academic science and awarded 52 percent of the doctorates, mainly in the life sciences, physical sciences, and engineering, the same fields that were receiving most of the federal research funds.[39]

Spurred on by the Russian launching of *Sputnik I* in 1957, the national government provided even more funds for basic research. Federal sponsorship of research increased every year from 1958 to 1968.[40] In that decade alone annual federal contributions to academic research increased fivefold from $1 billion to $5 billion (in 1988 constant dollars). As the federal investment increased, so did the universities' share of basic research, from one-third to one-half in that decade.[41] As a result the basic research expenditures of research universities tripled from $433 million in 1960 to $1.64 billion in 1968.

Thus, the post–World War II period clearly established that research was a separate function and operation largely paid for by the federal government, and that universities could perform a large share of the nation's research effort.[42] At the same time as higher education was perceived as having an increasingly legitimate research role, higher education enrollment rose from 3 million to 7 million students, doubling within doctoral granting universities, from 1.24 million to 2.5 million, for undergraduate and graduate levels combined. Annual Ph.D. production in science and engineering grew dramatically, from near 6,000 in 1958 to over 14,000 a decade later.[43]

The allocation of research funds by the national government has consistently exhibited two characteristic features: multiagency support and field-initiated competitive research grants. Federal sponsorship has entailed a clear presidential directive (Executive Order #10521 in 1954) that no single agency within the government should be given sole responsibility for distributing research funds. Rather, each federal agency should sponsor research related to its mission, be it health, defense, or energy. In 1959, 96 percent of federal sponsorship came from five agencies: Department of Defense; Department of Health, Education, and Welfare (largely the National Institutes of Health [NIH]), Atomic Energy Commission, National Science Foundation, and Department of Agriculture. Over 96 percent of the $1.4 billion spent that year went for research in the life sciences, physical sciences, and engineering, leaving the social sciences and, particularly, the humanities neglected.[44]

Although such expansion in research funds lacked a unified policy specifying purposes, funding has been indirectly and loosely coordinated by

peer review. The mechanism for reviewing research proposals and awarding research grants on a competitive basis became the primary vehicle
through which the national government thought it would insure support
and encouragement of the best research.[45] For the most part, although
some effort was made to disperse resources across geographic locations and
to smaller institutions, the federal agencies' priorities were to nurture excellence. The resulting pattern of funding reinforced the leading tier of research universities, which presently constitute only about 3 percent of all
U.S. institutions of higher education, and gave support primarily to the sciences, with life sciences and physical sciences accounting for over one-half
of the basic research budget.[46] In 1958 the top one hundred universities
spent 95 percent of all federal university R&D funds; a decade later their
share had fallen somewhat but it was still a hefty 86 percent.[47]

Similar to the expansion of federal basic research funding, the federal
support for doctoral education intensified, mostly for training science and
engineering personnel. Aside from short-term interests to advance science
and technology, the national government was mindful of improving the
country's research capacity and developing a longer-term pipeline of
trained scientists and engineers. The National Cancer Act of 1937, which
called for grants-in-aid to nongovernment scientists and direct student aid
in the form of fellowships, set a precedent for this twofold agenda. In the
1950s the National Science Foundation offered over five hundred prestigious
portable fellowships each year. A variety of mechanisms were employed to
attract and keep talented students in the pipeline: direct student aid (fellowships), student aid channeled through institutions (traineeships), and
individual project grants to individual faculty that included salary for
graduate student research assistants.[48]

Congressional response to the Soviet launching of *Sputnik* in 1957
reflected another surge in federal commitment to the improvement of research training. The National Defense Education Act of 1958 conveyed a
commitment to rebuild the nation's research capability and specifically to
support science education through a host of fellowship and traineeship
programs to be launched by a variety of federal agencies (NIH, NSF,
NASA). National Research Service awards, administered through three
federal agencies in the 1960s, constituted a second major initiative. These
training programs were deliberate efforts to attract talented students with
stipends for predoctoral and postdoctoral support as well as to improve the
training environment on campuses with institutional allowances. In the decade between 1961 and 1972 these programs assisted over 30,000 graduate
students and 27,000 postdoctoral scholars.[49]

With direct support of doctoral education through fellowships and
traineeships provided on a competitive basis, talent and support continued
to concentrate at the leading research universities where federally spon-

sored research was centered. The resulting consolidation of resources for both research and doctoral education gave these institutions a double competitive edge in attracting high-quality students and faculty. Thus, federal initiatives were instrumental in cementing the legitimacy of the interdependence between sponsored university research for its short-term R&D value and graduate education for its manpower training.

A New Era of Expansion for Graduate Education

Within the context of expanded, sponsored research opportunities and a shifting funding base, the graduate education system became dispersed into a wide range of doctoral and master's programs, both growing at a constant rate each decade. Doctorates increased from 6,000 in 1950 to 10,000 in 1960: more doctorates were granted in the decade of the 1950s than in all the years prior.[50] A dramatic threefold increase during the 1960s then brought the total up to nearly 30,000.[51] The expansion of master's degrees followed a similar pattern. From a base of about 25,000 granted in 1940, master's degrees dramatically increased to about 60,000 in 1950, 75,000 in 1960, and close to 300,000 two decades later.[52] Thus, while the concentration of Ph.D.'s in the top tier of universities has been most visible, a larger penumbra of institutions account for graduate education at the master's level.[53]

Both doctoral and master's degrees reflect an overall increase in degrees awarded across all fields of study, especially in the sciences and professional fields. In 1965 the physical sciences, the life sciences, and engineering accounted for close to one-half the doctorates; two decades later they still dominated, although the life sciences edged out the other two fields. The social sciences (including psychology) remained fairly constant at about 20 percent, humanities dropped from 20 percent to 10 percent, and education increased from about 15 percent to 25 percent, reflecting an increased professional orientation of graduate study.[54] The fields in which doctoral degrees are awarded have diversified tremendously. An already large number of about 150 at the end of the first World War grew to over 550 fields in 1960. In addition, forty-seven types of doctoral degrees besides the Ph.D. developed: e.g., doctor of education, doctor of social work, doctor of business administration, doctor of theology, doctor of arts.[55] A similar orientation to the demands of the marketplace is evident in master's degrees. Revealing a marked shift since 1965, roughly 85 percent of master's degrees reflect practitioner-oriented programs such as education (down from 40 percent to 30 percent), business (up from 7 percent to 23 percent), engineering (10 percent), and the health professions (about 6 percent), while only 16 percent were in research-oriented master's programs.[56]

The early 1970s brought an economic crisis that threatened even the strong research-training link of the sciences and the solid resource base of the most prominent research universities. An era of retrenchment, roughly between 1969 and 1975, began with a tightening academic labor market and inflation in the wider economy. Most important, the national government reduced funds to support the research infrastructure it had dramatically expanded in the postwar era. Between 1968 and 1971 the basic research budget fell over 10 percent in real terms.[57] Academic research expenditures contributed annually by the federal government declined from $5 billion in 1968 to $4.7 billion in 1974. The government's attention turned to short-term research, which would make scientific knowledge technologically relevant. As a result, cutbacks in funds meant that physical resources, such as equipment and campus buildings, were neglected.

As funds for academic science declined, so did support for graduate students; thus both became "victims of federal benign neglect."[58] Although doctoral degrees peaked in 1973 at 33,000, the government abruptly withdrew the bulk of its direct fellowship support to graduate students, especially in some of the larger programs of the National Institutes of Health. In the space of a few years, from 1968 to 1970, 57,000 fellowships and traineeships fell to 41,000.[59] As graduate fellowships were "cut back too fast and too far," a series of national reports conducted on the finance of graduate education cited the destabilizing effects of "stop-and-go" federal funds and the disadvantages of smaller-scale fellowships.[60] In place of the wider base of support, the government compelled the bulk of doctoral students to get direct support from loans and indirect support from short-term R&D assistantships.

Institutions responded with their own initiatives, with teaching assistantships and research assistantships drawing on institutional funds from endowments and tuition; public institutions drew from state revenues. Institutions also used their own funds to support research activities, including facilities and equipment improvement and stepped-up efforts to collaborate with industry. In seeking a broader base of funding in specialized areas of interdisciplinary and applied research, American universities have elaborated their organizational structures in the form of extradepartmental research units, with an increasing number of nonfaculty research personnel, who vary as to the extent of their involvement in graduate education.

CONTEMPORARY SYSTEM OF GRADUATE EDUCATION

Since the mid-1970s graduate education in the United States has grown to be an even larger and more diverse system. With an enterprise so vast, as the following chapter makes clear, there is tremendous variation in the actual educational experiences of graduate students in the same fields at different institutions as well as across departments within the same institutions. But that variation occurs within a larger framework of system sponsorship that is subject to the impact of shifts in primary funding sources.

The historical patterns that crystallized in the quarter-century immediately after World War II have remained prominent in the past two decades: the production of doctorates and the production of research are concentrated at the leading universities in the American system, although some decentralization of doctoral production has occurred at the base. Graduate education and postdoctoral work continued to be supported more heavily in the sciences than in other fields.

Master's degree programs have grown enormously since the mid-1970s, with education and business alone accounting for one-half of the total annual degrees conferred.[61] Although the majority of Ph.D. recipients (over 80 percent) hold master's degrees, increasingly the latter is taken as a terminal degree earned. Master's degrees in the professions account for 85 percent; the other 15 percent are in liberal arts.[62] Many of these master's programs, which are the highest degrees given in certain fields, do not fit into a linear sequence with undergraduate or doctoral programs. Some are in problem-centered areas, such as urban planning, social work, or counseling. Others are more directly linked to the demands of the marketplace, such as technically oriented computer science or nursing sciences. Unlike doctoral programs, the explicit focus of these programs is on training the student for practice rather than for theory or knowledge development. Consistent efforts have been made by the Council of Graduate Schools, which represents four hundred higher education institutions, urging standardization of master's degree programs.[63]

Overall enrollment in master's and doctoral programs totaled over 1.5 million students by the end of the 1980s, accounting for about 10 percent of all higher education enrollments in the United States. Roughly one-third of all science and engineering students are not U.S. citizens and hold only temporary visas; in some fields such as mathematics, engineering, and computer science, foreign students were over 40 percent of the graduate enrollment and about two-thirds of postdoctoral appointments in engineering.[64]

The distinctive American model for doctoral education has remained the same. Students begin with a few years of prescribed course work, classes, and seminars led by a faculty member. Passing examinations marks advancement to candidacy, when students undertake a dissertation that reflects original research under the guidance of a faculty committee. In the past decade, across the disciplines, doctoral students are taking longer to complete their programs, averaging 6.8 registered years, with humanities taking about eight years and engineering less than six years.[65]

During the Ph.D. program, across all fields, students and faculty establish some kind of apprenticeship relationship that is often formalized and tied to a form of financial support. Teaching assistantships are standard. Research assistantships, largely tied to federally sponsored research projects, are most prominent in the sciences. More than one position may be held at a time, although the convention is not to exceed half-time employment in order not to interfere with progress toward the degree. As we shall see in greater detail in chapter 8, in the sciences, where research is laboratory-intensive, a graduate student may work alongside or be closely supervised by a faculty advisor; the dissertation may arise as one piece of a faculty research project. In the humanities, where research is library-intensive, a student is more likely to work independently with infrequent contact with faculty supervisors or even graduate student peers.

Changes in the funding of graduate education and research during the 1970s and 1980s appear to have altered significantly the nature of the research-training experience. When the national government eliminated the bulk of its fellowship programs, it reduced support of graduate education as an intrinsically worthwhile activity and instead linked it more directly to the production of research. The funding base became centered more on research assistantships embedded in short-term academic research projects, supplemented by a variety of loan programs. The impact of changes in the funding mechanisms has been most evident in the research training experiences of Ph.D. students in the sciences.

One set of concerns focuses on the lengthening of time to completion. Students acquire more loan indebtedness the longer they defer employment and become discouraged from the loss of momentum. In an effort to speed up the process, several programs across the country are reducing requirements for course work so that students begin working on their dissertations earlier. The University of Chicago, for example, instituted a reduced course work policy in 1982 in order, a university report said, to encourage students "to engage in their doctoral research as quickly, as clearly and as self-consciously as possible," which will lead to "a healthier emphasis on the research stage of graduate student work."[66] The need for such a change is especially apt for the humanities, where the prior tendency has always been to handle knowledge changes cumulatively, with increasing amounts of material incorporated into graduate course work; in the sciences (for example, physics and biological sciences) the faculty revamp the curricula every few years instead. Along similar lines, the expectations for the dissertation are being revised, especially in the sciences, including economics, where shorter publishable articles are more important than a long treatise.[67]

Such changes may also reflect the recognition that many Ph.D.'s do not end up in research settings, or, if on an academic path, they tend to teach in a nonresearch university, thus rendered "forgotten scientists."[68] Even though those institutions offer the master's as the highest degree, they employ research-oriented faculty who earned doctorates from the country's leading research universities. As a case in point, San Diego State University is now encouraging research activity of its faculty through several mechanisms, including release time from teaching, summer funding, travel funds, graduate student assistantships, and so on.[69] Although it is not chartered as a research university nor is it doctoral granting, that institution is attempting to raise its research profile.

A second set of concerns focuses on the nature of student-faculty relationships during research training, especially for students in the sciences. The historical ideal envisioned a student working "at the bench" with a mentor. Since sponsored research has become the medium for supervision and potential collaboration, there is some critical concern that faculty have become more like project managers and administrators rather than mentor-professors, and that students are being supervised in a more directive manner, treated like employees and technicians rather than as apprentices. As a sociologist of science suggests, "the roles of faculty member (mentor) and principal investigator (employer) are becoming inconsistent, straining the incumbents. Principles and practices that the *mentor* would prefer are inconsistent with the needs of the scientist as *employer*."[70]

Graduate student research assistants face the exigencies of an increasingly competitive arena of research support: time schedules of short-term project grants mean less leeway for mistakes; less available grant money means more competition and pressure to produce better results; sharing capital-intensive instrumentation means long hours of work, often in other cities; increased size of research teams entails perfecting a technique on one part of a project rather than completing an entire project from beginning to end; and time spent in research is valued over time spent in the "burden" of teaching younger graduate students or undergraduates. The arrangements emphasize efficiency and productivity, which promote an organizational climate of a factory floor, or a "quasi-firm," rather than a learning arena.[71]

In the context of efforts to reduce the federal deficit, the Tax Reform Act in 1986 included a provision to tax stipends associated with research and teaching assistantships that had previously been excluded from income tax. In addition to requiring technical changes in the administration of financial assistance, this change has been cited by concerned scholars and practitioners as another sign that graduate students are increasingly conceived of as workers producing short-term R&D rather than as longer-term national investments whose advanced study and training is inherently worthy of support. Although universities and their representatives lobbied on behalf of themselves and their graduate students to have this legislation amended, the outcome was to deem as taxable income the assistantship stipends but not fellowships and tuition awards.

Other signs that graduate students have become more like academic laborers are evident in campus controversies that surface for public discussion, especially on campuses where graduate students have unionized. In some cases students perceive and faculty admit that advanced students are kept on in laboratories longer than is necessary for their training because of their productive contributions. In other cases disputes over academic authorship and ownership of intellectual property appear. The tensions are heightened with the blurring of boundaries in university-industry collaboration: if the exploitation of students for a faculty member's academic advancement is historically grounded in the university research system, it is another matter for a professor to profit financially from a student's work on a commercial venture.[72]

One organizational arrangement to mitigate these tensions is to expand the structure of research training. Moving away from a short-term, product-oriented conception of graduate training, the longer-term professional development of the student can be made explicit, as in science fields where postdoctoral positions have become the norm. In fact, it is now a necessary one-to-three-year component of research training after the doctorate in such fields as physics and biological sciences. The "postdoc" position is generally seen as an attractive opportunity to begin publishing and to refine research skills in a market that is increasingly competitive for both industrial and academic positions. Across the country in 1986 there were an estimated 24,000 postdocs, 90 percent of whom are located in the top one hundred universities and 30 percent in the top ten. One year later the number rose to 25,300, a 5 percent increase.[73] Even if the expansion of postdoctoral training has been praised mainly as a way of enabling young scientists to enhance their expertise and to gain a competitive edge, it may also have a hidden value for the graduate education and research system by providing a rationale for graduate students to patiently climb a longer ladder.

Another feature of the university research system that mitigates these tensions is widespread loan assistance programs. In compensating for the reduction in fellowship support, loans increased substantially in one decade alone, from 15 percent in 1974 to 44 percent in 1984 of all students enrolled in graduate programs.[74] In the latter year over 500,000 students working on graduate degrees borrowed $2 billion from the federal government in guaranteed student loans.[75] Graduate students also contributed more self-support, especially in the nonscience fields.

Indeed, the finance of graduate education entails major policy issues, with the quality of education and training at stake. Strains have been severe in the humanities and social sciences, where there has been little or no federal support. They have also increased in the sciences and engineering over the past fifteen years with the decline in federal funding of various types of studentships. Graduate education continues to be federally supported in an ad hoc and largely indirect fashion. The largest potential funding base, that of the national government, is essentially unstable. Professors are under pressure to develop lean research budgets, while at the same time including salaries for students. The trends in government financing during the 1970s and 1980s suggest a need to examine more closely what material conditions are required to sustain effective research training in universities as well as to consider what arrangements can safeguard the autonomy and creativity of institutions, faculty, and students alike.

CONTEMPORARY SYSTEM OF ORGANIZED RESEARCH

Research in the United States is performed in a variety of organizational settings: intramural government laboratories, industrial laboratories, non-profit research institutes, and universities. Shifting patterns of research sponsors and research performers over the past two decades point to two themes. First, the involvement of government and, increasingly, industrial sponsors has resulted in a blurring of boundaries, if not purposes, between academic researchers and external sponsors. Second, the proportion of basic research done in university settings may decline, unless industrial sponsorship replaces the federal involvement. Such contemporary trends in the organization of research have implications for the research training component of graduate education.

Of the total $130 billion national R&D effort in 1986, about one-half ($55 billion) was provided by the federal government and about one-half ($60 billion) by industry.[76] Most R&D funds go toward development. Federal funds of $14.5 billion went for basic research, making the national government the largest sponsor, at about two-thirds, in this category; industry was second largest sponsor at about $3 billion; and higher education institutions themselves were third at $1.5 billion.

The national government itself also performs about 10 percent of the country's R&D effort and employs 8 percent of the scientists and engineers.[77] Located in government laboratories, the amount of basic research conducted by the federal government ranks second to universities. Although generally perceived to be less effective than university labs in generating high-quality basic research, a few labs stand out as first rate, such as the National Institutes of Health (NIH), which allocates 15 percent of its research funds to intramural researchers on its own "campus."[78]

In contrast to government laboratories, industry performs about three-quarters of the total national R&D effort and employs 75 percent of all engineers and 50 percent of all scientists.[79] But as performers of basic research, industry ranks third behind university and government labs. Compared to other countries, industry's share of basic research in the United States is greater than industry's share in France but less than in Japan. Especially in American biotechnology research, small firms play a big role.

Nonprofit research institutes now perform about 3 percent of the total national R&D effort.[80] Several kinds of institutes fall into this classification, including applied research institutes (Stanford Research Institute), operating foundations (Institute for Advanced Study), endowed institutes (Brookings Institution, Sloan Kettering), and project institutes (Institute for Cancer Research, Bureau of Social Science Research).[81] Some institutes have merged with or converted into universities; others have acquired the right to award degrees: the Mellon Institute merged with the Carnegie Institute of Technology to form Carnegie Mellon University; the Woods Hole Oceanographic Institute in Massachusetts became a doctoral-granting enterprise.[82] Some institutes managed by universities that have been deeply involved in research sponsored by the Department of Defense have had to sever their university connections: SRI from Stanford, Electronics Research Laboratories from Columbia, and Draper Laboratory from Massachusetts Institute of Technology.[83] A closely related setting consists of federally funded R&D centers that together perform about 3 percent of national R&D.[84] Funded directly to meet the particular needs of a federal agency, such as the Department of Energy or the Air Force, many of these centers are administered, or hosted, by universities or nonprofit institutions.

Universities perform about one-half of all basic research. Sponsored research resources are concentrated: the top one hundred institutions account for over 80 percent of all academic R&D funds, the top fifty over 60 percent, the top ten over 20 percent. The distribution of academic R&D across fields has remained essentially the same over the past two decades, with the life sciences consistently receiving the largest share ($4.5 billion in 1987) of federal obligations for basic research and the physical sciences receiving the next largest share ($2 billion). The behavioral and social sciences have seen a decline from $1 billion in 1972 to $.78 billion in 1987.[85]

Whether basic research is done in academic or nonacademic settings makes a difference in programmatic autonomy. Usually, basic research is ideologically grounded in the norms of academic science, where professionals have autonomy to choose and conduct research projects, to communicate extensively with domestic and international colleagues, and to compete in a system of peer review. Universities ostensibly do research with a greater degree of independence than government or industry, which have more explicit political and commercial interests.

The organization of research in university settings has historically been anchored in the departmental structure, where departmental faculty work as both individual investigators and mentors to their advanced graduate students in the department's degree programs. The major persistent exception to this mode of organization in the contemporary period is the organized research unit (ORU).

ORUs are academic units outside departments and lacking degree-granting status. Prior to the twentieth century, ORUs were primarily observatories and museums, but in the post–World War II expansion of academic research, ORUs proliferated to meet new societal demands for research that did not correspond to instructional areas outlined by departments or that was disproportionate to departments in magnitude and expense. Funded by the national government, state governments, industry, and foundations, ORUs have extended university research into interdisciplinary, applied, and capital-intensive endeavors.[86] By the end of the 1980s, there were over two thousand of them on American campuses: they continued to emerge in new fields of biotechnology, microelectronics, material sciences, and artificial intelligence.

While the presence of external funds from a sponsor is often the impetus for a proposed ORU, other criteria include the presence of a critical mass of faculty and the availability of administrative support. Some ORUs even have explicit commitments to graduate education, such as graduate fellowships offered by the Stanford Humanities Center. ORUs can offer important advantages for graduate education. Intellectually, they can mediate between the world of disciplinary training and real world needs and problems.[87] Practically, they can provide dissertation support and stipends for graduate students. They may make available more and better research equipment. Finally, as an indirect benefit to graduate students, they employ specialists (postdoctoral or nonfaculty researchers) in a temporary home, akin to the departmental home, in which graduate students can participate.

The administration of research and training in ORUs evokes a new set of challenges, as it is increasingly incompatible with departmental organization. Full-time nonfaculty research personnel may supervise graduate student research assistants but do not have faculty status.[88] Generally, students and younger faculty want the opportunity to work in ORU settings, with trained researchers and up-to-date equipment. Older department-based faculty and administrators may feel threatened that these centers draw intellectual, organizational, and economic vitality away from departmental graduate programs and thereby jeopardize the continued viability of various departments. Not only do faculty loyalties become divided between organizational units, but budgets for research are overseen by different managers than those who handle departmental instructional budgets. Thus, a significant component of research training ends up staffed and financed by complex administrative arrangements in which faculty allocations and budget allocations may no longer be congruent with the actual practice of department-based graduate education. In short, the actual research training activity of graduate education may become organizationally less visible as it increasingly falls between the lines of departmental organization.

In recent years ORUs have become a highly visible and controversial receptacle for forthcoming industrial funds, especially as federal initiatives have been launched to encourage industrial contributions for larger-scale operations on campuses. Beginning with the mid-1970s, the NSF established the Industry-University Cooperative Research Projects; again in the late 1980s, NSF promoted proposals for Engineering Research Centers as well as Science and Technology Centers at universities. These programs were to be funded initially by congressional appropriations and to be gradually weaned from NSF funds through industrial contributions. Generating controversy across these programs was an explicit orientation for universities to aid in the nation's economic competitiveness.

Graduate education and research are affected in mixed ways by these kinds of initiatives that combine—or seek to replace—federal support with industrial sponsorship. Resources become not only more concentrated but less flexible, for once a center is established it has to be fed. Moreover, industrial sponsorship, whether formally arranged in these kinds of ORUs or as informal collaboration, carries some potential constraints in terms of the research process (for example, secrecy) and the product (for example, agreements on patents). However, by favoring new interdisciplinary and applied sciences and by bringing to the campus research personnel to staff those facilities, industrial sponsors provide graduate students with exposure to timely problems, to state-of-the-art research and techniques, and to internships that are job placement opportunities in industry, and they provide faculty with supplemental income.[89]

Attracting some university administrators and researchers to industrial collaboration or sponsorship is the recognition of a formidable problem: how will universities sustain the material conditions required for first-class, capital-intensive science? Direct appeals by universities to the federal government have brought limited results. With much lobbying on the part of university representatives, the federal government has reluctantly agreed to sponsor some of the rebuilding and replacement of campus research facilities and equipment that was neglected throughout the 1970s and insufficient as science became more capital-intensive in the 1980s. Both the NIH and the NSF participated in this revitalization through regular research grants and center grants.[90]

Another strategy for universities to recover the enormous costs incurred in campus research has been to renegotiate the indirect cost rate for overhead on research grants, although university administrators, campus-based researchers, and the federal agencies have been struggling to reconcile their conflicting interests. The indirect cost rate is a mechanism for distributing among sponsors and research projects the indirect costs the institution incurs through lighting, heat, libraries, and general maintenance of the campus. Since a university wants to recoup the maximum possible and the researcher wants as much as possible for the research process itself, administrators and researchers disagree. Universities vary considerably in their indirect cost rates, from Stanford University at over 75 percent to leading state universities at around 50 percent. The government wants more adequate justification of university expenses.[91] Underlying these discussions is a widespread perception that instrumentation in university labs compares poorly to government or commercial labs and the conviction that a decline in quality of instrumentation in research universities may cause a decline in research productivity of academic scientists as well as in the first-rate training opportunities for graduate students.

Overall, the concern is whether universities will be able to respond to interdisciplinary research and research training without reducing the strength of traditional, disciplinary graduate education. The fear is that if universities do not make, as put by Kenneth Hoving, "some realistic accommodation...an increasingly large portion of basic research and academic activity which is necessary to the quality of (graduate) education...will move outside the university structure."[92] In spite of universities' current role as the site of over one-half of American basic research, an increase in proportional shares may occur in industry, especially as industry decides whether to collaborate with universities or to keep funds for its own laboratories. Ultimately, the concern is that academic departments would no longer be on the frontiers of research and that the best researchers would be moved away from graduate students, thereby jeopardizing the premise of the whole system—that "the best and the brightest" produce the best science and scientists at centers of excellence.[93]

CONCLUSION

Over the past century graduate education and organized research have become so interwoven in American higher education that graduate education and research has emerged as the foremost explicit raison d'etre for universities in the top tier, as an increasingly noble aim for lower tiers to emulate, and as an implicit professional imperative for faculty devoted to the production of new knowledge and the preparation of new generations of knowledge producers. This distinctive linkage between graduate education and research has occurred fundamentally in the most visible top layer of doctoral training, which has helped raise the country to international eminence in science and scholarship but at the same time has overshadowed the vitality of a wide array of thriving master's degree programs.

As with the evolution of other social institutions, the forces establishing this arrangement differ from those that sustain it. Historical evidence on the organization and sponsorship of graduate education and organized research reveals that the linkage of doctoral education and research in the leading modern universities was created out of opportunities from major societal changes: the use of scientific research for national defense and economic priorities, the rise in the research budget of the federal government for R&D allocations and for basic research funds, the plurality of funding agencies to help stabilize university autonomy, and a system of peer review to insure distribution of resources for the best science. Universities became the main performers of basic research, with an abundance of funds unconnected to their instructional budgets, and the federal government became the dominant external source for funds.

As historical circumstances changed, sustaining this linkage between government and universities proved to be a fundamental challenge for research universities. Although still in a system without centralized planning, an array of factors have enhanced the structural partnership. First, public and private universities alike have become heavily dependent on research funds from the federal government and other patrons, given the capital-intensive requirements for university expansion. Second, protecting the legacy of excellence in doctoral education, universities have an incentive to retain a dominant role in the country's basic research enterprise, for otherwise they would be unable to attract talented faculty and students for doctoral study. Third, the many federal funding agencies maintain their instrumental course, ever vigilant that universities keep their end of the bargain by contributing to the production of knowledge and the preparation of trained science and engineering personnel.

At the same time, however, a changing social and economic climate has strained the university-government linkage. During the 1970s and 1980s, shifts in organization and sponsorship of university research produced a context of greater uncertainty, as funding sources and amounts reflected changing perceptions of the appropriate role of the federal government in sponsoring research and research training. Despite the immense post–World War II surge of funds, the government has become an unstable base of economic and political support for university research and graduate education.

There may be powerful negative consequences in sustaining what now seems to be a problematic partnership. Two sets of policy concerns have been most prominent in this regard. The first characterizes a federal fiscal presence less as one of support and more as one of regulation. Most obvious for university researchers and their doctoral students are the ways in which rhythms of federal research funding have come to dominate not only the conduct of university research and research training but its content. The second set focuses on the patterns of distribution of research funds across institutions as well as fields of study. Although concentration of funds enhances more concentrated activity and ultimately knowledge advancement, the perennial concern is that the dispersion of funds required for maintaining a broader base of activity across campuses and disciplines does not appear to enhance the current science and technology agenda.

At both levels of campus and national policy discussions, much of the discourse centers on strategies for sustaining the linkage while simultaneously protecting the autonomy of higher education institutions and the professionals who work within them. From the university perspective, the drive for competitive advancement makes the leading one hundred institutions most vocal. As research performers and trainers of scientific personnel, universities have competed to sustain a share of basic research funds. This is the modern research imperative, the vehicle whereby universities protect if not advance their institutional mobility, for the institution which is not steadily advancing is certainly falling behind."[94] These institutions have consistently and aggressively competed for talented faculty and graduate students, while simultaneously seeking to preserve their autonomy through stabilizing a base of support from a plurality of sources in external sponsors and internal revenues. Through their own initiatives, they have created increasingly complex organizational structures in order to minimize the skewing of institutional priorities toward the economic incentives of short-term R&D sponsors.

Somewhat less vocal and certainly less visible internationally, the vast majority (seven hundred) of institutions engaged in graduate education at master's and doctoral levels emulate the model of the leading tier of research universities. If at the leading institutions all fields could be covered within the aim of undertaking more sponsored research and expanding Ph.D. production, the less elite institutions have a lesser resource base in facilities, departmental funds, and critical masses of faculty and students and can invest their resources only in selected fields. Not until the 1970s did asserting a distinctive institutional mission become a strategy for gaining a competitive edge in specialized areas. These campuses have indeed become more research oriented, as they encourage and reward faculty to seek sponsored projects. Given the insufficient magnitude of scale, though, as the next chapter will reveal, these campuses are also vulnerable to the agendas of short-term R&D sponsors, in that fiscal support for applied research projects from government or industry provides a relatively larger boost to a smaller base, and thus more visibly may draw faculty away from their basic instructional missions.

Thus, throughout the American system, the contemporary era reveals an increasing disjuncture between nineteenth-century ideals and the exigencies of transforming campuses into modern research complexes. Universities have been continually challenged by an inherently unstable federal funding base that left direct support to doctoral education concentrated in the physical and life sciences, weak in the social sciences, and virtually nonexistent in the humanities. Particularly in the past two decades, the tension has become heightened as the national government has replaced many fellowships and traineeships with loans that are incurred by individual students, leaving the bulk of support as indirect, through research assistantships on R&D projects that strain the ideal mentor-apprentice research training relationship.

Substantial changes in the volume and nature of academic research as well as in the economic and political role of universities obscure the more significant issue: whether the support of graduate education is motivated by a desire to purchase short-term R&D labor or to make a long-term investment in the nation's research capability. During the 1970s and 1980s, the short-term view has been much in evidence among external sponsors, necessitating compensatory action by universities traditionally devoted to the production of knowledge for its own sake and to the effective training of future generations of scientists and scholars.

NOTES

The author gratefully acknowledges research resources from the Spencer Foundation, editorial suggestions from Burton R. Clark, and research assistance from Ronald Opp.

1. Rosenzweig, "Rationale for a Federal Role," p. 11.
2. American Council on Education, *1986–87 Factbook on Higher Education*; Glazer, *Master's Degree*; Hauptman, *Students in Graduate and Professional Education*.
3. Crane, "Scientists at Major and Minor Universities," p. 713.
4. For the rise of modern American science, see Bruce, *Launching of Modern American Science*. For the emergence of the research university, see Geiger, *To Advance Knowledge*, and Veysey, *Emergence of the American University*. For graduate education, see Storr, *Beginnings of Graduate Education in America*, and Berelson, *Graduate Education in the United States*. For an analysis of their interdependence, see Ben-David, *Centers of Learning*.

The strategy for this analysis finds its conceptual underpinnings in the social theories of Durkheim and Weber. Specifically, there are four conceptual anchors: a Durkheimian notion of the division of labor process; a Weberian notion that beliefs and structures together determine change; a Weberian view on the causes and consequences of social stratification; and an institutional view that the establishment of a new classification of social institutions is a social and political process of acquiring legitimacy.

5. Bruce, *Launching of Modern American Science*, p. 335.
6. Ibid., p. 337.
7. Ibid., p. 335.
8. Wolfle, *Home of Science*, p. 4.
9. Veysey, *Emergence of the American University*, pp. 149, 168.
10. Ibid., pp. 318–319.
11. Hofstadter and Hardy, *Development and Scope of Higher Education in the United States*, pp. 44–45.
12. Berelson, *Graduate Education in the United States*, p. 33.

13. Mayhew, *Reform in Graduate Education*, p. 6; Ben-David, *Centers of Learning*, p. 61.

14. Ben-David, *Centers of Learning*, p. 102.

15. Geiger, *To Advance Knowledge*, p. 37.

16. Veysey, *Emergence of the American University*, p. 177.

17. Geiger, *To Advance Knowledge*, p. 19. The original AAU institutions were: California, Catholic, Chicago, Clark, Columbia, Cornell, Harvard, Johns Hopkins, Michigan, Pennsylvania, Princeton, Stanford, Wisconsin, and Yale; they were joined by Illinois and Minnesota in 1907, and California Institute of Technology and Massachusetts Institute of Technology after World War I.

18. According to the Carnegie Classification (1987), the U.S. system may be differentiated vertically by sectors; roughly 800 institutions offer graduate programs of which the top 213 are distinguished for doing both doctoral education and federally sponsored research. The next sector consists of 595 comprehensive colleges and universities in which the master's degree is the highest level offered. NSF (1989) data for science and engineering doctorates in 1985–1986 show that the top sector of 213 universities produced 95 percent of the doctorates and 72 percent of the master's degrees. Within that sector the leading 104 produced 83 percent of the doctorates and 53 percent of the master's. The comprehensive sector awarded 1.2 percent of the doctorates and 23 percent of the master's.

19. Merton, "Matthew Effect in Science." The Matthew effect of the rich getting richer, as hypothesized by Merton, signifies a cumulative advantage in the allocation of rewards and resources, thereby enhancing one's already eminent position in the social system of science.

20. Veysey, *Emergence of the American University*, p. 312.

21. Trow, "Analysis of Status," p. 134.

22. DiMaggio and Powell, "Iron Cage Revisited." In this macrosocial theory of organizational change, institutional isomorphism is posited as part of a modernization in which the state and the professions come to replace bureaucratization as forces for rationalization.

23. Bruce, *Launching of Modern American Science*, pp. 329–334.

24. Rudolph, *American College and University*, pp. 425–427.

25. Berelson, *Graduate Education in the United States*; Geiger, *To Advance Knowledge*, especially pp. 140–173 for a thorough discussion of foundation giving and university-foundation relations in the interwar years.

26. Geiger, *To Advance Knowledge*, p. 166.

27. Rudolph, *American College and University*, p. 430.

As philanthropists became more prominent, some observers were uncomfortable, warning that these benefactors used their wealth to transform and redirect higher education through the funding of selected institutions. See Fosdick, *Adventure in Giving*. As a case in point, this was the procedure by which medical education, with its attention to basic biological and chemical science research, was established in its modern form. See Flexner, *Medical Education in the United States and Canada*; Brown, "Public Health in Imperialism," Sacks, *Caring by the Hour*, and Starr, *Social Transformation of American Medicine*, p. 120. Other observers were uncomfortable with philanthropic support, for its potential compromise of the ideals of scholarship toward business interests, including Veblen (1918) in his famous treatise, *Higher Learning in America.*

28. Rudolph, *American College and University*, p. 427.

29. See Geiger, *To Advance Knowledge*, especially p. 175 and p. 192. For a description of the role of private industrial support in the interwar years, see pp. 174–245.

30. Ibid., p. 262.

31. Bruce, *Launching of Modern American Science*, pp. 301–305 and 315–317. Quotation is on p. 315.

32. Geiger, *To Advance Knowledge*, pp. 13, 100, 165, 256. Geiger states that these elites met in

committees of the NRC, on the boards of the Carnegie and Rockefeller philanthropies, and as trustees of recipient [universities]. . . . Such gatherings brought together the elite of American science, the heads of the philanthropic world, research directors and corporate leaders of the major research-based firms of the day . . . [with] the enduring effect of bringing industry, foundations, and universities into closer cooperation and of consecrating the direction of science policy to a private elite that represented the leadership of those institutions. The federal government, which the NRC had originally been meant to advise, was pushed into the background during the 1920s. (p.100).

33. Ibid., p. 255.

34. All historical data here are from Starr, *Social Transformation of American Medicine*, especially p. 193.

35. Wolfle, *Home of Science*, p. 110, and Dickson, *The New Politics of Science.*

36. Rivlin, *Role of the Federal Government in Financing Higher Education*, p. 31.

37. Finkelstein, *American Academic Profession*, p. 24.

38. Geiger, *To Advance Knowledge*, p. 220.

39. Rivlin, *Role of the Federal Government in Financing Higher Education*, p. 47.

40. Dickson, *New Politics of Science.*

41. Government-University-Industry Research Roundtable, "Science and Technology in the Academic Enterprise."

42. Ben-David, *Centers of Learning*, p. 119.

43. Government-University-Industry Research Roundtable, "Science and Technology in the Academic Enterprise."

44. Knight, et al. *Federal Government and Higher Education*, pp. 135–137.

45. The peer review system places responsibility for allocating funds with the science community. The criteria used for judging scientific merit are: research performance competence, intrinsic merit of research, utility or relevance of research, effect of research on the infrastructure of science and engineering, including research education and the manpower base. The latter two criteria are often brought in with a dual system of peer review, where the first stage entails technical review by a panel of experts and a second stage in which both scientists and lay representatives from government or industry evaluate the research in terms of broader priorities, such as geographic distribution. NIH uses the dual review system as does the NSF's Engineering Research Center program. For critical analysis of peer review and the conduct of science, see Chubin and Hackett, *Peerless Science.*

46. National Science Foundation, *Science and Technology Data Book*, p. 17.

47. Wolfle, *Home of Science*, pp. 118–120.

48. The national government has also shown a preference for supporting indi-

viduals directly rather than institutions, as the history of financial assistance reflects.

49. Coggeshall and Brown, *Career Achievements of NIH Postdoctoral Trainees and Fellows*; National Academy of Sciences, *Personnel Needs and Training for Biomedical and Behavioral Research.*

50. Berelson, *Graduate Education in the United States*, p. 30.

51. Berelson, *Graduate Education in the United States*; National Research Council, *Summary Report 1986.*

52. Department of Education and National Center for Education Statistics, *Digest of Educational Statistics 1989*; Glazer, *Master's Degree.*

53. National Research Council, *Century of Doctorates*, p. 4; Berelson, *Graduate Education in the United States*, p. 93; Ben-David, *Centers of Learning*, p. 110; National Science Foundation, unpublished data 1989.

54. National Research Council, *Summary Report 1986.*

55. Berelson, *Graduate Education in the United States*, p. 35; National Research Council, *Summary Report 1986.*

56. Glazer, *Master's Degree.*

57. Government-University-Industry Research Roundtable, "Science and Technology in the Academic Enterprise."

58. Kidd, "Graduate Education," p. 43.

59. Wolfle, *Home of Science*, p. 256.

One estimate is that funds for federal fellowships and traineeships alone were cut by one-third. The National Research Service Awards were cut dramatically, so that by 1983 there were 11,500 positions and by 1985 the awards were under $200 million, which was down 17 percent in constant dollars from 1971. Given inflation and the substantial increase overall in national research expenditures, these cutbacks were devastating (National Academy of Sciences, *Personnel Needs and Training for Biomedical and Behavioral Research*, p. 8).

In the past, humanities fellowships have come from foundations, the leader being the Andrew W. Mellon Foundation. However, some major privately funded programs have been eliminated, including the Ford Foundation (which had 600 graduate fellowships), the Woodrow Wilson Foundation (which over twenty years supported 18,000 graduate students in humanities and social sciences), and the Danforth Foundation (which over twenty-eight years supported 3,500 students in the same fields). (See Bowen, "Graduate Education".)

60. See Kidd, "Graduate Education."

The major national reports exploring the federal role in graduate education were by the Carnegie Commission in 1968 and again in 1973, the National Science Board in 1969, President's Task Force on Higher Education in 1970 and in 1973, and the National Board on Graduate Education in 1973.

One of the earlier reports, by Alice Rivlin (1969), noted problems in the dependence on federal support, quoted in Kidd, "Graduate Education" (p. 46):

> The project system has many advantages and should be retained, but it has also generated some imbalances: a) decreases in professors' loyalty to institutions; b) inadequate attention to teaching; c) relatively weak support of humanities and social sciences; d) overconcentration of federal support in relatively few institutions.

61. Glazer, *Master's Degree*.

62. Ibid.

63. Mayhew, *Reform in Graduate Education*, pp. 81–82.

64. National Science Board, *Science and Engineering Indicators*, p. 44; National Research Council, *Foreign and Foreign-Born Engineers*. In 1987 foreign citizens constituted 43 percent of the science/engineering postdocs, 41 percent of those in the sciences, and 65 percent of those in engineering, as well as about 45 percent of all full-time graduate student enrollments, which is up from 36 percent in 1977 (National Science Foundation, 1989).

65. National Research Council, *Summary Report 1986*.

66. University of Chicago, "Report of the Commission on Graduate Education," p. 126.

67. Berger, "Slowing Pace to Doctorates Spurs Worry on Filling Jobs," *New York Times* (May 3, 1989): A-1.

68. Drew, *Strengthening Academic Science*; and Drew, "Finest Science Not Always Found in Fanciest American Universities."

69. Wanberg, "Encouraging Research and Scholarship," pp. 1–2.

70. Hackett, "Science as a Vocation in the 1990s," p. 267.

71. Etzkowitz, "Entrepreneurial Scientists and Entrepreneurial Universities in American Academic Science."

72. Kenney, *Biotechnology*.

73. National Science Foundation, *Academic Science/Engineering Graduate Enrollment and Support*, p. e-21; National Science Foundation, unpublished data, 1989.

74. Hauptman, *Students in Graduate and Professional Education*.

75. Ibid., p. 57.

76. National Science Board, *Science and Engineering Indicators*; National Science Foundation, *National Patterns of Science and Technology Resources*.

77. National Science Foundation, *National Patterns of Science and Technology Resources*, p. 1.

78. Newman, *Higher Education and the American Resurgence*.

79. National Science Foundation, *National Patterns of Science and Technology Resources*, p. 1.

80. Ibid.

81. Orlans, *The Non Profit Research Institute*, pp. 3–4.

82. Ibid., pp. 152–157.

83. Ibid., pp. 148–149.

84. National Science Foundation, *National Patterns of Science and Technology Resources*, p. 1.

85. National Science Foundation, *Science and Technology Data Book*; Gerstein et al., *The Behavioral and Social Sciences*, p. 251.

86. Geiger, "Organized Research Units." Research units can also be established by federal agencies where ordered to do so by Congress, bypassing peer review procedures. This type of "pork barrel" funding is criticized because it is not based on scientific merit. The White House has generated a "hit list" questioning the worthiness of apparently trivial projects, ridiculing some campus-based operations, such as the Berry Research Center at Rutgers University, a poultry laboratory at the University of Arkansas, and a center for wildflower research at New Mexico State Uni-

versity. See Cordes, "Berry Research Center at Rutgers, Ridiculed by Reagan, Will Get Funds After All."

87. Friedman and Friedman, "Organized Research Units in Academe Revisited."

88. The term "unfaculty" or "non-faculty" has been applied to academic researchers to signify their marginal status. See Kerr's *Uses of the University*. Estimates of the number of nonfaculty researchers now employed in universities range from 5,000 (National Science Board, *Science and Engineering Indicators—1987*) to over 30,000 (Kidd, "New Academic Positions"; Teich, "Research Centers and Non-Faculty Researchers," Government-University-Industry Research Roundtable, "Science and Technology in the Academic Enterprise"). Several issues concerning their rights and responsibilities have surfaced: Should they be permitted to participate in campus governance? Should they be granted tenure or its equivalent? Should they have principal investigator status? Should they be permitted to chair dissertation committees or even to be a committee member at all? See Kruytbosch, *Organization of Research*; Kidd, "New Academic Positions"; Teich, "Research Centers"; Smith and Karlesky, *State of Academic Science*, p. 237.

89. National Science Board, University-Industry Research Relationships; Irwin Feller, "University-Industry Research and Development Relationships."

90. Smith, *State of Graduate Education*; National Science Board, *Science and Engineering Indicators*, p. 84.

91. Association of American Universities, *Report on Instrumentation Needs*, p. 20. The perception by government and researchers is that administrative expenses were inadequately justified (Donchin and Wilson, "Negotiating the Indirect Cost of Research). The role of indirect cost in peer review is a matter of controversy. There is currently a dual system. At NIH the proposal review panels see only the direct cost; whereas at NSF the total amount is shown. If a university's ICR increases, and a multiyear award has a fixed total, the NSF grant would remove funds from the researcher's project operating budget, while the NIH grant puts pressure on the federal agencies to make up the difference. It is not surprising that the federal government prefers the NSF approach because it puts pressure on the researchers and universities to keep the indirect cost rate down (White House Science Council, *Renewed Partnership*, p. 220).

92. Hoving, "Interdisciplinary Programs, Centers and Institutes," p. 2.

93. Kruytbosch, "Future Flow of Graduate Students into Scientific Research"; Smith, *State of Graduate Education*, pp. 29–30.

94. Rudolph, *American College and University*, p. 329, quoting James Angell, president of the University of Michigan in 1871. On the possible negative consequences of embracing research, see Gumport, "Research Imperative."

BIBLIOGRAPHY

American Association for the Advancement of Science. *Research and Development FY 1990, Report XIV*. Washington, D.C., 1989.

American Council on Education. *1986–87 Factbook on Higher Education*. New York: Macmillan, 1987.

Association of American Universities. *Report on Instrumentation Needs*. Washington, D.C., 1980.

Ben-David, Joseph. *Centers of Learning: Britain, France, Germany, United States*. New York: McGraw-Hill, 1977.

Berelson, Bernard. *Graduate Education in the United States*. New York: McGraw-Hill, 1960.

Bowen, William G. "Graduate Education: Prospects for the Future," *Educational Record* (Fall 1981): 20–30.

Brademus, John. "Graduate Education: Signs of Trouble and Erosion," *Change* 16, no. 2 (March 1984): 8–11.

Brown, E. Richard. "Public Health in Imperialism: Early Rockefeller Programs at Home and Abroad," *American Journal of Public Health* 66, no. 9 (1976): 897–903.

Bruce, Robert V. *The Launching of Modern American Science: 1846-1876*. New York: Alfred A. Knopf, 1987.

Carnegie Foundation for the Advancement of Teaching. *A Classification of Institutions of Higher Education*. Princeton, N.J.: Princeton University Press, 1987.

Chubin, Daryl, and Edward Hackett. *Peerless Science*. New York: SUNY Press, 1990.

Clark, Burton R. *The Higher Education System: Academic Organization in Cross-National Perspective*. Berkeley, Los Angeles, London: University of California Press, 1983.

Coggeshall, Porter, and Prudence Brown. *The Career Achievements of NIH Postdoctoral Trainees and Fellows*. NIH Program Evaluation Report by Commission on National Needs for Biomedical and Behavioral Research Personnel and Institute of Medicine. Washington, D.C.: National Academy Press, 1984.

Cordes, Colleen. "Berry Research Center at Rutgers, Ridiculed by Reagan, Will Get Funds After All." *Chronicle of Higher Education* (July 20, 1988): A17–A19.

Crane, Diana. "Scientists at Major and Minor Universities: A Study of Productivity and Recognition." *American Sociological Review* 30 (1966): 699–714.

Department of Education and National Center for Education Statistics. *Digest of Education Statistics 1989*. Washington, D.C.: U.S. Government Printing Office, 1989.

Dickson, David. *The New Politics of Science*. Chicago: University of Chicago Press, 1984.

DiMaggio, Paul, and Walter Powell, "The Iron Cage Revisited: Institutional Isomorphism and Collective Rationality in Organizational Fields." *American Sociological Review* 48 (April 1983): 147–160.

Donchin, Emanuel, and Linda Wilson. "Negotiating the Indirect Cost of Research." *American Psychology* 40, no. 7 (July 1985): 836–848.

Drew, David Eli. "Finest Science Not Always Found in Fanciest American Universities." *Los Angeles Times* (October 18, 1987): 3, 6.

————. *Strengthening Academic Science*. New York: Praeger, 1985.

England, J. Merton. *A Patron for Pure Science: The National Science Foundation's Formative Years, 1945-1957*. Washington, D.C.: National Science Foundation, 1982.

Etzkowitz, Henry. "Entrepreneurial Scientists and Entrepreneurial Universities in American Academic Science." *Minerva* XXI, no. 2/3 (1983): 198–233.

Feller, Irwin. "University-Industry Research and Development Relationships." Paper prepared for the Woodlands Center for Growth Studies for Conference on Growth Policy in the Age of High Technology: The Role of Regions and States, 1988.

Finkelstein, Martin. *The American Academic Profession.* Columbus: Ohio State University Press, 1984.

Flexner, Abraham. *Medical Education in the United States and Canada.* New York: Carnegie Foundation, 1910.

Fosdick, Raymond. *Adventure in Giving: The Story of the General Education Board, a Foundation Established by John D. Rockefeller.* New York: Harper & Row, 1962.

Frances, Carol. "1984: The Outlook for Higher Education," *AAHE Bulletin* 37, no. 6 (February 1985): 3–7.

Friedman, Robert S., and Renee C. Friedman. "Organized Research Units in Academe Revisited." In *Managing High Technology: An Interdisciplinary Perspective,* ed. B. Mar, W. Newell, and B. Saxburg. North Holland: Elsevier Science Publishers, 1985. Pp. 75–91.

Geiger, Roger L. *To Advance Knowledge: The Growth of American Research Universities in the Twentieth Century, 1900–1940.* New York: Oxford University Press, 1986.

———. "Organized Research Units: Their Role in the Development of University Research." *Journal of Higher Education* 61, no. 1 (January/February 1990): 1–19.

Gerstein, Dean, R. Duncan Luce, Neil Smelser, and Sonja Sperlich, eds. *The Behavioral and Social Sciences: Achievements.* Washington, D.C.: National Academy Press, 1988.

Glazer, Judith S. *The Master's Degree: Tradition, Diversity, Innovation.* ASHE-ERIC Higher Education Report No. 6. Washington, D.C.: Association for the Study of Higher Education, 1986.

Government-University-Industry Research Roundtable. "Science and Technology in the Academic Enterprise." Washington, D.C.: National Academy Press, 1989.

Gumport, Patricia J. "The Research Imperative." In *Culture and Ideology in Higher Education: Advancing a Critical Agenda,* ed. William Tierney. New York: Praeger, 1990. Pp. 87–105.

Hackett, Edward J. "Science as a Vocation in the 1990s." *Journal of Higher Education* 61, no. 3 (May/June 1990): 241–279.

Hauptman, Arthur M. *Students in Graduate and Professional Education: What We Know and Need to Know.* Washington, D.C.: Association of American Universities, 1986.

Hofstadter, Richard, and C. Hardy. *The Development and Scope of Higher Education in the United States.* New York: Columbia University Press, for the Commission on Financing Higher Education, 1952.

Hoving, Kenneth. "Interdisciplinary Programs, Centers and Institutes: Academic and Administrative Issues." Paper presented at the annual meeting of the Council of Graduate Schools. Washington, D.C., December, 1987.

Kenney, Martin. *Biotechnology: The University-Industrial Complex.* New Haven, Conn.: Yale University Press, 1986.

Kerr, Clark. *The Uses of the University.* New York: Harper & Row, 1963.

Kidd, Charles V. "Graduate Education: The New Debate." *Change* (May 1974): 43–50.

———. "New Academic Positions: The Outlook in Europe and North America." In *The Research System in the 1980s: Public Policy Issues,* ed. John M. Logsdon. Philadelphia: Franklin Institute Press, 1982. Pp. 83–96.

Knight, Douglas, et al. *The Federal Government and Higher Education.* Englewood Cliffs, N.J.: Prentice-Hall, 1960.

Kruytbosch, Carlos. "The Future Flow of Graduate Students into Scientific Research: A Federal Policy Issue?" Paper presented at annual meeting of Council of Graduate Schools, Orlando, Florida, December 5–7, 1979.

———. *The Organization of Research in the University: The Case of Research Personnel.* Ph.D. Dissertation. University of California, Berkeley, 1970.

Mayhew, Lewis B. *Reform in Graduate Education.* SREB Research Monograph No. 18. Atlanta: Southern Regional Education Board, 1972.

Merton, Robert K. "The Matthew Effect in Science." *Science* 159, no. 3810 (January 1968): 56–63.

Metzger, Walter P. "The Academic Profession in the United States." In *The Academic Profession: National, Disciplinary, and Institutional Contexts,* ed. Burton R. Clark. Berkeley, Los Angeles, London: University of California Press, 1987. Pp. 120–208.

National Academy of Sciences. *Personnel Needs and Training for Biomedical and Behavioral Research.* The 1985 Report of the Committee on National Needs for Biomedical and Behavioral Research Personnel and the Institute of Medicine. Washington, D.C.: National Academy Press, 1985.

———. Panel on Science and Technology Centers. *Science and Technology Centers: Principles and Guidelines.* Washington, D.C., 1987.

National Research Council. *A Century of Doctorates: Data Analyses of Growth and Change.* Washington, D.C.: National Academy of Sciences, 1978.

———. *Outlook for Science and Technology: The Next Five Years.* San Francisco: W. H. Freeman & Co. 1982.

———. *Humanities Doctorates in the United States: 1985 Profile.* Washington, D.C.: National Academy Press, 1986.

———. *The New Engineering Research Centers: Purposes, Goals and Expectations.* Report of Cross-Disciplinary Research Committee and Commission on Energy and Technical Systems. Washington, D.C.: National Academy Press, 1986.

———. *Summary Report 1986: Doctorate Recipients from United States Universities.* Washington, D.C.: National Academy Press, 1987.

———. *Foreign and Foreign-Born Engineers in the United States: Infusing Talent, Raising Issues.* Washington, D.C.: National Academy Press, 1988.

National Science Board. *University-Industry Research Relationships: Myths, Realities and Potentials.* Washington, D.C.: U.S. Government Printing Office, 1982.

———. *Science and Engineering Indicators—1987.* Washington, D.C.: U.S. Government Printing Office, 1987.

National Science Foundation. *Federal Support to Universities, Colleges and Selected Nonprofit Institutions, FY 1985, Detailed Statistical Tables.* Washington, D.C., January, 1987a.

———. *Science and Technology Data Book, 1988.* No. NSF 87-317. Washington, D.C., 1987b.

———. *Academic Science/Engineering Graduate Enrollment and Support: Fall 1986, Detailed Statistical Tables.* Report No. 88-307. Washington, D.C., 1988a.

———. *Proposal Review at NSF: Perceptions of Principal Investigators.* Report No. 88-4. Washington, D.C., February, 1988b.

———. Science/Engineering Degrees Awarded by Carnegie Category and Degree Level, 1985-86. Unpublished data. Washington, D.C., 1989.

————. Division of Science Resource Studies. *National Patterns of Science and Technology Resources, 1986.* Report No. 86-309. Washington, D.C., March, 1986.

Newman, Frank. *Higher Education and the American Resurgence.* Princeton, N.J.: Carnegie Foundation for the Advancement of Teaching, 1985.

Office of Science and Technology Policy. White House Science Panel on the Health of the U.S. Colleges and Universities. *A Renewed Partnership.* Washington, D.C., February, 1986.

Orlans, Harold. *The Non Profit Research Institute.* New York: McGraw-Hill, 1972.

Queval, Francoise Alice. *The Evolution Toward Research Orientation and Capability in Comprehensive Universities. A Case Study: The California State University System.* Ph.D. Dissertation, University of California at Los Angeles, 1990.

Rivlin, Alice. *The Role of the Federal Government in Financing Higher Education.* Washington, D.C.: Brookings Institution, 1961.

Rosenzweig, Robert M. "The Rationale for a Federal Role in Graduate Education." *Change* 16, no. 2 (March 1984) 11–13.

Rudolph, Frederick. *The American College and University: A History.* New York: Vintage/Random House, 1962.

Sacks, Karen B. *Caring by the Hour: Women, Work and Organizing at Duke Medical Center.* Urbana and Chicago: University of Illinois Press, 1988.

Smith, Bruce L. R., ed. *The State of Graduate Education.* Washington, D.C.: Brookings Institution, 1985.

Smith, Bruce L. R., and Joseph Karlesky. *The State of Academic Science: The Universities in the Nation's Research Effort.* Vol. I. New York: Change Magazine Press, 1977.

Starr, Paul. *The Social Transformation of American Medicine.* New York: Basic Books, 1982.

Storr, Richard. *The Beginnings of Graduate Education in America.* Chicago: University of Chicago Press, 1953.

Teich, Albert H. "Research Centers and Non-Faculty Researchers: A New Academic Role." In *Research in the Age of the Steady-State University,* ed. Don Phillips and Benjamin Shen. AAAS Selected Symposium Series, no. 60. Washington, D.C.: American Association for the Advancement of Science, 1982. Pp. 91–108.

Trow, Martin A. "The Analysis of Status." In *Perspectives on Higher Education: Eight Disciplinary and Comparative Views.* ed. Burton R. Clark. Berkeley, Los Angeles, London: University of California Press, 1984. Pp. 132–164.

U.S. General Accounting Office. *University Funding: Assessing Federal Mechanisms for University Research.* RCED 86-75. Washington, D.C., 1986.

University of Chicago. "Report of the Commission on Graduate Education," *University of Chicago Record* 16 (May 3, 1982): 2.

Veblen, Thorstein. *The Higher Learning in America: A Memorandum on the Conduct of Universities by Business Men.* New York: Sentry Press, 1918.

Veysey, Laurence. *The Emergence of the American University.* Chicago and London: University of Chicago Press, 1965.

Wangberg, Elaine. "Encouraging Research and Scholarship in Master's Only Institutions." Paper presented at the annual meeting of the Council of Graduate Schools, Washington, D.C., December 4, 1987.

Weber, Max. "Science as a Vocation." In *From Max Weber: Essays in Sociology,* ed.

H. H. Gerth and C. Wright Mills. New York: Oxford University Press, 1958. Pp. 129–156.

Webster, David. "America's Highest Ranked Graduate Schools 1925–1982." *Change* 15, no. 4 (May/June 1983): 14–24.

———. *Academic Quality Rankings of American Colleges and Universities.* Springfield, Ill.: Charles Thomas, 1986.

White House Science Council. *Renewed Partnership.* A Report of the White House Science Council on the Health of U.S. Colleges and Universities to the Office of Science and Technology Policy. Washington, D.C., 1986.

Wolfle, Dael. *The Home of Science: The Role of the University.* New York: McGraw-Hill, 1972.

Zumeta, William. *Extending the Educational Ladder: The Changing Quality and Value of Post-Doctoral Study.* Lexington, Mass.: Lexington Books, 1985.

EIGHT

Graduate Education and Research Imperatives
Views from American Campuses

Patricia J. Gumport

American graduate education and research are more strongly linked on some campuses and in some disciplines than in others. In an enterprise involving eight hundred campuses and 1.5 million students, tremendous variation occurs among diverse campus settings and disciplines. This chapter closely examines that variation, describes the links between graduate education and research, and identifies the conditions that sustain or weaken that linkage.

In the previous chapter I suggested that certain national economic and political changes had direct effects on the strength and organization of research and research training in American universities. The post–World War II surge in federal support for university research and graduate education fueled dramatic expansion through the 1960s. Major research universities greatly extended their capital-intensive research infrastructure, thereby securing their position as international centers of excellence. In this expansion process the need for research assistants by faculty who were engaged in sponsored university research became a major determinant of size and kinds of graduate programs.[1]

The early 1970s brought sharp declines in direct federal support of doctoral education and a reorientation of federal basic research funds toward economic competitiveness and growing industrial collaboration. This shift provided formidable challenges for the research and research training activities of universities. As Joseph Ben-David observed, reduction of the massive federal support was "inevitable, but...the system was entirely unprepared for it when it came."[2] How universities managed to achieve stability, let alone thrive, in a national context of declining support is as compelling an analytical concern as how the higher education system as a whole has nurtured excellence while sustaining a wide range of viable graduate education programs across disciplines and institutional settings.

By the late 1980s universities regained the numerical losses of doctoral output in the 1970s: annual production stabilized above 33,000, surpassing the 1973 peak. Disaggregated by field of study, however, the data are mixed: there was an increase in the number of natural sciences and engineering doctorates, a marked decline in the humanities, and slightly less of a decline in the social sciences.[3] Also, the length of time to complete a doctorate has increased over the past two decades, a trend that observers link directly to declines in federal support.[4]

The financing of graduate education also underwent a dramatic change at both master's and doctoral levels. Since federal support declined in the early 1970s, graduate students found alternative sources: loans, an increased reliance on self-support (especially for humanists) and on university support (especially for humanists, but also for scientists). Universities have compensated for declines in federal fellowships in part by expanding state-funded or institutionally funded teaching assistantships. These changes in sources of support have already been noticed in a group of recent doctorates. In 1986 loans for doctoral education were supplemented by support that was generally more labor-intensive: about one-half received teaching assistantships, over one-third research assistantships, about one-fifth university fellowships, under one-tenth federal fellowships, and less than one-twentieth had nonfederal national fellowships.[5]

Campuses have had varying success in responding to the changes in the finance of graduate education and university research. Broad-based institutional initiatives by administrators to protect the quality of graduate education and faculty research take place in the context of faculty authority that is radically decentralized: the ultimate integration of graduate education and research depends on departmental practices, where faculty and their graduate programs are anchored. Thus, the distinctive feature responsible for resilience in the American system of higher education lies in strong local organization.

Case study data from four campuses and over one hundred and fifty interviews show the significance of local contexts.[6] Tremendous variation exists, not only in the educational experiences of graduate students across departments within the same institutions but also in the same fields at different institutions. This analysis reveals how faculty, students, and administrators worked within the larger framework of shifting system sponsorship.

DISCIPLINARY DIFFERENCES

Ph.D. programs in the United States are distinctive for having a period of prescribed course work followed by a supervised dissertation. Among the many hurdles encountered by doctoral students across the disciplines, one emerges as paramount: the transition from course work to the dissertation, which transforms the student from a consumer to a producer of research. The research training component is clearly central to this transition and thus to successful program completion across the disciplines.

Different disciplinary interpretations of research training prevail. Most common are the laboratory-intensive apprenticeship model of the sciences and the library-intensive individualistic model of the humanities. In the sciences students are trained in laboratories while they contribute to professors' ongoing research projects; in the humanities students work independently with little or no faculty contact unless they initiate it, often for months at a time.

These distinct patterns of social relations are, in part, intrinsic to the disciplines and tied to professional norms, the nature of disciplinary inquiry, and the type of research technology.[7] Beyond such intrinsic factors, the arrangements for research training are intensified given the underlying funding base, which reflects societal values. As seen in the sciences, the presence of research funding facilitates research training. The national government has attempted to insure this instrumental linking of research training with its sponsored research agenda. Alternatively, in disciplines with an absence of research funds, like the humanities, the question becomes whether a research training component can be adequately provided without the substantive and symbolic support of funding. Without a collective research agenda or a reinforcing social structure of the laboratory setting, students are free agents who either develop independently or not at all.

To look more closely at these disciplinary differences, I examine arrangements for course work and research training, as well as the underlying funding base, in four disciplines: physics, biological sciences, history, and economics. Two basic patterns emerge: at one extreme, in the sciences, graduate education and research are tightly linked and formalized in structural relations supported by funding; at the other extreme, in the humanities, graduate education and research are unevenly linked and informally accomplished.

Physics

Physics, of all the disciplines, commands great national prestige along with the grants and contracts to support its capital-intensive instrumentation needs. Applied physics and large-scale high energy physics (projects requiring particle accelerators) have become visible multimillion- and multibillion-dollar projects sponsored by the national government. One high energy physicist explained that funding is essential: "In my field you can't do anything unless you're supported. I was raised in the tradition of asking for money. If you don't ask, you won't get." A condensed matter physicist revealed a similar orientation: "I fire proposals anywhere and everywhere." Funding has become more competitive; a physicist with twenty-five years of experience said, "It's no longer getting funding for the best projects; it's only half the best projects get funded."

Although research funding has become visibly strained, physics is where graduate education, research training, and funding are thought to articulate most easily as compatible systems. This is true for large-scale, high energy, experimental physics as well as for smaller-scale, condensed matter physics. Theoretical physics deviates from experimental physics in that less funding is available, but more of the course work required of doctoral students is directly applicable to their research training.

Students are generally admitted into Ph.D. programs immediately after receiving undergraduate degrees, usually in physics. Some programs require that students declare a subfield for their specialty at this stage. One department chair said, "There are more wanting to do theoretical physics than we have support for. If you want to do experimental physics, it's easier to get into the program." On some campuses an advisor is assigned temporarily for one year, while the student sorts through the options for specialization. In other cases an early match between student and faculty advisor may endure throughout the program.

Physics programs require about two years of prescribed course work. According to one department chair some programs recently revised their curriculum to "redefine the minimum core and decide the boundaries of physics." The revision was also intended to eliminate redundancy in courses in physics, applied physics, and material sciences programs, since "a continuum of physics activity" usually is found on any given campus.

The first year of the two-year course is often remedial in part, making it boring and too easy for some: faculty and students alike say the content of the first-year curriculum is not an attractive feature. Beyond reviewing basic principles of physics and homework assignments of practice problems, course work is meant to expose students to an overview of subfields. The work culminates in an exam that tests mastery of the knowledge covered in the required courses. From one-third to two-thirds of a cohort pass; students may have two or three tries before being asked to leave the program with a terminal master's degree.

During the first year, physics doctoral students may have a teaching assistantship. This is less prominent a feature of doctoral education than it is for the other three disciplines in this study. The assistantship may entail supervising undergraduates in the laboratory once a week or helping them with homework problems. After having been teaching assistants for a semester, they are eager to spend their time in the laboratory, a place "where you really learn, where you get the tools."

The rotation through faculty laboratories is a major component of the first year; usually one moves on to a new one every three months. The options for a laboratory vary dramatically across campuses. On a small campus a student may choose among a few departmental faculty who have small-scale projects, most common in areas of condensed matter physics. On a large and more affluent campus, a student may have the option of working in four subfields within the department as well as in an applied physics laboratory or at a particle accelerator, either on or off campus. Opportunities are more abundant in departments with a large faculty, abundant research funds, and a tight connection between the physics department and applied physics centers on campus.

A student stays in a laboratory if the research project is interesting, the atmosphere is congenial, and the faculty member commits to supporting the student. The student's research training will then be tied to a research assistantship that pays a half-time stipend, although the actual work in the laboratory may be fifty to sixty hours a week. If a faculty member's project is between grants or if proposals are not successful, departments may have unrestricted funds to cover student salaries during funding gaps. Generated from indirect cost rebates or from the sale of old equipment, these funds are "essential for maintaining an even keel," according to a department chair.

Interaction between faculty and students in a laboratory is frequent (daily) and often directive in nature. A student might need help with techniques of instrumentation, measurement styles, or design of equipment; there may be a leak or a conceptual problem to solve. One faculty member said, "I have to set up the harder parts of the experiment myself. But when it breaks, they fix it. I say 'this is the last time, so watch.'... It's like having a child learn to walk. You watch and you catch 'em. As they get better, they go off on their own more." According to students, some days are better than others: "Some days you're a peon. Other days you know how... and you're king for a day."

The nature of research training also varies by subfield. In contrast to the intimate, small-scale laboratory setting of low temperature experimental physics, the elementary particle physics laboratory may be far from the department or off campus entirely, perhaps across the country, requiring travel for data collection when "the beam is on." Thus, patterns of interaction also differ: research assistants may leave the campus for eight months at a time or may never see the beginning or end of an experiment, since several years are often required for completion; they may learn research out of sequence—data analysis, instrumentation, design—depending on funding circumstances and access to a particle accelerator.

At the other extreme, research training in high energy theory involves calculations, which students do either independently or in pairs. Students check in with a faculty supervisor periodically to see if their computations are correct. As one faculty member described it: "I try to teach them a set of skills. The biggest one is to know when you're right and when you're wrong. It's common for them to miss it when they're wrong. After a while they can see it. It's intuitive partially." That students usually do not have research assistantships to work full-time on research is justified as follows: "You can't do calculations all day or you'd become fuzzyheaded." Students in theoretical physics have a conception of apprenticeship that differs from "working at the bench" in a laboratory. A fifth-year theoretical physicist at a well-funded university said that he did not see working with his advisor as an apprenticeship: "You mainly need an advisor to tell you what's worth doing and what's already been done, what's easy enough that you can do it and hard enough that someone else won't do it first."

Beyond course work and the acquisition of specific research skills, the dissertation is expected to be a student's original contribution to the field, yet student research emerges from faculty projects and is funded from that source as well. One faculty member said that "I have a list of interesting things to look at. Most often I suggest one and they go along with it; other times we negotiate and agree on something else they are more capable of." Similarly, a high energy experimentalist who had recently returned from a session at a particle accelerator said proudly, "I'm sitting on a huge amount of data right now, enough for ten or fifteen graduate students." From the student perspective, the line between a research assistantship on a faculty project and one on dissertation research is blurred. "Those two things run together. The dissertation idea came from him. Anything sounded good to me at the time. I just wanted a project of my own, but it's . . . part of the whole project, a subtopic."

Faculty in both small-scale and large-scale research settings observed that the increasingly competitive nature of funding has constrained research training. According to one, "The funding is a tricky balancing act when you're training graduate students. You have to give them leeway to make mistakes, yet unless you make progress in the laboratory, there's no funding. In recent years the funding is tighter so you have to keep the students on a tighter leash. This is bad for their education, but you live with it." Another said, "Given today's funding picture, . . . there's no way to proceed slowly. Funding would dry up. . . . The price has been independent thinking and autonomy, which were more pronounced twenty years ago. . . . We can't give them as much leeway or rope."

Nonetheless, physics students perceive that they are given some leeway, permitted to make some of their own decisions and mistakes, or allowed to explore a pathway that may or may not be the most profitable. "I feel like an employee, but I like it . . . an employee on a long leash." Another student expressed a similar conception: "It's certainly not a sink-or-swim model here, but they do give you enough rope to hang yourself." Physics students do not move out on their own until after the thesis. This practice contrasts sharply with historians' methods. History graduate students are obligated to work on their own. It is significant, no doubt, that the post-doctoral position has replaced the Ph.D. as the terminal degree in physics. Seeing it as an extended two- or three-year commitment, students look forward to enhanced responsibilities, greater professional autonomy, learning about managing a laboratory, obtaining their own research funds, publishing, and supervising students.

Of the four disciplines physics most clearly has a formalized research training component that relies on an adequate funding base. The funding is a necessary but not a sufficient condition for connecting graduate students with faculty research projects. The disciplinary norms involve students with current research so they will acquire specific laboratory skills. The early work serves to some extent as paying their dues or proving themselves, but the more advanced work entails more autonomy.

Biological Sciences

On the surface the biological sciences resemble physics, given the stable funding base for biomedical research and the national priority for trained personnel in the life sciences. Like physics, doctoral education in the biological sciences is laboratory-intensive and culminates in postdoctoral positions. But a closer look reveals that the rapidly changing knowledge base in the biological sciences makes doctoral education less discipline-driven and less department-based than in physics, although training experiences are still tied to the research specialties of funded faculty members. Faculty in the biological sciences are expected to carry out sponsored research and to support graduate students as research assistants. In the words of one department chair, "In the sciences, students are apprentices. . . . It's a full-time job."

Admission to doctoral programs in the biological sciences is the most complicated of the four disciplines because the organizational units for biology have been reorganized at a rapid rate. A student no longer simply applies to a biology department, but selects a doctoral program from among as many as a dozen departments, including molecular and cellular biology, zoology, botany, microbiology, and the neurosciences. The situation is complicated because faculty in various departments may work on the same kinds of projects. Departments in the biological sciences, according to one faculty member, are "nothing more than mailing addresses for paychecks."

Admission to doctoral programs has become more competitive, and strong applicants may be heavily recruited. To make offers more attractive, stipends are often a combination of a research assistantship and institutional fellowship funds. Although students are asked to specialize at the outset, they can switch subfields and even entire programs as new ones emerge on campuses. Unlike the other disciplines, seeking a master's degree is a common and legitimate route, although master's students are not recruited or financially supported. Doctoral students expect the program to take five to six years, and the completion rate of students in well-financed programs is as high as 90 percent.

Like physics, biological sciences require prescribed courses for two years, building on undergraduate backgrounds in biology, chemistry, and physics. According to one biologist, even two years of graduate courses are insufficient: "With the knowledge explosion you can't do more than scratch the surface. So instead we teach students to think and develop their own basis of information, a breadth of what are the important problem areas in biology and later how to do research in a given specialty area." In one department this is accomplished with a required first-year course where different faculty members come in each week to describe their research specialties, which range across plant biology, marine biology, molecular biology, neurobiology, population biology, and ecology.

The teaching assistant requirement is a component of the first stage of a doctoral program as it is in physics, but perhaps more prominent. Since biology undergraduate enrollments are usually higher than in physics, doctoral students may supervise laboratories for a few years if a program is short on resources. Students tend to accept the arrangement in a good-natured way: "The teaching assistant work is part of the apprenticeship. . . . I'm glad I did it, but it will keep me here a year longer."

As in physics, laboratory rotation is a crucial component of doctoral education and a primary introduction to skills entailed in research training. Students are expected to be in three different laboratories during their first year, each one for three months. Unlike physics, biological sciences offer a range of settings to a student, more and more often outside the department. The increasing interdisciplinarity of biological science requires intrainstitutional cooperation, so that faculty in other departments may take on research assistants not enrolled in their home departments. An explicit tension is obvious in some programs because as boundaries are increasingly blurred, budgetary accommodations tend to lag behind.

Students spend as many as sixty to eighty hours per week in laboratories. A workable size for a laboratory depends on the space, but one faculty member may have five to ten graduate students, two to five postdoctorates, one to three technicians, and a dishwasher. Not all faculty actually do research in the laboratory; some spend more time in their offices but are available for students' questions. The norm is a weekly laboratory meeting, as in physics.

The nature of student-faculty relations in research training reflects a greater range than in physics. Of the directive kind, a faculty member said, "When they walk in my door I say you can work on this or this. . . . Generally they are relieved. . . . Otherwise students wouldn't know where to begin, they'd flounder." Some students are "handed a problem and it is their responsibility to take it and run with it." In this less directive interaction, students ask faculty for help "when we reach a crossroads and need advice" or "when we need a sounding board." Some faculty members explained that they try to achieve a balance in training students to do independent research. Part of the rationale in encouraging students to be more self-directive from the beginning is that the rapid knowledge changes in biology call for less emphasis on skill training, which will be obsolete in a few years anyway, and more emphasis on acquiring conceptual foundations for the significance of research questions.

As in physics, dissertation topics are funded as an extension of the research done on a faculty project, yet they convey more of a sense of ownership. As one student said, "I'm being paid to work in her laboratory but it's my research. It's my project and ultimately it's for the laboratory." Following the dissertation, students in biological sciences tend to find postdoctoral positions in arts and sciences departments or in medical schools, although nonacademic options, such as industrial laboratories, where research for product development occurs, and government intramural laboratories, including the high-prestige National Institutes of Health, are available.

Doctoral education in the biological sciences reveals a strong integration of research training and faculty research, much like the physics model. Laboratory relations are structured and facilitated by research funds for project grants or federally funded traineeships. Students seem to have more autonomy and professional self-direction than they do in physics. They also sense that their skills will soon be obsolete, which lends an air of urgency. Since the nature of the subject matter is living organisms, the rhythm of work is tied to the demands of the experiment rather than to individual discretion. Even in crowded laboratory arrangements, a cooperative ethos prevailed within departments and, in the best cases, across biological sciences departments.

History

History, at the other end of the continuum from the sciences, garners little national support for research. The main source of funding is highly competitive fellowships from such private foundations as Guggenheim, Ford, and Rockefeller as well as from the government's small National Endowment for Humanities. Even though the fellowships bring a faculty member and a department high prestige—"We encourage it," a department chair said, "because it's a mark of excellence for our department"—the funds are for leave time away from teaching responsibilities. When history faculty members do get funds, they are used to support themselves rather than their students, in contrast to science faculty who hustle for funds because their "students are mouths to feed." Generally, history faculty do not see writing proposals as worthwhile: "We're really on our own here. It takes time to write a proposal for twenty-five hundred dollars. I lose time by applying, when I could use that time to work on an article or book chapter."

Limited external funds render the finance of graduate education problematic. Although admissions to doctoral programs in history have improved since the 1970s, the number of doctoral students a program can admit is still limited to availability of financial support, the bulk of which comes from loans, self-support, and state and institutionally funded teaching assistantships rather than from sponsored research assistantships. One chair said, "We feel suspicion and rebuke from other departments for not paying our way. We're a debit on the books."

Aside from the scarcity of external funds, the pace of knowledge development results in a different dynamic from the sciences. Knowledge change is slower, but it is also cumulative. The emergence of social history, and more recently women's history, for example, generated historical material over the past two decades which is now being added to the curriculum. The result is an increased body of knowledge to master, rather than efforts to revamp the curriculum into a coherent, concise view. As one faculty member noted, "What it means to be a historian has expanded since the 1950s. There's more published and the number of problems and subspecialties has increased. So there's more to know about. It's a good thing, but it results in a deeper obscurity for training. Only the best [students] are quick enough and competent enough to make their own way." Given a finite period of course work in doctoral programs, the expansion of what is considered a topic or method in history causes controversy over what material should be covered.

Students tend to complete the prescribed course requirements in two years. The courses aim to "map out what's been done" in the discipline. Some students experience the first two years as an extension of undergraduate courses, as "a chance to fill in the gaps," as "massive catching up to do." Others do not see it as remedial. Instead, they see it as an opportunity to gather and master material for their teaching repertoire. Students are encouraged to have some specializations in mind early on, in order to promote their expertise in subfields. Some major areas are: U.S. history, European history, Latin American history, Renaissance and Reformation history, and Asian history. The third year (and sometimes beyond) is devoted to reading for the exam, usually in a vast list of books in a few chosen subfields. From the student perspective this exam, which advances them to candidacy, is the biggest hurdle in the doctoral program, although faculty do not tend to see it as that. Most students pass by the second attempt, although the exam may weed out the weak students who leave the program with a terminal master's degree. (Students may be accepted for the master's as a terminal degree: often they are older adults.)

Lacking the rotation found in physics, history has no explicit research training component; if not for one or two required doctoral seminars, training would be structurally invisible. The purpose of the seminars is to provide "a warm-up for the dissertation," according to one faculty member. "We give them a dose of substance so they have a common base of knowledge; we try to be systematic by covering the basic fields." Faculty also "give them a dose of methodology, which is basically a discussion of how to marshall evidence. They are taught that they can't be definitive, but they can be persuasive in arguing with peers." The seminar usually requires a sizable research paper and often sessions in the library with archivists to learn about sources. A shared belief is that "historians learn how to do research by reading other historians doing history. It's largely trial and error by imitation."

Aside from seminars, research training is accomplished informally, one-on-one with students and faculty. Another historian explained his intentions: "We're trying to train them to think. We train them to know what sources are available and what are their limitations, where to find them and how to manipulate them. We do this in the classroom and orally one-on-one as well as in writing when I critique their papers." However, many students reported that this contact provided no training in how to do research. One student described his experience with his advisor: "At no point has he or anyone else trained me to do research. . . . He is my intellectual mentor but not my research guide." Similarly, a fifth-year student just beginning her dissertation stated: "I feel like an apprentice although I don't know to whom—maybe to the field of history. . . . We used to joke about it, as it's just do-it-yourself graduate school."

Thus, history students become de facto free agents in developing their own research interests—perhaps too much so, since they claim to need more guidance from faculty. The ways in which students choose dissertation topics reflect a tension between faculty-encouraged development of student autonomy and student floundering for several years or, worse yet, never finishing. History faculty see the dissertation as an opportunity to encourage independent thinking and self-determination in their students: "We want students to take control of their own lives, not do our work," said one. A colleague said: "We want them to learn how to read books, how to criticize them, how to construct their own questions, how to consider what's professionally worthwhile." Said another faculty member, "I won't tell a student what to work on. If they won't take responsibility to come up with a topic they're interested in, then I won't work with them. . . . One lives with that decision for about ten years—three, five, seven doing the dissertation and another three making it a book."

The ideal of independence implicit in history is further revealed in the social relations between faculty and students. As one historian put it: "The practice of history is a solitary endeavor. It takes a long time in terms of gestation and production. That's how we do it. We replicate that practice in training graduate students. We give them an assignment to go off and do on their own. I don't hire them to do work or pay for their time." The absence of an employer-employee dynamic in research training is noteworthy. One faculty member said he would not know what to do with a research assistant: "I'm bad at that. I never know how to use them. There's just no connection between my research and the work of graduate students."

Although graduate students are not employed in their research training, they are treated like employees in their teaching assistantships, where they may have to meet as many as four classes a week as discussion leader and grade eighty to one hundred students. Some students say that this relationship is beneficial to their professional development, since it is an opportunity to "master the material in an intense way." Others define it as exploitation, since the teaching is unrelated to their research: "It's a lot of work for a little money"; "We're just doing time," lightening the teaching loads of faculty and thereby subsidizing their research. Still other students spend anywhere from twenty to fifty hours per week working off campus in jobs that may not relate at all to history. A faculty member said students "live like dogs, not like decent human beings," since they have to take on second and third part-time jobs to meet living expenses. Given these structural obstacles, it is not surprising that doctoral students in history take the most time to completion and have the highest attrition rates of the programs examined.

In spite of its inadequacies, the uneven guidance provided by history faculty and the sporadic student-faculty contact seem to lead to independence and the formulation of intellectual agendas by students. However, the potential for research training is framed within an organizational context in which the faculty have no structural incentives or stake in the particular dissertation research or in the launching of a student's career, other than the internalized professional imperative that such support is intrinsically rewarding. In a pragmatic sense, supporting graduate students may be incompatible with faculty pursuing their research interests. A department chair said, "The greatest tension in our lives is between teaching and research. If we're conscientious about graduate education, then we have less time to devote to our scholarship. I try to protect myself from being overloaded with students."

Unlike the sciences, history does not seem to require a critical mass of faculty in a department, except to provide subfield coverage, nor a critical mass of students to sustain a peer culture. Since doctoral education is largely a solitary endeavor, small numbers are sufficient. Research training is incorporated into seminars and one-on-one student-faculty meetings over a student-initiated dissertation topic. Some history faculty convey early that they view their students as colleagues and autonomous professionals, although the students do not express this sense of themselves until they have nearly completed their programs. Working as teaching assistants probably contributes to delay in the evolution of student self-conception: it gives them a professional but subservient role that categorizes them as classroom teachers rather than scholars.

Economics

Economics demonstrates characteristics of both the sciences and history. Different patterns occur by subfield: in the empirical and experimental fields economics resembles the physics model of research training and teamwork; the theoretical fields are like the autonomous training in history. Additional differences follow from individual faculty conceptions. Of the four disciplines in this study, economics is the most internally differentiated in both ideals and practices of doctoral programs.

Economics has gained such high prestige nationally that it is funded by federal agencies as well as by private donors. Economics research is supported in considerable part because its instrumental value is clear; in this sense it is closer to the natural sciences than history. One economist remarked about the potential practical utility: "Economics is like plumbing. You've got to fix the pipes in society, so people need to learn the skills to be productive members of society." Research funding may be either grants for faculty projects as in the sciences or fellowships for time off as in history.

Within economics there is an internal pecking order to the subfields, so that macroeconomics, public finance, and econometrics are more highly regarded than Marxist theory or history. The pecking order is communicated to graduate students who are introduced to specialties from the beginning. According to one professor: "Economics is a profession that has too many specialties. Just look at the specialized journals. . . . Mathematical economists address one another and not economics per se. . . . We have to be careful of this with graduate students. They pick up these cues."

Applications to doctoral programs in economics have become quite competitive at the top universities. Commenting on which universities do most of the training, one department chair noted that even though 120 universities offer Ph.D.'s, the top 20 do half of the Ph.D. production. He added that the highest quality graduate students are concentrated in the top ten universities, but the top faculty are in the top fifteen. Unless a student attends one of those programs, he or she is likely to be "out of the running for a good job." Another chair said the average completion rate in economics is 25 percent; some programs admit doctoral students to "exploit them for a few years as teaching assistants," while other programs deliberately do not do so in order to have a completion rate of 70 to 80 percent.

When students are admitted to a program they are temporarily assigned a faculty advisor and, sometimes, a committee of three faculty members to advise them on courses. When they are more advanced in the program and choose a specialization, it is common to change advisors and to reconstitute the committee for the dissertation.

The prescribed course work in economics is about two years. The first year covers broad areas of the field and major questions that frame the discipline. The second year has advanced coursework. In this regard it is similar to physics: a written exam at the end of the two years covers the content of the courses. The exam may weed people out of the program: one-half may fail and leave with a terminal master's degree.

Economics programs reveal a common challenge in doctoral education—the transition from course work to doing research, "from being a coursetaker to a research-doer," as a faculty member suggested. This problem emerges in the third year, which is often "a wasteland" for students who do not know how to make "the quantum leap into research"; they may spend "a year of aimless wandering, waiting for a big insight." Faculty have devised different mechanisms to ease the transition. In one program they do "more hand-holding" in the second year and require students to do a research paper. Another program eliminated field exams in order to "get students involved in our research earlier." Informal advising seems helpful. According to a faculty member, his advisees "wander in all the time and use me as a sounding board to help define their interests."

Most doctoral students in economics are required to be teaching assistants. Undergraduate enrollments are large, and teaching assistants help staff lecture courses. On one campus economics was "the gut major," so all doctoral students were required to be teaching assistants for a whole year, staffing sections a few times a week, holding office hours, and grading exams. In departments with more resources, doctoral students may teach for only part of a year. Some programs have two distinct tracks of students, those who are teaching assistants and those who are research assistants. Differentiation between the two is reinforced financially, as research assistants usually get a summer stipend but teaching assistants do not.

For students who end up "falling between the tracks," research training is difficult to obtain. Unlike physics, economics has no systematic rotation through laboratories. As in history, economics students initiate one-on-one contact with faculty, a challenge that may require perseverance. Some students reported "going door to door literally to find out who would be interested." Other students "lay low and remain invisible for a few years." It is more difficult if the student tries to jump from the teaching to the research track. One student recognized that "being a research assistant is essential for your training as an economist, while being a teaching assistant isn't"; he even wrote book reviews as a sign of his research potential, hoping to gain faculty approval.

The nature of research training varies widely from computer programming and mathematics in subfields with a technical bent to library work and more rarely, data collection and statistics. In economic theory, a faculty member explained, "you can have related projects but you can't take an idea and break it down easily." In econometrics, however, large-scale projects are possible, similar to those involving a small-scale physics team. The variation also depends on individual faculty preference: some faculty members prefer to use students for clerical chores, doing "go-fer" work, such as proofreading or checking mathematics; others see students as possible coauthors. Both extremes are found within one department and even within subfields of economics.

Faculty-student relationships concerning the dissertation also vary among individual faculty members. The dissertation idea can be initiated by the student and carried out in a self-directed manner, as is common in history. One economist said, "I prefer the topics to be self-generated. . . . They should go out and find a problem on their own"; students ought to rely on the advisor for technical help only. The other extreme is choosing a topic generated by faculty. Between the two is a mix, perhaps reflecting an underlying ambivalence: "I want them to be on my wavelength. I want the main thrust of their work to be along the lines of my work. They'll choose a topic of their own interest though."

The length and content of the economics dissertation has shifted away from being a book-length manuscript to three shorter pieces. One chair said, "Books don't count in our profession," and one of the three reports can be used "as a job market paper." Students are encouraged in some programs to have expertise in more than one subfield. According to one chair: "In our program we encourage students to work in a traditional subfield as well as in [a newer one]. . . . They have two strings in their bow that way."

Ideals about faculty roles in the research training process differ among individuals. One faculty member said that "a good research supervisor is someone that helps you learn research. . . . You can't get it any other way." She actively tries to get research projects that will support graduate students' research training and funds that can be also used to support their dissertation research. "I put a lot of energy into writing proposals that will support graduate students. As a student, being a research assistant was a crucial experience for me; people gave me a lot of rein to pursue my own ideas. But even rote work like coding. . . which is menial and tedious . . . can be good to learn new skills." In contrast, another faculty member said he did not actively seek external funds to support dissertation research.

From the student perspective an advisor's accessibility is important, although one pragmatic student spoke favorably of his advisor, who "was not accessible in terms of advice on technical research problems" but "had lots of money, and he had great connections" in job placement.

Graduate students in economics, as in other disciplines, choose not only the kinds of economics they will do, but must decide with which faculty members to work. Sometimes students take three to four years to "know where they fit." Faculty acknowledge that "we have a huge influence on what students think," so there are "strong pressures." Some emphasize potential for innovation: "A good Ph.D. program trains students to do what you can't—to go beyond what you do, to show them what you do and encourage them to use their imagination. . . . If you treat them like colleagues, they'll become so." Still others emphasize the developmental dimension of training: "It's more like a teenage child because the name of the game is differentiation."

Economics displays the most internal variation of the four disciplines discussed, even within the same department on a given campus. This lack of consensus may be attributed in part to subfield variation in the nature of inquiry and the technology used in the research. Economics is also situated at the intersection of several other disciplines and heavily influenced by their norms. One pattern of doctoral education looks more like mathematics or history with less formalized research training relationships and a solitary or self-directed unfolding; another looks similar to applied sociology or statistics, with more structured interaction through funded research assistantships and substantive contributions to faculty projects.

To summarize, graduate education and research across the disciplines are practiced differently depending on the funding context, the knowledge base, and the professional ideals internalized by individuals. Physics and biological sciences reveal the closest integration of course work and research apprenticeships. The training relations are formalized and structurally supported by academic science. History reflects a weaker linkage, where research training ideals tend to be informal and uneven; when some funding is available, faculty use it for leave time rather than for graduate student support. This points to the resilience of disciplinary norms and the tendency for faculty to reproduce the system that spawned them. Different from the other three disciplines, economics offers a wider range of practices for graduate education and research. An internal differentiation reveals strong disciplinary influences from mathematics, history, and statistics. Economics illustrates a dynamic in the system which is often overlooked: although graduate education is a department-based responsibility, it is implemented by individual faculty members accountable to the students they select to train. This radically decentralized faculty discretion leaves open the possibility for greater differences in interpretation about ideal practices for graduate education when faculty in a discipline do not share a coherent research tradition.

INSTITUTIONAL DIFFERENCES

Although the organization of disciplines into departments provides a common framework across campuses in the American system, important differences exist among universities in graduate education practices and the administration of sponsored research. In four universities, ranging from the very prominent to the nearly invisible, faculty research activities and research training methods vary in tandem.

The first campus is a leading research university in the top ten nationally, the pinnacle of the sector that does the bulk of Ph.D. training and sponsored research. With abundant resources and a reputation for excellence, the integration of graduate education and research is assured across the disciplines. The second university has recently been ranked about twenty-fifth in receipt of sponsored research dollars, but it lags in the amount and quality of doctoral education. The third university is ranked at about one hundred. It is smaller and is strong in only a few fields. The fourth campus is not primarily in the business of doctoral training or sponsored research as generally recognized by American standards, although it aspires to those two missions nonetheless.

University One

As a leading research university in the United States, it is also internationally known for excellence in scholarship across a wide range of disciplines. This university has made deliberate, consistent efforts to integrate graduate education and research. An abundance of resources together with a sustained institutional will to be the best have provided the organizational and financial means for this achievement.

The university annually brings in over $200 million in federal contracts and grants, an increase of 50 percent (in constant dollars) over the past ten years. Roughly one-third of these funds come from the Health and Human Services Agency (mostly from the National Institutes of Health) and 15 percent from the Department of Defense. About one-third of research funds are in the form of research grants, leaving two-thirds as contracts, most of both kinds going to sciences and engineering.

Sustaining a high-quality graduate program is viewed as vital to the functioning of its departments, which are small—twenty to forty faculty— by American standards. As a self-conscious national exemplar, this institution encourages research training that urges students to be innovative in their research interests and to take intellectual risks. "They want to be famous, but they hate to be wrong," said one department chair in explaining that students often support each other through initiating their own peer review activities. This dynamic was most prominent in the biological sciences department where there is a high ratio of "discovery research" to "follow-up research."

The university offers about seventy master's and seventy doctoral degree programs. The overall graduate enrollment is about 6,000 students, one-quarter of whom are foreign. About 2,500 are full-time graduate students in engineering and 1,500 in the sciences. Life sciences and physical sciences each have about 10 percent of the graduate enrollment. The campus has over 600 postdoctoral researchers. Last year 2,500 graduate degrees were granted, among them over 500 Ph.D.'s. The number of doctoral degrees conferred has remained consistent over the past decade, in spite of the depression of the 1970s. This stands in dramatic contrast to the other three universities, where some departments virtually disbanded their graduate programs for a few years. Most master's degrees are awarded as terminal degrees either for students who are weeded out of doctoral programs or for undergraduates who extend their study into a fifth year.

The finance of graduate education reflects a strong university commitment to doctoral education. Incoming students are guaranteed four years of full support to cover tuition and a stipend throughout their research training—an $80,000 commitment by the university (in 1990 dollars) for every graduate student admitted. This arrangement enables departments to recruit the most sought after applicants and ends up providing not only a psychological cushion but also a structural vehicle for completing their programs. Departments can augment the stipend level, a practice most common in the sciences where funding for twelve instead of nine months is offered. The additional funds come from several federal agencies in physics, the National Science Foundation and private sources in economics, and National Institutes of Health Training Grants in biology. The best students are able to secure support in the fifth year and beyond through such prestigious national competitions as the National Science Foundation Fellowships, or from foundations supporting humanities. With an abundance of funding, most students are covered, although those in the sciences have higher stipends; this can result in as much as a $4,000 annual difference in income between departments. A few students, usually under 5 percent in any department, do not have financial aid and may pay their way. The policy is to admit those students who can be financially supported.

At this university new recruits to graduate school begin their professional lives; there the program is not simply an extension of undergraduate education. For faculty, there is an abundance of things they value most—time to do research, research facilities, student-faculty interaction. "The ability to get funds builds on itself. It's easier to get funds here due to a supportive infrastructure already in place," said a scientist. In this milieu the message is clear that the aim of graduate education is to train researchers and scholars, not teachers. Upon completing doctorates "almost all of them find good academic jobs" was an assessment by all department chairs.

In interviews graduate education and research were often linked together closely, as if the activities were inseparable. Administrators, faculty, and graduate students alike were consistent in expressing an entrepreneurial spirit and a fast pace of work. Flexible organizational arrangements are the key ingredient to the university's ability to adapt to rapidly changing knowledge bases in the disciplines. "We can whip something up fast," boasted the dean. New programs are created if faculty resources are present in the home departments; according to the dean, "it takes just a few good people." But it also helps to have physical space and financial support for graduate students. Graduate education is enhanced in these forward-looking programs because research training opportunities cross departmental boundaries and, often, facilities. The activities on this campus come closest to the traditional ideals of linking research and graduate education. Not only has there been a consistent track record, but the future is promising; the university has the institutional will and an ability to generate resources.

University Two

Unlike the first university, where graduate education and research has been closely integrated across a range of fields for some time, the second one has only recently achieved this linkage, and mainly in the sciences. This campus has been "on the move" for the past twenty years and is "still climbing"; it is rising from "a mediocre university" to "a research-compulsive" one. The downside of this momentum, for some observers, is that it seems to pull "graduate education away from being an educational enterprise" toward being "a research factory engaged in research training."

Initially a land grant institution devoted to teaching, research, and public service, this campus has sharply raised its research profile. It now ranks about twenty-fifth nationally in sponsored research activity; in 1987 it brought in $125 million in external research funds, up from $60 million five years ago and $40 million ten years ago (in constant dollars). About 75 percent of the research funds are from the federal government; about one-quarter of them are located in the biological sciences. The National Institutes of Health and the National Science Foundation are prime supporters. Grants and contracts are also raised from the National Aeronautics and Space Administration, the Department of Agriculture, and the Department of Defense. The campus is dramatically expanding its facilities and is planning for several science buildings to house new interdepartmental programs.

The university now offers 150 master's and about 100 doctoral programs.

The 1987 full-time graduate enrollment was about 7,500. Science and engineering programs enrolled 4,000 students, about three-quarters of whom were full-time. About one quarter of the graduate students were in the life sciences. Although enrollment is higher than in the first institution, this university confers fewer master's and doctoral degrees. There are more part-time students, who take a longer time to completion. Since 1970 physics granted twenty-six Ph.D.'s. that took between 5.5 and 14.5 years to complete; history has produced nine doctorates whose completion time ranged from 6.5 to 15 years.

A major part of this university's strategy is to achieve upward mobility by leading in the sciences, first with thriving faculty research and then with graduate programs.[8] A change in faculty hiring has been so marked that it divided the faculty between the "old and rusty" and the "stars," the "younger faculty with a research orientation." Many in the first group are referred to as "deadwood." As an administrator noted, "Twenty years ago this was a mediocre university. Many people hired then wouldn't stand a snowball's chance in being hired now. None of them have anything to do with graduate programs now. They teach undergraduates or do consulting." But the younger faculty wish to establish a track record, so "their research agenda is at the forefront."

The biological sciences have been a major focus of this research investment and related changes: their graduate programs have been revised three times since 1966. In 1989 the biological sciences are found in thirteen discipline-based departments and seventeen interdisciplinary programs. Criteria for establishing a new program are simple. "We want to maximize resources and avoid duplication," and "there is a need for it, the faculty is good, and there is no other like it on campus." Interdisciplinary programs are assisted by a special budget managed by the graduate dean.

Because research in the pure and applied sciences is emphasized, some faculty and former administrators believe that graduate programs in other disciplines flounder. They assert that the research enterprise has become the campus's main identity at a cost to graduate education and humanistic values, citing for example, the major improvements still needed for the library, due to neglected acquisitions in the 1960s and 1970s. Humanities faculty are most vocal in reporting they have had to "hunker down" as if waiting for a storm to pass. According to a former dean, "Graduate education went downhill and became subservient to the research enterprise. The only way to get graduate education stable funds [is] to link it to research funding. I'm embarrassed to say this but graduate education is research now."

The lag time between achieving high quality in faculty research and high quality in graduate programs is mentioned often. A department chair explained the cycle: "You get research assistants to do the work you don't want to do. That enables you to get publications. The publications enable you to get more research funds and more prominence and then you can attract better graduate students. . . . The better students go to where the better faculty are unless the stipend differences are so large they can't ignore it."

In some disciplines the finance of graduate education is dependent upon federal funds for research assistantships. In others university funds are allocated for teaching assistantships where high undergraduate course enrollments warrant them. Each department negotiates the teaching assistant stipend level with the graduate dean annually, so that those trying to compete with other departments outside the university for talented new students get a higher stipend. Although the funding enables them to admit new students as teaching assistants, it is "a mixed blessing," said a department chair, because students arrive unprepared. "We need the bodies to staff the sections even if they are not ready. And many of them are not."

Overall, as this university has become upwardly mobile, some faculty raised concerns about an exaggerated emphasis on research training at the expense of breadth and thinking skills. "A person might be taught to think," one faculty member said, "but I'm not so sure it happens here in the sciences," due to the emphasis on "technical skills." A former dean also expressed concern: "As a research-compulsive institution, can it stay true to graduate education? If not, it will have failed." A related fear is that the university will "sell its soul" to external sponsors by establishing interdisciplinary science programs that will become the core of the campus rather than buffering the core from sponsors' agendas.

In spite of these concerns, this case illustrates how to move up in the competitive system by linking research and graduate education as an ideal as well as a reality. While trying to enact the ideal, the mere assertion of it helps. According to a former dean, "If you want to stay in the coterie of leadership, you must repeat the tribal mythology of 'excellence in graduate education and research.' It's like a script."

University Three

Less competitive and smaller, the third university has tried to be distinctive in a few areas of excellence. If graduate education and research are clearly stated ideals, the enactment of those ideals is fully possible only in some areas. Generally in the pure and applied sciences, and in a distinctive social science department as well, the campus is known for having some nationally recognized faculty, but not for producing high-quality doctorates. Unlike the first two field sites, this campus has no construction in progress. A long period of deferred maintenance is evident in the decaying physical plant, including "ripped up floors, leaky pipes." As one scientist said, "It's not terrible. It just doesn't make you happy to be here."

The campus enrolls about 20,000 undergraduates and 6,500 graduate students and employs fifty postdoctoral researchers. Of the graduate enrollment, two-thirds are in professional schools. Two-thirds of these are part-time, and many are older. Financial aid rests on an unstable and uncertain foundation, since most financial aid comes in the form of state-supported teaching assistantships, and the state faces a huge budget deficit. Some externally sponsored research enables faculty to support research assistants. Most of these funds are in the sciences and engineering. Faculty-sponsored research brings in $50 million annually; about three-quarters of that sum is from the federal government. Unstable funding for teaching and research assistantships causes low morale among students and faculty. Students receiving no assistantship do not get the tuition waiver all half-time research assistants and teaching assistants receive; they are also denied office space and a key to the mailroom!

The central administration actively encourages faculty to get external research funds both to increase the research visibility of the university and to support graduate education. A symbolically important move was to create a new position of vice provost for research and graduate education, filled by a charismatic and outspoken person who aspires to a leadership role. The vice provost is known for asserting the inseparability of research and graduate education as well as the campus's competitive drive. In his words, "Graduate education and research are inseparable. If there's no research in it, there's no place for graduate education. There is no tension in that at all. The only tension arises between the 'haves' and the 'have-nots' with regard to external funding sources. . . . If it's good for research it's good for graduate education. . . . Graduate education and research are one and the same. The best teachers are the most productive scholars. The biggest trouble we have is the poor undergraduate teachers; they are not good teachers nor active scholars." The associate dean commented that linking graduate education and research is "symbolically important, even if it is too big for us to do well. . . . Change comes slowly and from the bottom up. . . . We're still feeling our way."

Like the second university, faculty authority over graduate programs is decoupled from the central administration; however, a recent change in administrative leadership has generated a negative response among faculty. Their perception of this change is noteworthy. Prior to it, "The graduate school was something you passed papers to, lots of memos. They just approved stuff. . . . They're doing more to encourage faculty research. And they're angry with faculty for not getting more research funds, . . . but they don't get to determine the character of graduate education on this campus." These discussions were infused with emotion, even animosity. Interviews with administrators and faculty reveal a gulf between them.

Faculty and graduate students are more realistic about the current scene and lack an idealism or optimism about the future. The university currently offers about fifty doctoral programs. Decisions about whether to establish or eliminate a Ph.D. program are based more on the market of student enrollment than on the cutting-edge programs at the top research universities. In 1987 the university granted close to nine hundred master's degrees and just over three hundred doctorates. The productivity has increased after a long period of inactivity, when doctoral student admissions were limited. In the past fifteen years about seventy-five Ph.D.'s. have been granted by history, but only six were given in the last four years; physics has granted twenty-one doctorates in the past four years. The length of time to degree completion is long across all disciplines.

Faculty research activity prevails across departments at this university, but there are only a few pockets of excellence; it is in those rare places where graduate education and research are most strongly integrated. This campus, in contrast to the second university, has a smaller-scale operation and lives with a daily acknowledgment that it falls short of its ideals. It tends to protect its position rather than to advance to the upper echelons of the country's leading universities.

University Four

Reflecting the greatest disjuncture between graduate education and research, the fourth campus is a small public university that was originally founded as a normal school, an early pedagogical mission that has had a lasting imprint on campus practices. Graduate education and research have become ideals espoused in the mission, although in reality these enterprises are quite limited. While the first university was excellent across the board, the second campus had several major areas of excellence, and the third attempted innovation and good research training in some areas, the fourth site has established only small groupings of doctoral activity, referred to as "research strengths . . . in selected areas."

The graduate education program at this university is the smallest of the four sites—a total graduate enrollment of about 3,500 students, 2,000 or so in master's programs, with a large part-time enrollment for both degree levels. Offering about twenty-five Ph.D. programs, the campus has increased its doctoral enrollment by 16 percent and decreased its master's enrollment by 7 percent in the past seven years. Annually, the university produces just under a thousand master's degrees and one hundred Ph.D.'s.

Since the graduate level is small by American standards, the university cannot cover all disciplines (there is no economics Ph.D. program), nor can it cover all subfields within a discipline. Usually a department has one faculty member per specialty, leaving gaps in physics, history, and biology. There are more full-time doctoral students in the sciences: the size of graduate enrollment in any department depends on the availability of financial assistance for their applicants. As on other campuses, undergraduate enroll-ments boost the number of teaching assistantships allocated.

Graduate education strengths and faculty research interests have been limited to selected areas where (according to its publications) the uni-versity is inclined to support graduate programs that "show promise of achieving distinction and which will fulfill vital societal needs of the state in the areas of basic and mathematical sciences, health sciences, business and technology, professional education, communications, and the applied and performing arts."

In research activity, the campus ranks about two hundred nationally in university R&D expenditures. The total for the entire campus is less than that for many departments at the first university and some at the second. Over the past decade the growth has been dramatic, a fivefold increase in R&D expenditures, mostly attributed to the expansion of physics: by 1988, the R&D expenditures were up to $5 million, about $3 million from federal sources. Over one-quarter goes to physics, including funds for a research center that was characterized by one distant observer as "really more en-gineering than physics," and less to biological sciences. The professional schools (business and speech) amount to about one-half.

As on other campuses, faculty seek outside funds to support graduate students as research assistants, but fewer are involved in that pursuit than on the other three campuses. Although faculty are encouraged to pursue sponsored research by the central administration and department chairs, they cite their location as a hindrance in national competition: the campus has neither the reputation nor the concentration of faculty or physical re-sources that would lend it appeal. This is especially difficult for academics in physics and biology, for whom external funds are a necessity in the financing of their research. As one biologist explained, "We don't compete very well. When we line up against Stanford, Washington, Minnesota, Wis-consin, and eastern schools, we can't compete. Our faculty is as good as theirs. We publish in the same journals, have been trained in the same places, we work just as hard, but when it comes to getting proposals funded, we don't get money. Now it may be that the panels at NSF think that the probability of completing the project with results that are going to move this idea farther is more likely to happen at Stanford than [here], and I guess they're right." At the same time that faculty are expected to do re-search or get research funds, they teach heavy course loads, normally three (in physics, two) courses per semester.

This lack of funding is a hardship for students because they must "search for" research assistantships. In the pure and applied sciences, according to an administrator, "students aim to be a research assistant somewhere along the line. In [the] humanities it's almost unheard of." Only two-thirds of the students are supported with some kind of financial aid; three-quarters of the biology students are funded, but summer appointments are handled separately and are not guaranteed. In physics one-half of the doctoral students are teaching assistants and one-half are research assistants. There are discrepancies between their stipends across fields. The associate dean remarked that the university provided "$7,200 for nine months in natural sciences, less in humanities—as low as $4,500. We're not proud of this discrepancy. . . . [We] respond to market pressures."

The portrait that emerges from this fourth campus is that it aspires to distinctiveness but establishes research activity and doctoral training in only a few areas. Seeking research resources from federal, state, and industrial sources and reaching for quality graduate students as levers for institutional mobility, the campus finds both beyond its grasp. Trying to sustain a research training component in graduate education is a stretch, even in biology and physics. While the university may produce a scholar/scientist who receives national recognition or acquire research resources in a science specialty, that is the exception. It produces people with doctoral and master's credentials, many of whom remain in the area and teach or go elsewhere to be teachers. This small university, with its graduates and applied research projects, provides services to the region, but both its graduate education and research activities are uneven and somewhat disengaged.

To summarize, the four universities vary in size and scope and in the integration of graduate education and research through the use of sponsored research funds. The case studies illustrate how graduate education and research are most easily connected when an abundance of human, physical, and financial resources concentrate in an institution devoted to being the best. Farther down the line, the campuses reveal how asserting excellence in graduate education and research can serve as powerful levers for institutional mobility, even if it remains merely a stated ambition. The variation across these campuses serves as a significant reminder that in the United States, disciplinary differences are mediated through the filter of institutional differences.

THE SIGNIFICANCE OF STRONG LOCAL ORGANIZATION

The department is the major operating unit of graduate (and undergraduate) education. By selecting students and providing them with course work and research training opportunities, it is the intellectual, social, and administrative home of graduate programs. Over the past two decades, however, a centralized institutional structure has emerged to formally oversee the administration of graduate education and research. Different attempts have been made to coordinate these campuswide activities. Two arrangements are most common. One pattern separated the responsibilities by specifying a dean for research and a dean for graduate studies. The graduate dean is reputed to have no (or little) power, authority, or leadership with respect to departments. He or she serves primarily to rubber-stamp the work of departments. An administrator remarked that "if research is separated from graduate education, the graduate dean is nothing but a bean counter." A second pattern provided for a dean (or vice provost) for research *and* graduate education. This arrangement has been more common at the leading research universities, and the position is usually occupied by a physical or life scientist. When the two responsibilities are combined, it is commonly acknowledged that research issues consume most of the dean's attention, such as providing assistance with sponsored project proposals and acceptances, serving as a liaison to external sponsors, and negotiating about indirect cost rates or intellectual property rights. An associate dean is charged with the primary responsibility of overseeing graduate education. Oriented toward internal campus relations with departments, the associate dean allocates funds for teaching assistantships and tries to standardize department practices that are benchmarks of degree progress.

In recent years, especially at leading research universities, the arrangement of linking the administration of research and graduate education under one office has changed; the two elements have been separated once again. Issues in each arena are becoming more complicated and divergent. In research, concerns center on technology transfer and patenting activities of faculty. In graduate education, new issues are how to cope with rapid knowledge changes, including whether or not to create new organizational units and degree programs to pursue interdisciplinary research and training. Such rearrangements in the central administration of graduate education and research do not appear to substantially alter the day-to-day activities of departments; rather they reflect administrative attempts to standardize a radically decentralized system of faculty authority.

The department, then, remains the building block of campus administration, a convenient unit for the distribution of operating funds that coincides with faculty expertise in the disciplinary specialization of knowledge. Reflecting the professional standards and expertise of the discipline, faculty in each department oversee the undergraduate curricula and graduate program, the latter including admitting graduate students, determining requirements for coursework, providing classroom instruction and research training, giving financial support, and supervising student progress to degree completion. Not only do departments have authority over most academic matters, especially curriculum and faculty hiring, they also have discretion over the allocation of resources they receive from external sponsors and from the central administration. Receiving externally sponsored research funds enhances a department's power with respect to both the central administration and to other departments.

A department becomes more independent when it receives externally sponsored research funds. Such funds provide discretionary resources to cover operating expenses not tied to the instructional budget. These funds are either directly received for research costs or indirectly received from overhead rebate. The locus of support for a department then shifts to sponsors outside the university, which makes the department less dependent on the internal administration for providing funds to finance faculty research, summer salary, research facilities, and the research component of graduate education. From the perspective of the central campus administration, grant-seeking and grant-getting activities of faculty are highly desirable, for they expand the resource base of the campus and can contribute to faculty salary, the finance of research activities and facilities, as well as the finance of graduate education.

Departments that do not seek and find funds (the humanities are an example) are seen as "a drain" on institutional funds. This intraorganizational strain is most apparent in the finance of graduate education. Departments are usually allocated teaching assistantships on the rationale that graduate students contribute to the instructional mission of the undergraduate curriculum. The larger the undergraduate enrollment in department courses, the greater the number of teaching assistantships granted a department to assist with teaching and grading. The work of graduate students as teaching assistants enables the university to offer large lecture classes of several hundred students, releasing faculty from some teaching. Departments without external funds for research assistantships rely on the campus for teaching assistantships as the sole source of support for graduate students, but a department with funds can provide higher-paying research assistantships as well as supplement the stipend levels of teaching assistantships to help recruit higher quality graduate students in a competitive market.

External research funds not only enable a department to be more self-reliant in relation to the central administration but also to gain leverage with respect to other departments. Although all departments are ostensibly equal, some are clearly more equal than others. In the past two decades the physical and life sciences have risen to the top of campus structures, both in leadership positions (president, vice provost, dean) and in allocation of discretionary resources (especially for start-up costs and facilities expansion). One reason to invest more heavily in scientists is purely pragmatic—let those in the know lead—as campuses seek to protect their position or become upwardly mobile as modern research complexes. This arrangement is sensible; it would be ill-advised for humanists to try to navigate through the turbulent seas of the science-driven funding world. Another reason is the symbolic message sent to the campus community, making visible the institutional position regarding the desirability of external sponsorship and big science. Even humanists are encouraged to seek similar support to bring prestige to their departments and greater national recognition to their campuses.

Departmental organization permits a critical mass of faculty to have the major responsibility for overseeing a graduate program: its curriculum; research training opportunities through course work or laboratory rotation; financial assistance to maintain adequate stipend levels; student performance on comprehensive examinations; and length of time to completion. With a group of scholars responsible from the outset, instead of an individual as in chair systems, there is opportunity for some complementarity, even some solidarity. Departmental organization enables faculty to pursue individual research agendas while still mobilizing collectively to shepherd the next generation of disciples. This arrangement allows for the harmony of two strands of faculty authority in the modern academic profession, a combination of guildlike autonomy and bureaucratic autonomy. Graduate education programs are then both a personal and collective responsibility. Faculty can establish their own research agendas and preserve the possibility for individual patronage/apprenticeship relationships, while simultaneously holding themselves and colleagues responsible for the collective welfare of a department program. Department-based graduate programs allow for both autocratic and collegial tendencies among faculty. Departments permit differentiation of academic specialties while insuring some lateral integration within any given department.

As departments have grown in size from eight or nine faculty to twenty or forty, or even eighty or ninety, research has also become more specialized. Ben-David has observed that a department can function like a professional school, with each professor having a specialty.[9] Since subject matter has increased in scope and specialization, the premise of sharing the same interests has given way to the premise of compatible interests. An organizational vehicle for mediating this shift has been the emergence of intradepartmental research groups. Often an overlooked feature of campus arrangements, these groups of faculty and their selected students serve to strengthen the graduate education–research linkage.

When departments are large enough—a staff of twenty or more—faculty divide into clusters that reflect their subfields of expertise. History will have a group of Americanists, physics a group of high energy experimentalists. The tasks of the department are then decentralized. A cluster of two or more faculty may be responsible, in their specialty alone, for reviewing applications for the next entering graduate class, allocating research assistantship funds, and advising students. Students also are clustered in these faculty-led research groups. They may establish weekly meetings, larger in size than laboratory sessions, or organize colloquia or preprint discussion groups. Offices of faculty in a research group are often in close proximity, especially in the sciences, where laboratory space and equipment may also be shared. Such research-group interaction is more formalized and more frequent in the sciences than in the humanities. Nonetheless, across the disciplines faculty and students alike identify themselves as members of a subgroup as well as a department. A student is not just a doctoral student in the physics department; she works in Dr. Long's laboratory and is financially and intellectually cared for by him, while perhaps at the same time serving as a member of the high energy experimentalist group that Long, Alkin, Pedersen, and Bruno run.

The organization of faculty and graduate students in research groups is an intradepartmental solution to powerful tensions that may result from relying on external sponsorship of research for the finance of graduate education. Several strains have become apparent in sponsored research, especially in relying on federally funded R&D support. If these strains are most apparent in the sciences, variations are evident in applied social sciences, including economics. The research groups are a strong counterforce against the following problems: faculty can build individual fiefdoms with uneven pockets of wealth within a department. Their time and attention can move so much to grant seeking that they give limited access and attention to students. The short duration of funding cycles imposes a time constraint on faculty and student research with pressure to finish work quickly or to apply for renewals. Research funds for individual projects tie a student to one laboratory, or, conversely, if funds are withdrawn a student may have to find another laboratory and start on another research project for financial support. Critically, if research is increasingly tied to an agenda that is applied or interdisciplinary, it pulls the intellectual and social center of gravity away from the department and traditional canon of the discipline. Dependence on federally sponsored research, if unchecked, potentially threatens departmental cohesion and weakens the graduate education–research linkage. The nesting of research groups within departments encourages a collective will that balances the individualistic nature of outside funding.

To summarize, strong organization at the local level keeps the locus of faculty authority within department-based graduate programs. Graduate education and research become linked and reinforced by formal and informal decision making within the department. As departments have grown in size and proliferated into subspecialties, the emergence of intradepartmental research clusters of faculty and students has strengthened the research component of graduate education. These groups also mediate between the faculty's personal research agendas and collective orientations to the graduate program.

CONCLUSION

Campus arrangements in the contemporary era reveal a mix of material conditions and reinforcing beliefs that enable graduate education and research to be integrated. Without intending to overshadow the tremendous variation in the American system, it is instructive to simply describe two basic patterns that occur in two different campus and disciplinary settings for doctoral education.

At leading research universities and in the sciences, administrators and faculty are compelled to provide sufficient funds for the necessary material conditions for research training. Sustaining quality graduate programs that train excellent researchers is seen as vital to the life of the department. The climate reflects a grant-seeking agenda as a way of life—both for faculty and graduate students. Concerns about personal and institutional advancement reflect a competitive ethos, one grounded in the knowledge that research contributions are socially valued and heavily supported with fiscal resources.

Alternatively, at less prestigious institutions and in nonscience disciplines, the absence of funds presents an underlying dynamic of scarcity if not organizational invisibility. Not only is it virtually impossible to advance one's competitive position, but funds are simply insufficient to integrate graduate education and research. There is not a sufficient research infrastructure to support doctoral programs. Departments often need to contend for mere survival, and they earn it by undergraduate course enrollments. These organizational settings are particularly characterized by unwanted cleavages: distinctions among faculty (the few research "stars" and the "deadwood"); hierarchies among graduate students of the "haves" versus "have nots" (usually research assistants and teaching assistants respectively).

These two patterns illuminate structural and normative conditions that sustain the research foundations of graduate education: an abundance of externally derived funds for faculty research; a professional imperative for faculty to reproduce their disciplines; and a rapid pace of knowledge change. Departments with abundant research resources provide a stable basis of financial support for students, enabling them to take advantage of faculty's research training opportunities. At the same time, faculty reproduce the kind of training they received. Motivated by compelling incentives in the academic reward structure, doctoral students and faculty together seek to be at the forefront of knowledge developments.

Paradoxically, these same conditions may weaken the educational foundations of doctoral programs. Although sponsored research funds provide a structural vehicle for apprenticeship relationships, the increasingly competitive nature of government funding constrains those relationships, bringing ever more stringent expectations for efficiency and productivity in research output at the expense of a broader intellectual agenda. Moreover, as faculty are tied to external support, their professional norms reflect increased acceptance of sponsors' agendas, thus modeling less professional autonomy for their students. Finally, the rapid pace and direction of knowledge change quickly renders the knowledge base for doctoral study obsolete. It generates controversy over what constitutes the disciplinary canon and, portending yet unfathomed changes, how the swell of extra-departmental research training opportunities can be integrated with a department-based doctoral program.

Among the many "master's only" institutions, graduate education faces a different normative, structural, and funding environment than in those institutions offering doctoral training. With fewer resources for research, and historically committed to instructional missions, institutions that grant the master's as the highest degree are engaged in a more market-driven enterprise of producing practitioners rather than researchers. In spite of a subtle, small-scale drift to emulate the more prestigious research institutions, these master's-oriented campuses display fewer research foundations. Neither disciplinary reproduction nor the advancement of knowledge are central aims. The funding base for graduate student assistance is highly problematic; the funding of faculty research is not a high priority.

Institutions engaged in the broad sweep of American graduate education display different and differently valued functions in the production and transmission of knowledge. In a national context that nurtures sciences over humanities, that values research training over scholarship, and both of those over teaching, recent strains in the arrangements for doctoral education in the top tier of research universities have commanded greatest attention in policy discussions. These are the flagship campuses that have most of the resources for university research and gain international reputations as centers of excellence. If advocates of a system that has such a prominent and successful sector find it hard to imagine organizing it any other way, critics have suggested that the prevailing notions of excellence and quality benefit a few institutions rather than the system as a whole.[10]

Even though the major universities have thus far reacted successfully to dramatic funding changes, major underlying questions remain about the goals and conditions for graduate education and research: how many and what kinds of students ought to be trained? What kinds of research and how much of it should be performed? Where should resources be allocated and what is the proper amount to be spent on research? How should research be integrated with teaching and professional training for research? Obviously normative in nature, these questions are not just about efficient means but also about desirable ends.

In a higher education system as decentralized as in the United States, such fundamental questions about the purposes and means of doctoral education have yet to be addressed, let alone resolved, from a systemwide perspective. Instead incremental local solutions are attempted to abet structural strains. The result is a persistent underlying ambiguity of purpose that lies close to the surface across the disciplines and various campus settings, with little collective deliberation on the future organization and sponsorship of graduate education.

NOTES

The author gratefully acknowledges research resources from the Spencer Foundation and editorial suggestions from Burton R. Clark. Data collection at one of the four campuses studied was conducted by Ronald Opp, a research assistant at UCLA.

1. Ben-David, *Centers of Learning*, p. 117.

2. Ibid., p. 124.

3. By 1986 the annual number of physics Ph.D.'s conferred was over 1,100, in economics about 850, in history about 550, and in biological sciences 3,800. The presence of foreign students varied from 40 percent in physics, to 45 percent in economics, to 15 percent in history, to 20 percent in biological sciences. The gender composition of each of these disciplines varied: physics was 90 percent male, economics 80 percent, history 65 percent, and biological sciences 65 percent. Data on national trends can be found in the survey of earned doctorates. (National Research Council, *Summary Report.*)

4. The median number of registered years for each discipline from 1970 to 1986 increased as follows: 5.7 to 6.3 years in physics, 5.2 to 6.3 years in economics, 6.3 to 8.5 years in history, and 5.3 to 6.3 years in biological sciences. History is the most striking change, taking two years longer. (National Research Council, *Summary Report.*)

5. Within national R&D funds for science and engineering, three agencies now allocate the bulk of the doctoral support: the National Science Foundation allocated the highest proportion of research funding as research assistant support (9.2 percent), followed by Health and Human Services at 2.4 percent and Department of Defense at 4.0 percent. Research assistantships by those three agencies amount to over 21,000: 9,075, 7,710, and 4,628 respectively. Each of these agencies also grants fellowships, traineeships, and training grants at $25.2 million, $204.3 million, and $.5 million, respectively, to well over 60,000 doctoral students. (National Research Council, *Summary Report.*) No federal predoctoral support for humanities was offered, except the new Javits program, which is minuscule given the magnitude of funding to the sciences and engineering.

6. The data were collected from 1987 to 1989. After a pilot study, four universities were selected for their representativeness of the stratification in the American system (different levels of federally sponsored research activity and different levels of doctoral production). The four case studies included over 150 campus interviews with administrators, faculty, and graduate students in four disciplines: physics, history, economics, and, because of heavy national investment in biomedical research,

biological sciences. Primary and secondary data sources are not specified in order to conceal the identity of the informants and institutions. Data were analyzed with a grounded theory approach. (Glaser and Strauss, *Discovery of Grounded Theory*.)

7. For discussion of disciplinary differences, see Snow, "Two Cultures"; Becher, "Cultural View"; and Metzger, "Academic Profession in the United States."

8. For discussion of the strategies employed in institutional upward mobility, see Gumport, "Research Imperative."

9. Ben-David, *Centers of Learning*, p. 109.

10. See, for example, Astin, *Achieving Educational Excellence*.

BIBLIOGRAPHY

Astin, Alexander. *Achieving Educational Excellence*. San Francisco: Jossey-Bass, 1987.

Becher, Tony. "The Cultural View." In *Perspectives on Higher Education: Eight Disciplinary and Comparative Views*, ed. Burton R. Clark. Berkeley, Los Angeles, London: University of California Press, 1984. Pp. 165–198.

Ben-David, Joseph. *Centers of Learning*. New York: McGraw-Hill, 1977.

Glaser, Barney, and Anselm Strauss. *The Discovery of Grounded Theory: Strategies for Qualitative Research*. New York: Aldine, 1967.

Gumport, Patricia J. "The Research Imperative." In *Culture and Ideology in Higher Education: Advancing a Critical Agenda*, ed. William Tierney. New York: Praeger, 1991. Pp. 87–105.

Metzger, Walter P. "The Academic Profession in the United States." In *The Academic Profession: National, Disciplinary, and Institutional Settings*, ed. Burton R. Clark. Berkeley, Los Angeles, London: University of California Press, 1987. Pp. 123–208.

National Research Council. *Summary Report 1986: Doctorate Recipients from United States Universities*. Washington, D.C.: National Academy Press, 1987.

Snow, C. P. *The Two Cultures*. Cambridge and New York: Cambridge University Press, 1959.

PART FIVE

Japan

Introduction

To search for the research foundations of advanced education in Japan is to be struck not only by the overwhelming importance of national setting but also by the seemingly sheer perversity of human institutions. Here is a country that has exhibited outstanding strength in elementary and secondary education. High school graduates compete strenuously for access to the best universities. A bachelor's degree is clearly a valued item. The country is also known for striking industrial and economic performance, suggesting significant R&D investment and effective training of scientists and engineers. But graduate education, it turns out, is small and relatively weak. System incentives seem to wind down: individual motives become seriously dampened at the door of the graduate school and especially at the entry to doctoral programs. It is all very odd to foreign eyes and more than a bit of a puzzle to Japanese observers. Why does this educationally robust country not have a vigorous commitment to education beyond the bachelor's degree?

The story of constraints on Japanese graduate education is complex. A long chain of interacting conditions are rooted in history and in the ways of industry, government, and the general culture. Industry is clearly eager to employ young people as soon as they have the bachelor's degree and sees relatively little value in prolonged university education. The many private universities, heavily dependent on student tuition, are undergraduate-centered. The main public universities are thoroughly nationalized, but they are atomized at their operating level around chairs. The funding system of the central ministry of education sharply limits the number of master's and doctoral students that each chair can have. The doctoral degree has, historically, served as an honorary award to be possibly achieved later in life for a body of scholarship or long service. Even today it can be taken without serious work in a doctoral program. Conversely, those who go through a doctoral program typically emerge without the degree in hand. To add to the interaction, senior professors often do not have doctorates and see little reason why faculty recruits need them.

As Morikazu Ushiogi and his colleagues detail in chapters 9 and 10, Japanese universities divide considerably at the most advanced level between strong science and engineering and relatively weak humanities and social science disciplines. The greatest strength is found in engineering at the master's level. Engineering is so powerful in university organization that it tends to swallow applied science—for example, the applied side of physics. In contrast, all the constraining conditions of saturated job markets and bureaucratic specifications hit hardest on the humanities and social sciences. In these fields mere handfuls of students make their way through to doctoral degrees, and then with long-delayed dissertations.

Across the disciplines, but especially in the humanities and social sciences, the graduate level is plagued with the problem of smallness noted in the case of Britain. There are generally too few students in a given specialty in a university to justify instruction and systematic course work. Overall, there are many graduate schools but relatively few students.

Will Japan yet develop more robust graduate schools? The problem has been on the national agenda for some years. In 1990 new efforts are underway to seriously decentralize control from ministry to university. But Japanese industry continues to work its powerful ways in building its own research capability, attracting young talent, and making its own educational investment.

NINE

Graduate Education and Research Organization in Japan

Morikazu Ushiogi

Graduate education in Japan is an anomaly, a marginal segment in an otherwise highly developed system of education. Well known for its intense commitment to education, Japan has a huge educational structure. Virtually all—about 95 percent—of the graduates of the country's nine-year compulsory education pursue a secondary education; about 35 percent then enter higher education. But less than 2 percent of the age group and only 6 percent of the first-degree graduates go on for graduate work. Students do not find such advanced education attractive. Professors and employers have their doubts about the value of the doctoral degree. As Japanese industry invests in basic and applied research and development, the research base of graduate education becomes problematic. A peculiar combination of historical developments and contemporary structural arrangements, including government funding, has placed Japanese graduate education in a position of neglect. Its past and present distortion presents serious problems for its future development.

THE HISTORICAL LEGACY

Graduate education in Japan can be traced back to 1886, just a decade after Johns Hopkins was funded as the first true American research university. An enacted Imperial University Ordinance stipulated that Japan's first university was to be composed of two major components: an undergraduate level devoted to teaching, and a graduate school dedicated to research. Here was clear governmental recognition from the outset that the university was to incorporate research as well as teaching and that the graduate school was to serve as a home for the research function.[1] The ordinance stipulated that a specified number of students were to be admitted from the undergraduate schools, that the term of the study should be five years, and that all candidates who passed a final examination were to be awarded a degree.

When this historic ordinance was written, the only university in Japan was the University of Tokyo, founded in 1877 by the national Ministry of Education. The university had absorbed in its earliest years several schools already in existence under other ministries, namely a law school founded and run by the Ministry of Justice and a school of engineering operating under the Ministry of Industry. When the 1886 ordinance renamed the university "the Imperial University," it was formally defined as consisting of five schools: law, medicine, engineering, humanities, and natural science. Four years later, a school of agriculture was added. Thus the structure and orientation of what was to be Japan's "flagship" university was closer to the European than the American model. The professional school components were significant from the outset, unlike the American situation, where the liberal arts were the intellectual core to which research and graduate level training were added.

Seven imperial universities of this type were established by the Second World War. Private universities were also created: several of them, preeminently Keioh and Waseda, were older than Tokyo University, but the government did not grant them university status until 1919. The University Reform Ordinance of that year also authorized the establishment of graduate schools. Universities grew in number from one in 1890 to sixteen in 1920 and forty-seven in 1940; student enrollment in those years increased from 1,312 to 21,915 to 81,999. The number of graduate students increased gradually but quite irregularly: from 23 in 1886, to a first peak of 966 students in 1909, then a drop to 293 in 1914, and an increase again to a second peak of roughly 2,600 in the 1930s. After another decline to 2,000 in the late 1930s, the pre-1945 peak of 2,687 was reached in 1944.[2]

Graduate students remained a small minority throughout the prewar period. For example, in 1935, a peak year, the proportion of graduate students to undergraduates was only 3.7 percent. If undergraduate students numbered 103 per 100,000 inhabitants, those at the graduate level numbered fewer than 4. An international comparison for that year indicated that Japanese higher education overall had already greatly expanded. There were 110 German university students (including those in the *Technische Hochschule*) per 100,000 inhabitants at the time, while the numbers for France and the United Kingdom appeared as 196 and 104 respectively.[3] The Japanese undergraduate base had clearly developed, but the graduate level did not flower. As the graduate programs failed to become well rooted in the academic community, a pattern of weakness developed and still exists today. Students were not strongly committed to graduate study. Gradually, they began to use the graduate level as a place for extra study time to prepare for higher civil service examinations or as a place to tarry as they looked for better jobs.

As an example of this lack of commitment, Tokyo University had 966 graduate students in 1909, with 500 of them in the law school; five years later the total had dropped to 293 and the number in the law school was down to only 51. This devastating decrease was caused by the abolition of a free tuition system. Until then graduate students were not required to pay tuition; once they learned they were obliged to foot the bill, they left graduate school without hesitation. Most had registered not for the sake of academic study but to prepare themselves for the civil service examinations. When a second boom occurred in graduate education between 1925 and 1935, with the number of graduate students increasing two and one-half times in a decade, the dramatic rise was largely the result of the troubled job market caused by the Great Depression.

All early documents indicate that organized course work especially designed for graduate education did not exist. Graduate students were either left to study independently, or they helped professors, apprentice-style, to do research. In spite of its early promising beginnings, graduate education became a neglected part of the educational scheme. This unsuccessful development was closely related to the peculiar qualities of the emerging doctoral degree. The Japanese doctorate, in contrast to those of most other countries, was not well connected with graduate education. Although graduate school enrollments expanded slowly, the number of awarded degrees increased very rapidly. In the five years between 1935 and 1939, roughly six thousand doctoral degrees were conferred. But only 15 percent of these degrees were earned through graduate training; the remaining 85 percent were otherwise awarded. In what way did this come about? For what purpose? How did this critical disjuncture emerge?

The Degree System

In 1887, the year following the enactment of the Imperial University Ordinance, a Degree Ordinance was enacted. The degrees were specified by field, as for example, law, medicine, engineering—a pattern that corresponded to the structure of schools within the university. No Ph.D. was created that could encompass an array of subjects. Critically, the ordinance provided three alternative routes leading to a doctorate. The first specified that a person was to undergo five years of training at the graduate level, pass a final examination, and submit a dissertation. The second bypassed the course work requirement entirely but required the submission of a dissertation, which had to be approved by the university senate. The third pathway stipulated that the Minister of Education could confer a degree on a person even without a dissertation. This latter procedure had to meet the approval of two-thirds of the members of the university senate. Thus a route was opened for gaining a doctoral degree without any graduate training at all.[4]

This first Degree Ordinance continued for eleven years, until 1898, during which 139 doctorate degrees were conferred. Four recipients (3 percent) had taken the first route of graduate course work; nineteen (14 percent) earned the degree by submitting the dissertation alone; and the remaining 116, or over 80 percent, were awarded degrees without any training and without submitting a dissertation.[5] This latter type of award became understood as a special honor to be bestowed on outstanding scholars for long careers of service to scholarship and science.

The Degree Ordinance was changed in 1898 to grant doctorates in a wider range of fields—in pharmacy, agriculture, forestry, and veterinary medicine, along with the old categories of law, medicine, engineering, humanities, and natural science. The routes for earning a degree were also modified somewhat and a fourth added. The first path continued to be by graduate training; the second, by dissertation only. The third and fourth paths toward a doctorate came about by recommendations—one by a national association of degree holders (*Hakase-kai*) and the other by the Minister of Education on the endorsement of university presidents. By this time Kyoto University was functioning as the second imperial university. It was now possible for professors at both universities to earn a doctoral degree solely on the recommendation of their university presidents; most imperial university professors who were awarded doctorates received them in just this fashion.

Except for the few who had studied abroad for long periods, professors at the time had had little chance to earn doctoral degrees: both the graduate school and the degree system were still in utero during their student days. After taking the first degree, most of them had enrolled at the graduate level to wait for the opportunity to study abroad on a government stipend. After two or three years at an American or European university, usually not long enough to earn a foreign doctorate, they returned to Japan to eventually become professors. The recommendation of their university presidents provided their main chance for getting the degree.

But sharp censure surfaced. One journalist criticized those doctorate-holders who were popping up only through the recommendation of their university presidents as "bamboo-shoot doctors": they mushroomed everywhere. These degrees-by-recommendation even became unpopular within the academic community, leading to their abolition in 1919. Two avenues for acquiring a degree then remained: two years of graduate training plus the dissertation was one; the other required submission of a dissertation only. The majority preferred the latter way.

In medicine, for example, after completing the undergraduate course, students worked in the university hospital as unpaid trainees and did research during their off-duty hours. This research could be compiled and submitted as a dissertation. The university hospital rather than the graduate school functioned as the cradle for doctoral candidates. In the humanities and social sciences students became paid assistants at the university or took positions as professors in the high schools that corresponded to the upper classes of the *gymnasium* in Germany or the *lycée* in France. They usually carried out research by themselves—an effort that could stretch over many years—and then submitted a dissertation.

Before World War II, the total number of Japanese graduate students never exceeded three thousand. Until 1915 there were fewer than one hundred doctoral degrees per year; they increased to more than one hundred after 1915, and passed the one thousand mark after 1935. But the pattern had become entrenched in which most degrees were conferred without training at graduate schools. During the 1920s and 1930s more than 80 percent of the doctorates were conferred just by submitting the dissertation. Graduate schools were thereby denied a central role in the education and training of scholars, researchers, and professional practitioners who would hold the country's highest degree.

The Disciplinary Cleavage

As the sharp increase in the annual production of doctorates was taking place after 1920, substantial differences among fields developed. Medicine became preeminent, offering as much as 70 percent of all doctorates, or about one thousand M.D.'s each year after 1935. Law, during the 1920s and 1930s, in contrast, awarded only about ten doctorates a year. Medicine was followed by the natural sciences, engineering, and agriculture. Between 1920 and 1940 the number of awarded degrees in the natural sciences increased by eightfold; in engineering, by five. Doctorates in the humanities remained rare, with only ten a year at most for the entire country.[6] Sharp and long-lasting differences in the use and meaning of the doctoral degree became fixed. Natural science degrees became in effect professional certificates for young scientists; degrees in the humanities and the social sciences remained a high honor bestowed only on a few authorities in the disciplines.

These different perceptions and uses became reflected in age differences: degree earners in the humanities and social sciences were mostly older than those in the natural sciences. Among the degree earners in the humanities, from 1927 to 1936, 90 percent were older than forty, while only 22 percent of those in medicine were that age. Strikingly, 47 percent of degree earners in the humanities were even older than fifty, compared to only 3 percent in medicine.[7]

The "honors" tradition also continued to have lingering negative effects on the production of doctorates in the humanities and social sciences and related professional fields. In the post-1920 degree system, if a doctoral degree was sought, even very senior professors were obliged to write a dissertation and submit it to the university for approval. This new system was incompatible with the self-definition of those professors, particularly in the humanities and social sciences, who considered themselves well-established scholars and were already recognized as authorities. Hence many professors in these fields did not pursue the degree. In 1940, only 52 percent of the humanities professors had a doctorate; among law professors at Tokyo University the figure was only 20 percent. In sharp contrast, 82 percent of professors in the School of Natural Science at Tokyo and 95 percent in the School of Medicine held doctoral degrees.[8]

This disciplinary gap has become deeply entrenched. After World War II, the granting of the doctorate continued to occur far less frequently in the humanities and the social sciences than in medicine, natural science, engineering, and agriculture. This fundamental difference among fields of study is reflected in the situation found in the 1980s in which almost 80 percent of the doctoral students in the natural sciences and science-related professional fields (medicine, engineering, agriculture) are able to finish a projected five-year effort with an earned degree in hand, while only 2 percent in the humanities and only 6 percent in the social sciences do so.

The Role of Assistantship

In a situation where the systematic training of doctoral candidates was impoverished, the recruitment and training of future academics became located in a system of assistantships. Each school selected some of its most promising students and appointed them to the position of assistant (*joshu*) directly after they finished the undergraduate program. Differing from U.S. teaching and research assistants, Japanese assistants were and are full-time academic staff. They are mostly free from teaching responsibilities but are presumed to assist professors in research, particularly in the natural sciences. Many of them are also free from this responsibility in the humanities and social sciences, and they are expected to devote themselves exclusively to their own research. The years of assistantship are considered a crucial "incubation period" for determining whether young scholars can successfully enter the academic community. After several years of work, assistants can be candidates for promotion to lecturer or associate professor at their own university or elsewhere.

This academic pathway was worked out and institutionalized when the Japanese academic community was quite small. In 1940 the total number of teaching staff at forty-seven universities was only seven thousand. Such a small academic community hardly needed a grand scheme of systematic training. For the replacement of teaching staff, the recruitment of some promising undergraduate students, trained as assistants in an apprenticeship style, was sufficient. Whether they had a doctorate or not was largely immaterial.

THE CONTEMPORARY SYSTEM OF GRADUATE EDUCATION

After World War II the Japanese educational system underwent a thorough face-lifting under the powerful influence of the United States. An American-style graduate school was initiated, providing master's as well as doctoral programs, a separation that did not exist in the prewar graduate school. In an overall system of higher education that underwent tremendous expansion, the number of universities with graduate schools increased sixfold in the three decades between 1955 and 1988, from 47 to 294. In the latter year, among 490 four-year institutions (leaving aside two-year junior colleges), 202 (41 percent) offered both master's and doctoral work and another 92 (19 percent) had master's courses alone. During the 1960–1988 period, master's students increased from 8,305 to 56,596, a sevenfold increase; doctoral students increased from 7,429 to 25,880, a threefold increase.[9]

The Drive to Develop Graduate Schools

Several factors underlie this rapid expansion. First, a graduate school offers higher status to a university and boosts the prestige of its professors. In the Japanese system a university that plans to establish a graduate school submits an application to the Ministry of Education. The ministry then asks the University Chartering Commission, a body composed of representatives of the national, municipal, and private universities (*Daigakusettishingikai*), to examine the application. A positive evaluation by the commission is considered an endorsement of university quality. Therefore, on grounds of reputation alone, more and more universities became eager to upgrade themselves to "graduate school university."

Second, salary benefits are involved. In the national universities the teaching staff engaged in master's programs receive a 4 percent salary supplement and those engaged in doctoral courses 8 percent. In the private universities professors in charge of graduate school programs are also paid a higher salary than professors who are involved only in undergraduate education. Third, and most critical, in the case of national universities large differences appear in the basic budget allocation, including differing amounts of research funds for professors. As seen later in detail, professors in charge of doctoral programs have access to a budget nearly double that of those who teach only undergraduates.

Many professors at the older universities, especially the former imperial universities, were dissatisfied with the new postwar university system. During prewar times, the university could offer three years of relatively advanced study at the undergraduate level following three years of general education in the higher secondary schools (*Koutougakkou*). Postwar educational reforms condensed the three years of general education and the three of advanced work into four-year university programs in which the first two years are devoted to general education and the remaining two years are given over to specialized work in such fields as law, engineering, science, and economics. Professors have long complained that the latter two years are too short to give sufficient advanced training. Repeated efforts were made to reduce the time devoted to general education. When these efforts were blocked, strategy shifted to extending training upward, essentially by combining the last two undergraduate years with two years in master's courses as a period devoted to specialized education. This upward extension became especially prevalent among schools of the natural sciences and engineering. It became another major motivating factor for establishing graduate schools.[10]

The boost in university prestige, the budget increases for salary and research funds, and the study time necessary for sufficient advanced training have all worked to motivate universities to raise themselves to the status of the graduate school university. This academic spiral caused a rapid expansion of graduate schools.

But international comparisons of student numbers provide a very different picture. A 1984 comparative analysis compiled by the Ministry of Education indicated that the number of graduate students per one thousand inhabitants was 4.9 in the United States, 2.8 in France, 0.9 in the United Kingdom, and only 0.5 in Japan. The proportion of graduate to undergraduate students was 14.5 percent for the United States, 17.8 percent for the United Kingdom, 20.2 percent for France, but 4 percent for Japan. The number of doctoral degrees conferred each year per ten thousand inhabitants was 1.5 for the United States and 2.2 for West Germany, but only 0.5 for Japan.[11] The disciplinary cleavage already well in place before World War II apparently continued to deepen in the postwar decades. Engineering, medicine, and the natural sciences have become even more dominant at the graduate level, with the humanities and social sciences quite stunted. Over 40 percent of Japan's students at the master's level are enrolled in engineering, which makes up the largest sector of Japanese graduate education. On the doctoral level over 40 percent of the students are in the health sciences, mostly in medicine (table 9-1).

The Master's Level

Each graduate school in both public and private universities has a prescribed admission quota approved by the Ministry of Education. But the application ratio differs widely from subject to subject. Master's programs in engineering are able to attract many qualified applicants; recently, there

TABLE 9-1   Number of Graduate Students, by Field of Study, Japan, 1987

Field of Study	Master's Students		Doctoral Students	
	Number	Percentage	Number	Percentage
Health sciences	2,272	4.2	10,581	43.1
Humanities	5,896	10.8	3,297	13.4
Engineering	23,862	43.9	3,196	13.0
Natural sciences	5,388	9.9	2,678	10.9
Social sciences	4,988	9.2	2,533	10.3
Agriculture	5,472	10.1	1,318	5.4
Education	4,240	7.8	641	2.6
Fine arts	1,379	2.5	81	0.3
Other fields	855	1.6	237	1.0
Total	54,352	100.0	24,562	100.0

SOURCE: *Annual Report of the Ministry of Education,* 1987.

were 1.6 times more applicants than the quota assigned to them. Other fields do not fill their quotas. Roughly two-thirds of the admission quota for master's work in the social sciences remains unoccupied. Indeed, there are more applicants than the prescribed quota, but only one-third are judged to be qualified for admission. A similar situation exists in the humanities, where about 40 percent of the admission quota remains unfilled.

After students are admitted to the two-year master's program, they are required to earn thirty credits of course work, to write a master's thesis, and to defend the thesis in an oral examination at the end of the two years. One and one-half hours of course work per week for a year (two semesters) is worth four credits; students have to average at least 3.5 courses a year to earn fifteen credits or thirty in two years. The students are not usually encouraged or allowed to take courses outside of their departments or at other schools within the university (unless they submit petitions). Then, too, most Japanese universities with graduate schools are structured in a chair system (discussed later) that tends to bind graduate students to the chair. Hence it is quite difficult for master's students to obtain a broad knowledge in subjects related to their majors.

Instead, from the very beginning, Japanese graduate students tend to specialize. At entry they ought to have had a certain amount of expertise and to be semi-independent researchers who have mastered the basic skills of research. Their task is to develop their interests more deeply through taking graduate seminars or engaging in laboratory work. Most graduate courses in the humanities and social sciences are offered in a seminar style: each student is required to give class presentations or reports on the basis of reading assignments. There are few lecture courses. In the Graduate School of Humanities at Nagoya University, for example, a graduate student majoring in oriental history usually takes two seminars each year in this subject taught by either a professor or an associate professor, and a two-credit course taught by a visiting professor. By repeating the same pattern in the second year, the student can earn as much as twenty credits, exclusively in oriental history. In the natural sciences and engineering, however, graduate courses are offered in the form of a combination of some lectures and many laboratory experiments, which may be part of advisors' ongoing research projects.

At the same time they fulfill course work requirements, students are also required to write a master's thesis. Those who wish to enter the three-year doctoral program must take another entrance examination largely based on the thesis. This exam determines a candidate's capability as a future researcher. Because the thesis rather than the course work is the key to entering the doctoral course, every school requires one and stresses its importance. Since doctoral degrees have not become standard requirements for academicians, especially in the humanities and social sciences, a master's degree is sometimes considered as sufficient qualification for a researcher. As a terminal degree or as a pathway to a doctoral program, students and their advisors attach great importance to the master's thesis. In extreme cases students spend as long as four years in writing their theses, twice the normal number of years and the maximum period allowed. Some students write theses of five hundred pages (approximately 70,000 words in English sentences); others produce fewer than one hundred pages.

The Doctoral Program

The doctoral programs are more problematic. For virtually every field, including engineering, the number of candidates does not meet the prescribed admission quota. For all fields admitted students are only about 55 percent of the quota, leaving almost one-half of the openings unfilled. Table 9-1 shows that medicine is overwhelmingly the largest field at the doctoral level. Basic medical schooling, including the undergraduate period, lasts six years. Many who complete this curriculum go on for a doctoral degree: in medical practice it enhances one's reputation and raises the confidence of clients.

Because course work is not emphasized and the possibility of obtaining a degree without taking courses exists, "doctoral students" in Japan means doctoral candidates in the American sense. Although most doctoral students do take courses, the main tasks are to submit a doctoral dissertation and pass an oral examination within three years (*Katei-hakase*). Here again the disciplinary cleavage is quite apparent between the natural sciences and engineering and the humanities and social sciences. The essential quality needed for doctoral students in the natural sciences and engineering is the ability to finish writing a doctoral dissertation. The dissertation is emphasized; it is expected to be equivalent in quality and quantity to several articles acceptable to professional journals. Doctoral students in these fields are also expected to advise undergraduates and to teach them how to write theses. Qualified students are a quintessential part of the departments and schools of natural sciences and engineering. The research productivity of these units is influenced by the number of qualified doctoral students as well as the quality of professors.

But the status of doctoral students in the fields of humanities and social sciences is extremely vague and problematic. Unlike the departments or schools of natural sciences and engineering, those of humanities and social sciences do not have clear standards concerning the conferring of doctoral degrees. And even if clear, the standards tend to be too high and too difficult for young doctoral students to attain. The results are astonishing in that the overwhelming majority of students in these fields leave graduate school without receiving the doctorate: in 1987, 85 percent in the humanities and 78 percent in the social sciences, compared to 34 percent in the natural sciences and 32 percent in engineering. This is part of the pattern in which some senior scholars submit doctoral dissertations only after they spend twenty or thirty years of study on a topic (*Ronbun hakase*). Some departments—psychology and economics are examples—are attempting to shift their criteria closer to those of the natural sciences and engineering. This movement may signal a break with the traditional "tightfisted" custom that has prevented young scholars in their twenties and thirties from submitting their dissertations.

Writing a dissertation, usually considered the central task of doctoral students, is not regarded as an essential step in pursuing a career as a researcher in the humanities and social sciences. Rather than encouraging their doctoral students to write and submit dissertations, most professors in these fields advise students to contribute many articles to professional journals and to make regular presentations at academic conferences soon after entering the doctoral program, as a way of broadening their reputation and enhancing their chances for securing research positions. Despite the privilege of conferring doctoral degrees, doctoral programs in the humanities and social sciences are largely nominal and underdeveloped.[12]

Labor Market Demand

The unbalanced popularity between graduate school in the humanities and social sciences and that in engineering is strongly related to the labor market. For master's graduates in the humanities and social sciences, the market is very limited, mainly consisting of high school teaching. Because the high school age population is declining, the present and future prospects for such employment are hopeless. Seventeen percent of the humanities master's graduates and 14 percent of the social sciences master's were unemployed in the late 1980s. Having little choice, many of these students continue to attempt to gain entry to doctoral programs but, as we have seen, they have been mostly unsuccessful. The situation is quite different in engineering, where 90 percent of the master's graduates immediately find a job in industry. Graduates in the natural sciences and agriculture also do quite well.[13] The master's program in the natural sciences and engineering operates as a training institution that supplies highly qualified scientists and engineers to industry; in the humanities and social sciences it serves primarily as a preliminary step for doctoral work. The function of graduate schools in the natural sciences and engineering is closer to that of professional schools in the American context.

The job market for doctoral program graduates is limited almost entirely to the academic profession. Neither private enterprises nor government departments show any interest in hiring those who have doctorates: they consider them to be overspecialized and lacking in adaptability to the workplace (certain types of teaching and research excepted). Graduates have little choice other than to find academic positions.

For the natural sciences and engineering, the difference in research conditions between the university and private enterprises is another factor that makes doctoral studies unpopular. Most master's graduates from these fields go into the research and development branches of industrial firms. Research conditions are better in the private sphere: they have more research funds and more up-to-date equipment than most universities. The employed university graduates, if they choose, are still able to earn a doctoral degree in the near future without bothering with the course work, by working up and submitting a dissertation.

Thus if they choose to go into industry, the master's graduates have an immediate stable income, good research conditions, and a chance to earn a doctoral degree in the future. If they choose to pursue the doctorate, they have to study three or more extra years without income, pay tuition, and face the unpleasant possibility of unemployment. Under these conditions, doctoral programs in the natural sciences and engineering cannot attract enough students, even with substantial enrollments at the master's level.

The Ronbun Doctor

According to university regulations, if students do not submit their dissertations within three years after completion of course work they cannot qualify for the doctoral degree. However, an alternative way is still open, in the form of "*Ronbun* doctor" (a degree earned by submitting a thesis), as contrasted to "Katei doctor" (degree earned upon completion of course work and thesis). According to a 1986 report, 78 percent of the doctoral degree

TABLE 9-2   Doctoral Degrees Awarded, by Field of Study, Japan, 1987

Field of Study	Number	Percentage
Health sciences	5,657	61.8
Engineering	1,547	16.9
Natural sciences	837	9.1
Agriculture	715	7.8
Social sciences	149	1.6
Humanities	102	1.1
Other fields	149	1.6
Total	9,156	100.0

SOURCE: *Annual Report of the Ministry of Education*, 1987.

recipients in the humanities and social sciences were "ronbun doctors."[14] Although no official information exists on the age of these degree earners, a very wide age range is apparent. Some students earn degrees in their middle thirties; others are older than sixty before they have the degree in hand. By contrast, most students in science and engineering earn the degree within the prescribed three years or close to it. This high completion ratio results from their more structured training system.

The disciplinary cleavage in place before World War II still remains: the share of the conferred doctoral degrees in different major sectors of study is enormously uneven. In 1987, 9,156 doctoral degrees (including both ronbun and katei doctors) were conferred. Sixty-two percent of them were in medicine, 17 percent in engineering, and 9 percent in the natural sciences. The humanities and social sciences together made up only 3 percent of the total (see table 9-2).

Government standards stipulate that the doctoral degree is the minimum qualification for full and associate professors. But in the humanities and social sciences, this requirement is widely ignored. Most students in these fields complete their graduate education without earning the degree; most do not finish their dissertations within the prescribed period. While enrolled, they are usually waiting for a job as a research associate or lecturer: the three-year doctoral program in the humanities and social sciences is an interim waiting room for those who wish to enter the academic profession. Earning the doctorate is not a critical step, nor is it even a routine part of the early stages of an academic career. Institutionalized over many decades, this system continues to discourage graduate students from devoting themselves to early completion of dissertations. It leads to extremely low productivity of doctorates in these fields.

Japanese universities have been eager to upgrade themselves to the recognized status of graduate school university. But, with few exceptions, they cannot attract enough students. The majority of graduate schools are "empty show-windows."

THE RESEARCH SYSTEM

The production (and development) of new knowledge in Japan is carried out in various locales, principally universities, government research institutes, and industrial laboratories. Before World War II, the universities were the main sites for research. But during the last half-century, the center of gravity has shifted to industry.

In 1986–1987, Japan spent nearly ¥9 *trillion* ($62 billion) or about 3.5 percent of the gross national product (GNP) for research and development (R&D), employing over 400,000 researchers. In total expenditure and the number of researchers, it was exceeded among the democratic nations only by the United States. Its proportion of the GNP so invested was the highest. This situation differs enormously from that of three decades ago when Japan spent merely ¥40 *million* ($276 million) for research, a sum equal at the time to only 13 percent of the research expenditure of the United Kingdom. Japan was then far behind the other major powers covered in this study. The current huge investment for R&D is also largely for nonmilitary purposes. Centered in industry, it has led to a high level of technology, while basic research has lagged.[15] Recent data (1986–1987) indicate that only about 13 percent of national R&D is expended for basic research; 24 percent is for applied research and 62 percent goes for development.[16] These allocations vary greatly among the major research sectors. Industry invests most of its funds for development (72 percent); universities expend 54 percent for basic research, 37 percent for applied research, and less than 10 percent for development. Standing between industry and universities, research institutes spend 59 percent for development and 27 percent for applied research, and hence less than 15 percent for pure science.

Industrial Laboratories

Industry plays a crucial role in research advancements in Japan. Industrial firms are the major financial sources, recently funding 80 percent of the national R&D; they are the largest performers, expending 73 percent of total funds, and the largest employers of scientists and engineers, supporting 62 percent of all researchers. Some fourteen thousand companies, overwhelmingly in manufacturing, engage in research. They emphasize the development of future products rather than basic and applied research; the proportion of funding for basic research increased only from 5 to 6 percent between the mid-1970s and the mid-1980s. But in the late 1980s industry experienced a laboratory boom, and many of the newly created laboratories were investing in pure research.[17] The commitment to R&D overall remains very high.

In spite of economic difficulties caused by the high appreciation of the yen, the ratio of industrial research funds to sales set its highest level (2.57 percent) in 1986–1987. Japanese industry knows well that Japan has few natural resources and must rely on its brain power. Most members of the R&D staffs in industry hold master's or doctoral degrees in engineering or science. Some leading manufacturing companies recruit more than one hundred master's graduates each year. Recruits customarily expect to stay on with the same company rather than move elsewhere; their companies then have particularly strong reasons to invest in their further training. The firms send their R&D personnel to graduate schools abroad; they cycle them back to Japanese graduate schools; and they allow them to earn doctoral degrees while working.

The relationship between universities and industrial laboratories is strengthened through personal connections built around graduate recruitment. Companies interested in the ongoing research of a particular department or chair attempt to employ its graduates. If they find the research leading toward practical outcomes, they invite the involved professors to be consultants. By such means private companies can maintain very useful personal ties with university personnel. At the same time, the industrial laboratories are rivals to universities, not only in research resources and productivity but in research manpower. If they provide an active market for the master's level graduates, they have been highly instrumental in the ongoing weakness and withering of the doctoral programs.

Research Institutes

This sector of the research system includes institutes owned by the national government (94) and by local governments (601); it also includes institutes in essentially a nonprofit sector, variously designated as private institutes (404) and special corporations (7).[18]

These research institutes are mainly engaged in "big science," such as nuclear power development (Japan Atomic Energy Research Institute) and space development projects (National Space Development Agency of Japan), *or* "local science," related to the promotion of local industry. Doing R&D for both "sciences" is a difficult task for industry to attempt alone because the research is either too extensive or too specific. The research institutes carried out 14 percent of the total national R&D effort in 1986–1987 (¥1.7 trillion, $12 billion), with most of their funds (72 percent) provided by national and local governments. Overall, as indicated earlier, they expend most of their funds for applied research (27 percent) and for development (59 percent), leaving less than 15 percent for basic research.

But the major types of institutes vary considerably. Those supported by the national government emphasize basic research: in 1986–1987, expending ¥236.7 billion ($1.6 billion), they reported 32 percent for basic research, 35 percent for applied research, and 33 percent for development. Local government institutes are centered in applied research (12 percent for basic, 65 percent for applied, and 23 percent for development, out of ¥193.6 billion ($1.3 billion). Private institutes, and especially the special corporations, are oriented toward development. Not entirely "private"—the government provides almost one-fifth of their funds—the private institutes expended 58 percent out of ¥360.4 billion ($2.5 billion) for development, and the special corporations as much as over 90 percent in this category, out of ¥382.3 billion ($2.6 billion).

Under rapidly changing economic, social, and international conditions, government-owned laboratories are increasingly expected to engage in trendsetting research toward developing new technologies for Japan. Research laboratories are increasingly considered for their potential in revitalizing local economies. Many local governments are now attempting to bring research laboratories, not new factories, to their regions.

Universities and Colleges

Before World War II, universities in Japan were nearly the only institutions engaged in research. The Institute of Physics and Chemistry (*Rikagaku kenkyuujo*) and the Ohara Institute for Social Problems (*Ohara Shakai Mondai kenkyuujo*), both established around 1920 under philanthropic support, were two of the few exceptions. Today the universities are just one of a group of institutions engaged in research; they are losing the leading position they once enjoyed.[19]

In total research funds the university sector is a minor player, expending only 13 percent of total national R&D in 1986–1987. In research funds per researcher, the impoverished situation of the universities stands out clearly. If a researcher at a research institute received in 1986–1987 some ¥36 million ($248,000) on the average for research, and one in an industry laboratory had ¥24 million ($166,000), a researcher at a university received only ¥9 million ($62,000). Furthermore, 60 percent of the funds for the university researchers went for salaries, leaving an even smaller amount left for research as such.[20]

One group of analysts has compared 1978 research expenditures in pharmacy between national universities, government-owned research institutes, and a typical leading industrial laboratory. The money spent per researcher was roughly ¥1 million ($7,000) in the universities, ¥2 million ($14,000) in the research institutes, and ¥9 million ($62,000) in industry laboratories run by leading companies.[21] Furthermore, university researchers on the average have fewer assistants: 0.3, compared to over 1.0 at the research institutes and about 0.8 in industry.

Why have universities lost their monopoly over R&D? As educational institutions, they must obviously devote a large share of their resources to educational objectives. They cannot only intensively recruit researchers in a few particular fields but instead are obliged to hire a varied group of teachers to accommodate divergent academic subjects. Further, budget and staff allocations, especially for national universities, are based primarily on numbers of students rather than on research priorities. This system guarantees all researchers at universities and colleges a definite amount of funding each year, without sudden fluctuation, but it also means that the universities cannot compete with large industrial laboratories and research institutes in devoting resources to particular research topics. Also, graduate schools in universities are not organizationally independent of undergraduate colleges. Professors exclusively in charge of graduate courses are exceptional. Where graduate schools exist, the professors supervise both undergraduate and graduate students.

But universities and colleges are still indispensable for the advancement of science because no other institutions carry out as much basic research; universities devote over half of their funds to basic research as well as engage in the training of future researchers.

Although professors at all universities and colleges are expected to engage in research and also teach, institutions can be placed in a hierarchy according to the magnitude of research activity. Adapting the Carnegie classification used widely in the American system, Ikuo Amano, a leading higher education researcher, classified 443 universities and colleges (1979), leaving aside junior colleges, into five clusters.[22] Only 24 institutions were distinguished as "research universities," that is, universities that had doctorate programs in all schools and a ratio of graduate to undergraduate students higher than 9 percent for national universities, 6 percent for private universities (which usually have bigger undergraduate colleges), and 20 percent for medical colleges. Among these 24 institutions, 7 former imperial universities and 2 private universities, Waseda and Keioh, stood out as the most research-oriented. These 9 universities enrolled over 45 percent of the doctoral students, even though they represented only 2 percent of the total universities and enrolled only 7 percent of the undergraduate students. They conferred nearly 80 percent of all doctoral degrees, other than doctor of medical science.

Beyond the research universities, the Amano classification grouped 121 universities, mostly private, as "Doctorate Granting 1" universities with doctorate programs in all schools but with a ratio of graduate students to undergraduate students which was lower than that found in the research universities. Another 35 universities fell into a "Doctorate Granting 2" category, places that have doctorate programs in some but not all schools, followed by 85 "Master Granting" universities, which have only master's programs, and a remaining 178 "college" or undergraduate institutions.

The universities with graduate schools are organized primarily around chairs. As the basic operating unit, a chair usually consists of one full professor, one associate professor, and one to three research associates. In the national universities an annual budget is allocated to each chair. But research is not necessarily done by the chair as a unit: sometimes it is carried out by several chairs together, and sometimes it is done by individuals within the chair. The major universities also have many research institutes that are organizationally independent from schools and chairs and even have their own faculty. Exclusively devoted to research, they do not have undergraduate programs, but they may have graduate programs and professors involved in graduate training. For research purposes they are in a more favorable position than the schools. The conditions for these institutes may worsen, however, since the government introduced in the late 1980s a "scrapping and rebuilding" policy. Those institutes assessed as useless or outdated are being forced to reorganize, merge with other institutes, or become defunct. At some of the university institutes established recently, professorships involve ten-year appointments or less, not permanent tenure. Given such conditions, university institutes seek increasingly to develop graduate programs to secure the more stable and secure organizational base graduate schools possess.

Recent Developments

In the early 1990s, two new developments may significantly affect university research. First, unlike most foreigners' perceptions of a close relationship between universities and industry in Japan, these two sectors have not been formally involved with each other. The national universities have had a strict tradition of academic independence. Recently, as a part of a broad government effort to privatize, the Ministry of Education introduced two innovations that may substantially influence the nature of research at universities. One is the establishment of Centers for Cooperative Research in Advanced Science and Technology at some universities; their aim is to promote research in these fields with the cooperation of private companies and public and private research institutes. The other is the introduction of chairs endowed by private companies.

Recently, a completely new type of graduate school has been established. Chartered in late 1988 and opened in early 1989, this new graduate school, the Graduate University for Advanced Studies (*Sougou Kenkyuu Daigakuin Daigaku*), consists of six research institutes administered by the Ministry of Education. This institute-cum-school is defined as a university with just a few advanced students; chartered as a graduate school, it can enroll only doctoral students—a very favorable setting for the research and training of advanced students. Its emergence poses a threat to university professors in traditional sites who, in addition to their research work, have to teach undergraduates as well as master's and doctoral students.

THE FUNDING BASE

Funding mechanisms—especially in the national universities—for general institutional finance, research subsidy, and graduate student support play a significant role in determining the nature of academic science and advanced education. In a country where university finance is considerably national-ized, ministerial bureaucratic categories define the financial underpinnings of much of the university system.

The National Universities

For professors at national universities, the main sources of research funds are the budgets of their own chairs, allocated by the Ministry of Education without any application procedure; research grants for which they can apply, administered by the Ministry of Education and reviewed by mem-bers of the national Science Council; and research grants procurable from private foundations. The Science and Technology Agency, the Ministry of Trade and Industry, and other national government departments also have their own research funds, which are available mainly for the natural sci-ences and technology-related fields. Professors in engineering and medicine who carry out cooperative research with private companies may obtain funds from them. Everyday research activity, then, is supported by a mix-ture of sources. Salaries for all academic personnel, as in nationally unified systems or sectors in other countries, are handled separately as a systematic component of "civil service" employment. The allocations here discussed are in addition to salary subsidy.

For most disciplines and professional fields, however, the chief source by far is the chair budget. Automatically allocated every year by the Ministry of Education, it is the most stable source of funding. In the past professors depended entirely on this "institutional" line of support to carry out their research. This is increasingly less true today. But the nationally determined allocations for chairs are central components in the budgets of universities. To explain their role, a description of the budget allocation system for national universities follows.

University Allocations. The Ministry of Education allocates a budget to each national university based on both students and teaching staff. It calcu-lates the unit cost per student by degree level and field. Combining the two

TABLE 9-3   Unit Cost per Student, Japan, 1988

Degree Level and Field of Study	Yen	(Dollars)
Doctoral program		
Humanities and social sciences	142,800	(985)
Natural sciences and engineering	262,600	(1,811)
Medical science	262,600	(1,811)
Master's program		
Humanities and social sciences	99,700	(689)
Natural sciences and engineering	183,700	(1,267)
Medical science	183,700	(1,267)
Education	155,700	(1,074)
Undergraduate program		
Humanities and social sciences	26,700	(184)
Natural sciences and engineering	53,300	(368)
Medical science	57,700	(398)
Education	44,500	(307)
General education program	38,400	(265)

SOURCE: Information provided by the Ministry of Education, 1989.

criteria, students are classified into twelve categories. The resulting allocations vary enormously (see table 9-3). They are much higher for graduate students than for undergraduates, and much higher for the sciences, engineering, and medicine than for the humanities, social sciences, and education. At the extremes, doctoral students in natural sciences, engineering, and medicine add seven times as much to a university budget as do undergraduates in the general education courses that occupy the first two years of study.

Unit costs for teaching staff are figured as budgets for chairs, which are also differentiated by degree level and type of discipline. Chairs involved in doctoral and master's programs (in addition to undergraduate teaching) are placed in two higher categories with much greater unit costs than chairs that handle only undergraduate courses. Even more important, chairs are formally classified by the Ministry as experimental, nonexperimental, and clinical. All chairs in the natural sciences and engineering are defined as experimental; the majority of chairs in the humanities and social sciences are classified as nonexperimental. However, some of the latter—psychology, sociology, and archaeology—have managed to get themselves described as experimental. All medical school chairs are defined as clinical. The highest unit cost is for the clinical chair in charge of a doctoral program, the lowest is for a nonexperimental chair involved only in undergraduate teaching (table 9-4). As in the definition of unit cost per student, the differences in

TABLE 9-4   Unit Cost for Chairs, Japan, 1988

Degree Level and Type of Field	Yen	(Dollars)
Chair for doctoral program		
Nonexperimental	1,903,000	(13,124)
Experimental	7,443,000	(51,331)
Clinical	8,078,000	(55,710)
Chair for master's program		
Nonexperimental	1,048,000	(7,228)
Experimental	3,955,000	(27,276)
Chair for undergraduate program		
Nonexperimental	958,000	(6,607)
Experimental	3,400,000	(23,448)

SOURCE: Information provided by the Ministry of Education, 1989.

defined unit costs of chairs are very great, in the order of 8.5 to 1 between the two extremes.

Internal University Allocations. The Ministry of Education allocates a budget to individual universities by multiplying the number of students and chairs by the defined unit costs for each. Using its own scheme, each university allocates a budget to each of its schools, retaining a certain amount for central administration. At the school (*gakubu*) level, a certain percentage of the allocated budget is pooled for management common to all of its departments (*gakka*), and each department does likewise in distributing funds to its chairs (*koza*). After this series of pooling arrangements, the research budget of each chair is fixed, approximating 50 percent or even less of the unit cost first defined by the ministry. Taking the doctoral program experimental chair as an example, out of an original allocation of over ¥7 million, approximately ¥3 million is at the disposal of the chair members—a group composed of a full professor, an associate professor, and one to three research associates.

This basic budget may be used to buy books, word processors, and laboratory equipment and to hire part-time secretaries. Chair holders can use it for academically related purposes; travel expenses, however, belong to another budget item. This is the basic fund for research activity, institutionalized and guaranteed in annual allocation. Other sources are less stable, since they depend on grant proposals that may win or lose as they undergo peer review or some other form of evaluation. Whether or not the chair budget is sufficient to carry out research depends on the research activity and style of individual professors. Some professors are satisfied with it, others are not.

The allocation formulas make clear that the standard research fund at the disposal of professors differs greatly between universities with graduate schools and those without. Beyond the prestige differential lies this very considerable budgetary one that motivates universities to include graduate schools. This differentiation of institutions affects the mobility pattern of professors. Professors generally prefer universities with graduate schools over undergraduate institutions. If they have the opportunity to move to a university with a graduate school, they usually accept the offer. This tendency is strongest in the natural sciences, engineering, and medicine; in these fields research productivity depends much more on the availability of research funds and equipment.

If professors wish to have additional research funds, they submit applications to the Ministry of Education. The ministry has another line of research funding, officially called "Grants-in-Aid for the Scientific Research Program" (or simply the research grant program). The budget for this program amounted to ¥45 billion ($310 million) in 1987. It is allocated to researchers on the basis of competitive application; in 1987 roughly 57,000 applications were submitted, with 17,000 accepted. These applications are evaluated by a committee, composed of university professors, of the national Research Council. The program contains six categories: the keypoint research grant; the general grant; the promotion grant; the experimental grant; the foreign country exchange grant; and the grant for research publications. The keypoint grants support large-scale research projects that arise from pressing national concerns, such as nuclear fusion, accelerator science, space science, ocean science, earthquake and volcanic eruption prediction, antarctic observation, bioscience, and cancer studies.[23]

Government policy in the 1980s has restricted the increase of the standard fund based on students and teaching staff and has increased the budget for competitive research grants. Since 1983, in spite of inflation, the unit costs per student and per teaching staff have never been reviewed. Meanwhile, the budget for competitive research grants increased in absolute sums from ¥40 billion ($276 million) in 1983 to ¥53 billion ($366 million) in 1989, itself not much of an increase when inflation is taken into account. The intent of this policy is to promote the meritocratic principle in research activity and to distribute research funds more effectively, dependent on the evaluation of research output. If distribution of the standard research fund is automatically based on the number of students, teaching staff, and types of chairs, the competitive research grants are distributed after peer review of proposed projects, and supposedly reflect reputation and past contribution of applicants.

The Contribution of Private Foundations. The third source of research funds is grants from private foundations; in 1987 they numbered 118. Private grants to national universities alone increased rapidly in the mid-1980s, from ¥12 billion ($83 million) in 1983 to ¥24 billion ($166 million) in 1986. Well-known examples of such foundations, to name a few, are the Toyota Foundation, the Nihon Seimei Foundation, and the Casio Scientific Foundation. They play an increasingly important role in supporting university research, with grants around ¥1 million ($7,000) in the humanities and social sciences and two to three times that amount in the natural sciences and engineering.

Research activity at the national universities is carried out by a combination of these three major lines of research funding. Some professors are satisfied with the standard funds; others seek to combine the standard fund, the competitive research council grants, and research funds from private foundations.

The Private Universities

Japanese private universities enroll almost 80 percent of all undergraduate students; they employ about 50 percent of the full-time teaching staff of the four-year institutions, but they enroll only about one-third of the graduate students. The Ministry of Education provides some subsidy, now approximating 16 percent of their operating costs; the ministry also has a special budget designed to assist them with their research activities, which in 1987 totaled ¥230 billion ($1.6 billion). This research support is distributed to individual universities through the Foundation for Promoting Private Education (*Shigaku Shinkou Zaidan*).

The allocation of research funds to professors at private universities is not as systematically structured as it is in the national universities. No official national information is available regarding these funds, but they are known to be considerably less than for professors at national universities involved in doctoral programs. If professors in private universities are not satisfied with institutionally allocated funds, they too can apply for grants from the ministry's research grant program and for grants from private foundations.

Financial Support for Graduate Students

Graduate study in Japan is increasingly expensive, especially in the large cities where the major universities are located. A 1986 Ministry of Education report showed that master's students on the average spent ¥1,358,400 ($9,370 per year) and doctoral students ¥1,690,900 ($11,660). Since sharp rent increases have occurred in large cities since then, the 1990 cost of living is higher; hence a greater proportion of expenses must be used for everyday living. At the same time the Japanese government has introduced a plan to raise the tuition for national universities every two years to narrow the tuition gap between them and the private institutions. Along with the appreciation of the yen, these factors have caused Japanese graduate schools to lose their reputation of being comparatively inexpensive.[24]

The high cost of graduate study does not deter wealthy students or students with full government scholarships. But the national government scholarships awarded by the Japan Scholarship Society (*Nihon Ikueikai*), a subsidiary of the Ministry of Education, for master's students covers only one-quarter of their expenses on the average; parental support covers more than one-half. For doctoral students, the government stipend covers about one-third of expenses and the parental contribution decreases to about one-fourth. Both master's and doctoral students engage in part-time work out of necessity. Unlike American universities, however, Japanese universities have not yet institutionalized such on-campus jobs as teaching and research assistantships. Graduate students are generally engaged in off-campus work as private tutors to younger students during their notorious examination ordeal; the drawback here is that much precious study time is lost.

The scholarship system in Japan is not well developed. About one-half of the master's students and over two-thirds of the very limited number of doctoral students are awarded scholarships, chiefly by the Japan Scholarship Society. Scholarships for graduate students from private companies or foundations exist but these are rare and quite limited in amount. Even at a large institution such as Nagoya University, only twenty private scholarships are available for graduate students and the amount of the stipend is at most ¥50,000 ($345) a month. Individual national universities do not have any funds for scholarships. Accordingly, professors and advisors cannot provide scholarships for their graduate students; they may, however, recommend them to the scholarship society. Critically, the scholarships awarded by the society, and some of those offered by private foundations, are not really grants but loans that have to be paid back. If the scholarship recipients accept certain jobs after graduation, such as teaching positions at universities or research positions at research institutes, they are not required to pay back their "grants." But those who get jobs in industrial laboratories or become civil servants in national ministries have to pay off their award at a fixed annual rate.

Graduate students in Japan are obviously heavily dependent financially on parents and part-time jobs. Because the scholarship society makes its awards strictly according to the income level of students' families (in 1987, only those students whose annual family income was below ¥6.5 million—$45,000—were eligible to apply), students from middle-class families find it especially difficult to continue their studies. To improve this situation, the Japanese government in 1986 initiated a scholarship program that provides selected doctoral students with ¥1,476,000 annually ($10,200), an amount more or less sufficient to cover their cost of living, and a few postdocs were awarded ¥2.5 million ($17,200). But these special scholarships are few—

only about two hundred for the entire country. Competition for them is fierce, especially in the humanities and social sciences. And stipends that just about cover the cost of living do not compare with the salaries of former classmates who took jobs in private companies after earning a bachelor's (or master's) degree.

CONCLUSION

The number of graduate schools in Japan has expanded greatly in recent decades, due largely to the efforts of universities to upgrade themselves to the more prestigious and financially more rewarding category of graduate school university. But with the principal exception of the master's program in engineering, most schools have not succeeded in attracting sufficient students. A set of related reasons conspire to produce this graduate school weakness: a better job market for undergraduates than for higher graduates; little or no income advantage for those who take the higher degrees; inadequate financial support for graduate students; an unclear rationale for advanced training, particularly in the humanities and social sciences; better conditions for research outside the university; and, in particular, the existence of alternative ways to earn the doctoral degree. As a result, in the vast majority of fields prescribed admission quotas go unfilled.

At the same time, a few doctoral programs have become factories of jobless doctoral degreeholders called "overdoctors." These graduates are not so much victims of overproduction as they are of sharp institutional hierarchy. A handful of prestigious research universities provide relatively attractive conditions for research, but the vast majority of institutions offer weak research environments. The young researchers want jobs in the leading universities, especially in the natural sciences, engineering, and medicine, where research depends heavily on scientific equipment and apparatus. If they are willing to accept positions at low-prestige institutions, it is not impossible for them to obtain employment. But instead they seek to stay on at the university where they did their work, there to serve as unpaid trainees. In some fields and institutions they accumulate year after year. They then serve as "scarecrows" for young students, discouraging them from pursuing the doctorate.

In a country where the demand from the academic teaching profession itself is limited, the success of graduate programs depends on the strength of outside labor markets. Master's programs in the pure and applied sciences are a success because their graduates enter a vigorous market in industry. The humanities and social sciences have virtually no such market; they still send most graduates into the very constrained market of higher education itself. Industry does not expect to gain highly qualified manpower from such fields. Even professional schools in such areas as business and law, in contrast to the United States, have remained underdeveloped or virtually absent from the scene.

If graduate education in the natural sciences and engineering is relatively successful, it is a success limited to the master's level of recruitment and training. With industry so powerfully attractive in so many ways, the abler students do not stay on for the doctoral programs. The universities are then poorly positioned to obtain even the small number of top scholar researchers they need to staff and strengthen the academic profession. Most critical for the relationship between research and advanced education, the center of gravity for research continues to shift from the universities to the industrial laboratories. Advanced teaching also flows in that direction, away from the halls of the university. In Japan there is much that is deeply problematic in the involvement of higher education in advanced training and research, and in the interaction between the training system and the research system.

NOTES

1. Ookubo, *Nihon no Daigaku*, pp. 301–338; Nakayama, *Teikoku Daigaku no Tanjou*, pp. 130–169.

2. Ministry of Education, *Annual Report*, 1886, 1890, 1909, 1914, 1920, 1935, 1940, 1944.

3. Ushiogi, *Kindai Daigaku no Keisei to Henyou*, pp. 147–242.

4. Tokyo Daigaku, *Tokyo Daigaku Hyakunenshi*, vol. 1, pp. 949–974.

5. Amano, *Henkakuki no Daigakuzou*, pp. 194–210.

6. Ministry of Education, *Annual Report*, 1920, 1925, 1935, 1940.

7. Calculated from the list of degree recipients in *Teikoku Daigaku Taikan*, ed. Teikoku Daigaku Gakuyuukai.

8. Calculated from *University Calendar* 1940, Tokyo Teikoku Daigaku.

9. Ministry of Education, *Annual Report*, 1955, 1988.

10. With the revision of *University Standards* in 1970, one-third of general education credit could be used for professional education and for foreign languages.

11. Ministry of Education, *Kyouikushihyou no Kokusaihikaku*.

12. It is common for graduate students to make presentations at annual meetings of national academic associations; in fact they are encouraged to do so. See chapter 10.

13. Ministry of Education, *Annual Report*, 1988.

14. Ministry of Education, *Daigaku Shiryou*, no. 109.

15. Kagaku Gijutsu Chou, *Kagaku Gijutsu Hakusho*, 1988.

16. *Ibid.*, 1989. These data pertain to the natural sciences only.

17. Kagaku Gijutsu Chou, *Kagaku Gijutsu Hakusho*, 1987.

18. *Ibid.*

19. Ministry of Education, *Wagakuni no Gakujutsu*.

20. Kagaku Gijutsu Chou, *Kagaku Gijutsu Hakusho*, 1988.

21. Uemura, *Daigakuin Mondai nikansuru Chousa Kenkyuu*, pp. 214–216.

22. Keii, *Daigaku Hyouka no Kenkyuu*, pp. 57–111.
23. Ministry of Education, *The University Research System in Japan*.
24. Ministry of Education, *Gakusei Seikatsu Jittai Chousa*.

BIBLIOGRAPHY

Amano, Ikuo. *Henkakuki no Daigakuzou* (The image of the university in a time of change). Tokyo: Rikuruuto Shuppan, 1980.

Kagaku Gijutsu Chou (National Agency for Science and Technology). *Kagaku Gijutsu Hakusho* (White paper on science and technology). Tokyo: Ookurashou Insatsukyoku, 1987, 1988, 1989.

Keii, Tominaga, ed. *Daigaku Hyouka no Kenkyuu* (A study on university evaluation). Tokyo: Tokyo Daigaku Shuppankai, 1984.

Ministry of Education. *Monbushou Nenpou* (Annual report). Tokyo, 1886, 1890, 1909, 1914, 1920, 1925, 1935, 1940, 1944, 1955, 1988.

———. *Wagakuni no Gakujutsu* (Arts and sciences in Japan). Tokyo: Nihon Gakujutsu Shinkoukai, 1975.

———. *Gakusei Seikatsu Jittai Chousa* (Survey on student life). Tokyo, 1985.

———. *The University Research System in Japan*. Tokyo, 1986.

———. *Daigaku Shiryou* (University and college data). Tokyo, September, 1988.

———. *Kyouikushihyou no Kokusaihikaku* (International comparison of educational indices). Tokyo, 1988.

Nakayama, Shigeru. *Teikoku Daigaku no Tanjou* (The establishment of the imperial university). Tokyo: Chuuoukouronsha, 1978.

Ookubo, Riken. *Nihon no Daigaku* (Universities in Japan). Tokyo: Sogensha, 1943.

Teikoku Daigaku Gakuyuukai, ed. *Teikoku Daigaku Taikan* (The encyclopedia of the imperial university). Tokyo: Teikoku Daigaku Gakuyuukai, 1939.

Tokyo Daigaku. *Tokyo Daigaku Hyakunenshi* (The centennial history of the University of Tokyo), vol. 1. Tokyo: Tokyo Daigaku Shuppankai, 1984.

Tokyo Teikoku Daigaku. *University Calendar*. Toyko, 1940.

Uemura, Yasutada, ed. *Daigakuin Mondai nikansuru Chousa Kenkyuu* (Research on the issues of graduate education). Tokyo, 1981.

Ushiogi, Morikazu. *Kindai Daigaku no Keisei to Henyou* (Formation and change in the modern university). Tokyo: Tokyo Daigaku Shuppankai, 1973.

TEN

The Education of Advanced Students in Japan
Engineering, Physics, Economics, and History

Tatsuo Kawashima and Fumihiro Maruyama

Chapter 9 made clear that despite Japan's impressive commitment to elementary, secondary, and higher education, students have not been strongly attracted to the graduate level. The country's many graduate schools remain relatively undeveloped and underused. Then, too, although three-quarters of the undergraduate students are enrolled in private universities that became the main providers of mass higher education during the recent expansion, the advanced programs are concentrated in the public sector. A high degree of institutional hierarchy reflects and shapes the distribution and strength of these programs, with just nine institutions serving as the main producers of the limited number of advanced degree holders. The many other institutions that are formally involved in the graduate education business award degrees in only a few fields and have very small enrollments. The very substantial difference between the few major graduate schools and the many small ones was portrayed in chapter 9 in the twin metaphors of "factories of overdoctors" and "empty show-windows." Finally, the major universities are substantially divided between relatively strong departments and schools in science and engineering and weak counterparts in the social sciences and humanities.

Small size, public-sector development, much institutional concentration, science and engineering emphasis—these are primary features of Japanese graduate education. Building upon this macro explanation, we explore in greater detail in this chapter how the graduate education and research training of advanced students actually takes place. As part of the common framework used in this volume, we report on the disciplines of physics, economics, and history. Because of its strength and prominence, we also examine engineering, located at the high end of a continuum of differences in disciplinary strength. We begin with the historical development of each of these four fields. We then pursue similarities and differences across these disciplines in the patterns and processes that currently constitute the Japanese mode of linking research with academic teaching and advanced university study.

THE FOUR DISCIPLINES

Each field we studied has a genetic imprint established in earlier years; each also has characteristics found in common with disciplines in other national settings blended with features that stem uniquely from the Japanese context.

Engineering

In the historic European tradition, engineers were generally trained outside the university system. Seen as a practical field, along with agriculture and commerce, engineering or technology was usually not included in universities devoted to pure science or *Wissenschaft*. In Japan, in contrast, engineering started as a scientific discipline and early established a major niche in the university system. The School of Engineering (*Kouka-daigaku*) was part of the University of Tokyo, the first Japanese university, from the beginning, and for some time it surpassed the School of Natural Sciences (*Rika-daigaku*) at that university in status as well as size.[1] Expected to contribute significantly to Japan's industrialization, engineering was not only seated at the university table but was placed at the end where the important fields congregated.

Beginning in the Meiji era, research in engineering became focused on the reproduction of the basic materials needed to manufacture goods invented outside of Japan. In the early decades of the twentieth century many technological innovations emerged in the advanced industrial nations. Because Japan was lagging in technology as well as science, the country strengthened its practice of importing ideas and skills and using engineering research to turn them to practical use. Before and during World War II, Japan also invested in military technology in a major way, establishing a technological base that was transformed into civil technology after the war; this contributed markedly to Japan's swift economic development. Warship construction helped to make Japan, during one postwar period, the best shipbuilder in the world; aircraft production technology was put to use in the manufacture of automobiles.[2]

Engineering research in the universities is expected to couple basic research in the sciences and development research in industry. In this context, as noted in chapter 9, the Ministry of Education has recently established a major Center for Cooperative Research in Advanced Science and Technology with units located at many national universities (fifteen in

1989). Surprisingly, no formal connection previously existed between the national universities and industry. At this center, university staffs and visiting professors from the industrial sector will jointly carry out large projects requiring industrial leadership. In addition a new type of graduate school for science and technology was established in 1990. Its aim is to enroll not only university students but also engineers, with or without the master's degree, who are employed in industrial firms. The hope is that the engineers will be able to complete a doctoral program in a relatively short time and then return to the R&D departments of their companies.

Physics

Physics has enjoyed high prestige in the Japanese academic community. The first Nobel prize laureate in Japanese history (1951) was a physicist; three out of the seven Nobel prizes won by Japanese academics have been in this field. The physical sciences have been relatively good fields in Japan in which to attempt to win international reputation and recognition; for over three decades, the government has invested in physical science research and in the expansion of natural science and engineering departments. In 1957 plans were made to expand the admission quota for these departments by eight thousand during the following five years—the first instance after World War II of higher education planning that was based on a forecast of future manpower demand. When this goal was attained in three years, a second expansion, based on the Master Plan for Doubling the National Income during the 1960s, was established. The idea here was to increase the admission quota for the natural sciences and engineering departments by 16,000 during the next seven years. Again, the goal was attained in a shorter period than originally projected.

The 1960s were a time of unprecedented economic growth: national income per capita more than doubled; the governmental budget increased even more rapidly, making it possible to invest more in higher education. The expansion of natural science and engineering departments was in step with the growth of the economy and industry. During that decade the enrollment in these departments nearly tripled, increasing from 16,000 to 42,000. But in the 1970s physics undergraduates and graduates found jobs less easily. The problem of the so-called overdoctors—those who finished the doctoral program and received doctorates but could not find jobs—became serious, particularly in physics. This problem has continued.

Three features of research in physics in contemporary Japan stand out. First, the scale of research steadily grows larger: to construct an accelerator, for example, costs hundreds of millions of yen. This means that only central government can afford such "big science" and that it then becomes more involved in scientific research. Physicists must negotiate with the government and other interest groups; their research cannot help but be affected by politics and broad economic trends.

Second, partly because of the high cost, the government is trying either to establish independent research institutes or to integrate research institutes attached to several universities into one independent institute—*and* to establish graduate programs in these organizations, especially the three-year doctoral program. Financial and human resources, including graduate students, may thus be shifted from the universities to nonuniversity or independent research institutes.

Finally, research in physics is rapidly becoming more internationally competitive as well as cooperative. Physics has moved ahead of other disciplines in Japan. Its main academic journal, *Journal of Physics Society of Japan*, published a series of articles, as early as 1961, on how to write papers in English. Today many young physicists with doctorates take jobs abroad as postdocs or researchers.

Economics

Economics as an academic discipline also essentially began after the Meiji Restoration. At the time economics research barely existed; instead academics commonly tried to introduce classical economic theory. At first a course in political economy was offered in the School of Humanities (*Bunka-daigaku*) of the University of Tokyo, along with courses in political science and philosophy. However, classical economic theory that emphasizes the "invisible hand" of the market or the freedom of economic activity did not fit the economic situation of the Japan of that time; strong state leadership was the way chosen to catch up with the great powers. Classical economics prospered only briefly at the University of Tokyo, the flagship national university, which was supposed to respond to critical state needs and to produce talented people. It was to become located more at such private universities as Waseda, Keioh, and Dohshisha. For a while a German social policy school influenced Japanese academics, leading to the absorption of economics into "state science." Accordingly, the chairs in economics at the Imperial University of Tokyo were moved in 1886 to the School of Law (*Houka-daigaku*). Then, in turn, at Tokyo in 1908, a department of economics was created independently from the department of political science; and, in 1919, the School of Economics (*Keizai-gakubu*) was made autonomous from the School of Law.[3]

Today, a school of economics usually consists of a department of economics and a department of management. But the latter does not offer a professional program, even at the graduate level, like the M.B.A. program in the United States. Both departments are academically oriented. The undergraduate programs of the two departments send their graduates to both the public and private sectors to become white-collar employees.

Broadly speaking, the present-day discipline of economics in Japan has several notable features. First, there are two schools of thought that seem irreconcilable: Marxist economics and modern economics. The Marxist

approach was introduced in the 1930s, while modern economics did not
enter significantly until the 1950s. Most departments of economics belong
to either one or the other. The division runs so deep that two economics
classes are sometimes offered for a course in a department, one taught
by a Marxist economist and the other by a modern economist. This highly
partisan nature of Japanese economics was acutely criticized in a review
of Japanese social sciences carried out by the Organisation for Economic
Co-operation and Development in the mid-1970s.[4]

Second, among the social sciences, economics has the strongest connection to government and society. Economists are often selected to be
members of government committees and to give advice to parliamentary
committees. Economic methods of quantitative analysis are used to make
long-term economic plans. Economists are also more active than other
social scientists in journalism; they contribute articles and essays on the
economy to newspapers and magazines. Finally, compared to sociologists
and political scientists, Japanese economists are more active in the international academic community. The younger generation especially tries
to contribute papers to American and European economic journals and to
present the results of their research at international academic meetings.

History

Among the ruling dynasties in Japan, the compilation of official historical
documents was for a long period a significant task that helped to secure
their legitimacy. The Meiji government was no exception. Upon recaptur-
ing sovereignty from the Tokugawa Shogunate in 1867, it immediately
established within the government the Office for Compilation of Orthodox
Japanese History. This office was very political as well as ideological: its
main task was not historical research as such, but rather the compilation
of appropriate books and documents. However, a decade later, upon the
founding of the University of Tokyo, an organization for historical research
and training of historians was established in the form of the country's first
department of history. Because of a lack of talented professors who had
broad knowledge of Western history and a shortage of students wishing to
study history, this department was abolished several years later. Courses in
Japanese and Chinese history were offered in departments of Japanese literature and Chinese literature, with the curriculum biased toward ancient
Japanese thought and Confucianism.

In 1886 when the University of Tokyo was renamed the Imperial University, a department of history was reestablished within the School of
Humanities (Bunka-daigaku). Chaired by a German professor and oriented
toward European or Western history, the department introduced modern
history and a positivist approach to historical research. One year later the
Office for Compilation of Orthodox Japanese History was moved from the

government to the Imperial University and renamed the Institute for Compilation of Historical Documents (*Siryo-hensanjo*): it was to be used by university researchers and the public. Because prominent historians at the office also moved to the university, a department of Japanese history was established in 1888 and the department of history was strengthened. Furthermore, in 1909 a new department of oriental history was separated from the department of Chinese studies. Thus, by 1910, the prototype of the contemporary structure of history departments in Japan had emerged. They were broadly differentiated into Japanese, Western, and Chinese history.[5]

Certain features of historical studies in contemporary Japan separate it markedly from the other disciplines. First, because the spectrum of subjects in history is broad, individual history departments cannot cover the entire field, especially at national universities where staff numbers are strictly controlled by the Ministry of Education. The Ministry has therefore deliberately established special chairs in the less popular subjects. Osaka University has, for example, a chair for Asian history (but excludes China); Tsukuba University, a chair for Latin American history. These chairs are the only ones in these specialized subjects in the national universities. If graduate students and their advisors think it profitable for students to take courses not offered at their universities, they can register at the chosen university for up to one academic year.

Second, although history is not a large academic discipline, it has a broad base of outside participants and supporters. In the late 1980s, for example, one society specializing in Japanese history had over 2,400 members, of which about 950 were located in universities and research institutes. The vast majority were elementary and secondary schoolteachers, students, journalists, other professionals, white-collar workers, and housewives.[6] Criticism from outside the university is believed to stimulate and benefit historical research. This wholesale interpenetration of insiders and outsiders—academic historians and "Sunday historians"—is not generally found in other disciplines.

The national parliament passed an Archives Law in 1987 that requires local governments to take measures to preserve official documents, to establish archives to store them, and to hire archivists. This law may prove highly significant for history, since the graduate program, especially the master's, is expected to train professional archivists.[7]

THE BASIC PATTERNS OF GRADUATE EDUCATION

In broad outline the general structure of Japanese graduate education is much like the American. A four-year undergraduate program is followed by a two-year master's, which in turn is followed by a three-year doctoral program. Those universities with both master's and doctoral programs often designate the former as the first term and the latter as the second term of the doctoral sequence; the doctoral work is simply added on to the master's program. Since the prescribed admission quota for the doctoral program is usually about one-half that of the master's program, the master's program is implicitly a screen for the doctoral program, or more precisely for the second term of the doctoral program. Only a few universities have organizationally separated a two-year terminal master's program from the five-year doctoral effort, except in engineering. Graduate study is also defined as a full-time endeavor: part-time students who are working full-time and attending classes at night or weekends are exceptional. To help provide for more part-time study, the Ministry has recently encouraged some graduate schools to open their doors at night and over the weekend.

Despite this clear formal structure, the role of each stage, especially the nature of the master's program, and the relationship of the two stages are problematic. This is partly because the master's program was introduced for the first time after World War II, long after the nature of the doctoral commitment had solidified, and partly because the purposes and standards of graduate education, as prescribed by national organizations or the central government, have been changed several times. In 1949 the Japan University Accreditation Association (*Nihon Daigaku Kijun Kyoukai*)—a voluntary organization of national and private universities and colleges—defined the purposes of both master's and doctoral programs. The master's program was given a decidedly scholarly cast and research orientation in that it was to deepen scholarship and to develop research ability; the doctoral program was to further develop academics to the point where they could produce new knowledge and direct research activity. These definitions were part of the framework used by the University Chartering Committee (*Daigaku Setthi Singikai*) in 1952, when it established guidelines for approving the establishment of graduate schools.

But only a few years later, in 1955, the accreditation association revised its Standard of Graduate Education (*Daigakuin Secchi Kijun*). The purpose of the master's program was then changed to develop the ability to carry out both "theoretical and applied research" in each discipline. Then again in the early 1970s the Ministry established an ordinance for graduate education in which the purposes of master's programs were broadened. They were to develop the capability to carry out research in a discipline *or* to instill advanced knowledge necessary for professional practice; the doctoral programs were to continue to develop the research ability necessary for independent research activity and to cultivate scholarship. Now it was understood that the master's program had two functions, namely, to train future researchers and to prepare professionals.

As of 1990 there is no disagreement about the purposes of the five-year doctoral program: in the four disciplines under review, all must train future researchers. The two-year master's program is the preparatory stage, and the three-year doctoral program is the principal stage of research activity. In engineering, however, we find a clear distinction between the five-year program and a two-year master's program designed for the professional training of engineers. Within engineering and across all disciplines the engineering master's is the most successful in attracting students, presenting a coherent program, and placing students. The University Council (*Daigaku Shingikai*) and the Ministry of Education are trying to extend to other fields the conception of the master's program as a place for professional education. But in the other disciplines and specialties the older tradition is still dominant: master's as well as doctoral programs are oriented to the training of future academic researchers.

Opportunities for Graduate Education

Considerable institutional differences exist in the opportunity for graduate education. As already noted, the larger comprehensive universities can offer more research training opportunities in more fields than the smaller ones. In economics, for example, among 95 national universities only 8, less than 10 percent, have doctoral programs; among 357 private universities, just 40, again about 10 percent. The universities with major economics doctoral programs are mostly the former imperial universities or such large comprehensive private universities as Keioh and Waseda. Further, across the disciplines, about 80 percent of students accepted by graduate schools are graduates of the same institution.[8] The site of undergraduate education significantly determines both the possibility of future graduate education and also the institutions in which it will occur.

Opportunities for graduate education also depend on disciplinary differences. A 1985 report of the National Universities Association (*Kokuritsu Daigaku Kyoukai*) showed that the ratio of the actual number of matriculated doctoral students to the prescribed admission quota at the seven former imperial universities, together with the Tokyo Institute of Technology and Hitotsubashi University, differed considerably from discipline to discipline. The highest ratio was found in the humanities (105 percent), followed by the natural sciences (78 percent), engineering (34 percent), and economics (33 percent).[9] Two reasons have been given for the low number of students admitted compared to the prescribed admission quota in economics and engineering: in the vibrant Japanese economy, industrial and commercial firms entice holders of bachelor's degrees in these fields with good job offers, and departments in these fields were voluntarily practicing "birth control" in order to avoid overproduction of graduates with higher degrees.

Patterns of Training

All master's students, regardless of subject, have to take at least thirty credits of course work; doctoral students do not have any course work requirement at all. Generally speaking, research training begins at entry to the master's program and runs for at least two years. All master's students must submit theses, which in turn are crucial for admission to doctoral programs, especially in the humanities and social sciences. In these latter fields most course work takes the form of seminars in which participants are expected to present book reports or reports on the thesis topic. The engineering and physics reports are discussions of experiments or laboratory work. Most graduate seminars and laboratory experiments are opened for both master's and doctoral students: there are no separate sequential series of numerically labeled courses for the master's students and doctoral students. Even economics, the most institutionalized of the social sciences in the sense of core requirements, standardized textbooks, and established methodologies, does not require separate courses for the two groups. Graduate students who feel the necessity to master certain basic analytical tools, for example, multivariate analysis, may have to learn them individually. An important exception to this pattern is the master's program in engineering, where much more emphasis is placed on lectures than on seminars and experiments.[10]

Although research training theoretically begins at the master's level, courses are not structured enough to actually constitute "course work." Japanese graduate students mostly receive loosely structured academic training while they do independent research initiated at the beginning of the master's program. This system of graduate education falls between the American, which emphasizes training by requiring highly structured course work for all students at the beginning of their graduate work, and the British system, which has considered graduate students to be "research students" and has not until recently offered "taught courses."

The reasons for the lack of a formal training system in Japan vary somewhat across the disciplines. It is easier in every country to provide systematic instruction in fields where the core body of knowledge—an example is physics—is well-articulated, cumulative, and clearly divisible. It is more difficult in history, a "soft" field, where knowledge is holistic and requires interpretation and understanding rather than explanation.[11] One history professor we interviewed believed that the only training he could give his graduate students was how to read the ancient Chinese characters! But formal training is difficult in Japan for another reason: the universal small scale of the operating units. Even in the largest departments, the instructional staff for each research unit, assembled around one or a few chairs, is at most five. The entering graduate students also number about five, with perhaps only one student in a particular specialty. Highly structured sequential curricula are then clearly not feasible. The organizational setting calls for relatively informal and unstructured ways of training.

PROCESSES WITHIN GRADUATE EDUCATION

Recruitment and Selection

Student recruitment is a crucial issue for the chair, the lowest operational unit, since its prestige and research productivity depend considerably on the quality and quantity of graduate students. The chair that succeeds in attracting many brilliant graduate students can establish a favorable reputation not only in the national academic community but also in the department in which the chair is located. But the motivation of students to go on to the graduate program differs from discipline to discipline as well as from institution to institution.

In physics and engineering, master's students are easily recruited. Although the less prestigious graduate schools had difficulty in attracting students in these fields a decade ago, it is increasingly the norm, especially in the major research universities, for abler seniors to advance to the master's programs. Students know well that the master's degree enables them to find better jobs than will an undergraduate degree. In contrast, the job market for master's students in economics and history has steadily grown worse. The market for undergraduates in these fields is now strong due to the labor shortage caused by the recent economic boom. Although the academic year ends in March, most seniors succeed in finding jobs as early as the fall of the previous year. Almost all of them have located a position six months before graduation.

Graduate programs in history and economics have generally been satisfied with small numbers of strongly motivated students. Their mission has been to train the next generation of the academic profession. They never expected to have many students. But the economic boom of recent years has trapped them in a difficult situation. The professors we interviewed frequently spoke about the difficulty of attracting competent students to their graduate programs. A prestigious history professor remarked that until ten years ago he was in the favorable situation of having a small number of highly motivated students. Since academic positions in history were very limited, he emphasized quality rather than quantity. But the situation has changed: the better and more ambitious students now prefer jobs in private companies or in journalism. Only those who were not able to get work outside applied to graduate schools. Another professor said that the graduate school was now becoming a "hospital" for the youngsters who were afraid of the real world and lacked energy to get into it.

Graduate education has long been seen as a long, painstaking process. Students are anxious about their future. We met many undergraduates who once had planned to go on to graduate programs but were persuaded by parents and classmates to abandon this intention.

This negative attitude toward graduate education is partly related to the timing of selection. Seniors usually begin searching for a job soon after the end of their junior year, commonly in August. Nationally a gentlemen's agreement among major private companies specifies the period of recruitment and of job offers, but because of the labor shortage many companies cheat and attempt to secure new graduates as early as possible. In September most seniors choose the company for which they will plan to work the following April. But seniors who intend to advance to the graduate program have to prepare for entrance examinations, typically held in January and February. A student remarked that it was almost intolerable to continue studying for the examinations, isolated from classmates who had already accepted jobs and anxious about the results of the pending hurdles. He stated: "I can't do it. It is impossible to work on two foreign languages and my specialization with my eyes closed to happy classmates around me and my ears shut to my parents who want me to get a job at a company."

To solve this timing problem, many university departments have moved their examinations up to the fall months. This early selection has been adopted by numerous physics and engineering departments; those seniors who pass the entrance examination can go on to graduate school, those who fail can still enter industry. But in history and economics, this practice has not been accepted by the professors. Both departments usually require graduating seniors to submit theses that are not finished until December or January. The theses range from 50 to 150 pages. Since students know that the quality of the thesis is crucial for admittance to a graduate program, those who wish to go on usually write 100 to 150 pages. The theses are then taken as the most important measure of academic ability. One economics professor said: "We have many occasions to meet students at lectures and seminars. It is not hard to sense the ability of each student. But it is too risky to judge academic ability before reading their graduation theses." The emphasis on the thesis is most conspicuous in history. A history professor remarked that the senior thesis was the beginning of a long period of academic training. "Our contact with students is limited. We are with them for just one year. Although their presentations at the seminars are a good opportunity for me to know their academic capabilities, selection in the autumn is too early. We cannot use the written exam as they do in physics. The best way for us is to scrutinize the senior thesis."

Timing in the selection process is just one of many elements that causes disciplines to lose talent to private companies. Even more critical is student support. Under the present system it is impossible for professors to encourage promising students to enter the graduate programs with offers of financial assistance. Students cannot apply for scholarships before entering:

therefore they cannot be guaranteed a scholarship at the time of entrance. Further, selections made by the Japan Scholarship Society (*Nihon Ikuei kai*), the largest source of student support, are not based on merit but on need. Universities, excepting certain private ones, do not have their own funds to support graduate students. Hence professors have no financial means of encouraging students to enter graduate schools.

An economics professor, trained in the United States, offered a pointed comment: "The situation is quite irritating to me. Once I met a very talented student. He was the best student I have encountered in the past ten years. I invited him to the doctoral program. If the situation had occurred in the United States I could immediately have offered him a research fellowship." In a centrally administered student support system professors cannot offer even the ablest of students financial assistance.

Poor research conditions at the universities, compared to those at the industrial laboratories, also negatively affect the recruitment of master's students to doctoral programs in physics and engineering. An engineering professor at one of the former imperial universities said with some scorn: "The amount of the chair budget was two million, five hundred thousand yen [$17,200] in 1970, and it is now six million yen [$41,400]. It has increased only two-point-five times while other prices have increased more than several times in the same two decades. What makes the situation worse is that all four chair members—one professor, one associate professor and two research associates—have to share this amount of the chair budget. Under these circumstances, I cannot recommend that promising master's students pursue an academic career anymore."

Professorial prestige depends not only on personal academic excellence but also on how many distinguished disciples one has trained. Professors, especially at the less prestigious graduate schools, face a delicate dilemma. They need a minimum number of graduate students to promote active discourse. But if they accept too many students, they face the difficulty of finding scarce academic jobs for them. Since it is the responsibility of the chairholder to provide academic teaching positions for students, the production of too many "overdoctors" is a form of professional failure. It is hard for anyone to forecast how many graduate students are needed to fill future vacant positions, which are created considerably by chance. Except for some influential chairholders who have access to a wide academic market, most history and economic professors suffer from this dilemma.

A chair can officially accept two master's students and one doctoral student each year. If a chairholder accepts up to this prescribed number each year, he can have seven graduate students in total. But this officially prescribed admission quota has no meaning in history and economics. Since only one of the two master's students in each cohort can go on to the doctoral program (its second stage), one of them must leave at the end of the master's program, with a degree that has no outside market value. Therefore, those who fail to be admitted to the doctoral programs— "overmasters"—apply to the doctoral program the following year. For compelling reasons, most professors hesitate to accept two master's students a year: the "birth control strategy" is widely seen among chairs in history and economics.

Recruitment of doctoral students is under a similar strain. At a time when higher education is no longer expanding, even professors of physics and engineering have to be very careful about accepting too many doctoral students, although they need them as research staff. The admission quotas for these doctoral programs in most graduate schools tend to remain unfilled.

Until recently the central government did not confront this delicate and perplexing problem. But in the late 1980s it began to ascertain how much the prescribed admission quotas were filled. When a university attempts to set up a new graduate program, the Ministry of Education checks to see the degree to which the existing programs are filled. If the quotas are considered unfilled, the university is required to explain. The Ministry may well indicate also how the situation ought to be improved.

In physics and engineering the ratio of matriculated students to the prescribed quota is used as an indicator in the allocation of special funds for expensive research equipment. The likelihood of being judged to be a "center of excellence" may hang in the balance. A similar predicament exists in history and economics at the national universities: when they attempt to set up a new chair the Ministry checks the number of graduate students. The numbers play a crucial role in central approval. Thus, professors stand in the midst of contradictory pressures from the central government and the marketability of graduate students. On this score, an economics professor confessed that his life has been continual failure: "Sometimes, fearing the bad job situation, I did not accept excellent students, and other times I had no doctoral students to send for a good position." This type of disappointment is common among history and economics professors.

Unlike the American system of graduate education in which institutions generally select students in part on the basis of the national Graduate Record Examination (GRE), the Japanese system does not have such a standardized examination for graduate schools. Each department administers its own entrance examination. Although there are some minor differences in detail, the entrance examination to the master's programs usually consists of three parts in all disciplines at all institutions: foreign language(s), usually English, German, French, or Chinese; subject fields; and an oral interview.

The examination consists of two- to three-hour sessions, usually lasting several days. On the first and second days, all applicants take the foreign language examination, which primarily tests the ability to translate into Japanese an article (or part of it) originally written in English, German, or French, extracted from academic journals or books in the discipline. Students also take the subject examination. In engineering and physics, where knowledge is cumulative, the emphasis is on the mastery of defined basic knowledge and methodological skills, a relatively straightforward requirement. One physics graduate student reflected that, although the entrance exam was competitive, he had only to review and summarize the content of the lectures and seminars in the undergraduate program. In economics and history, on the other hand, the subject exams are of the essay type, with one topic common for all applicants and the other drawn from the applicant's specialty. The applicant must not only show mastery of the broad knowledge of a field but also demonstrate the capability to integrate concepts and theories in a consistent essay. It is difficult to prepare for this type of entrance examination—one more reason why graduate programs in the humanities and the social sciences are not very attractive in Japan.

On the third day each applicant is interviewed by a group of faculty members consisting of the professor and associate professor of the chair in which the applicant wishes to major, and two to three faculty members in neighboring subjects. Here the applicant is examined more deeply on scholarly capability and is questioned about a research plan for the master's program. This probing theoretically allows the faculty to judge the applicant's basic knowledge as well as more specific expertise. One history professor complained that since specialization has become so advanced, it is increasingly difficult to pose common questions for all applicants and to judge an applicant's competence in subject areas other than the declared specialties. It is often said that the foreign language tests are the most critical item because they at least offer clear minimum standards of competency. Now, however, some departments are attempting to reduce this requirement from two languages to one—mostly English—to make graduate programs more attractive and accessible to older bachelor's-degree holders.

At the close of the examinations period, scores are calculated and the faculty decides whom to pass and admit. The natural sciences and engineering graduate schools commonly allow applicants to nominate three or four subfields in which they might specialize. The determination of the actual specialty is then based on performance on the entrance examination. Those students who score highest may opt for their first choice; those scoring lower, but high enough to be admitted, are assigned to chairs (kozas) covering the various specialties according to second and lower choices. Although the final decision is made in the name of the faculty as a whole, the actual decision is made by individual chairholders, who consider many factors such as the potential academic job market and the balance of students among chairs. In short, the professors in charge of graduate programs exercise considerable authority in the selection of students. This is especially true at the private universities, where each professor in charge of a graduate specialty may partially ignore the examination procedure by admitting one or two students solely on personal judgment and recommendation.

Because the depth and breadth of subject expertise is examined when applying for entrance to graduate school, those who have majored in other subjects during their undergraduate years have virtually no chance of being accepted to a particular master's program. Those who are determined to change their major at entry to graduate school may have to spend one or two more years preparing for the entrance examination. This obstacle adds to the "closed" character of the graduate education system, adding to the constraints resulting from the institutional inbreeding of students mentioned earlier. These features combine to lessen the drawing power of graduate education, a strong contrast to the enormous popularity of the university undergraduate programs.

Upon completion of the master's program, those who wish to go on to doctoral work must take another examination. If the master's degree has been at the same institution, the applicant is usually examined on the content of the master's thesis at the interview. This serves both as the criterion for passing or failing a master's degree and as the entrance examination to the doctoral program. Those who apply from other institutions usually have to pass a foreign language examination as well as be interviewed. Such differential treatment for "insiders" and "outsiders" is one more obstacle that restricts the movement of students from one institution to another to find the best training and conditions for research. Such "in-house" barriers contrast notably with the extensive interinstitutional mobility of students at the more advanced levels of the American system.

Choice of Topic for the Master's Thesis and the Doctoral Dissertation
In the humanities and social sciences, for example history and economics, where it is difficult to get the doctorate within the prescribed period of graduate training, the choice of a topic for the master's thesis is crucial. In the natural and applied sciences, such as physics and engineering, where the doctorate has been somewhat institutionalized as a qualification for an academic researcher, the choice of topic for a doctoral dissertation is decisive.

Most professors we interviewed in economics and history agreed that the students themselves must decide on topics for their theses. Since most departments require each applicant to submit a research proposal, which is examined at the entrance interview, most master's students have their own topics clearly in mind at the time of entrance. It is quite rare for professors to provide topics for the master's theses or to suggest a major change of topic. However, since teaching staff and courses are quite limited, and since many students come from the same institutions and have taken undergraduate courses taught by the same staff, the students cannot help selecting topics for master's theses which are similar to the specialized interests of their advisors. Without any explicit direction by advisors, students will tailor the topic and scope of their theses accordingly. At the beginning of every academic year, each master's student also has to inform the department about the thesis topic and obtain approval of the faculty. It may then become clear at the beginning of the second year that the topic was too broad and would require many years to complete. Based upon intensive discussions with advisors as well as with graduate student peers, the student may then petition to change the topic to a narrower, more feasible one. Although most departments do not have preconditions for preparing a master's thesis, some departments, especially in private universities, require students to take qualifying examinations that test for competence both in foreign languages and the subject area.

For engineering and physics the general picture is quite different. The master's thesis topic and the doctoral dissertation topic are often decided upon by the professor or the associate professor of the chair to which the students belong, as a part of a large ongoing research project. Since such topics are so fragmented, some students complain that they cannot find any significance in what they do.[12] Often the material conditions control the choice of topic: except in theoretical physics, where graduate students are allowed to choose their topics, research in physics and engineering is increasingly dependent on huge experimental apparatus and other valuable equipment. Teamwork is increasingly more necessary, partly to utilize the limited research budget more effectively. Professors are then virtually required to regulate and coordinate the research activities of graduate students. One engineering professor who has accepted many foreign students warned that this limitation on the choice of topics for master's theses and doctoral dissertations should be explained to foreign students when a chair decides to accept them. If the student does not understand the situation, many serious problems may result because they cannot do what they expected to be able to do at the outset and what they as individuals would like to do.

Pattern of Interaction Between Advisors and Students

The organization of the chair system in Japanese higher education is profoundly significant. The chair remains the fundamental organizational unit for teaching, research, budget allocations, and general management. Graduate students, most intensely in the humanities and social sciences, are selected primarily by the chairs on the basis of admission quotas allocated to them. Upon admission, the students become closely linked to the chairholding professor and other members of the chair unit. The relationship is often very personalized: it is quite common to refer to a chair by using the professor's family name. Indeed, the chair can be readily likened to a family in which the full professor is the father, the associate professor the mother, the research associates the older brothers or sisters, and the graduate students the younger ones. Like siblings, the research associates and graduate students are often very closely attached to one another. Many graduate students pointed out that research associates in daily discussion strongly influenced their choice of research topic; often they consulted with research associates first when problems arose. The koza is the home. The everyday activities of the graduate students are organized around it.

The nature of the interaction between advisors and graduate students does vary somewhat from discipline to discipline. In history and economics, where independent research activity is often required, the interaction may be intermittent and individualistic because graduate students and advisors meet once or twice a week in a seminar or meet by appointment when students need advice. Otherwise, they seldom meet; at the doctoral stage, contact becomes even less.

In contrast, for physics and engineering students, especially those in experimental subfields, interaction is continuous and group-oriented. Experiments are done by a team consisting of a professor, a research associate, and several graduate students, or a team of an associate professor, a research associate, and several graduate students. Professors, graduate students, and sometimes undergraduate students work together more than ten hours a day, often continuing late into the night in the laboratory. Throughout this process of hard work and cooperation, the students cultivate such traits as industriousness, punctuality, problem-solving abilities, and loyalty to their own koza. These personal characteristics are exactly what industrial companies are looking for. The anomaly is the theorist in physics who mostly works alone. But even here a considerable amount of interaction may occur in the research colloquia that bring students and teaching staffs together weekly for discussion or to hear guest speakers. In interviews students and professors unanimously judge this type of discussion and communication to be a key part of research and training.

However, physics and engineering units do exhibit some differences in style. Like their American counterparts,[13] Japanese physics professors are more liberal than those in engineering; in fact some we interviewed were so egalitarian that they attempted to treat graduate students as peers of the staff. For example, some physics departments hold departmental conferences where teaching staff and all graduate students participate; everyone is given an equal voice in determining the research funds allocated to each group and in the selection of staff members. A professor justified such "democratic" departmental management as indispensable to stimulate and cultivate the initiative of young scientists. Only in a democratic climate, he maintained, could the creativity and originality of the graduate students be cultivated. In turn, however, this brand of equality required graduate students to perform miscellaneous duties involved in the management of the chair and to coach undergraduate students without payment. A physics doctoral student complained that he was so busy with trivial routine duties that he did not have enough free time to think about his own research.

In contrast, the relationship between professors and graduate students in engineering is more paternalistic. Here, in the classic pattern, the professor stands as the parental figure at the top and coordinates the work of staff and graduate students. Because they work together with graduate students for long hours in the laboratory, engineering professors felt they could closely assess students' abilities and hence effectively recommend them to various companies or to continue in the doctoral program.

The Role of Academic Societies and Study Groups

Each discipline has academic societies that play an important part in the lives of graduate students. As they begin their graduate work they are expected to be active members of one or more societies. Very early, after attending a few meetings, they are obligated to make a presentation, usually on their master's thesis research. By attending these annual meetings students learn about the latest trends in research topics and methodologies and how to make a clear presentation and how to answer questions. They also meet researchers in other institutions, a valuable networking maneuver. The personal contact allows them to be evaluated before they actively seek a job. No formal interviews for jobs take place during these meetings.

Along with these national societies, graduate students commonly form their own study groups (*Jishu-zemi*), usually within a department but sometimes across departments and institutions. Especially at the doctoral stage in economics and history, activity is centered more on these voluntary groups than in the formal seminars. Professors are "invited" to study-group meetings and asked to give suggestions. Many departments even give financial support for the graduate students to publish their own academic journal.

These formal and informal groups not only promote research in general but also function as an "invisible graduate school." By such participation students who are not offered a variety of courses in their own departments, because they are too small, have an opportunity to explore ideas more broadly, exchange opinions with others, and be evaluated by experts from other institutions. Japanese graduate students thereby deepen their knowledge in subject areas represented in their own departments while widening it at association meetings held on a larger stage.

The Time Span and Nature of Doctorates

As chapter 9 indicated, doctoral degrees have typically and traditionally been awarded in Japan to outstanding scholars later in life rather than at the outset of their careers. This tradition has been maintained most strongly in the humanities and social sciences. It has been changed the most in the natural sciences, engineering, and medicine, where the degree is now perceived as a minimum qualification for younger scientists. Economics is moving in this direction. These differences in the definition and use of the doctorate in different subject areas entail large differences in doctoral training and in the length of time it takes to get the degree. In the natural sciences and engineering, students are likely to receive the doctorate in a relatively short time; most faculty members in these fields are holders of the degree. The doctorate has become a requirement for faculty employment. In the social sciences and humanities, since it normally takes much longer to earn the doctorate, the number and proportion of degree holders in faculties are much lower.

Generally, in every field, including engineering, students who have matriculated in the doctoral program are not required to take further course work. In engineering their main tasks are to engage in a joint research project within their own koza, to work on a related dissertation, and to prepare papers for delivery at meetings of academic societies to which they belong; these papers will be published in refereed journals. The departments commonly require their doctoral students to write two to five articles for international as well as domestic journals as a prerequisite for a doctoral degree. In most cases, a doctoral candidate finishes the dissertation and offers its final defense within three to four years after the completion of the master's program. In interviews in engineering little or no difference was reported among departments and students in the minimum standards and the time needed to complete a dissertation.

Schools of engineering also confer a doctoral degree upon those who, after acquiring a master's degree, become employed at various outside research institutions. This is the *Ronbun hakase* route—the earning of a doctoral degree by submitting a dissertation without continuing at the university. Matriculation is not necessary; just the submission of a dissertation will do. This route is quite common among researchers in the R&D laboratories of private companies. Of course, as one might suspect, the dissertation is not simply dropped off in a mail chute in the middle of the night. Those planning to submit a dissertation have normally had some informal contact with the professor(s) involved. Opinions vary considerably among professors about the appropriateness and value of this route that so clearly bypasses the university-housed program. Some professors view research activities at industrial laboratories as equal to or more effective than university settings in training top-level researchers. They believe that graduate schools should not be reluctant to award the doctorate to those who have shown outstanding academic accomplishment, regardless of whether they followed the official doctoral route. Others are more negative. They note that the existence and use of the Ronbun hakase makes master's students in engineering reluctant to go on to doctoral programs, thereby causing these programs to lose students.

Students in physics also complete their work at a relatively rapid rate. They too are advised by their supervisors to present papers at meetings of relevant academic associations and to submit papers to various professional journals. They can then compile those papers into a dissertation. Their research is thus continually exposed to outside evaluation; supervisors also become informed on how the students are coming along in the eyes of colleagues at other universities. Many students in physics thereby participate in a larger "invisible college."

Economics and history are quite different. Almost none of the students in those programs earn the doctoral degree within the prescribed three years after completing the master's program. Even the best students require at least two more years after the three-year period to finish the dissertation. During the additional years, such students are usually employed as a *joshu*, a research associate, the lowest rank in a faculty. Although the role of joshu is defined as the support of full and associate professors' research and teaching activities, they are relatively free to do their own research because in most cases they do not have to give lectures and there is less teamwork in which they must take a part. The joshu position is considered an important step in a research career.

In economics a doctoral degree is not a requirement for finding a job in most universities. Even though some economics departments require it as a minimum qualification for promotion from research associate to associate professor, others do not. Those who take jobs at the less prestigious universities after completing doctoral programs also find it difficult to maintain a strong motivation to pursue the degree. In these places the ethos of research is less emphasized, and the teaching load is heavier. Not having the degree is not a particular disadvantage. Also operating as a serious constraint on doctoral output is the simple fact that many graduate schools try to maintain very high standards in conferring degrees. In one interview a professor showed us a recent dissertation on which he had been an examiner. It was based on more than ten papers that had appeared in refereed journals, including major American ones.

In history, as in the other graduate programs, there are no formal requirements of course work for doctoral students. Although most doctoral students participate in some seminars, officially they must only submit a dissertation and defend it at an oral examination within six years after enrolling to earn the doctoral degree, namely the Doctor of Humanities

(*Bungaku-hakase*). Completion within this time frame is rare throughout the humanities. Most doctoral students devote themselves to writing papers to submit to journals and thereby build a record of scholarship that is a virtual requirement for obtaining an academic post. Most history students leave graduate school without a doctoral degree: in American terms, they are "ABDs" (all but dissertation).

In conferring degrees, history is at the other extreme from physics and engineering. Behind its lower productivity lingers the tradition of considering the doctoral degree as an honorable reward for the great scholar and not as an entry qualification. Young scholars, mostly lecturers and associate professors, seldom hold degrees. For the most part this is not a disadvantage. But some differences appeared in our fieldwork. One professor reported that his department followed an informal rule not to promote a candidate to full professor unless the nominee held a doctoral degree. The rule functioned as an incentive. Currently, that department also encourages competent students to get the degree as soon as possible and assists them with some financial support. But other departments were not yet taking this route of requiring higher standards. And most history departments offer little encouragement for the expeditious attainment of a doctoral degree.

CAREER POSSIBILITIES

As suggested briefly in chapter 9, students who obtain master's degrees in engineering have exceptionally strong job possibilities in industry, followed by master's graduates in the sciences. Graduates in the social sciences and humanities trail so far behind in securing private-sector employment that their situation is qualitatively different. They must look to the academic world, where the job market has also been weak in recent years.

In engineering, private companies have been employing the graduates of master's programs in considerable numbers since at least the late 1960s. Private companies and schools of engineering have been on good terms. What the companies expect from these graduates is not the qualities of the first-rate researcher but those of the high-level technician, one who can adapt flexibly to the demands and needs of the companies. These newly minted engineers are hired primarily for research and development divisions. They are also assigned to production units. Unlike their peers in America and Europe, the best engineering advanced-degree graduates do not hesitate to work in such units. Their attitudes differ from those of other graduate students in that they are little oriented toward the academic world and are strongly motivated to enter private companies.

Historically, firms have had no interest in engineering doctoral graduates, but change now seems underway. As the pace of R&D has intensified and more international ties and exchanges have formed, companies have gradually started to recruit from this higher level of training. Doctoral graduates in engineering can now look for good job opportunities at research institutions managed by private firms instead of waiting for scarce research jobs at the universities. Private companies also have started sending their promising researchers to doctoral programs, while paying them a full salary. When firms have research contracts with engineering schools, their researchers participate in joint projects and publish together with university researchers. In the late 1980s more than a dozen major companies also had financed chairs in schools of engineering, establishing yet another form of linkage.

Compared to engineering graduate students, physics students are more strongly oriented toward the academic world. They have been reluctant to go to private firms: their private-sector job market has been quite limited. However, here too the situation has been changing. Private enterprises have become more eager to hire master's level physics graduates, in part because of a shortage of engineering graduates relative to the large appetite of Japanese industry. Physics graduate students then face a critical career choice. They may prefer the doctoral program and the pursuit of an academic career, but prolonging their training may lead them only to the door of a poor academic labor market. The private firms offer stable positions and incomes, without further travail, but to choose them is to give up the main pathway to research careers in physics. More than ever, physics graduate departments stand to lose able students. Some professors we interviewed indicated that they had no difficulty in attracting promising students to the doctoral program in the past but that the recent changed behavior of private companies made the doctoral program less attractive. Along with the doctoral program in engineering, pure science then faces more of a "brain drain" to industry. And as private firms put more emphasis on basic research, they also look more kindly upon physics doctoral graduates, broadening considerably their job market. As a result, some physics professors feel that the era of oversupply of doctoral graduates is rapidly passing, that it was a short-term phenomenon that stretched from the middle 1970s to the middle and late 1980s.

Unlike that in engineering, the training function of graduate work in economics is restricted to preparing future university teachers and those few individuals who will engage in their own research. As they begin their master's programs, most students are looking primarily toward an academic career: the others have in mind self-employment or employment as an accountant. Economists sort themselves into two groups: those who work at universities and colleges and those who are "economists in bureaucratic organizations," engaged in research in major banks, insurance firms, and local and central governments. The former are largely trained in graduate schools; the latter are trained on the job after finishing an undergraduate education, and hence seldom hold more than a bachelor's degree. Rarely do students with master's or doctoral degrees in economics, or even in management and accounting, enter the business world. Japanese firms are reluctant to employ them, fearing that they are "overeducated" for business activities. But this does not mean that firms do not need specialists who can analyze local and world economies and comprehend economic policies at home and abroad; banks and insurance companies in particular do indeed want to employ those who understand modern economics and foreign languages. But they traditionally have trained such employees on the job, *or* they have sent them to foreign graduate schools on full salary. The education costs of Japanese students in business schools in the United States are covered by their employers.

In history, a graduate who leaves the university with a master's degree in hand is generally seeking a post as a high school teacher. High school teaching does not necessarily mean a nonacademic career. Those who get jobs as high school teachers may continue their own research and attend annual meetings of history societies. Japanese high school teaching is lodged somewhat between academic and nonacademic. Of those who go on to complete doctoral *programs*, as we have stressed, only a minority actually gain a doctoral *degree*. They too, more often than not, are destined for high school posts. They need the work, and it is still possible for them to carry out historical research and obtain the degree later. In fact, as we have seen, the Ronbun hakase type of doctorate can still be earned without benefit of any course work simply by submitting a dissertation. Some graduate students in history reported that they did not care if they did not find a position at a university and had to work for a high school. The high school location might be more favorable for historical research because it gave access to local historical materials. And upon completing the dissertation while doing secondary teaching, there was still a chance to be recruited by a university or a junior college. For historical research, especially in Japanese history, location at a university does not matter as much as in the other fields we have considered.

In all fields, graduate students who choose the academic pathway generally seek first to become a research associate. Those who land on this first rung of the academic career ladder are more often than not recruited from within the same school. Unlike posts with similar titles in American universities, these positions usually provide tenure, but they carry no guarantee of promotion in the same university to the next rank of associate professor. While assisting in research projects, the associates need to look for opportunities in other universities or research institutes. The lucky few who appear to be doing the best work may be offered associate professorships at their own institutions. Associate professors who then become full professors—the heads of chairs—generally come from within the chair. This makes the recruitment of an associate professor a critical event in the management of a chair.

Scientists in particular have a tough pathway to negotiate when they are determined to fashion an academic career. In physics, for example, the best position for doctoral students is a teaching position in one of the ten universities with a doctoral program. These universities have better research equipment and more research funds; they offer more chance to carry out research with the help of graduate students. With world-famous professors on the staff, and as the main training grounds of such professors, these universities have strongly inculcated the academic ethos in their graduates. The crush of applicants is therefore great and the chances of winning a post are very limited. To improve their chances, many graduates, even after earning the doctoral degree, will try to remain in their home graduate school for some years as unpaid research workers. A second choice is to get a job in a local university, one that at best has only a master's program at the graduate level and often no graduate program at all. This move carries the risk of isolation from the main research centers and a loss of daily communication with research colleagues. In experimental physics the isolation entails separation from experimental equipment. And the many private universities have very little to offer: physics departments of any major kind are generally beyond their means.

RESEARCH AND GRADUATE EDUCATION

Our analysis of four disciplines in this chapter extends the basic point made in chapter 9 of the great differences between engineering and the sciences on the one side and the humanities and the social sciences as a second major component in Japanese universities. The differences extend from styles of training to relationships between students and supervisors to the general orientation of whole schools and departments.

In each discipline it is widely accepted that the goal of graduate education is to train future researchers in such a way as to encourage originality. But quite different paths of training are emphasized in the effort to realize this goal. Some professors claim that creativity and originality can be best cultivated in a liberal atmosphere that stresses student independence, while others assert that much structured training is necessary. These two directions need not be contradictory, of course, in that graduate training in any discipline may increasingly require both extensive course work and room for the demonstration of individual capability. But at present, due in part to the intrinsic characteristics of disciplines, one direction or the other tends to dominate.

As we have seen, engineering is at one extreme in emphasizing systematic training; physics also tends in this direction. A systematic and well-supervised training system is built up around chairholders. Students are involved in parts of the larger research projects undertaken by their supervisors. Large research topics are systematically broken down into various subtopics, which are assigned to teams of students. Students have little freedom to choose the topics for their master's and doctoral theses: their everyday research work then has some similarity to the tasks of manual workers in modern large-scale factories. But at the same time a close blending is achieved between graduate education and ongoing research.

Those who doubt the effectiveness of this style of training warn that early involvement of students in specialized topics is purchased at a loss in basic knowledge and broad research experience. This opinion has become stronger as the international recognition of Japanese technology has increased: sharpened international competition has strengthened the longstanding criticism that Japanese technologists lack originality and creativity. Innovative graduate training is sought to provide more broad interdisciplinary programs. New programs combining engineering, biology, and several other subjects are responses to this concern.

In physics the training style varies somewhat from subfield to subfield. Theoretical physics has tended to emphasize independent study, while experimental physics has been similar to the training style of engineering. Throughout the field, supervisors stress that students' originality and creativity is critical for the development of the discipline as a whole. But some see their role as directing student research while others prefer to function mainly as a stimulator of students' ideas and creativity. The latter approach, we noted, is sometimes reflected in extremely "democratic" department management in which graduate students and teaching staff are treated as equals.

In contrast, the emphasis on independent self-study is dominant throughout nearly all the humanities and much of the social sciences. Since research in these fields is so often an individual endeavor, students ought to learn how to study by themselves, the argument goes, and not depend on being spoon-fed by supervisors. For the most part supervisors do not assign research topics for master's and doctoral theses. This traditional approach clearly leads to a lack of structured training and close supervision, and it contributes to the low production of doctorates.

In our field interviewing the emphasis on independent self-study showed up in history at the master's as well as at the doctoral level. Because the master's thesis is decisive in the selection of doctoral students, the master's students concentrate their time and energy on writing good theses. When pressured, they save time for thesis writing by not attending prescribed seminars and lectures. Especially near the end of the academic year, they do not appear in seminars, a practice that supervisors find they can overlook.

As we have detailed, training styles in economics are much in conflict and undergoing much change. Compared with other disciplines in the social sciences and the humanities, it tends toward the styles of the sciences, in part because the extensive knowledge base of the field requires some systematic accumulation of theory and technique, and in part because many economics professors have been trained in American graduate schools where they became accustomed to highly structured training. But here also selection to doctoral programs is made largely by the evaluation of master's theses. Students are put under stress both to attend seminars for course credits and to write good theses. Without a job market in industry, students in economics who fail to be selected for doctoral programs may end up jobless. They may want to commit to classroom activity, but above all they need theses that will move them through the doctoral gateway.

As a final note on the involvement of graduate students *in* research and their training *for* research, our field interviewing revealed a basic way in which Japanese students make up for various deficiencies occasioned by the formal arrangements of the national system, the individual universities, and the operating units, preeminently the chair. They create their own study groups within and across chairs and local sets of institutions. From the beginning they participate frequently and intensively in meetings of national disciplinary associations. The many serious constraints placed upon Japanese graduate education virtually cry out for countermeasures. Voluntary association is one such compensatory device.

All these differences and specific tendencies occur, of course, in the larger context of the macro features highlighted in chapter 9. Japanese universities have been eager to have graduate schools, but positions for master's and doctoral degree holders have been few. Industry basically trusts its own on-the-job training, which is more relevant to the individual needs of firms than graduate school work. Behind this emphasis lies the historic pattern of low mobility of Japanese workers across companies. In a country where interfirm transfer has not been frequent, companies need not fear the loss of an "educational investment" in their personnel. Instead they actively invest in upgrading their employees. They increasingly do research, including basic research. They expand the ways to do advanced training, most of which skirts formal and prolonged university study.

Doctoral programs continue to be unattractive. As graduate schools fail to attract the cream of the crop, they remain trapped in a vicious circle of weak inputs and outputs. Only time will tell whether various incremental reforms introduced in recent years will gradually turn a vicious cycle of interaction into a virtuous one of heightened attractiveness, widely appreciated training, and good jobs for graduates. Meanwhile, doctoral programs are roundly avoided, and the doctoral degree has yet to become a highly valued credential. As long as it is not, the research foundations of graduate education will remain comparatively weak.

NOTES

We deeply express our gratitude to our colleagues Professor Morikazu Ushiogi, Toru Umakoshi, Koujiro Imazu, and Misao Hayakawa for their cooperation and valuable suggestions. Our research was supported by funds from the Spencer Foundation, through Professor Burton R. Clark, and by the Monbusho International Scientific Research Program.

1. Nakayama, *Teikoku Daigaku no Tanjou*, pp. 74–88.
2. Osatake, "Gijutsu Kakushin to Daigaku."
3. Tokyo Daigaku, *Tokyo Daigaku Hyakunenshi*, pp. 873–954.
4. Organisation for Economic Co-operation and Development (OECD), *Social Science Policy: Japan*.
5. Sakamoto, *Nihon no Shuushi to Shigaku*, pp. 245–250.
6. *Nihonshi Kenkyuu*, no. 313 (Sept.), 1988: 71.
7. *Shigaku Zasshi*, vol. 97, no. 5, 1988: 1–5.
8. Ministry of Education, *Gakkou Kihon Chousa Houkoku*.
9. Kokuritsu Daigaku Kyoukai, *Kyuusetsu Daigakuin no Kaizen nituite*, p. 56.
10. Kokuritsu Kyouiku Kenkyuujo, *Daigakuin no Kenkyuu-2*, p. 37.
11. Becher, "Disciplinary Shaping of the Profession," pp. 277–281.
12. Tanaka, *Kenkyuu Kateiron*, pp. 120–121.
13. Ladd and Lipset, *Divided Academy*, p. 64.

BIBLIOGRAPHY

Becher, Tony. "The Disciplinary Shaping of the Profession." In *The Academic Profession: National, Disciplinary, and Institutional Settings*, ed. Burton R. Clark. Berkeley, Los Angeles, London: University of California Press, 1987. Pp. 271–303.

Fujino, Shouzaburou. *Daigakukyouiku to Shijoukikou* (Market mechanisms of university education). Tokyo: Iwanamishoten, 1986.

Kokuritsu Daigaku Kyoukai. *Kyuusetsu Daigakuin no Kaizen nituite* (On the improvement of graduate schools of former imperial universities). Tokyo, 1985.

Kokuritsu Kyouiku Kenkyuujo. *Daigakuin no Kenkyuu-2* (Graduate education study-2). Tokyo, 1979.

Ladd, Everett Carll, Jr., and Seymour Martin Lipset. *The Divided Academy: Professors and Politics*. New York: McGraw-Hill, 1975.

Ministry of Education. *Gakkou Kihon Chousa Houkoku* (Basic school survey). Tokyo: Ookurashou Insatsukyoku, 1988.

Nakayama, Shigeru. *Teikoku Daigaku no Tanjou* (The establishment of the imperial university). Tokyo: Chuuoukouronsha, 1978.

Organisation for Economic Co-operation and Development (OECD). *Social Science Policy: Japan*. Paris, 1976.

Osatake, Tonau. "Gijutsu Kakushin to Daigaku" (Technological innovation and universities). In *Nihon no Daigaku* (Universities in Japan). Tokyo: Tokyo Daigaku Shuppankai, 1968.

Sakamoto, Taro. *Nihon no Shuushi to Shigaku* (Compilation and research in Japanese history). Tokyo: Shibundou, 1958.

Tanaka, Hajime. *Kenkyuu Kateiron* (An essay on the research process). Sapporo: Hokkaidou Daigaku Toshokankoukai, 1988.

Tokyo Daigaku. *Tokyo Daigaku Hyakunenshi: Bukyokushi 1* (The centennial history of the University of Tokyo: Departmental history 1). Tokyo: Tokyo Daigaku Shuppankai, 1986.

Conclusion

Burton R. Clark

Modern nations increasingly confront a complicated mix of crosspressures and countertrends among the ways of science, higher education, and government. Scientific advance generates its own imperatives in university conduct, ones made abundantly clear in the rewards of specialized publication and the disciplinary attitudes of research-oriented academics. Intrinsic motivation flows from the creation of knowledge for its own sake; extrinsic reward is found in national and international status based more upon disciplinary standing than on university location. Institutions of higher education in turn operate under mandates systematically at odds with the interests of science. When involved in the broad, initial education of students or the direct training of nonscience professionals, academic staff are steered by expectations and duties that have little to do with the pursuit of research or the training of future researchers. The dissemination of established knowledge comes to the fore. Positioned in political offices and bureaucratic departments, governmental patrons in turn are oriented by a wide range of interests, some as broad as the pursuit of equity and others as narrow as accountability in the purchase of laboratory equipment. Those who provide the money are sorely tempted to set research priorities, generating tension between mandated science and disciplinary science. They are inclined to assert responsibility for steering higher education, against the institutional claims of necessary autonomy, the eternally asserted professorial doctrines of freedom of research and teaching, and the student belief in freedom of study.

Much of the three-way interaction between science, higher education, and government becomes located in the arrangements for the most advanced programs of university education. It is no simple matter to fashion academic entities—universities and their base units—that offer advanced training, provide a home for science, and respond to the interests of government. Hidden in the intricate relations of academic life, the essential conditions for effective linkage are hard to identify. In any national system the first-degree level has historical primacy, predominates numerically, and possesses a deep hold on traditional thought and practice. It comes first in budget determination, public attention, and the concerns of government. Graduate or advanced education is then prone to develop at the margin, as an add-on of a few more years of unstructured work for a few students. A balance has to be sought in which a graduate emphasis on research activity and research training can prosper in addition to the first-degree commitments.

The extensive accounts of research underpinnings of university advanced education in Germany, Britain, France, the United States, and Japan in the earlier chapters reveal vast differences in national structures and practices. We observe elaborate configurations replete with national peculiarities. Confronting the heavy hand of history and context, we are necessarily struck by particular features and the unique texture of their connections. But amid the comparative confusion into which we are plunged by rounded accounts, certain common trends and basic tensions appear. Everywhere in industrial societies and in the more advanced developing societies we witness a transition from elite to mass higher education. This trend has broad effects, either in place or in the offing, on the most advanced level of university education as well as on the initial years of study. Everywhere we witness a growing tension between institutional concentration and diffusion of the advanced level. How many universities in the national system are going to mount expensive doctoral programs? In a few fields or many?

To integrate a portion of the country accounts, I set forth in the first section of this chapter common trends and tensions that are manifest in the previous chapters or lie just beneath the surface of our descriptive knowledge. Common features offer the beginning of a unifying framework. But common trends and tensions do not dictate common responses. Due to their separate histories, varied societal contexts, and accumulated unique patterns, national systems of advanced higher education possess different adaptive capabilities and tendencies. Organization does matter, and the systems are organized quite differently; governmental sponsorship also matters, and such patronage takes different forms. Between the stimulus provided by trends and tensions and the response of an embedded system stands a large institutional mass of actors and agencies who are not passive and inert. Oriented by ideas and interests determined historically, socially, and finally individually, they react to common trends and tensions by constructing different answers.

In a second, following volume, I set forth in fuller comparative detail the national configurations of research organization, advanced education, and funding in the five countries we have here reviewed. That analysis further disentangles the tendencies that fragment the relation of research to teaching and study and the countertendencies that help hold together these three activities. Central in that understanding is the graduate level of the American system, which, after much early experimentation and tentative development, achieved international prominence in the last half century. Both in the American context and in international perspective, the American unplanned evolution of strong organizational underpinnings for master's and especially doctoral programs is a relative success story. It stands in contrast in important ways to the undergraduate level of the American system where confusion reigns eternal over the composing of general or liberal education. There, as in the late 1980s, open warfare occurs frequently in the humanities, especially in literature and cultural history. At the graduate level in the arts and sciences, American university professors are much more confident about their fields and what should be done, for then they are free to specialize, to commit to research, to train disciplinary journeymen and apprentices. In line with the more extended analysis presented in the second volume, a brief statement in the second part of this chapter of the American model of second-tier organization suggests the nature of its distinctive capability. We find a graduate level operating on a grand and diffuse scale that also manages in some locales to concentrate resources and talent and provide the intimate settings necessary for scholarly and scientific centers of excellence.

In a third section I offer an example drawn from contemporary practice of the Humboldtian ideal of the unity of research, teaching, and study. Although this case is taken from an American university, similar instances can be found in various niches in the other four national systems. The chapter then concludes with the basic issue of how small settings and intimate mentor-student relations can be maintained in universities and national frameworks that become larger, more bureaucratic, and quite impersonal.

COMMON TRENDS AND TENSIONS

Within and among both highly industrialized countries and developing societies, four broad trends set a changing stage for the most advanced level of university education and its relationship to research and research training: the ongoing shift from elite to mass to universal participation; the widening labor market for highly educated experts; the self-amplifying, explosive expansion of knowledge; and the increased role of government representatives in support and supervision. While these primary trends bear on all of higher education, they affect in particular ways the research-teaching-study nexus, which, if found at all, is located mainly at the graduate or advanced level.

The Evolution of Mass Participation

It was not long ago—the 1950s in many European systems—that 5 percent or less of the age group entered higher education. Mary Henkel and Maurice Kogan (chapter 3) noted that even after much expansion from a low base the proportion entering the British university sector at the end of the 1980s was still as low as 6 to 7 percent, with the university and non-university sectors together admitting only about 14 percent. Sharply limited access is hardly buried in the past in Britain. But the trend there as elsewhere is clear: there are more students now than there were, and in the future there will be even more of them. The other nations reviewed in this volume have already moved deeper into mass involvement: first in lower secondary education, then in upper secondary, next in first-tier programs in higher education, and finally in increasing but quite varied degrees at the graduate level. The higher education systems of continental Europe currently have age-group participation rates that generally range between 20 and 30 percent. In Japan it is over 30 percent. With open-access colleges as well as selective institutions, and with enrollments in excess of twelve million, the United States has closely approached universal higher education. From this base it has clearly moved into a stage of mass graduate education. The advanced level in the United States is hardly elitist any longer when, at the end of the 1980s, postbachelor enrollment totaled nearly 1.5 million students and degrees awarded annually numbered 300,000 master's (both arts and sciences); another 70,000 master's and doctoral degrees in professional fields, the Master of Business Administration (M.B.A.) and the Doctor of Medicine (M.D.), for example; and 35,000 Ph.D.'s. Against a base of about one million bachelor's degrees, the advanced degrees totaled 400,000, a ratio of four to ten—a stunning indicator of the major place taken up by the graduate level in the American system, particularly when we keep in mind that the higher degrees have both more prestige and more value in the marketplace than does the bachelor's degree.

The rising tide of participation greatly broadens the enrollment base of higher education systems. When a system moves from 5 to 25 percent of the age group, or over a longer period, as in the United States, from 5 to 50 percent, there are five- to tenfold more entering students. With the students also more varied in educational background and academic sophistication than in the past, the need for introductory teaching is enormously expanded and intensified. Professors may want to spend their time on research and in the company of advanced students, but if old structures are kept and adaptations not soon made, they perforce need to spend more time teaching first-degree students. The enlarged scale of operations also presses hard for a shift from old patterns of intimate personal relationships that could stand alone to more formal, wholesale arrangements that can accommodate much larger numbers of students and students more varied in background, first at the introductory level and then even at the most advanced level. Rather than involvement in research, the vast majority of students primarily need systematic, sequential course work.

Less selection at the doors of higher education also means that more selection will necessarily take place within the system somewhere between points of entry and the awarding of the higher degrees. If the best research talent in the pipeline is to be identified, nurtured, and passed on to the locales of the best academic researchers, more pathways of student mobility are required: more degree levels and more types of degrees serve as gate-keepers and markers of competence. The French arrangements observed by Guy Neave may be the most Byzantine, due to the interweaving con-nections between *grandes écoles*, universities, and research laboratories, but in all countries the tendency toward mass advanced education promotes a more intricate arrangement of selection and transition from first-degree to higher degree programs.

Labor Market Demand for Advanced Education

While mass access changes systems of higher education from the input side, the widening occupational demand for highly educated experts stretches the system on the output side. More professions, semiprofessions, and would-be professions establish training footholds in the system, even if to do so they exaggerate their requirements in knowledge and skill. Postsecondary educa-tion accommodates a professionalization of everyone. In the European models first-degree work itself is seen as specialized study leading histori-cally to professional qualification or the right to take a professional exam-ination at a level approximating the American master's degree. In the American system most serious specialized study has been raised to the graduate level. In Japan, where employers seek out university students as they take the bachelor's degree, and now increasingly in engineering and the sciences when they have the master's degree in hand, the employing firms take over the task of further specialized training, even to the extent of subsidizing employees for extended study in foreign universities. There, too, training is elongated, stretching beyond the bachelor's degree, even if it is not located in formal doctoral programs. In short, the market demand for expertise is widened and deepened. If not met in the universities, that demand can be answered largely through education and training offered in nonuniversity or foreign channels, as it is in Japan.

Clark Kerr has cogently argued that at least 25 percent of all employees in an advanced industrial nation are now in the categories of professional, technical, and administrative personnel for which postsecondary training is appropriate. Factoring in equity pressures from the access side, and allowing for dropouts, effective systems accommodate 30 percent or more of upcoming age groups. By the end of the 1980s, the 30 percent figure was already well surpassed in the United States, Canada, Japan, the Soviet Union, and Sweden.[1]

As the spread of high occupational expertise intensifies the need for advanced programs in a widening number of fields, it also presses for longer training periods. The creation of a postdoctoral tier of research training in American universities is a dramatic example of this stretching response. In the biological and medical sciences and in some of the physical sciences, the "postdoc" has become in a decade or two the rule, not the exception. These one-to-three-year research training appointments, beyond the work of the Ph.D. program, have also become more frequent in the social sciences and even in the humanities. A weak academic job market in the late 1970s and 1980s encouraged their growth to help support and retain a generation of young scholars and researchers. But the growth of postdocs is more generic than their role as a temporary substitute for regular faculty and research positions. They offer additional expertise, sponsorship, and competitive advantage.

These two first trends, acting on the input and output sides of higher education systems, are forces for "reactive growth," growth that follows as a reaction to external demands.[2] Together they powerfully press for more teaching, irrespective of whether the teaching has research foundations. More students need more systematic instruction to be introduced to university level specialties and to achieve professional expertise. Their teachers need not be researchers, and their studies need not be an introduction to research. The access trend and the labor market trend so magnify the teaching and study components of the traditional research-teaching-study nexus as to encourage some separation from research in the system at large.

Knowledge Expansion

Internationally and nationally higher education over the decades continually undergoes "substantive growth," growth in faculty and academic units— the "tribes" of academe—generated by the development of knowledge.[3] In a self-amplifying cycle of effects, research and scholarship steadily fashion more specialisms and interdisciplinary subjects. The adherents of these cognitive domains push on toward new perspectives, interpretations, and clusters of knowledge, while intensifying and diversifying the major disciplines and the wider research enterprise. The "high knowledge" components of higher education systems, spurred by the drive for new knowledge, steadily become more esoteric. Intense, diverse, and esoteric, these components exist as substantive concentrations that require concentration in research resources, research infrastructure, and research-related personnel. It becomes difficult, if not impossible, to develop and maintain all these needed concentrations in the traditional locales of teaching and study.

The modern-day logic of the research imperative thus contains a divisive tendency. Potentially, it can best be served by research-dedicated groups that do not target teaching programs and student needs as goals. This logic may promote a drift of research from normal university teaching locales to university research units without teaching responsibilities, centers and institutes operated by full- and part-time research staff. Where research comes first, science education and even research training and research infrastructure may take a backseat. These concerns may be seen as second- and third-order priorities or as falling into another domain rather than as the responsibility of those who directly focus their energies in research activities. In the American system the National Science Foundation has experienced considerable internal difficulty in supporting science education, vis-à-vis direct support for scientific research. Biological and medical scientists have at times split sharply with university administrators, both in policy and funding circles in the national capital and on university campuses, over the share of grants and contracts that should be apportioned for university overhead and for the long-term construction of research infrastructure compared to the share that goes to investigators for direct use in research.

Research drift toward nonteaching concentrations need not stop at the boundaries of universities. As research groups form around cognitive domains in other sectors of society, substantive growth becomes a societal phenomenon, not one occurring just in higher education. Research becomes a common activity in industry, civilian government agencies, the military establishment, and the nonprofit sector, all structurally divorced from the university. In the last half of the twentieth century, research is still relatively an elite function, with sharp requirements for entry and bounded hierarchies of accomplishment and status. But in its multiplication and diffusion, it has become an activity in which many nonuniversity institutions are involved and in which vast arrays of knowledge workers can claim a role. From medicine to fashion design, every profession or would-be profession develops a research wing. Within such ever-widening peripheries, research undergoes its own version of massification.

In sum: the expansion of knowledge at the hands of research creates research settings that leave teaching and study behind. Within and beyond the grounds of universities, research finds homes where little or no teaching goes on and where few if any students are found. Research is intrinsically a restless activity that encourages followers to move out in many directions from old settlements to new frontiers. The consolidation of its accomplishments into the knowledge base of teaching and study may trail considerably behind.

Increased Governmental Patronage and Supervision

Interacting closely with these forces of reactive and substantive growth are the impulses of governments. Acting as *the* patrons of modern systems of higher education, governments in every country have concerns that push hard against the historic frameworks of research and advanced education. One concern is to contain cost. A second is to construct internationally competitive centers of research. A third irresistible inclination is to effect change on a political timetable.

The Concern to Limit Costs. Near the end of the twentieth century the Humboldtian principle is an increasingly expensive ideal. In a day of endlessly expanding knowledge, particularly in science, research programs have insatiable appetites for enhanced budgetary support. The cost of attempting to give all advanced teaching and study a sturdy research foundation, let alone teaching and study at the much larger preadvanced stages, presents a bill that governments are unwilling to pay. With expenditures in mind, they are prone to advocate and support the less costly nonresearch, full-teaching sectors. They find the costs of undergraduate instruction more to their liking than the outlays for hugely expensive graduate programs. Financial backers look to costs as reason to distinguish several types of universities funded differentially by extent of research commitment. Cost containment is also an important reason to differentiate fellowship and other financial aid for advanced students whereby only a few students obtain full support while others must take loans, engage in outside work, and otherwise support themselves.

At the beginning of the 1990s various governments are questioning sharply their support of universities by means of a main "institutional line" of funding that blends the costs of teaching and research. Despite the protests of academics and their institutions that such funding is the most appropriate way to support activities that are in fact mingled in the daily work of professors and the operation of the base units, economizers in funding circles are tempted to fund teaching and research separately. Mature universities do indeed contain slack that is buried in lump-sum budgeting. Critics also steadily point out that much academic research is "useless," especially when research activity is intensified, seemingly without limit throughout the humanities, the social sciences, the professional schools, and even the arts.

Hence a common drift in government circles is to take support for research, including subsidized time for research, wholly or partly out of the institutional line and to put it into a research council line, where funds will be awarded on a competitive basis by peer review of the merits of submitted proposals. Governmental actions in Britain, France, and Japan during the late 1980s reported in the earlier chapters are prominent examples of this general tendency. In the American system, a partial separate support of research has long been institutionalized. The federal investment in research grants and contracts is additional to the general institutional line of support for teaching and research built into the funds the fifty states give their main university campuses *and* additional to the support provided by institutional funds—from tuition, endowment, annual gift-giving—private universities autonomously have at their disposal.

Commonly, when research funding is separated, some academic fields are favored, while others are given little or no support. Even in the favored fields, only some academics obtain support for their research; the others, perhaps even a majority, receive little or nothing. And from medical school to classics department, those who do not obtain grants are expected to do more teaching. By such means the budgetary constraints exacted by governments in support of higher education systems tend to cut deeply into the research underpinnings of teaching and student learning. A government conception may readily develop in which economy and efficiency are seen as a product of less research across the board and more teaching in settings where research has been reduced or eliminated.

The Concern to Concentrate Research. Governments have numerous reasons to concentrate research by removing it from the base units of universities that are invested in teaching and study. Some scientific specialties are now so expensive that their work must be concentrated in a few laboratories or institutes too large to be placed under department management. Involved scientists often agree that concentration should triumph over scatteration: champions of "best science" are rarely found on the side of wide distribution of equitable shares. They often become centralizers. The desired research concentrations, large or small, may be located on university grounds, even formally listed as research units of the universities. But they are formally and spatially set apart from the teaching units. Some graduate students may find their way to these concentrations, brought over by professors serving in a dual capacity as research director or taken on as employed research staff, part-time or full-time. But only a minority, not all advanced students, are so admitted.

The research concentrations may also be located entirely outside the university. Ostensibly, they can be better managed if placed on their own and allowed to focus all energies on their research tasks. Off campus they escape the traditional, often heavily encrusted bureaucratic and professional practices of the universities. Research accountability is clarified; assessment of research productivity can be less clouded when research performance is separated from teaching and training activities. Governments find such reasoning especially tempting when cost containment is high on their agendas. They also push in this direction when they distrust the political climate of the universities, especially those with a pattern of antiregime faculty and student activism. Why give "them" more money? Why pour more good money down "that bottomless pit," or "that rathole"? Reform frequently entails bypassing traditional institutions: top-down reform of scientific research may offer the opportunity to move research out of "the university mess" and into scientifically safer as well as more concentrated locales.

The Concern for Short-run Action. Academics may maintain that there is nothing so useful as a good idea, and then point out that such ideas are best produced by unfettered research supported by stable, dependable funding oriented to the long run. Further, to protect the future capability of the scientific community, they may also maintain that teaching and training must be supported and integrated with the ongoing flow of unguided research. However, both elected and unelected government officials may well maintain that in the long run we will all be dead and point out the importance of shorter deadlines. If academic research can seemingly help with so many economic and social problems plaguing each nation, then the need to move faster is pressing. The self-interests of politicians and bureaucrats also dictate deadlines of a few years, which parallel the reelection campaigns on which political careers depend and the reviews of accomplishment in administrative posts on which bureaucratic careers are built.

Such time horizons bear significantly on the willingness of governments to leave research in the unguided, "soft" settings of university teaching departments. The need for responsible government actors to implement projects in a definable time span strongly supports the concern to concentrate research in what appears to be immediately productive settings. This need encourages a bias toward specialized institutions over comprehensive ones, for research units that can be funded and evaluated on a five-year cycle instead of university departments whose blend of research, teaching, and training is fixed in budget categories established in earlier days which seem to go on forever. National planning will nearly always have a relatively short time horizon—one year, three years, five years—which necessitates at least the promise, if not the production, of results in the definable here and now. To leave research to the ways of academic staff committed to the long-term and enmeshed in the slow processes of education then appears as a risk best not taken. In the urgencies of political agendas and executive actions governments find additional potent reasons to attempt to steer research and support it in concentrated centers.

Common Tensions

As these four primary trends steadily alter the context of advanced university education, they induce common problems that cannot be escaped or permanently solved. One is the problem of balancing commitment to first-tier and advanced-tier higher education. A second is the tug-of-war between concentrating and diffusing advanced education and academic research among academic institutions and disciplines. A third is the opposition between "research in" and "research out," the maintenance of basic research within higher education and its diffusion among outside locales. A fourth is the problem of combining central steering with the competition among institutions, departments, and individuals that stimulates advances in science and scholarship. Briefly identified here, these systemic problems are analyzed at greater length in the second volume of this study.[4]

The Balance of "Undergraduate" and "Graduate" Commitment. The historical structuring of degree levels generally emphasizes one level over the others. In Germany, France, England, and Japan the first major degree has received the greater emphasis. In Germany and France earlier chapters indicated that graduate education is neither a concept nor a distinctive level. The first major degree is overwhelmingly *the* degree. In England and Japan, for quite different reasons, the graduate level is marginalized. Academic attention and energy in Britain has long been centered on the three-year honors degree. In Japan selection to an undergraduate program is the most important marker for a student's life chances. With the name and status of the university behind the awarded bachelor's degree, the student is then off to the job market. In the balance between first degree and advanced degree, between undergraduate and graduate, these four systems, in their quite different ways, tend to be first-tier centered.

The system in the United States stands in contrast. Its vigorous graduate education has long been the pride and joy of its universities. Parents, students, and government officials may continue to largely perceive the undergraduate realm when they gaze upon universities, but the academic staff long ago—in what Christopher Jencks and David Riesman called "the academic revolution"[5]—settled upon doctoral programs and research involving graduate students as the center of their individual, departmental, and institutional identity. The university system is relatively second-tier centered.

Each type of imbalance has its defects. First-degree emphasis provides a weak platform for strengthened performance in academic research and research training. Solutions to the problem of "catching up with the Americans" in these critical matters of research and doctoral productivity requires the development of stronger systematic advanced programs analogous to the American. In contrast, the second-tier emphasis of the American university system leaves the undergraduate program, especially the first two years of implied general education, as an Achilles heel. Hence the constant pressure in the American setting to at least incrementally improve upon the time, attention, and quality of effort that academic staff devote to the beginning level. The relatively small leading private universities come closest to achieving a steady balance. The large state universities undergo greater strain in simultaneously maintaining the graduate base of research acclaim, supporting an elaborate structure of postbachelor professional schools, and mounting an effective undergraduate program for twenty thousand or more undergraduates—the latter effort, in the eyes of critics and reformers, set against the imagined ways of independent liberal arts colleges of one to two thousand students.

The modern trends identified earlier deepen this problem of balance across successive levels of higher education. They push systems toward more levels, more divergent degrees at the higher levels, and more pathways of student entry, progress, and certification.

Concentration Versus Diffusion of Advanced Education. Tension between concentration and diffusion in systems of graduate education is inescapable, first among institutions and second across disciplines and professions. Institutional tension is observable everywhere. Certain areas of science dependent on highly limited equipment have for a long time exhibited high institutional concentration, for example, research in astronomy based on the use of telescopes. As more specialties become expensive Big Science, involving major buildings and large equipment, they too become concentrated in a few locales rather than scattered widely among institutions. They cannot be divided into small pieces by a ministry or central committee as fair shares for all, nor can they be seized by a large number of universities in a competitive struggle. The problem soon ranges beyond the requirements of Big Science to the expensiveness of academic research and advanced research training in general, and it encourages differentiation among universities and would-be universities in how much they are able to invest themselves in graduate education. Japan has many graduate schools, but only about ten are fully invested. Britain is struggling to differentiate its universities either formally in several major categories or informally along a continuum of involvement in research and research training. The system in the United States has long been highly differentiated in this regard, first among its over two hundred doctoral-granting universities and then among another six hundred institutions that award master's degrees and do a little research.

Disciplines are similarly concentrated and diffused. Comprehensive universities concentrate many fields in one locale under one official identity. Pretenses of equality among fields can then be maintained; humanities professors can mingle with science professors in the academic senate and in other all-campus bodies; invidious comparisons may be made to bring the salaries and work conditions of the poor disciplines closer to those of the rich fields. But the concentration of diverse subject areas in comprehensive universities runs squarely against the desire of many fields to separate from others and the wishes of patrons to sponsor on a highly selective basis. Notable is the fascinating change, highlighted by Guy Neave in chapter 5, which took place in French universities since the 1968 reform. Before the reform the individual universities each had a full complement of four major faculties embracing medicine, law, the humanities and social sciences, and the sciences. But once turned loose to reconstitute themselves from the bottom up, the universities have become more specialized, with scientists particularly anxious to compose universities entirely around a set of scientific fields. The disciplines are thus diffused from one another, as the sciences cluster in scientific universities, the humanities and social sciences in other universities, and certain professional fields in yet others.

Everywhere there are signs of limits being placed on the comprehensiveness of universities. Current opinion has it that henceforth no university will be able to cover all disciplines and their many specialties, that even the richest universities, for example, Harvard and Stanford in the United States, will need to clearly and decisively choose *not* to have research, research training, courses, and degrees in an increasing number of fields. The spreading of fields differentially among institutions then becomes an important part of institutional differentiation, one that shapes graduate education much more than first-tier programs. Notably, the increasing gap among disciplines, especially between the "hard" sciences and science-based professional fields and the "soft" fields of the humanities, social sciences, and related professions, is likely to be more represented among institutions.

Research In—Research Out. The French National Center for Scientific Research (CNRS) is the prototype in the Western world of the major academic subsystem that places much basic research in a research enterprise formally separated from the university system. Along with analogous French organizations created in recent decades, the CNRS represents a distinct willingness of the French government and its science planners to hold the universities responsible for teaching and learning and for the general support of humanistic high culture, while a separate sector concentrates resources and personnel in research. The effort to relate these two sectors has resulted in an elaborate set of arrangements, effectively drawn out by Neave, that offer pathways of advancement for research-minded students.

Japan prototypically lodges research in the industrial or business sector, with a tendency for research and research training to drift from the relatively poor and weak universities to the rich and powerful corporations. This tendency has been accompanied and furthered by the approval by graduate schools of dissertations written from industrial research without doctoral program participation. As in France, research performed in an outside sector has been linked to the educational functions and privileges of universities. But in each case the advanced level of the universities has been denied sturdy research foundations. Internal university deficiencies have been compensated for in part, but only in part, by intersector relationships.

Basic as well as applied research will increasingly find nonuniversity locations in all developed societies. Substantial research is carried out in sectoral government agencies in Britain, in the government-funded non-profit sector in Germany, and in mission-oriented government laboratories in the United States. But in Britain, Germany, and the United States the historic strong footing of basic research in the higher education system has offered much resistance to the outflow. The Humboldtian ideal became institutionalized in the very orientation of the system.

Central Steering Versus Autonomous Competition. The foregoing chapters have offered ample evidence of strong influence, real and potential, of national funding mechanisms and bureaucratic categories in determining the nature of advanced education and its relation to research. Close state control over higher education and the research system in France has led to enormously complicated central organization and center-to-field lines of influence. Central bodies have engaged in constant controversy and then remedial action. Large, unanticipated effects of massive state action have included an unintended de facto divorce between university appointment and research experience and capability that developed inadvertently during the 1970s with the emergence of an "instructor class." The gradual elaboration of control by a ministry of education in Japan has made national bureaucratic categories fundamental in the support and steering of the national universities, for example, the detailed formulas reported in the chapters on Japan that, across the board, base funding on student numbers, level of program, and nature of the discipline. Japan is an extreme case of the bureaucratic determination of academic research support.

In the Federal Republic of Germany, where higher education has been a *Land* (state) as well as a national responsibility, academic traditions have been considerably national in scope, and recent decades have seen national bodies and *Land* officials increase their top-down influence. Their actions have had broad, systemic consequences: salaries are standardized across the country; teaching loads for all university professors have been made uniform; and institutional competition for faculty has been reduced. Most of all, a national tradition of free student choice of university and field of study has been largely maintained for all students who pass a particular secondary school-leaving examination (the *Abitur*). Such choice leaves the universities and their departments with little or no power to select their students, hence reducing their capacity to build distinctive strengths, compete, and differentiate. When students are so fully in command of university admission, it is difficult to evolve a productive differentiation in the university system. Without such differentiation, elite functions that need groups of specialists are more likely to end up outside the universities.

The British transition during the 1970s and especially the 1980s from autonomous university to *dirigiste* state control has been a dramatic case of increased centralization and concentrated control among major Western systems. The national legislature and especially the national executive branch of government have clearly come to play a much larger role. A plethora of central bodies directly under the government have become instruments of official steerage. Planning bodies and funding councils have told universities to undertake this or to do that, to abandon certain fields of study or to amalgamate in the name of system economy and efficiency. Her Majesty's Inspectors (HMIs), long used for national supervision of elementary and secondary education, have been found in the hallways of academe. By the end of the 1980s, however, the national government was of two minds on control and autonomy. While exercising more detailed, direct supervision, it was also attempting more broadly to point the universities toward a more competitive life in "the market." Universities were encouraged to become entrepreneurial, reducing their dependence on the national purse by raising more of their funds from nongovernmental sources and then spending those funds according to their own choosing. A "successful" institution became one that received half or less of its funds from the Department of Education and Science.

The strain between increased central steering and the governmental demand that British universities behave like autonomous competitive actors has left the universities and their staffs confused and feeling battered. The passing stage of the 1980s may be seen later in history as an important move toward encouraging British universities to again become fairly independent enterprises, to compete and maneuver among multiple sources of support. But the short-term damage to the integrity of the universities has been considerable, and some vicious cycles of effects have been set in motion that seemingly lower the capability of British academic science to do research and train research specialists. As of 1990 the tension between university and state is great; the future of British academic science is quite problematic.

State control versus institutional autonomy has always been *the* perennial issue in higher education. The effects of mass involvement, heightened labor market demand, and knowledge expansion serve to deepen the problem. Governments clearly have more at stake: planning and steering follow. But increased supervision soon becomes dysfunctional when it does not produce desired results and turns academia into a hostile camp. Central officials as well as others then turn to the promise of initiative exercised not at the national level but by the universities themselves. Can the universities become dynamic actors able to stand considerably on their own feet? Can they adapt to a changing environment according to their own perceptions of what needs to be done and what fruitfully can be done? Thoughts turn to "competition" and "the market," especially as means of promoting an interplay between scientific advance and the improvement of advanced education. The experience of American higher education becomes internationally a point of reference. Let us turn to a brief overview of the American provision of advanced education, in which competition is indeed the distinctive if not the central element.

THE DISTINCTIVE CAPABILITY OF AMERICAN GRADUATE EDUCATION

Compared with the German, English, French, and Japanese national systems, and with all others, American higher education is strikingly large, decentralized, diversified, competitive, and entrepreneurial. Further, over two hundred private and public institutions have become doctoral-granting universities, and over six hundred more universities and colleges offer master's degrees. This huge, diversified advanced system is the unplanned product of a long evolution in which institutions freely competed, imitated, and diverged. Graduate education early received structural and symbolic distinction in formal graduate schools in the arts and sciences, which were erected as a second tier on top of the historic four-year college. The emergence of universities in the American system in the last quarter of the nineteenth century made the graduate school a special place for research and research training. The graduate school in the basic disciplines also became distinguished from the professional school more clearly than in Europe and in Japan.

The habits and styles of American graduate schools were also considerably shaped by private foundation sponsorship of research and research training, particularly during the 1920s and 1930s, before the patronage of science by the federal government after World War II.[6] Grants were selective and competitive. Systematic allocation in the form of fair shares for all was nowhere in the picture and soon was not expected. Federal support of research then provided a substantially expanded financial base during the 1950s and especially the 1960s, but the contribution always varied tremendously across the growing numbers of universities and institutions that offered at least master's level work. On their end the institutions steadily diversified the financial base of their graduate schools as they drew entrepreneurially upon various private and public channels of support. The result has been a large number of leading universities—a top ten, a top twenty, a top fifty—which are positioned financially and operationally to provide strong research foundations for graduate education. They combine systematic instruction in disciplines with participation in ongoing faculty research, which may or may not also be the research required for the doctoral dissertation. They do so on a competitive basis, always mindful of ranking in a reputational hierarchy of institutions.

Other nations look to American higher education primarily to understand the effectiveness of its graduate level of university education and research training. Acting as a magnet in attracting talent internationally, the graduate level for the last half-century has turned the American system into the most important international center of research-based higher education, assuming the role the German system occupied during the nineteenth century and into the twentieth up to 1930. Five features, briefly identified here, have been primary in the evolution of this capability.

First is the sheer scale of advanced education. It is located in large departments in large universities in a large national system. The benefits of such size in an age of mass demand and ever-expanding knowledge stand out particularly in contrast to the small scale of the British and Japanese systems, in the form of thousands of substantial departments in hundreds of universities and colleges. Second is the organizational footing provided by the distinctive graduate school, which became a home for science a whole century ago. This organized segment is capable of handling myriad programs and large numbers of students. Able to reach across numerous disciplines and specialties, it has readily accommodated growing substantive diversity.

Third is the great advantage of long-standing department organization over the traditional chair system of continental Europe and Japan. If the chair concentrates power in the individual senior professor, the department spreads authority and patronage. If the chair atomizes base units, the department expands to incorporate multiplying specialties. Critically, the American department commonly brackets undergraduate and graduate levels, its academic staff teaching in both realms. Since financial and personnel resources are related to student numbers and hence are produced considerably by undergraduate enrollments, American departments typically cross-subsidize from the less expensive undergraduate level to the more expensive graduate work, especially in the allocation of faculty time.

Fourth, more clearly and decidedly more strongly than elsewhere, the driving force of the research imperative, with all its incentives and rewards, is directly expressed at the graduate level. The system does not pretend the first-degree level is a home for science and a place for research. The undergraduate realm is for general or liberal education, delayed choice of major, introductory specialization, the development of the student's personality, and the enjoyment of sports and other social features of "the college life." Efforts to integrate research, teaching, and learning are largely reserved for the seminars and laboratories that compose the educational infrastructure of master's and especially doctoral programs.

Last and arguably the most important factor is the enormous competitive initiative of American universities in institution building, which is hooked first to research capability. Institutions operate in a deeply competitive environment. In cross-national comparison intense institutional competition is not only singular but stands out as a fundamental driving force in graduate education.

At the beginning of the 1990s, there is little doubt that American elementary and especially American secondary education are relatively weak, even systematically flawed. Long-standing qualitative impressions have been increasingly supported by quantitative comparisons. As we move up the educational ladder into postsecondary education, the story changes. The American undergraduate level is quite varied in quality, but it serves effectively by combining open access to some institutions and sharp selection to others, a pattern that produces concentrations of talent. The graduate level is also increasingly varied, but with its many concentrations of diverse talents it stands far in front internationally as a success story in research productivity and research training. The graduate school is where the American system finally overcomes the comparative disadvantages of its K-12 system and becomes an international pace setter.

THE IDEAL TYPE OF RESEARCH-CENTERED GRADUATE EDUCATION

Amid all the differentiation and complexity that moves higher education far from the Humboldtian principle of the unity of research, teaching, and study, we still find sturdy locales in which the principle, in modern dress, finds virtually ideal expression. One setting is a recognized, sustained research group in a large science department in a major American research university. Leadership is provided by a senior figure of considerable stature, who selects the members of the group and guides, if not dictates, their choice of research problems. The graduate student members of the group are also members of the larger department. Before and during much of their research work, they take courses taught by other faculty in the department and meet departmental requirements on courses, credits, examinations, residency, and degrees. But their lives as advanced students intent upon research are centered in the daily activities of the research group. This is their home; this is where, if they are successful, research effort and activity will become an intrinsic motivation and a reward in itself; this is where careers begin.

The principal American national association of graduate school deans, the Council of Graduate Schools, offered in 1989 "a very cogent statement of graduate education at its best" in a description prepared by Donald Cram, a Nobel laureate chemist at the University of California, Los

Angeles (UCLA), for presentation at a meeting of the regents of the University of California.[7] In this statement we can note at the outset the substantial size of the research group and the mingling of postdoctoral scholars, advanced students, and beginning graduate students:

> My research group has, for about 40 years, been composed of 17 people, plus or minus three at any given time. Three of the group on average are postdocs and the rest graduate students working for their Ph.D.'s. The postdocs stay about a year and a half, and already are independent investigators, but work in my field of specialization. The graduate students spend an average of four years doing their thesis research, the first two years of effort being blended with their teaching duties and the courses they take. The last two years, they work up to 70 hours a week on their research problems.

Around their simultaneous involvement in several research studies, the students are very involved with one another and especially with the faculty mentor. They are soon writing research reports, drafts of journal articles, and determining which materials will best compose a thesis. The group publishes a great deal, in the style of laboratories in chemistry in which the senior figure is commonly first author:

> Each investigator has two or three problems he or she is working on. Usually one of these turns into thesis material. I act as their consultant, critic, judge, advisor, and scientific father. . . . When a project is finished, these students write a detailed report or a thesis describing it. These reports serve as the basis of research papers. I usually write these from parts of reports or theses, which the co-workers then criticize. The better graduate students and co-workers write the first drafts of research papers, which I then rewrite. In this way, our group has published about 370 research papers over the years.

The whole enterprise depends considerably on the work of the graduate students:

> Although professors and postdoctoral fellows are important to a research group, the graduate students are the heart of the research effort. If they are talented and motivated, they make excellent teaching assistants and research assistants. They stay long enough to provide continuity and leadership and group memory. They form, during their graduate student days, friendships and contacts that last throughout their lives.

There is the output of trained researchers, large but differentiated:

> If the papers constitute the research group's legacy, our immediate products are our freshly-minted Ph.D.'s and postdocs. Of the two hundred-plus of them from my lab, about 60 are now professors in academic work, about 12 work for government, about 5 left chemistry to become dentists, doctors, mothers, or businessmen, and the rest do research or research administration in the chemical, pharmaceutical, or oil industries. Of these, about half keep in touch

with me at least on a yearly basis. Of the first 80 or so Ph.D.'s in my group, about 10 were female. Currently there are more females in my group than males.

Finally, the Ph.D.'s produced by the group are scientifically competent. A few are outstanding:

> I would judge almost all of these students to be operationally creative; that is, they can solve problems. Only about 5 to 10 percent, however, are conceptually creative. They are the ones that formulate research objectives. It is this small, latter percentage that will shape the changes in our society. They are the elite of the elite. They not only know how to get things done, but they know what should be done.

The Cram statement is an ideal description of a virtual ideal type: it was not designed to offer a full accounting of student life in a research group and thereby to cover failure as well as success, pain and suffering as well as health and happiness. But its straightforward description helps highlight the specific operational conditions which, at the end of a chain of nested supportive settings in the national system and in the host institution, support an intimate blending of research activity with faculty teaching and student learning. The immediate larger setting is the department that was only lightly mentioned in the above description when Cram noted at the outset that "the first two years of effort" on the part of students in his group were "blended with their teaching duties and the courses they take."

The American departmental framework, especially in cross-national perspective, is decidedly important. The Cram group is nested in a department of chemistry and biochemistry of over fifty faculty members, thirty-five of whom are full professors—the latter a staggering number, especially when considered against the very limited number of senior people found in chair-based organization of disciplines in other countries.[8] The department offered in 1990 about fifty undergraduate courses—twelve in the first two years of study ("lower division"), thirty-eight in the last two years ("upper division")—and even more courses, fifty-five, at the graduate level. It had a large undergraduate base, with about 700 students majoring and taking their bachelor's degree in chemistry and enrollments in individual courses approximating 4,000 during any week of the academic year. Its graduate student population numbered about 250, 98 percent of whom, in 1989–1990, had financial support that averaged $16,000 per student per year. At the end of the 1980s this one department received about one hundred and fifty research grants or awards from external funders each year, which totaled about $10 million, all in addition to the support provided by the state of California and whatever special funds the university had accumulated for its own disposal and allocation to this particular department.

Like others in the American system, this department has an elaborate framework for admission, study, and awarding of advanced degrees. It is the department that "offers programs of study and research leading to the M.S. and Ph.D. degrees." It is the department, not the research group, that admits graduate students in chemistry and biochemistry: it even has its own "Graduate Office." For each student admitted to graduate standing, the department gives "orientation examinations at the beginning of the first term in the division of study and a second area selected from physical, organic, and inorganic chemistry." It sets numerous course requirements for both the master's and the doctoral degree. It gives all Ph.D. candidates "a series of written tests called cumulative examinations" that are "designed to encourage and test the continued growth of professional competency through coursework, study of the literature, departmental seminars, and informal discussions with colleagues." Students are required to enter the examination pathway by the middle of the first year ("second term in residence") and continue until they have passed five exams.

At the end of the first and second years, overall progress is "evaluated by the graduate study committee, taking into account performance in courses, cumulative examinations, and research." This committee, acting on behalf of the department, recommends that the student proceed to the oral qualifying examination from which he or she can move on to the dissertation stage of the doctoral program or be "redirected to the M.S. program" or "be terminated." The dissertation stage then calls for a doctoral committee. Meanwhile, "one year of teaching experience is required"; it is normally fulfilled as a teaching assistant. These many rules and regulations are partly department-specific and partly general. The central office of the graduate school keeps its own records, exercises some uniform requirements, and administers funding for graduate students. The "graduate council" of the campuswide academic senate reviews every department graduate program on an eight-year cycle.

In short the Cram research group is well nested in a strong departmental and university (graduate school) framework. From such settings is international preeminence made. The UCLA chemistry department stands in the top ten to fifteen of nationally ranked departments in the United States.

Conditions that equal or even surpass those described here exist in thousands of disciplinary locales in fifty to one hundred American universities. As described in the foregoing chapters, there are specific institutional settings in Germany, Britain, France, and Japan where the daily practice of advanced education thoroughly blends research, teaching, and learning. The question is whether such operational locales in universities, and indeed in some nonuniversity settings, are rare exceptions or a common occurrence. Ample system and institutional pressures exist to make them more infrequent. One such pressure noted by Patricia Gumport in the United States chapters is the need of some faculty researchers to use graduate students as workers who perform narrow tasks in funded research projects that contribute little to their learning. Whether or not the students' cumulative learning then takes a backseat depends considerably on the departmental environment, especially on a sequence of courses and research projects that together transform rank neophytes into accomplished scholars.

SCALE, FORMALIZATION, AND THE MAINTENANCE OF APPRENTICESHIP

The reactive growth of departments and universities that follows from the input and output trends identified earlier, along with the substantive growth induced by the expansion of knowledge, causes science and higher education to be caught up in large, formal frameworks. The national system becomes more elaborately structured, the university decidedly more bureaucratic. In numbers of faculty, students, and staff, and the amounts of money, equipment, and buildings needed to teach many more students, and especially needed to do research and to train more research specialists, the university becomes big business. Organizational frameworks capable of supporting activities on a much larger scale evolve; the mechanisms of bureaucracy and organized profession grow. There are more "science administrators," "project managers," nonfaculty "support personnel," offices to process grants and contracts, vice-chancellors for research, and vice-chancellors for graduate education *and* research. In turn, within the university, departments and laboratories grow larger, and, in many scientific specialties, the labs and research groups form teams that involve managers and employees, professors of various ranks, full-time researchers, support personnel, postdoctoral scholars, and graduate students. The dominant science model becomes one of collaboration within specially funded projects. All along the line, from the national ministry to the local laboratory, more formalization must be expected, driven by size, complexity, and cost.

International competition of national systems and institutional competition within each system adds to the pressure for growth and formalization. The immensity of the American system becomes a virtue over the smallness of the British counterpart. Limited "old-fashioned" scale and organization can well become a major handicap, inducing a vicious circle of effects in which a brain drain today is a self-perpetuating brain loss tomorrow. It can cause a major country to become a minor player in research and advanced education. Hence, growth and its attendant formalization cannot be escaped. Britain, like other countries, has to evolve frameworks suitable for greater numbers of students, larger faculties, more research, and transactions that multiply geometrically. The evolution of such new supportive structures in Britain or elsewhere is normally slow and painful: they may take two or three decades or more to develop. And any new underpinnings for graduate education must be devised in universities where attention is first fixed on numerically predominant first-degree education, which more fully determines the overall resource base and remains the first object of public attention and governmental concern.

But an always increasing scale of organization in the support of science and higher education can be in itself a hollow framework. It offers no guarantee of productive academic research and effective transition of advanced students to scholarly adulthood. Expanding systems need an infrastructure of relationships that are more personal than impersonal, more informal than formal. At the undergraduate or first-degree level, of course, it remains possible for universities in various countries to batch students in lecture halls of five hundred. Particularly in the European tradition, the grand lecture still has its place. Grand or not, it is widely used in the large universities of the American system. But nowhere does the lecture hall have a prominent place in the execution of research and the training of researchers. The chosen instruments, the laboratory and the seminar, form relatively small settings. Students are "at the bench" with a practicing scientist or are seated around a table with a professor. There is much one-to-one consultation, especially when students are in the dissertation stage. The teacher-student relationship is often prolonged over several years. Tacit aspects of perspective and technique are transmitted by means other than the spoken word.

The dilemma associated with growth and formalization is how to be simultaneously large and small, formal and informal. Little doubt remains that transmission of the intricacies of research still requires small-scale settings where neophytes are closely related to experts—a feature widely observed in the small British system. Hence the struggle in increasingly complex modern universities is to maintain an organizational balance in which the whole is substructured into considerably smaller working groups: in departmental specialties, laboratories and centers, seminars and colloquia, and in mentor-apprentice pairings that resemble the traditional craft. At the cutting edge knowledge is not separable from the minds that create it.

What conditions and structures are essential if research activities are to be related effectively to the teaching activities of professors and the study activities of students? A fuller, detailed answer to this question is the focus of the second volume of this study. But a brief, capsule answer here is that strong organization is required at two local levels. It is required in the university as a whole, there promoted by wise state policy that turns universities loose under broad subsidy and especially by the institutional initiative characteristic of competitive settings. It is required even more within universities at the operating level of department, laboratory, and research cluster. The great importance of the degree and form of organization at these two local levels is not particularly apparent when we remain at home, encased in the traditional provisions of our own system, our eyes glazed over by the grandeur of the Big Picture. But cross-national comparison reveals how much specific organization matters. It matters a great deal to have formally organized graduate schools. It matters considerably to have departments rather than chairs as the primary operational units. It matters to have research clusters subsumed within teaching settings but also capable of raising much of their own funding. It matters that universities, departments, and research groups compete for prestige and resources.

Cross-national comparisons also lead to a richer understanding of the special nature of research, advanced teaching, and advanced study as human activities. We learn to appreciate how much their integration requires special organizational supports. We then see more clearly that macro frameworks of national systems are rational and effective to the degree they generate and support the best micro settings. There are no shortcuts in massive planning and bureaucratic organization which can bypass the need to have thousands of individually composed small worlds in which, as Humboldt stressed, the professor and the student join hands in the pursuit of knowledge.

NOTES

1. Kerr, "Critical Age."

2. The concept of reactive growth has been taken from Metzger, "Academic Profession."

3. On substantive growth, as different from reactive growth, see Metzger, "Academic Profession." On academe consisting of academic tribes and cognitive territories, see Becher, *Academic Tribes and Territories*.

4. Clark, *Places of Inquiry*.

5. Jencks and Riesman, *Academic Revolution*.

6. Geiger, *To Advance Knowledge*; Rosenzweig, *Universities and Their Patrons*.

7. Council of Graduate Schools, *CGS Communicator*.

8. The following data and quotations were taken from UCLA administrative records and the *UCLA Catalog, 1990–91*.

BIBLIOGRAPHY

Becher, Tony. *Academic Tribes and Territories: Intellectual Enquiry and the Cultures of Disciplines*. Stony Stratford (Milton Keynes, England): The Open University Press, 1989.

Clark, Burton R. *Places of Inquiry: Graduate Education in Advanced Industrial Societies* (tentative title). Forthcoming.

Council of Graduate Schools (U.S.). *CGS Communicator* (April 1989): 1, 8.

Geiger, Roger L. *To Advance Knowledge: The Growth of American Research Universities, 1900–1940.* New York: Oxford University Press, 1986.

Jencks, Christopher, and David Riesman. *The Academic Revolution.* Garden City, N.Y.: Doubleday & Co., 1968.

Kerr, Clark. "A Critical Age in the University World: Accumulated Heritage Versus Modern Imperatives." *European Journal of Education* 22-2 (1987): 183–193.

Metzger, Walter. "The Academic Profession in the United States." In *The Academic Profession: National, Disciplinary, and Institutional Settings,* ed. Burton R. Clark. Berkeley, Los Angeles, London: University of California Press, 1987. Pp. 123–208.

Rosenzweig, Robert M. (with Barbara Turlington). *The Research Universities and Their Patrons.* Berkeley, Los Angeles, London: University of California Press, 1982.

INDEX

Britain (*cont.*)
examinations in, 134–135; expansion of,
71, 72, 86–87, 358; foreign students in,
92–93, 123, 124, 125, 136, 137; funding of
students in, 88–89, 90, 91, 94, 100, 101,
121–122, 125, 133, 142–143, 144; funding
of universities in, 69–70, 76, 78, 79, 80–
82, 84, 88, 89, 99–102, 106, 107, 108,
120–121, 149; gender as factor in, 91–92;
government policy on/autonomy over,
69–70, 76–82, 87, 88, 98, 99–102, 103,
107–108, 120–121, 122, 125, 133, 142–
143, 144, 149, 369, 376; history in, 102,
103, 116, 117, 120, 122, 123–124, 125,
126, 127–128, 129, 130, 131, 132, 133,
137, 140, 141, 143–144, 146, 149–150; inbreeding in, 124; interinstitutional consortium in, 120, 132; manpower planning in,
104–106, 109; master's degree in, 72, 86,
87, 91, 92, 93, 94–95, 99, 100, 103, 118–
119, 123, 136, 141, 142, 145, 148, 149,
150; monitoring procedures of, 103–104,
107, 133–135, 139, 141–145, 147; part vs.
full-time students in, 87, 89, 91; physics
in, 102, 116, 117, 120, 122, 124, 126, 127,
128, 129, 130, 131, 132, 133, 136, 137,
138, 140, 141, 144, 146, 147, 150–151;
polytechnics in, 71, 80–81, 88, 89–90, 91,
93, 97; postdoctoral work in, 95–96, 144;
recruitment in, 123–124, 147; research
component of, 35, 72–85, 87, 98, 99–102,
108–109, 116, 117–118, 119, 120, 128,
131–132, 137–138, 140–141, 145–148,
377; selectivity of students in, 69, 70, 71,
72, 90–91, 115–116, 123, 124–125;
staffing in, 96–98, 104, 105–106; status of,
within Britain, 116; student's perspective
of, 35, 135–140; teaching in, 119, 133;
tutorial system in, 127; undergraduate
education compared to, 71, 90, 96–98,
110, 115, 166
Britain, research in: applied vs. basic, 82, 83;
concentration of, 84–85, 108; councils for,
73, 74, 75, 76, 77–79, 80, 81, 83, 84, 85,
87, 88–89, 91, 94, 95–96, 98, 99–102, 104,
105, 107, 119, 122; funding for, 73, 74, 75,
79–82, 83, 88, 91, 94, 99–102, 116, 143,
312, 362; government policy on, 69, 70,
71, 72–79, 80, 81, 82–83, 84–85, 107, 116,
362; by industry, 73–74, 77, 78, 82, 83,
107, 116, 243; isolation in, 137–138, 140,

141; on manpower needs, 105; mission-
directed, 73; near-market, 83; outside university, 80, 82, 368; in physics, 84;
strategic, 82–83, 108; university's role in,
35, 72–85, 87, 88, 98, 99–102, 108–109,
116, 117–118, 119, 120, 128, 131–132,
137–138, 140–141, 145–148, 377
British Academy, 91, 99–100, 144
British Royal Society, 73
Bush, Vannevar, 235
Business studies. *See* Economics
Bruce, Robert V., 233

California Institute of Technology, 232
Cambridge University, 86, 127
Carnegie, Andrew, 231
Carnegie classification, 251 n.18, 315–316
Carnegie Corporation (United States), 231
Casio Scientific Foundation (Japan), 321
Center for Cooperative Research in
Advanced Science and Technology
(Japan), 316, 327–328
Centre National d'Etudes Spatiales (France),
170
Centre National de la Recherche Scientifique
(CNRS) (France), 168, 170, 178, 193,
367; authority/power of, 173–174, 176,
179–180, 183, 194; budget for, 175–177;
concentration of resources in, 177; disci-
plinary bias of, 195, 196, 217; in economics, 194, 195; funding by, 157–158, 162,
171, 172, 179–180, 194, 195, 196, 217;
peer evaluation by, 180; recruitment in,
181; staffing of, 171, 172; university links
to, 157, 171–172, 176–177, 179–180, 182,
209
Centre National de Recherche en Informatique et Automatique (France), 170
Centre National pour l'Exploitation des
Océans (France), 170
Chair system, in Japan, 297, 307, 316, 317,
318, 319, 331, 335, 337–338, 339–340,
341–343, 350, 371
Chemistry, 372–376
Clark University, 227, 228, 229
Cluster system, in France, 211, 212, 218
CNRS. *See* Centre National de la Recherche
Scientifique
Completion rates/times: in Britain, 103–104,
108–109, 121, 122, 133, 135, 136, 141–
143, 146–147, 150; in France, 205, 210–